STRATEGIC VIEW OF MARKETING

A detail study of Strategic Marketing (TEXT AND CASES)

JAYANT ISAAC
M.B.A. (Marketing & Systems), M.Sc. (Physical Chemistry)
Senior Faculty,
Shivalik Institute of Management Education and Research (SIMER)
Durg, Chhattisgarh.

Himalaya Publishing House

MUMBAI • NEW DELHI • NAGPUR • BENGALURU • HYDERABAD • CHENNAI • PUNE • LUCKNOW • AHMEDABAD • ERNAKULAM • BHUBANESWAR • INDORE • KOLKATA • GUWAHATI

First Edition : 2012

Published by : Mrs. Meena Pandey for **Himalaya Publishing House Pvt. Ltd.,**
"Ramdoot", Dr. Bhalerao Marg, Girgaon, **Mumbai - 400 004.**
Phone: 022-23860170/23863863, Fax: 022-23877178
E-mail: himpub@vsnl.com; Website: www.himpub.com

Branch Offices :

New Delhi : "Pooja Apartments", 4-B, Murari Lal Street, Ansari Road, Darya Ganj, New Delhi - 110 002. Phone: 011-23270392, 23278631; Fax: 011-23256286

Nagpur : Kundanlal Chandak Industrial Estate, Ghat Road, Nagpur - 440 018. Phone: 0712-2738731, 3296733; Telefax: 0712-2721215

Bengaluru : No. 16/1 (Old 12/1), 1st Floor, Next to Hotel Highlands, Madhava Nagar, Race Course Road, Bengaluru - 560 001. Phone: 080-32919385; Telefax: 080-22286611

Hyderabad : No. 3-4-184, Lingampally, Besides Raghavendra Swamy Matham, Kachiguda, Hyderabad - 500 027. Phone: 040-27560041, 27550139; Mobile: 09390905282

Chennai : No. 8/2, Madley 2nd Street, Ground Floor, T. Nagar, Chennai - 600 017. Phone: 044-28144004/28144005; Mobile: 09345345051

Pune : First Floor, "Laksha" Apartment, No. 527, Mehunpura, Shaniwarpeth (Near Prabhat Theatre), Pune - 411 030. Phone: 020-24496323/24496333; Mobile: 09370579333

Lucknow : Jai Baba Bhavan, Church Road, Near Manas Complex and Dr. Awasthi Clinic, Aliganj, Lucknow - 226 024 (U.P.). Phone: 0522-2339329, 4068914; Mobile: 09307501550

Ahmedabad : 114, "SHAIL", 1st Floor, Opp. Madhu Sudan House, C.G. Road, Navrang Pura, Ahmedabad - 380 009. Phone: 079-26560126; Mobile: 09377088847

Ernakulam : 39/176 (New No: 60/251) 1st Floor, Karikkamuri Road, Ernakulam, Kochi - 682011, Phone: 0484-2378012, 2378016; Mobile: 09344199799

Bhubaneswar : 5 Station Square, Bhubaneswar - 751 001 (Odisha). Phone: 0674-2532129, Mobile: 09338746007

Indore : Kesardeep Avenue Extension, 73, Narayan Bagh, Flat No. 302, IIIrd Floor, Near Humpty Dumpty School, Indore - 452 007 (M.P.). Mobile: 09301386468

Kolkata : 108/4, Beliaghata Main Road, Near ID Hospital, Opp. SBI Bank, Kolkata - 700 010, Phone: 033-32449649, Mobile: 09883055590, 07439040301

Guwahati : House No. 15, Behind Pragjyotish College, Near Sharma Printing Press, P.O. Bharalumukh, Guwahati - 781009, (Assam). Mobile: 09883055590, 09883055536

DTP by : Sri Siddhi Softtek, Bengaluru.

Printed at : M/s. Padmaja Printers Pvt.Ltd., Hyderabad. On behalf of HPH

Dedication

This book is dedicated to my son Jason Moses Isaac who inspired me to write this book.

Jayant Isaac

PREFACE

There is always a better strategy than the one you have; you just haven't thought of it yet

Sir Brian Pitman, former CEO of Lloyds TSB, Harvard Business Review, April 2003

In today's scenario it is very much necessary to be competitive because of the changing technology; customer needs and challenges of global competition. To attain competitive advantage it is necessary that the companies must have strategic marketing skills to market their product in the competitive environment. The concept of strategic marketing plays a crucial role in determining the success of any company in the competition. In other words it can also be said that to have success, the companies must understand the competition and act accordingly to it in a strategic comportment.

This book is an attempt to understand marketing from strategic perspective where the overall concept of strategy is explained so that it will facilitate the reader to understand the deep meaning of strategy and its connection to marketing. The objective of writing this book is to make students understand the Indian & International approach on various aspects of strategic marketing. This book has been specially written for the post graduate students and the subject matter in this text has been presented in such a way that it can be easily grasped by a student and also by an advanced reader. This book will prove useful for all the postgraduate students in general and in particular the students of MMS (Masters of Management Studies) from Mumbai University for meeting their academic requirements related to Marketing Strategy. This book would also be appreciated by an advanced reader by providing sufficient knowledge about strategic marketing. The book contains clarity of expressions, thoroughness of content so as to make reading this book a pleasure.

The book offers new ideas, insights and a reliable perspective on strategic marketing formulation. The book is organized into seven chapters. Chapter-1 deals with the concept of strategy and strategic management in which an overall view of strategic management is explained from the ground level. This chapter will certainly help the student or reader to understand the strategic management from the elementary level. In addition to this an overview of marketing strategy is also included including the concept of the pillars of marketing i.e., STPD strategies. A deep discussion about market situational strategies and marketing planning is also facilitated in this chapter. The opening and closing case with the discussion questions will be adding value to the whole chapter.

Chapter-2 covers an introductory part of strategic marketing. In this chapter the concept, origin and aspects of strategic marketing is discussed in profound manner. The portfolio management analysis is also discussed in this chapter. The opening and closing case with the discussion questions will be adding value to the whole chapter. This chapter will certainly help the student to understand the strategic marketing and its difference with marketing management.

Chapter-3 gives a brief insight about product and service strategies. The opening and closing case with the discussion questions will be adding tremendous value to the whole chapter. The BCG and GE McKinsey matrix were also discussed including the new product strategies related to innovation, market entry and product line extension strategies. In this chapter the concept of product and service strategies is discussed from the ground level and hence due to this it has become a user friendly book for the readers.

Chapter-4 gives an understanding about the meaning of competition and its types. In this chapter the concept of competitive intelligence, competitive advantage and turnaround strategy is discussed which has added value to the chapter. The Porters five forces model and Porters generic strategies are also discussed which has given the idea of competition analysis and sustainable competitive advantage. The opening and closing case with the discussion questions will be adding tremendous value to the whole chapter.

Chapter-5 tells us about the concept of distribution and the strategies involved in distribution process. This chapter also describes the channel structure strategy and distribution scope strategy in detail. The last part of this chapter deals with managing the conflict that occurs in channel which made this chapter more interesting and informative.

Chapter -6 describes the corporate strategies and in this chapter the nature, scope and concerns of corporate strategies is discussed. The concept of innovative strategies is also discussed in this chapter. The opening and closing case with the discussion questions will be adding tremendous value to the whole chapter.

Chapter-7 covers various strategies in action including strategic customer relationship management (S CRM) which deals with the strategic orientation and framework for CRM. In addition to this various other strategies are also undertaken like communication strategy, brand building strategy, pricing strategy and advertising and sales promotion strategies. The opening and closing case with the discussion questions will be adding tremendous value to the whole chapter.

The opening and closing cases also acted as a helpful instrument to understand the topics more clearly and giving a practical and real understanding of the subject. In addition to this some more case studies are also incorporated at the end of this book which will give the reader a clear vision of strategic marketing.

A large work is difficult because it is large, even though all its parts might singly be performed with facility; where there are many thing to be done, each must be allowed its share of time and effort, in the proportion only which it bears to the whole; nor can it be expected, that the stones which form the dome of a temple, should.be squared and polished like a diamond of a ring.

I would like to gratefully thank the almighty Jesus Christ from the depth of my heart for anointing me with wisdom which helped me in successful completion of this book.

It will be a success story if this book would satisfy the need of the reader for whom it is meant.

JAYANT ISAAC

ACKNOWLEDGEMENT

It is very much difficult to accomplish this project without the active support from various resources. It is a matter of fortune that I have received many inputs from different directions to complete this project. I would like to take this opportunity to put on records my immense gratefulness to my former teachers who taught me about strategic marketing management and because of their efforts I am in this position to write a book on strategic marketing.

I would also like to thank my colleagues and the students of MBA at SiMER who directly or indirectly helped me through their discussions.

Above all, my appreciation must go to my wife Shweta and my Parents who not only made it achievable for me to live through the experience but also gave me support and motivation in innumerable ways.

Finally, I extend my sincere thanks to Mr.Niraj Pandey, Director of Himalaya Publishing House Pvt. Ltd., for supporting and motivating me by providing guidance during the preparation of this book on several aspects.

JAYANT ISAAC

Contents

OPENING CASE: SINGAPORE AIRLINES

There is something about Singapore Airlines. Over the past four decades, it has earned a stellar reputation in the fiercely competitive commercial aviation business by providing customers with high-quality service and dominating the business-travel segments. SIA has won the World's Best Airline award from Conde Nast Traveler 21 out of the 22 times it has been awarded and Skytrax's Airline of the Year award three times over the past decade.

What's not so well known is that despite the quality of its services, SIA is also one of the industry's most cost-effective operators. From 2001 to 2009, its costs per available seat kilometer (ASK) were just 458 cents. According to a 2007 International Air Transport Association study, costs for full-service European airlines were 8 to 16 cents, for U.S. airlines 7 to 8 cents and for Asian airlines 5 to 7 cents. In fact, SIA had lower costs than most European and American budget carriers, which ranged from 4 to 8 cents and 5 to 6 cents respectively.

It is intriguing that SIA has combined the supposedly incompatible strategies of differentiation - which it pursues through service excellence and continuous innovation - and cost leadership. Few enterprises have executed a dual strategy profitably; indeed, management experts such as Michael Porter argue that it is impossible to do so for a sustained period since dual strategies entail contradictory investments and organizational processes. Yet pursuing dual strategies is becoming an imperative. The demand for value-for-money products and services has shot up since the recent recession, particularly in developed countries, so even producers of premium offerings have to figure out how to grab opportunities in the middle and the low end of the market. Moreover, multinational corporations face competition from rivals - many of them from emerging markets - that use new technologies and business models to provide good-enough offerings at attractive prices. Incumbents can fight back by cutting prices or further differentiating products and services, but it is often a losing battle. Price wars typically hurt leaders more than they do challengers and relentless differentiation is tough to sustain. Adopting a dual strategy is often the only choice.

Our research suggests that dual strategies are embraced more readily in Asian countries. Many Western executives believe that, for instance, cost leadership and differentiation, globalization and localization and size and agility are fundamentally contradictory and can't be reconciled. But SIA and other companies such as Banyan Tree, Haier, Samsung and Toyota operate as though the dualities are opposites that make up a whole; that is, they complement, instead of contradicting, each other. This way of thinking is embedded in Eastern thought; the concept of yin and yang in Taoist philosophy, for instance, encapsulates the idea. To be sure, pursuing two strategies will result in organizational paradoxes, but executives in Asian markets tend to realize that opposing insights present the full picture and develop policies to manage both of them.

No company executes a dual strategy better than SIA. The airline has delivered healthy financial returns since its founding, in 1972, never posting an annual loss. It has almost no debt and except for its initial capitalization, it has funded growth through retained earnings while consistently paying dividends.

We have been studying SIA for the past nine years and have found that it executes a dual strategy by managing four paradoxes: providing service excellence cost-effectively; innovating in both a centralized and a decentralized manner; being a technology leader and a follower; and achieving standardization and personalization in its processes. SIA's self-reinforcing system is difficult to imitate, yielding sustainable competitive advantage. As we shall see in the following pages, the dual strategy has become part of the airline's organizational DNA over the years.

Achieving service Excellence Cost-Effectively

SIA has two main assets - planes and people - and it manages them so that its service is better than rivals and its costs are lower. Unlike other airlines, SIA ensures that its fleet is always young. For instance, in 2009, its aircraft were 74 months old, on average - less than half the industry average of 160 months. This triggers a virtuous cycle: Because mechanical failures are rare, fewer takeoffs are delayed, more arrivals are on time and fewer flights are canceled. New planes are more fuel efficient and need less repair and maintenance; In 2008, repairs accounted for 4% of SIA's total costs compared with 5.9% for United Air Lines and 4.8% for American Airlines. SIA's aircraft spend less time in hangars - which mean more time in the air: 13 hours, on average, per day versus the industry average of 11.3 hours. And of course, customers like newer planes better.

Service is mostly about people, so SIA invests heavily in training employees. It schools its fresh recruits for four months - twice as long as the industry average of eight weeks - and spends around $70 million a year to put each of its 14,500 employees through 110 hours of retraining annually. The training includes courses on deportment, etiquette, wine appreciation and cultural sensitivity. SIA's cabin crews are trained to interact with Japanese, Chinese and American passengers in different ways. Trainees learn to appreciate subtle issues, such as communicating at eye level rather than "talking down" to passengers. The superior service that results not only delights customers but also reduces costs by minimizing customer turnover.

SIA's training program focuses as much on the necessity of keeping costs down as on the delivery of great service. Trainers, usually former senior crew member's innovation helps sustain service excellence, which requires that every part of a customer encounter be outstanding.

Frontline employees are particularly important in developing innovations that strengthen SIA's image - and torpedoing those that could damage it. For example, cabin crews demurred when the idea on lowing passengers to order food and drinks by using the in-flight entertainment system was floated. The crews felt they would not be able to respond to requests immediately after take-off, before landing and during planned services, harming their ability to meet customer expectations consistently. That killed the idea.

SIA does not try to be overwhelmingly best in class on every count. It focuses on incremental innovation in most areas because the overall experience matters most. This approach enables the airline to make a profit, without pricing itself out of the market.

Being Both a Technology Leader and Follower

SIA is often the first to innovate in order to enhance the customer experience. But unlike many market leaders that innovate in every aspect of their business, SIA engages in only small improvements in functions that do not touch the customer. Being a technology leader where customers can experience the benefits is essential to differentiation; being a follower in the back office contributes to cost leadership.

Over the years, SIA has developed the ability to execute high-risk innovation projects. For example, it takes a lot of expertise and courage to be the launch airline for a huge aircraft like the A380. Although things did go wrong when Airbus postponed the launch by almost two years, SIA did get a boost. Introducing the A380 not only strengthened its image as a pioneer but also gained enormous publicity for the company. People bid for seats in one of eBay's biggest auctions and some paid $100,000 for a seat on the flight from Singapore to Sydney. (SIA raised $1.3 million for charity in the auction).

SIA's deep pockets allow it to take calculated risks. For instance, in 1976, when it introduced slumberettes in first class, competitions demanded that it either charge more or withdraw the innovation. It did neither, in 1991 it became the first to introduce telephone and fax services on board and in 1998, SIA was one of the first airlines to set up a website where customers could book flights, choose seats and order meals. That was a no-brainer; SIA knew it would save costs by sending would-be travelers online.

However, SIA is a pragmatic innovator, quickly stopping the use of technologies that cause problems or that customers do not like. In 1981, it introduced slot machines in the upper decks of its Boeing 747s but removed them when the queues that formed became a safety risk. In the aftermath of the SARS epidemic in the early 2000s, many airlines added time-consuming check-in procedures to screen for the contagious illness. SIA introduced a check-in system based on biometric technology, which enabled passengers to clear immigration, check in and get their boarding passes in about 60 seconds. However, the airline discontinued the system's usage when data showed that few passengers were taking advantage of it and conventional immigration procedures had speeded up.

SIA is happy to be a back-office laggard. For instance, it wanted a revenue management system that it could deploy quickly and had a low chance of failing. It bought a largely off-the-shelf system, whereas other airlines, such as American Airlines and Lufthansa, developed expensive cutting-edge systems. In 2004, SIA outsourced many of its IT functions - such as its data center and end-user computing support - so it could focus on its core business. Many SIA executives told us that constant innovation on many fronts is risky; changing processes could spread resources and expertise thin and blur SIA's customers focus.

Using Standardization for Personalization

SIA's service processes, like those of most other airlines, are highly standardized. That's central to high-volume service operations, because it leads to predictability, safety and lower costs. It also leads to customer satisfaction, but it can't deliver a "wow" experience, partly because once customers have experienced something, they tend to discount its value. That is why SIA combines standardization with personalization to delight customers.

Doing so is cost-effective because it does not add permanent costs to standard processes. The airline institutionalizes personalization by creating a service culture that, as mentioned earlier, it sustains through recruitment, training and rewards. It instills in employees a certain pride in working for the company and they come to identify with its reputation. SIA's crew members and managers alike say that service is in their blood.

SIA personalizes the customer experience by relaying information about birthdays and preferences from its CRM system to cabin crew members. They address frequent flyers by name and know their favorite drinks and magazines. Usually, though, personalization is spontaneous. Most opportunities arise from unexpressed needs: A passenger may look unwell; another may have no book to read; yet another may have a laptop that has run out of power. Most airlines employees don't pay attention to these small things; but SIA's training programs such as Transforming Customer Service teach cabin crews how to anticipate or external experts, discuss the airline industry's fiercely competitive nature with employees every year. At town hall-style meetings and in internal communications, senior executive stress the fact that SIA must become more efficient in order to remain competitive. They emphasize both parts of the company's vision: providing air transportation services of the highest quality and maximizing returns for the benefit of shareholders and employees.

Cost considerations affect every decision made at SIA. In day-to-day operations, the aim is to reduce waste without compromising customer service. For instance, when cabin crews noticed that about a third of passengers don't eat dinner on late-night flights out of Singapore, they recommended carrying less food. Unlike other airlines, SIA offers two brands of champagne in first class and spends $8 million on champagne every year. But its cabin crew minimizes costs by pouring from whichever bottle is open unless a passenger specifically requests the other brand. No cost is too small to reduce. SIA recently decided not to place jam jars on every breakfast tray, because many people don't eat jam. Even SIA's bonus scheme, which extends to all employees, serves as an incentive for employees to worry about expenses. SIA's plan gives them the opportunity to earn bonuses of up to 50% of their salary depending on how profitable the company is.

SIA attracts first-class university graduates, who are hardworking and ambitious. They like the idea of working for a leading local company and they are also able to take on a lot of responsibility at a young age. Companies in other service industries are happy to hire SIA employees when they leave. SIA offers only average pay by Singaporean standards, which is low by global standards. Because of this, its 2008 labor costs were just 16.6% of total costs, whereas American Airlines were 30.8%. British Airways 27.5%, Lufthansa's 24.4% and United Airlines 22.5%. According to a 2002 study, SIA employees among airlines were the second most productive among airlines (measured by the available ton per kilometer for $1,000 of labor costs) - after Korean Airlines.

Anything that touches the customer must be consistent with SIA's premium positioning, whereas everything behind the scenes is subjected to control. For instance, the company has outsourced ticketing and payroll processing to a low-cost Indian provider. The company's headquarters is atop an old hangar at Changi Airport - not in a swank downtown skyscraper - and the number of headquarters staff is small. What is more, you won't find espresso machines, fancy carpets, designer furniture, gyms or swimming pools in its office. For its training programs, SIA uses its own facilities instead of sensing employees to resorts, and participants buy their lunch from company canteens. Hard-bargaining local managers negotiate hotel rates for crew members at SIA's destinations. Consequently, SIA's other costs (total costs less fuel, labor, depreciation and aircraft rentals) is, at 29.1%, lower than the other large airlines average of 38.2%. This flies in the face of the notion that companies that deliver quality service can't be cost leaders.

Fostering both Centralized and Decentralized Innovation

SIA has earned the reputation of being a serial innovator, bringing many firsts to the civil aviation industry: on-demand entertainment systems in all classes; Dolby sound systems; a book-the-cook service that allows business-and first-class customers to order their favorite meals before boarding; the widest business-class seats; and so on. It follows a 4-3-3- rule of spending: 40% on training, 30% on revising processes and procedures and 30% on creating new products and services every year. The few airlines that worry about innovation usually have a central innovation department; SIA sustains innovation by using a structured, rigorous, and centralized process along with an emergent, distributed and local process. The former is the skeleton, the latter the flesh and blood; together, they provide customers with a body of novel services at a low cost.

The product innovation department (PID) follows a highly structured process that includes opportunity identification, concept evaluation, design and development and launch. The PID has developed innovations such as a nonstop, all business class service between Singapore and New York and the induction of the Airbus A380 into the fleet in 2007. SIA engages frontline employees, customers, competitors and the media to create multiple feedback channels. A small number of executives rotate in and out of the department every three years. Only for megaprojects like the A380 induction to managers stay through the development cycle. Most employees regard being involved in new product development as prestigious and an opportunity to shine.

At the same time, SIA uses its distributed innovation approach for efficiency. The company fosters the idea that employees - especially those in customer - facing functions such as in-flight services, ground services and loyalty marketing - must innovate if SIA is to stay ahead. Every function responsible for improving its service and department heads must implement new ideas out of their budgets. Not only is this approach cost-effective, but the process ensures that innovations are developed in accordance with operational realities, making it easy to implement them. Tensions sometimes erupt between central and local innovation, but SIA encourages both because they complement each other. Distributed customers needs and enhance employees' ability to delight customers. For example, a passenger may request a vegetarian meal without having reserved one. Even when the menu has no vegetarian option, SIA's cabin crews know how to put together a vegetarian meal from the available food. If a passenger wants to discuss the wine he is drinking, a member of the crew who has taken a wine appreciation course will quickly materialize.

Standardization actually enables personalization. Because designs simple processes and trains people well, following procedures becomes second nature. Employees know their jobs so well that they have the mental space to "read" customers and respond to them in creative ways. However, it takes time and effort to go the extra mile, so SIA flights carry more crew members than competitors. That adds about 5% to costs, but these crews help the airline provide unmatched service, which allows it to charge premium prices.

The How-To of Dual Strategies

Emulating SIA is not just about following its best practices; it is about implementing two seemingly contradictory strategies. This involves four broad principles.

Harness the power of your people and culture. Your rivals cannot easily copy your people and organizations culture and those are the linchpins of getting a dual strategy right. Companies should select, develop and reward employees in ways that incorporate aspects of both strategies in their everyday work. That will create an environment in which making decisions in accordance with both strategies comes naturally. For instance, SIA's human resource processes induce employees to keep costs low and boost productivity. Employees also feel that they are all members of one family, so if they do not deliver great service, they are letting down the company and their peers. Culture is deeply rooted in an organization's history. SIA has been concerned about losing money since it broke off from Malaysian Airlines, in 1972. At the time, the Singapore government could not support a loss-making airline; besides, the city-state did not need an airline because it had no domestic routes. Employees are constantly reminded that things have not changed much today.

Make good use of technology. Technology can transcend apparent contradictions such as cost-effective service excellence. Companies often make investment decisions on the basis of industry trends, instead of implementing technology to attain dual goals. For example, SIA chose the widest possible seats for its Airbus A380s, but it also ensured that the seats have the fewest possible parts, such as motors, cables and switches, to keep the risk of malfunction and the cost of repairs low. This kind of thinking results in service excellence at a low cost.

Utilize the power of business ecosystems. Companies must create business ecosystems rather than value chains, which are linear. A business ecosystem involves networks of interconnected actors and creates virtuous circles that support dual strategies. For instance, SIA has tied up with leading hotels, restaurants and retailers to offer discounts to frequent flyers. It selects high-end partners, such as the Ritz-Carlton and the Banyan Tree Private Collection and uses its negotiating power to earn a commission every time a frequent flyer uses its partners' services. The discounts accentuate SIA's differentiation while the additional revenues mitigate costs.

Make investment decisions strategically. Strategic alignment, not financial returns, must guide investment decisions. Executives should ask; What investments should we undertake to achieve both strategies? This mind-set should prevail even when rates of return are difficult to calculate or when investments are large. For instance, a person's ability to taste food declines by about 40% at an altitude of 30,000 feet because of the dry air. SIA invested $700,000 to build, a facility that enables chefs to taste good in the sky and allows its chefs to get their dishes right the first time. It's often impossible to calculate the return on initiatives like this, but they are worth making because they contribute to differentiation and lower costs.

EXECUTING DUAL strategies is difficult that's what makes the approach so valuable. By being different in ways that customers like, companies that do so rise from the pits of commoditization and make profits even in highly competitive industries.

Chapter: 1

Strategy: An Overall View

Learning Objectives

This Chapter is focused on the following objectives:

- Meaning and concept of strategy and strategy management
- Understanding various levels of strategy
- The Strategic Management Process
- Benefits of Strategic management
- An Overview of Marketing Strategy
- Pillars of Marketing-STPD strategies
- Market situational strategy and marketing planning

CONCEPT OF STRATEGY AND STRATEGIC MANAGEMENT

Strategy, a word of military origin, refers to a plan of action designed to achieve a particular goal. In military usage strategy is distinct from tactics, which are concerned with the conduct of an engagement, while strategy is concerned with how different engagements are linked. How a battle is fought is a matter of tactics: the terms and conditions that it is fought on and whether it should be fought at all is a matter of strategy, which is part of the four levels of warfare: political goals or grand strategy, strategy, operations and tactics.

Building on the work of many thinkers on the subject, one can define strategy as a "fundamental pattern of present and planned objectives, resource deployment and interactions of an organization with markets, competitors and other environmental factors." The word strategy first became a popular business buzzword during the 1960s. It is suggested that a strategy specify:

(1) what (objectives to be accomplished),

(2) where (on which industries and product markets to focus) and

(3) how (which resources and activities to allocate to each product-market to meet environmental opportunities and threats and to gain competitive advantage).

Strategic management as a discipline originated in the 1950s and 60s. Although there were numerous early contributors to the literature, the most influential pioneers were Alfred D. Chandler, Philip Selznick, Igor Ansoff and Peter Drucker.

The following definition however, captures the essence of the term Strategic Management:

"Strategic management is an ongoing process that evaluates and controls the business and the industries in which the company is involved; assesses its competitors and sets goals and strategies to meet all existing and potential competitors; and then reassesses each strategy annually or quarterly [i.e., regularly] to determine how it has been implemented and whether it has succeeded or needs replacement by a new strategy to meet changed circumstances, new technology, new competitors, a new economic environment or a new social, financial or political environment."

Any organization needs strategy in the following constraints:

a. When the resources are finite.

b. When there is uncertainty about competitive strengths and behavior.

c. When the commitment of resources is irreversible.

d. When decisions must be coordinated between far-flung places and over time.

e. When there is uncertainty about the control of initiative.

LEVELS OF STRATEGY

So, Strategy for any organization is the pattern of major objectives, purposes or goals and essential policies and plans for achieving those goals, stated in such a way as to define what business the company is in or is to be in and the kind of company it is or is to be. Strategy is concerned with the development of potential for results and the development of a reaction capability to adapt the environmental changes. Quite naturally we find there are hierarchies of strategies and in most (large) corporations there are several levels of management. Strategic management is the highest of these levels in the sense that it is the broadest applying to all parts of the firm, while also incorporating the longest time horizon. It gives direction to corporate values, corporate culture, corporate goals and corporate missions. Under this broad corporate strategy there are typically business-level competitive strategies and functional unit strategies.

Corporate strategy refers to the overarching strategy of the diversified firm. Such a corporate strategy answers the questions of "which businesses should we be in?" and "how does being in these businesses create synergy and/or add to the competitive advantage of the corporation as a whole?"

Business strategy refers to the aggregated strategies of single business firm or a strategic business unit (SBU) in a diversified corporation. According to Michael Porter, a firm must formulate a business strategy that incorporates cost leadership, differentiation or focus in order to achieve a sustainable competitive advantage and long-term success in its chosen areas or industries. Alternatively, according to W. Chan Kim and Renée Mauborgne, an organization can achieve high growth and profits by creating a Blue Ocean Strategy that breaks the previous value-cost trade off by simultaneously pursuing both differentiation and low cost.

Functional strategies include marketing strategies, new product development strategies, human resource strategies, financial strategies, legal strategies, supply-chain strategies and information technology management strategies. The emphasis is on short and medium term plans and is limited to the domain of each department's functional responsibility. Each functional department attempts to do its part in meeting overall corporate objectives and hence to some extent their strategies are derived from broader corporate strategies. Many companies feel that a functional organizational structure is not an efficient way to organize activities so they have reengineered according to processes or SBUs.

A strategic business unit is a semi-autonomous unit that is usually responsible for its own budgeting, new product decisions, hiring decisions and price setting. An SBU is treated as an internal profit centre by corporate headquarters. A technology strategy, for example, although it is focused on technology as a means of achieving an organization's overall objective(s), may include dimensions that are beyond the scope of a single business unit, engineering organization or IT department.

An additional level of strategy called **operational strategy** was encouraged by Peter Drucker in his theory of management by objectives (MBO). It is very narrow in focus and deals with day-to-day operational activities such as scheduling criteria. It must operate within a budget but is not at liberty to adjust or create that budget. Operational level strategies are informed by business level strategies which, in turn, are informed by corporate level strategies

Today, most strategic action takes place at business unit level ,where sophisticated tools and techniques permit the analysis of a business; the forecasting of such variables as market growth, pricing and the impact of government regulation; and the establishment of a plan that can sidestep threats in an erratic environment from competitors, economic cycles and social, political and consumer changes. Each functional area of a business for example marketing makes its own unique contribution to strategy formulation at different levels.

STRATEGIC MANAGEMENT PROCESS

The strategic management process consists of three stages:

1. Strategy Formulation (strategy planning)
2. Strategy Implementation.
3. Strategy Evaluation

EXHIBIT 1.1 Strategic Management Process

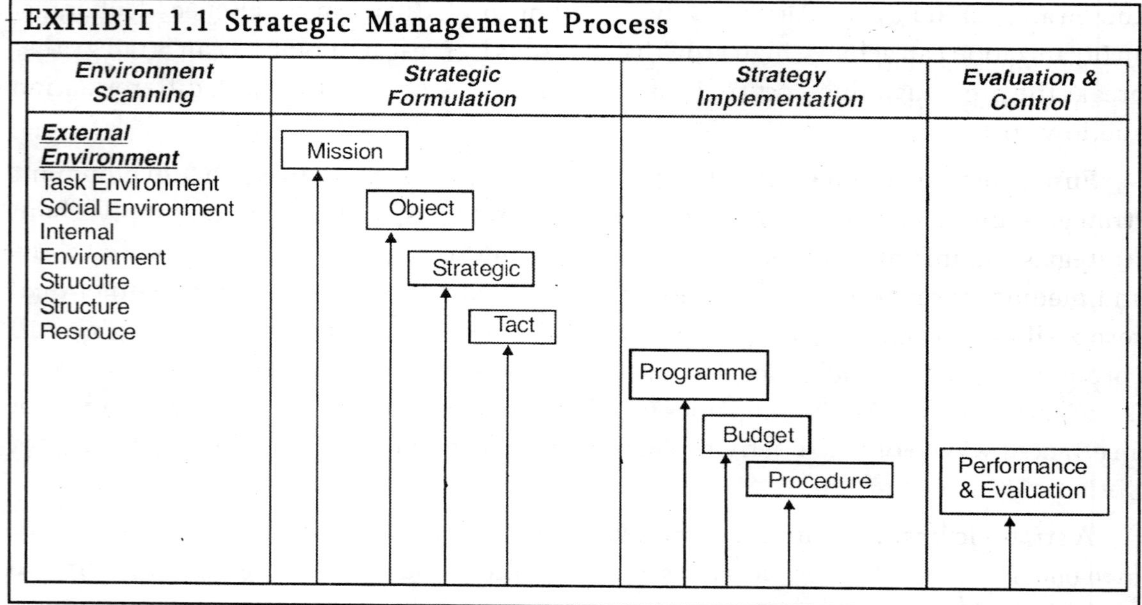

Strategic Formulation:

Strategic formulation means a strategy formulate to execute the business activities. Strategy formulation includes developing:-

i. Vision and Mission (The target of the business).
ii. Strength and weakness (Strong points of business and also weaknesses).
iii. Opportunities and threats (These are related with external environment for the business).

Strategy formulation is also concerned with setting ***long term goals and objectives***, generating alternative strategies to achieve that long term goals and choosing particular strategy to pursue. The considerations for the best strategy formulation should be as follows:

- Allocation of resources
- Business to enter or retain
- Business to divest or liquidate
- Joint ventures or mergers

- Whether to expand or not
- Moving into foreign markets
- Trying to avoid take over

Strategy Implementation:

Strategy implementation requires a firm to establish annual objectives, devise policies, motivating employees and allocate resources so that formulated strategies can be executed. Strategy implementation includes developing strategy supportive culture, creating an effective organizational structure, redirecting marketing efforts, preparing budgets, developing and utilizing information system and linking employee compensation to organizational performance. Strategy implementation is often called the action stage of strategic management. Implementing means mobilizing employees and managers in order to put formulated strategies into action. It is often considered to be most difficult stage of strategic management. It requires personal discipline, commitment and sacrifice. Strategy formulated but not implemented serve no useful purpose.

Strategy evaluation:

Strategy evaluation is the final stage in the strategic management process. Management desperately needs to know when particular strategies are not working well; strategy evaluation is the primary means for obtaining this information. All strategies are subject to future modification because external and internal forces are constantly changing.

ORGANISATIONAL MISSION AND PURPOSE

Strategists are individuals who form strategies and are most responsible for the success or failure of an organization. Strategists have various job titles, such as chief executive officer, president and owner, chair of the board, executive director, chancellor, dean or entrepreneur. Strategists help an organization gather, analyze and organize information. They track industry and competitive trends, develop forecasting models and scenario analyses, evaluate corporate and divisional performance, spot emerging market opportunities, identify business threats and develop creative action plans. Strategic planners usually serve in a support or staff role. Usually found in higher levels of management, they typically have considerable authority for decision making in the firm. The CEO is the most visible and critical strategic manager. Any manager who has responsibility for a unit or division, responsibility for profit and loss outcomes or direct authority over a major piece of the business is a strategic manager (strategist).Strategists differ as much as organizations themselves and these differences must be considered in the formulation, implementation and evaluation of strategies. Some strategists will not consider some types of strategies because of their personal philosophies. Strategists differ in their attitudes, values, ethics, willingness to take risks, concern for social responsibility, concern for profitability, concern for short-run versus long-run aims and management style.

Vision Statements

Many organizations today develop a "vision statement" which answers the question, what do we want to become? Developing a vision statement is often considered the first step in strategic planning, preceding even development of a mission statement. Many vision statements are a single sentence. For example the vision statement of Stokes Eye Clinic in Florence, South Carolina, is "Our vision is to take care of your vision." The vision of the Institute of Management Accountants is "Global leadership in education, certification and practice of management accounting and financial management."

Mission Statements

Mission statements are "enduring statements of purpose that distinguish one business from other similar firms. A mission statement identifies the scope of a firm's operations in product and market terms. It addresses the basic question that faces all strategists: What is our business? A clear mission statement describes the values and priorities of an organization. Developing a mission statement compels strategists to think about the nature and scope of present operations and to assess the potential attractiveness of future markets and activities. A mission statement broadly charts the future direction of an organization. An example mission statement is provided below for Microsoft. Microsoft's mission is to create software for the personal computer that empowers and enriches people in the workplace, at school and at home. Microsoft's early vision of a computer on every desk and in every home is coupled today with a strong commitment to Internet-related technologies that expand the power and reach of the PC and its users. As the world's leading software provider, Microsoft strives to produce innovative products that meet our customers' evolving needs.

External Opportunities and Threats

External opportunities and external threats refer to economic, social, cultural, demographic, environmental, political, legal, governmental, technological and competitive trends and events that could significantly benefit or harm an organization in the future. Opportunities and threats are largely beyond the control of a single organization, thus the term external. The computer revolution, biotechnology, population shifts, changing work values and attitudes, space exploration, recyclable packages and increased competition from foreign companies are examples of opportunities or threats for companies. These types of changes are creating a different type of consumer and consequently a need for different types of products, services and strategies. Other opportunities and threats may include the passage of a law, the introduction of a new product by a competitor, a national catastrophe or the declining value of the dollar. A competitor's strength could be a threat. Unrest in the Balkans, rising interest rates or the war against drugs could represent an opportunity or a threat. A basic tenet of strategic management is that firms need to formulate strategies to take advantage of external opportunities and to avoid or reduce the impact of external threats. For this reason, identifying, monitoring and evaluating external opportunities and threats are essential for success.

Environmental Scanning

The process of conducting research and gathering and assimilating external information is sometimes called environmental scanning or industry analysis. Lobbying is one activity that some organizations utilize to influence external opportunities and threats. In Environment scanning the management scans eternal environment for opportunities and threats and internal environment for strengths and weaknesses. The factors which are most important for corporation factor are referred as a strategic factor and summarized as SWOT standing for strength, weaknesses, opportunities and threats.

EXHIBIT 1.2

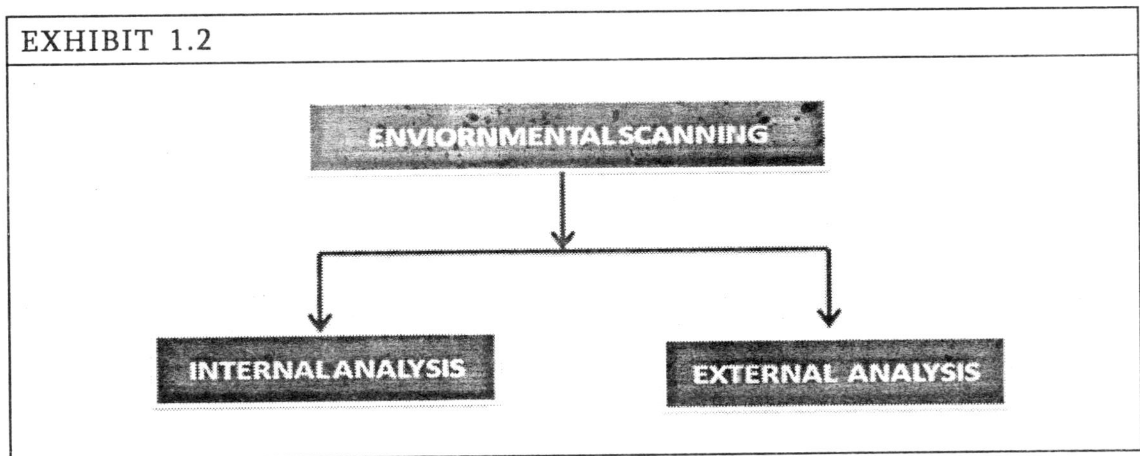

The external environment consists of opportunities and threats variables are outside the organization. External environment has two parts (Exhibit: 1.2):

- **Task Environment:** Task environment includes all those factors which affect the organization and itself affected by the organization. These factors affect the specific related organizations. These factors are shareholders community, labor unions, creditor, customers, competitors, trade associations.

- **Social Environment:** It includes those forces which do not affect in the short run activities of the organization but it influences the long run activities or decisions. PEST analysis are taken for social environment.PEST analysis stands for political and legal economic socio cultural logical and technological .

Internal Strengths and Weaknesses/Internal assessments

Internal strengths and internal weaknesses are an organization's controllable activities that are performed especially well or poorly. They arise in the management, marketing, finance/accounting, production/operations, research and development and computer information systems activities of a business. Identifying and evaluating organizational strengths and weaknesses in the functional areas of a business is an essential strategic-management activity. Organizations strive to pursue strategies that capitalize on internal strengths and improve on internal weaknesses. Strengths and weaknesses are determined relative to competitors. Relative deficiency or superiority is important information. Also, strengths and weaknesses can be determined by elements of being rather than performance. For example, strength may involve ownership of natural resources or an historic reputation for quality. Strengths and weaknesses may be determined relative to a firm's own objectives. For example, high levels of inventory turnover may not be strength to a firm that seeks never to stock-out. Internal factors can be determined in a number of ways that include computing ratios, measuring performance and comparing to past periods and industry averages. Various types of surveys also can be developed and administered to examine internal factors such as employee morale, production efficiency, advertising effectiveness, and customer loyalty.

THE STRATEGIC-MANAGEMENT MODEL

The strategic-management process best can be studied and applied using a model. Every model represents some kind of process. The framework illustrated in Exhibit 1.3 is a widely accepted, comprehensive model of the strategic-management process. This model does not guarantee success, but it does represent a clear and practical approach for formulating, implementing and evaluating strategies. Relationships among major components of the strategic-management process are shown in the model.

EXHIBIT 1.3 ***A Comprehensive Strategic Management Model***

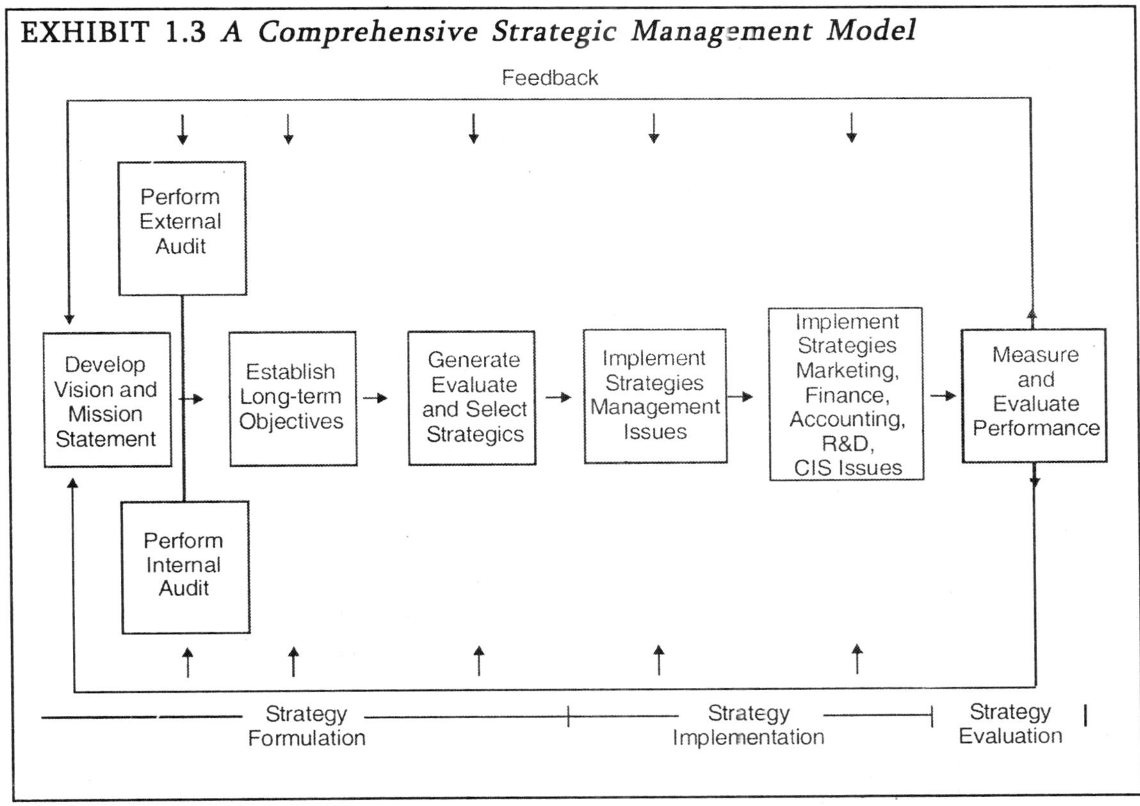

Source: Fred R. David, "How Companies Define Their Mission," Long Range Planning 22, no. 3 (June 1988): 40.

Identifying an organization's existing vision, mission, objectives and strategies is the logical starting point for strategic management because a firm's present situation and condition may preclude certain strategies and may even dictate a particular course of action. Every organization has a vision, mission, objectives and strategy, even if these elements are not consciously designed, written or communicated. The answer to where an organization is going can be determined largely by where the organization has been. The strategic-management process is dynamic and continuous. A change in any one of the major components in the model can necessitate a change in any or all of the other components. For instance, a shift in the economy could represent a major opportunity and require a change in long-term objectives and strategies; a failure to accomplish annual objectives could require a change in policy; or a major competitor's change in strategy could require a change in the firm's mission. Therefore, strategy formulation, implementation and evaluation activities should be performed on a continual basis, not just at the end of the year or semiannually. The strategic-management process never really ends. Application of the strategic-management process is typically more formal in larger and well-established organizations. Formality refers to the extent that participants, responsibilities, authority, duties and approach are specified. Smaller businesses tend to be less formal. Firms that compete in complex, rapidly changing environments such as technology companies tend to be more formal in strategic planning. Firms that have many divisions, products, markets and technologies also tend to be more formal in applying strategic-management concepts. Greater formality in applying the strategic-management process is usually positively associated with the cost, comprehensiveness, accuracy and success of planning across all types and sizes of organizations.

BENEFITS & IMPORTANCE OF STRATEGIC MANAGEMENT

Following are the major benefits of Strategic management:

- Proactive in shaping firm's future
- Initiate and influence actions
- Formulate better strategies (Systematic, logical, rational approach)

Financial benefits:

- Improved productivity
- Improved sales
- Improved profitability

Non-Financial benefits:

- Increased employee productivity
- Improved understanding of competitors' strategies
- Greater awareness of external threats
- Understanding of performance reward relationships
- Better problem-avoidance
- Lesser resistance to change

Research indicates that organizations using strategic-management concepts are more profitable and successful than those that do not. Businesses using strategic-management concepts show significant improvement in sales, profitability and productivity compared to firms without systematic planning activities. High-performing firms tend to do systematic planning to prepare for future fluctuations in their external and internal environments. Firms with planning systems more closely resembling strategic management theory generally exhibit superior long-term financial performance relative to their industry. High-performing firms seem to make more informed decisions with good anticipation of both short- and long-term consequences. On the other hand, firms that perform poorly often engage in activities that are shortsighted and do not reflect good forecasting of future conditions. Strategists of low-performing organizations are often preoccupied with solving internal problems and meeting paperwork deadlines. They typically underestimate their competitors' strengths and overestimate their own firm's strengths. They often attribute weak performance to uncontrollable factors such as poor economy, technological change or foreign competition. They typically underestimate their competitors' strengths and overestimate their own firm's strengths. They often attribute weak performance to uncontrollable factors such as poor economy, technological change or foreign competition.

Importance of Strategic Management

Strategic management becomes important due to the following reasons:

1. Globalization: The survival for business

First, global considerations impact virtually all strategic decisions. The boundaries of countries no longer can define the limits of our imaginations. To see and appreciate the world from the perspective of others has become a matter of survival for businesses. The underpinnings of strategic management hinge upon managers' gaining an understanding of competitors, markets, prices, suppliers, distributors, governments, creditors, shareholders and customers worldwide. The price and quality of a firm's products and services must be competitive on a worldwide basis, not just a local basis. The distance between the business sectors are becoming less due to the provisions of certain facilities. Although political boundaries are there but in order to become successful in business it is essential to laid stress on globalization.

2. E-Commerce: A business tool

A second theme is that electric commerce (e-commerce) has become a vital strategic-management tool. An increasing number of companies are gaining competitive advantage by using the Internet for direct selling and for communication with suppliers, customers, creditors, partners, shareholders, clients and competitors who may be dispersed globally. E-commerce allows firms to sell products, advertise, purchase supplies, bypass intermediaries, track inventory, eliminate paperwork and share information. In total, electronic commerce is minimizing the expense and cumbersomeness of time, distance and space in doing business, which yields better customer service, greater efficiency, improved products and higher profitability. The Internet and personal computers are changing the way we organize our lives; inhabit our homes; and relate to and interact with family, friends, neighbors and even ourselves. The Internet promotes endless comparison shopping which enables consumers worldwide to band together to demand discounts.

The Internet has transferred power from businesses to individuals so swiftly that in another decade there may be "regulations" imposed on groups of consumers. Politicians may one day debate the need for "regulation on consumers" rather than "regulation on big business" because of the Internet's empowerment of individuals. Buyers used to face big obstacles to getting the best price and service, such as limited time and data to compare, but now consumers can quickly scan hundreds of vendors' offerings. Or they can go to web sites such as www.comparenet.com that offers detailed information on more than 100,000 consumer products. The Internet has changed the very nature and core of buying and selling in nearly all industries. It has fundamentally changed the economics of business in every single industry worldwide

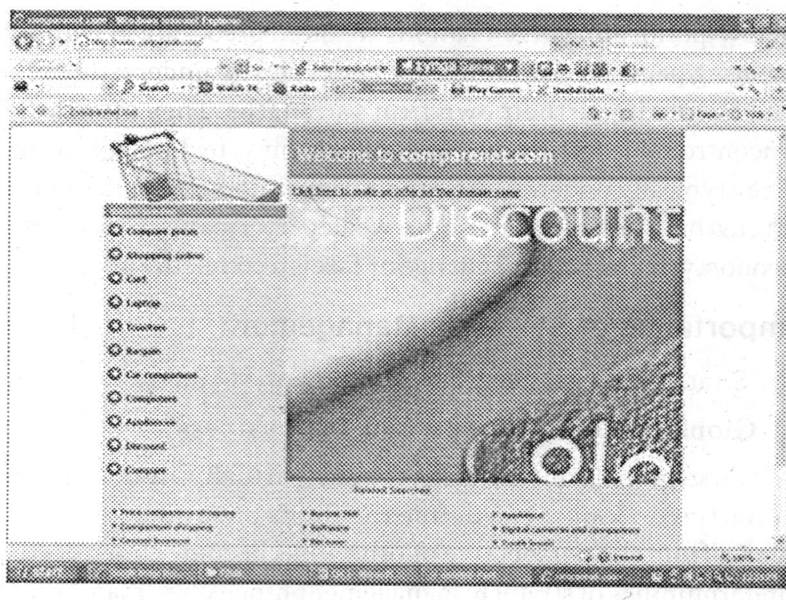

3. **Earth environment has become a major strategic issue**

A third theme is that the natural environment has become an important strategic issue. With the demise of communism and the end of the Cold War, perhaps there is now no greater threat to business and society than the continuous exploitation and decimation of our natural environment. The resources are scarce but the wants are unlimited. In order to meet the wants of the world, the resources should be efficiently utilized. For example, the use of oil resources or energy resources will make the people to use these resources for a long time.

MARKETING STRATEGY- OVERVIEW

Strategy is the crafting of plans to reach goals. **Marketing strategies** are those plans designed to reach marketing goals. A good marketing strategy should integrate an organization's marketing goals, policies, and action sequences (tactics) into a cohesive whole. The objective of a marketing strategy is to put the organization into a position to carry out its mission effectively and efficiently. Marketing strategies are dynamic and interactive. They are partially planned and partially unplanned.

Types of Marketing Strategies

Every marketing strategy is unique, but if we abstract from the individualizing details, each can be reduced into a generic marketing strategy.

1. **Strategies based on market Dominance** - Typically there are four types of market dominance strategies:
   i. Leader
   ii. Challenger
   iii. Follower
   iv. Nicher
2. **Innovation Strategies**- This deals with the firm rate of new product development and business model innovation. It asks whether the company is on the cutting edge of technology and business innovation. There are three types:
   1. Pioneers
   2. Close followers
   3. Late followers

3. Horizontal Integration

In microeconomics and strategic management, **horizontal integration** is a theory of ownership and control. It is a strategy used by a business or corporation that seeks to sell one type of product in numerous markets. To get this market coverage, several small subsidiary companies are created. Each markets the product to a different market segment or to a different geographical area. This is sometimes referred to as the horizontal integration of marketing. The horizontal integration of production is where a firm has plants in several locations producing similar products. Horizontal integration in marketing is much more common than horizontal integration in production

4. Vertical integration

In microeconomics and strategic management, **vertical integration** is a theory describing a style of ownership and control. Vertically integrated companies are united through a hierarchy and share a common owner. Usually each member of the hierarchy produces a different product and the products combine to satisfy a common need.There are three varieties of this: backward vertical integration, forward vertical integration and balanced vertical integration.

In **backward vertical integration**, the company sets up subsidiaries that produce some of the inputs used in the production of its products. For example, an automobile company may own a tyre company, a glass company and a metal company. Control of these three subsidiaries is intended to create a stable supply of inputs and ensure a consistent quality in their final product.

In **forward vertical integration**, the company sets up subsidiaries that distribute or market products to customers or use the products themselves. An example of this is a movie studio that also owns a chain of theaters.

In **balanced vertical integration**, the company sets up subsidiaries that both supply them with inputs and distribute their outputs.

Aggressiveness strategies (business)

Business strategies can be categorized in many ways. One popular method is to assess strategies based on their degree of aggressiveness. **Aggressiveness strategies** are rated according to their marketing assertiveness, their risk propensity, financial leverage and product innovation, speed of decision-making and other measures of business aggressiveness. Typically the range of aggressiveness strategies is classified into four categories:

1. Prospector
2. Defender
3. Analyzer
4. Reactor

1. Prospector strategy

This is the most aggressive of the four strategies. It typically involves active programs to expand into new markets and stimulate new opportunities. New product development is vigorously pursued and attacks on competitors are a common way of obtaining additional market share. They respond quickly to any signs of market opportunity and do so with little research or analysis. A large proportion of their revenue comes from new products or new markets. The risk of product failure or market rejection is high. Advertising, sales promotion and personal selling costs are a high percentage of sales.

2. Defender Strategy

This strategy entails a decision not to aggressively pursue markets. A defender strategy entails finding and maintaining a secure and relatively stable market.

In their attempt to secure this stable market they either keep prices low, keep advertising and other promotional costs low, engage in vertical integration, offer a limited range of products or offer better quality or service.

3. Analyzer

The analyzer is in between the defender and prospector. They take less risk and make fewer mistakes than a prospector, but are less committed to stability than defenders. Most firms are analyzers. They are seldom a first mover in an industry but are often second or third place entrants. They tend to expand into areas close to their existing core competency. Rather than expand into wholly new markets, they gradually expand existing markets. They try to maintain a balanced portfolio of products

4. Reactor

A reactor has no proactive strategy. They react to events as they occur. They respond only when they are forced to by macro environmental pressures. This is the least effective of the four strategies. It is without direction or focus.

PILLARS OF MARKETING-STPD

1. Segmentation(S)

Segmentation divides the market into distinct subunits of customers with similar needs. Market segmentation is a concept in economics and marketing. A market segment is a subset of a market made up of people or organizations with one or more characteristics that cause them to demand similar product and/or services based on qualities of those products such as price or function. A true market segment meets all of the following criteria: it is distinct from other segments (different segments have different needs), it is homogeneous within the segment (exhibits common needs); it responds similarly to a market stimulus and it can be reached by a market intervention.

The term is also used when consumers with identical product and/or service needs are divided into groups so they can be charged different amounts for the services. The people in a given segment are supposed to be similar in terms of criteria by which they are segmented and different from other segments in terms of these criteria. These can be broadly viewed as 'positive' and 'negative' applications of the same idea, splitting up the market into smaller groups.

Characteristics of Segmentation

- It facilities proper choice of market
- It is adapting offer to the Target
- Marketing efforts more efficient & economic
- Benefits to customer
- Consumer markets can be segmented and based on the following :
  - Geographic
  - Demographic
  - Psychographic and
  - Behavioral characteristics of customers

Geographic:

1. Nation

2. State
3. Region
4. City
5. Climate
6. Density (urban/rural)

Demographic

1. Age/Family size/Life cycle
2. Education
3. Income
4. Religion/Race/Generation
5. Nationality/Social class
6. Gender Occupation

Psychographic:

1. Lifestyle - culture, sports, outdoor, Page 3 etc.,
2. Personality - introvert, extrovert, compulsive, ambitious, authoritarian etc.,

Behavioral:

1. Occasions - regular, special
2. Benefits
3. User status - non user, regular
4. Usage rate - light, heavy
5. Loyalty status - medium, strong
6. Readiness stage - unaware, aware
7. Attitude towards product - positive, indifferent

2. Targeting (T)

Targeting identify the most profitable segments that its products and services can cater to. Targeting involves taking decisions regarding the choice of the segments on which the limited resources (include the marketing skills, managerial capabilities, technological innovations and the cost advantages) are to be focused.

The smart choice for the company to decide how it can deploy its resources to optimize efficiency, sales and profitability **For example, HUL started selling shampoos in sachets in order to tap the potential in rural markets.**

Targeting

- Single segment concentration - small car only
- Selective specialization - FM channel targeting all age groups with different programs
- Product specialization - one product selling to different segments (paint)
- Market specialization - many needs of 1 group - selling only to schools
- Full market coverage - Coke

3. Positioning(P)

Positioning is a term introduced by Jack Trout and Al Ries in 1969, means creating an image in the perception of the buyer in the target market about the product or service of a company with an advantage over the competition It is a combination of both market and psychological positioning

Positioning Concept

- A company can position its product based on various factors:
  - Positioning by attribute
  - Positioning by price/quality
  - Positioning by use or application
  - Positioning by with respect to a competitor
- Revamped Positioning Strategy
  - Assumption is that customers focus on the basic product or service and do not give much importance to the added features. Example.Air Deccan (provides only the basic)
- Break Free Positioning Strategy
  - According to this strategy, the product must be positioned in such a way that it escapes from categorization e.g. Dettol Soap
- Michael E. Porter has developed his 'Five Forces Model' to help managers to analyze the business environment. It discusses namely:
  - The Threat of new entrants
  - The Bargaining power of buyers
  - The Bargaining power of suppliers
  - The Rivalry among existing players and
  - The Threat of substitute products

4. Differentiation(D)

Giving something unique and innovative means differentiation. Here the business concentrates on achieving superior performance in an important customer benefit area, such as being the leader in service, quality, style or technology but not leading in all of these things. Intel, for instance, differentiates itself through leadership in technology, coming out with new microprocessors at breakneck speed.

MARKET SITUATION STRATEGIES: LEADERS, CHALLENGERS, FOLLOWERS, NICHERS.

Typically there are four types of **market dominance strategies** that a marketer will consider: These are Market leaders, Market challengers, Market followers and Market nichers

Market Leader

The market leader is dominant in its industry. It has substantial market share and often extensive distribution arrangements with retailers. It typically is the industry leader in developing innovative new business models and new products (although not always). It sometimes has some market power in determining either price or output. Of the four dominance strategies, it has the most flexibility in crafting strategy. The main options available to market leaders are:

- Expand the total market by finding
  a. new users of the product
  b. new uses of the product
  c. more usage on each use occasion
- Protect your existing market share by:
  a. developing new product ideas
  b. improve customer service
  c. improve distribution effectiveness
  d. reduce costs
- Expand your market share:
  a. by targeting one or more competitor
  b. without being noticed by government regulators

A market leader has considerable market share, significance presence in the industry and acknowledged as the leader by other firms. A market leader has to guard itself from competition. Competitors will always try to attack the leader at its weak spot or challenge in its strong area. Therefore they need to remain in that position by adopting certain strategies: e.g., Microsoft, Gillette, LG, Hero Moto Corp. (formerly Hero Honda).

Market Challenger

A market challenger is a firm in a strong, but not dominant position that is following an aggressive strategy of trying to gain market share. It typically targets the industry leader (for example, Pepsi targets Coke), but it could also target smaller, more vulnerable competitors. The fundamental principles involved are:

- Assess the strength of the target competitor. Consider the amount of support that the target might muster from allies.
- Choose only one target at a time.
- Find a weakness in the target position. Attack at this point. Consider how long it will take for the target to realign their resources so as to reinforce this weak spot.
- Launch the attack on as narrow a front as possible. Whereas a defender must defend all their borders, an attacker has the advantage of being able to concentrate their forces at one place.
- Launch the attack quickly and then consolidate. Some of the options open to a market challenger are:
    - Price discounts or price cutting
    - Line extensions
    - Introduce new products
    - Reduce product quality
    - Increase product quality
    - Improve service
    - Change distribution
    - Cost reductions
    - Intensify promotional activity

Example of Market Challenger:

1. Frontal attack -Amul
2. Flank attack(Target enemy's weak spot by geographical & segmental attack)e.g., LG
3. Encirclement attack(grand offensive on several fronts)

4. Bypass attack(diversifying into unrelated products/new markets/new technologies) e.g., Google over Yahoo
5. Guerilla warfare - Shivaji

Market Follower

Market followers prefer to follow the leader rather than attack it. Most follower firms manufacture products leveraging on the product innovations of the market leaders. If the follower attacks a market leader with the same quality offerings and at the same price, it might have to face severe attacks from the market leader. So, unless the follower firm has some strong point in its armor, it will not dare attack the market leader

A market follower is a firm in a strong, but not dominant position that is content to stay at that position. The advantages of this strategy are:

- No expensive R&D failures
- No risk of bad business model
- Best practices are already established
- Able to capitalize on the promotional activities of the market leader
- Minimal risk of competitive attacks
- Don't waste money in a head-on battle with the market leader

Examples of Market follower

1. Counterfeiter - Duplicate leaders market & sell in black market e.g., Pirated product
2. Cloner - emulates with slight variations e.g., LAVIS,PHILPS
3. Imitator - Copies something but maintain differentiation
4. Adapter - adapts from leader & improves

Market Nichers

In nicher strategy the firm concentrates on a select few target markets. It is also called a focus strategy. It is hoped that by focusing ones marketing efforts on one or two narrow market segments and tailoring your marketing mix to these specialized markets, you can better meet the needs of that target market. The nicher should be large enough to be profitable, but small enough to be ignored by the major industry players.

Profit margins are emphasized rather than revenue or market share. The firm typically looks to gain a competitive advantage through effectiveness rather than efficiency. It is most suitable for relatively small firms and has much in common with. The most successful nichers tend to have the following characteristics:

- They tend to be in high value added industries and are able to obtain high margins.
- They tend to be highly focused on a specific market segment.
- They tend to market high end products or services and are able to use a premium pricing strategy.
- They tend to keep their operating expenses down by spending less on R&D, advertising and personal selling.

Example - Logitech has become the king of nicher markets by making every variation of computer mouse.

CLOSING CASE:-SOUTHERN COMFORT RESTAURANT

Southern Comfort was the most happening South Indian restaurant in town. Its teak-and-ersatz banana plants décor was appealing; the food, authentically South Indian; and the service, excellent. Still, food was the last thing on the mind of T. R. Jagmohan, 46, the stubby, balding CEO of the Rs. 62-crore Coolex, the country's number one air-conditioner manufacturer.

However, it seemed to be the only thing that mattered to Jagmohan's table-mate, Ashish Mahapatra, 49. Yes, this was one of the foremost strategy thinkers in the world, a professor at the University of Southern California, who was in the country on a lecture-tour. The launch was Jagmohan's idea, but he had warned his friend from B-school that it was not to talk about old times. He watched with growing impatience as Mahapatra polished off the last of his adai, a pancake made of pulses.

"Some exercise for the brain after a good meal, I guess", sighed Mahapatra. "You want to pick my brains about strategy-planning. Tell me."

Jagmohan was only too willing. "Coolex was founded in 1965 by a group of technocrats. Professionally managed since its inception, it went public quite early. When I joined the company as a management trainee 14 years ago, we had a 55 per cent share of the local central air-conditioning business. Today, it stands at 40 per cent. The rest of the market is fragmented, with our closest competitor, Airtemp, accounting for a 15 per cent share. Still, everyday brings more competition. Airtamp itself is a new-comer, having launched its products only in 1994. And it is not just competition, even our customers are becoming increasingly unpredictable.

"And that worries you even more," Mahapatra finished for Jagmohan. "But what is your vision for Coolex?" have you defined it ever?"

"To become a one-stop national shop offering air-conditioning products, systems and services. We have set ourselves the goal of achieving a turnover Rs. 1,000 crore by 2002 by growing all our business: central air-conditioning, unitary air-conditioners and ducted systems."

"How much do each of these business contribute to your sales?" queried Mahapatra.

"We recorded a turnover of Rs. 620 crore in the year ended March 31, 1997. Seventy per cent of this came from central air-conditioning, 15 per cent from unitary air-conditioners, and 15 per cent from our trading operations."

"A 60 per cent growth rate over 4 years is a fairly conservative target," said Mahapatra. "Do you wish to discuss with me the strategy that can help you achieve this?"

"In part, yes," conceded Jagmohan. "What should our business-mix be? Can we achieve our goals faster by focusing on one or two business? Those are the questions our strategy needs to address. But I did not come to you for the answers; I wanted to reassure myself that we have the strategy-formulation processes to address this as well as any other issue we may later face."

"Describe them to me," said Mahapatra. "Every year, in January, I get my senior management team - the functional heads of Finance, Marketing, HR and Operations and the 3 heads of our business units - for a week-long discussion on the company's future course. We ask ourselves the kind of questions you'd encounter in any strategy-development process. Where are we today? Where do we want to be 3 years from now? How do we bridge the gap between our resources and our goals? Who are our competitors today? What is the competitive framework in which we operate? What are the strategies being adopted by our competitors? The answer from the basis of our strategy-formulation."

"Good," said Mahapatra, "you took the caramel-custard route. Just ask the questions every company has been asking itself since the time of Fredrick Winslow Taylor and you have a strategy. I hope you realize that the only reason this approach worked over the years are your historical advantage and familiarity with a regulated environment. And both are under threat now."

"I realize that," said Jagmohan. "We need to now look at the development in electronics and energy-management and incorporate them into our strategy-planning. But how?"

" What's wrong with the conventional approach," started Mahapatra, "is that it relies on a static picture of the competition, underplays the role of innovation, exaggerates the role of the environment and does not account for the varying resource-and competence-levels across companies. My experience with companies in several parts of the world indicates that your problems are not exclusive to Coolex. This malaise can, partly, be attributed to the fact that the planning process itself has become - as in your case - a mundane, annual ritual. Managers view it with no enthusiasm. It takes too much time without, often, leading anywhere and it is a waste to contemplate long-term strategy in an uncertain atmosphere, where even the next day may bring far-reaching changes. Traditional strategy-planning tools, like the Portfolio Models, have not really worked and synergy across business units remains elusive."

"What do I do? Dispense with it completely?" asked Jagmohan.

"No way. But you should try looking at it from a different perspective. Do not try to find the most advantageous strategic position in relation to the environment and your competitors. Instead, move towards building and exploiting your resources. Why do not you base your strategy on your core competencies instead of the environment and the industry"? Let me elaborate on the deficiencies of the latter. If you adopt the industry structure approach to quality, your strategy planning process becomes reactive. You look at your competitors, suppliers or customers - and react. This approach can work as long as the going is good. But it does have its limitations; it is after all, derived from a theory that sought to explain industry dynamics, not company competitiveness. However, if you adopt the competence based approach, you will look within your organization, find your core strengths and understand how you can leverage them to gain a competitive edge. It will help you realize which strategy is good for Coolex without blindly following every move that your competitors make. After all, you may not be able to emulate your competitors simply because you do not have the expertise to do whatever they are doing. Do what you do well; the rest will just fall into place."

There the luncheon ended. A satiated Mahapatra left to address a group of managers at a seminar organized by the Bombay Management Association. And a disturbed Jagmohan returned to work.

Spurted by his discussion with Mahapatra, Jagmohan convened a meeting of his brains-trust the next morning. "I have decided that we need to take a different approach to our strategy-planning," he told the 7 senior executives who assembled in the conference-room. "Let us find what our internal strengths are. I think there are 3 characteristics of strength. One, it needs to be unique to Coolex. Two, it should be difficult to emulate. And three, it should be internally sustainable over a period of time. For the next 30 minutes, we will not speak. Instead, we will put down our thoughts on paper. Then, we will take turns to speak. And, hopefully, we will have a clear idea of our strengths."

Thirty minutes passed. Avinash Vaidya, 38, Director (Finance), was the first to speak about, expectedly, finance: "Our working capital requirements are met by client-funds rather than bank finance. Loans constitute less than 5 per cent of our total working capital requirements. We have always ensured an optimal level of liquidity in our operations: by setting a modular schedule for each project, completing each module on time and collecting a part-payment at the end of each module. This sets us from our competitors. Their emphasis on unitary air-conditioners and ducted systems makes it difficult for them to emulate us."

A.V. Raman, 45, Director (Operations), was next: "Our core strength is our project management skills. We ensure the best deliverables, in terms of service and adherence to schedules." Raju Rastogi, the Head of the Ducting Systems business unit, agreed: "Our competitors do not have the capabilities that Coolex has in terms of engineering, procurement and construction."

Sanjeev Nanda, 43, Director (HR), predictably, picked people: "At Coolex, we have a disproportionately large share of the talent in the air-conditioning industry. With 650 qualified engineers and 1,200 trained technicians, we can boost of the largest concentration of specialists in the country. Their competence has contributed to our monopoly in central air-conditioning. That, in turn, enables us to attract talent."

Girish Wadhwa, 49, the Head of the Central air-conditioning business unit, picked relationship management: "We have built, over a period of time, excellent relationships with architects, interior designers, construction firms and suppliers. This network functions as an entry-barrier to competition."

Debashish Raña, 35, the Head of Trading Operations, stuck to his business unit:"We have the finest logistics support for our trading operations. Over the years, we have not only built and nurtured our distribution channels, but also diversified the range of products on offer. We have 200 dealers marketing products we source from 65 companies today."

THE CORE COMPETENCE AUDIT

A. Does the company have a core competence?

- Does the company possess one or more identifiable skills?
- Are the skills embedded in one or more groups of people?
- Do the skills lead to improvements in one or more processes?
- Does the company benchmark these processes against global standards?
- Do the results suggest that the processes are best-in-class?

B. Does the core competence add value?

- Does the customer think that the company's skills are stronger than its rivals?
- Do the competence lead to measurably superior results?
- Do those results add value to the products?
- Are those results central to the company's value proposition?
- Are those results boosting market shares and profits?

C. Is the core competence sustainable?

- Does the core competence steer the corporate power structure?
- Has it been ratified by the CEO?
- Are there continuing efforts to develop the competence?
- Has the competence been developed through a focused effort?
- Has it been transferred across the origination?

D. Is the company nurturing its core competent?

- Is the company retaining people with the core skills?
- Is it ensuring that too many decentralized initiatives are not taken?
- Is it continuously measuring the results of key processes?
- Is it setting rising targets for results from these processes?
- Is it trying to impart these core skills to new people?

"And," continued Gopal Menon, 41, Director (Marketing), "our strategy of going in for margins instead of volumes seems to have worked in our trading division. We choose products based on emerging technologies and develop the brands over a period of time. Several technology intensive products that we distribute have benefited from this. Given the number of inquiries we generate, we seem to be among the most sought-after distributors for any company manufacturing such products."

Jagmohan spoke last and he picked an unlikely strength: "Our major internal strength is our structure. We have just 4 layers of management and this has made decision-making flexible in contrast to our competitors. Given that pace is the fifth P, I think our structure gives us competitive advantage."

"But which of these is a core competence?" Jagmohan continued. "I believe that a company cannot have more than two or three core competencies. Going by that logic, our core competence is our turnkey abilities. Should we divest our interests in manufacturing and trading and focus on just this?"

"That would not make sense," countered Menon. "In most parts of the world, companies in our industry focus their efforts on manufacturing and marketing and outsource project management expertise. And the make for air-conditioners of less than 3-tons capacity is set to grow at 30 per cent a year, where Airtemp, market share of 30 per cent, is the leader. Should we not aim for a largest slice of that market?

Even as Jagmohan tried to think of an answer, Nanda spoke: "What is new in our perspective of strategy? I think we have looked at our internal strengths in our previous attempts at strategy-formulation. Only, we combined this with an analysis of the external environment which was and is critical. Even if we want to carry this approach to its logical conclusion, what should we focus on?

Questions:

1. Do you think that the core competence audit will give the positive results? Discuss
2. Analyze the above case and try to summarize in your own words.
3. "Our major internal strength is our structure. We have just 4 layers of management, and this has made decision-making flexible in contrast to our competitors. Given that pace is the fifth P, I think our structure gives us competitive advantage" - Justify this statement given by Jagmohan from strategic point of view.

SUMMARY & KEY TERMS

This chapter provides an overview of strategic management. It introduces a practical, integrative model of the strategic-management process and defines basic activities and terms in strategic management and discusses its importance. A strategy in a firm is the pattern of major objectives, purposes or goals and essential policies and plans for achieving those goals, stated in such a way as to define what business the company is in or is to be in and the kind of company it is or is to be. Strategy is concerned with the development of potential for results and the development of a reaction capability to adapt the environmental changes. Strategic management is the highest of these levels in the sense that it is the broadest applying to all parts of the firm, while also incorporating the longest time horizon. Under this broad corporate strategy there are typically business-level strategies and functional unit strategies.

The concept of strategic management process consists of three stages i.e. Strategy formulation, Strategy implementation and Strategy evaluation. Most of the large companies have made significant progress in last 10 or 15 years in improving their strategic planning capabilities. This chapter also focuses on the organization mission and purpose. Mission statements are "enduring statements of purpose that distinguish one business from other similar firms. In the process of strategy formulation it is very much essential that a company must go for the environment scanning. In Environment scanning the management scans eternal environment for opportunities and threats and internal environment for strengths and weaknesses.

The strategic management model shows the relationships among major components of the strategic-management process. This model does not guarantee success, but it does represent a clear and practical approach for formulating, implementing and evaluating strategies. The major benefits of Strategic management discussed in this chapter are increased productivity. High-performing firms tend to do systematic planning to prepare for future fluctuations in their external and internal environments. Firms with planning systems more closely resembling strategic management theory generally exhibit superior long-term financial performance relative to their industry. In this strategic role, the companies concentrate on the market to serve, the competition to be handled and the timing of the entry or exit is the major concern of the strategic management.

The objective of a marketing strategy is to put the organization into a position to carry out its mission effectively and efficiently. Marketing strategies are dynamic and interactive. They are partially planned and partially unplanned. Horizontal integration is a theory of ownership and control. It is a strategy used by a business or corporation that seeks to sell one type of product in numerous markets. Vertical integration is a theory describing a style of ownership and control. Vertically integrated companies are united through a hierarchy and share a common owner.

A market segment is a sub-set of a market made up of people or organizations with one or more characteristics that cause them to demand similar product and/or services based on qualities of those products such as price or function. Create and image or a specific identity for the product or brand in the minds of customers called positioning. Giving something unique and innovative is called as differentiation.

There are four types of market dominance strategies that a marketer will consider: These are Market leaders, Market challengers, Market followers and Market nichers. The market leader is dominant in its industry. It has substantial market share and often extensive distribution arrangements with retailers. A market challenger is a firm in a strong, but not dominant position that is following an aggressive strategy of trying to gain market share. Market followers prefer to follow the leader rather than attack it. Most follower firms manufacture products leveraging on the product innovations of the market leaders. In niche strategy the firm concentrates on a select few target markets. It is also called a focus strategy.

KEY TERMS

- Business Strategy
- Corporate Strategy
- Strategy
- Strategic Business Unit(SBU)
- Market Leaders
- Market Challengers
- Market Followers
- Market Nichers
- Task Environment
- Marketing Strategy
- Segmentation
- Social Environment
- Targeting
- Positioning
- Differentiation
- Horizontal and Vertical Integration

DISCUSSION QUESTIONS:

1. Is the concept of strategic planning relevant only to profit-making organizations? Can non-profit organizations also give importance to planning?
2. What is an SBU? What criteria may be used to divide businesses into SBUs?
3. Elucidate the various levels of strategy?
4. What do you mean by the strategic management model?
5. Write the importance and benefits of strategic management.
6. Define marketing strategy and also explain the types of marketing strategies.
7. Differentiate between horizontal integration and vertical integration.
8. Explain the Pillars of Marketing in detail.
9. What is market situational strategy? Discuss.
10. Write short notes on:
    a. Innovation strategies
    b. Aggressiveness business strategies
    c. Prospector strategies
    d. Market Nichers

OPENING CASE: GILLETTE'S STRATEGY

Gillette has had a strong business in Latin America since it began building plants there in the 1940s. Castro once told television interviewer Barbara Walters that he grew a beard because he could not get Gillette blades while fighting in the mountains.

The company targeted the developing world in 1969, the proportion of its sales that come from Latin America, Asia, Africa and the Middle East has doubled to 20 percent; dollar volume has risen sevenfold. The company's push into Asia, Africa and the Middle East dates to 1969 when Gillette dropped a policy of investing only where it could have 100 percent owned subsidiaries. That year, it formed a joint venture in Malaysia, which was threatening to bar imports of Gillette products. The company has added one foreign plant nearly every year in such countries as China, Egypt, Thailand and India and is now looking at Pakistan, Nigeria and Turkey.

The company always starts with a factory that makes double-edged blades - still popular in the Third World - and, if all goes well, expands later into production of pens, deodorants, shampoo or toothbrushes. Only a few ventures have gone sour; a Yugoslav project never got off the ground and Gillette had to sell its interest in Iran to its local partners.

In a few markets, Gillette has developed products exclusively for the Third World. Low-cost shaving cream is one. Another is Black Silk, a hair relaxer developed for sale to blacks in South Africa that is now being introduced in Kenya.

Gillette often sells familiar products in different packages or smaller sizes. Because many Latin American consumers cannot afford a seven-ounce bottle of Silkience shampoo, for instance, Gillette sells in it half ounce plastic bubbles. In Brazil, Gillettte sells Right Guard deodorant in plastic squeeze bottles instead of metal cans.

But the toughest task for Gillette is convincing Third World men to shave. The company recently began dispatching portable theaters to remote villages - Gillette calls them "mobile propaganda units" - to show movies and commercials that teach daily shaving. In South African Indonesian versions, a bewildered bearded enters a locker room where clean-shaven friend show him how to shave. In the Mexican one, handsome sheriff, tracking bandits who have nipped a woman, pauses on the trail to shave every morning. The camera lingers as he snaps double-edged blade into his razor, lathers his face and strokes it carefully. In the end, of course, the smooth faced sheriff gets the woman.

In other commercials, Gillette agents with oversized shaving brush and a mug of shaving cream lather up and shave a villager while others watch. Plastic razors are then distributed free and blades, which of course must be bought, are with the local storekeeper. Such campaigns may not win immediate converts, but in the long run, they should establish the company's name in the market.

Chapter: 2

Strategic Marketing: An Introduction

Learning Objectives

In this Chapter the main stress is given on:

- Understanding the concept of Strategic Marketing
- Origin of Strategic Marketing
- The various aspects of strategic marketing
- Planning process
- Strategic Analysis and Implementation
- Understanding the difference between Strategic Marketing & Marketing Management

CONCEPT OF STRATEGIC MARKETING

Strategic marketing is all about gaining competitive advantage on a continuous basis and finding out the strategies which will give companies such a competitive advantage. Let us call it Strategic Competitive Advantage. Planning strategic competitive advantage involves the following:

- Plan the business scenario: The shape and size of the market after three and five years.
- Plan market share on the basis of feasibility.
- Use resources including cash for maximizing the chances of achieving the objectives.
- Focus on core competencies of the firm and synergise efforts for fully exploiting them.

The core competencies of a firm are:

- **Technology:** Both production technology and product technology should provide the firm its cutting edge over competition. The technology advantage gets better if the firm enjoys exclusive patent.

- **Marketing:** The firm needs to be proactive in the marketplace, only then can it take full advantage of the business potential available in the market.
- **Finance:** The firm should be able to generate sufficient funds at lowest costs for growth and expansion.
- **Production:** The firm's manufacturing cost, including its time dimension should be better or at least comparable to that of competition. The firm should also find ways of reducing cost of manufacture by going in for economies of scale and experience curve, newer technology of manufacture and continuous training for the workers.
- **Human resource:** Personnel at all levels and in different functional areas should be geared to think and plan their moves for the benefit of the customer.
- **Government relations:** The firm should maintain good and healthy relations with the government and avoid confrontations at all times. The firm should be able to get government approvals where required at the shortest notice.

Once the firm gets the answers to these questions it is ready to take the following strategic marketing decisions:

1. Who are the firm's main competitors?
2. Where should be firm compete - in which markets, geographic areas and niche markets?
3. How should the firm compete - on the basis of price? Quality? Superior service? Availability of genuine spare parts?
4. What are the areas in which information is lacking and is needed? Is a one-off marketing research enough or should there be continuous flow of information?
5. How can product multiple be exploited? Bundling of products can help in selling slow-moving products.
6. Firms should plan business scenario for the next three to five years taking into consideration competitors, plans and likely changes in the business environment.

Strategic marketing decisions which need to be taken are listed below:

- With international players coming to India, technology is going to be rapidly changing. Indian firms would do well to either invest in R&D or purchase the state-of-art technology to keep abreast of the competition or even forge ahead of them.
- If the product is in the maturity stage of its life cycle and demand has stagnated, it may be necessary to go for penetrating pricing to maintain market share or build brand equity to the extent that it can ask for and get a higher price than competition. Price sensitivity of the market needs to be understood and decision on pricing taken accordingly.

- If new entrants are likely to enter the market with better product, technology and brand image, the existing firms may be required to invest in the product and the market through extra discounts, increased coverage and if possible, joining hands with a technology leader in the product.
- The customers of tomorrow are looking for: (i) product performance improvement, (ii) technical superiority, (iii) easy availability of the product, (iv) financial assistance like leasing.
- Firms should know the benefits, the customers are seeking from the product. It should be understood that no one buys a product, the customers buy only the benefits, which they get from the product.

Exhibit 2.1 shows the role that the marketing function plays at different levels in the organization. At the corporate level, marketing inputs (e.g. competitive analysis, market dynamics, environmental shifts) are essential for formulating a corporate strategic plan. Marketing represents the boundary between the marketplace and the company and knowledge of current and emerging happenings in the marketplace is extremely important in any strategic planning exercise. At the other end of the scale, marketing management deals with the formulation and implementation of marketing programs to support the perspectives of strategic marketing, referring to marketing strategy of a product/market. Marketing strategy is developed at the business unit level.

Within a given environment, marketing strategy deals essentially with the interplay of three forces known as the strategic three Cs: the customer, the competition, and the corporation. Marketing strategies focuses on ways in which the corporation can differentiate itself effectively form its competitors, capitalizing on its distinctive strengths to deliver better value to its customers. A good marketing strategy should be characterized by (a) a clear market definition; (b) a good match between corporate strengths and the needs of the market; and (c) superior performance, relative to the competition, in the key success factors of the business.

EXHIBIT 2.1 *Marketing's Role in the organization*

Organizational Level	**Role of marketing**	**Formal name**
Corporate	Provide customer and competitive perspective for corporate strategic planning	Corporate marketing
Business Unit	Assist in the development of strategic Perspective of the business unit to direct its future course	Strategic marketing
Product/market	Formulate and implement marketing programs	Marketing management

Together, the strategic three Cs form the marketing strategy triangle (see Exhibit 2.2). All three Cs -customer, corporation and competition - are dynamic, living creatures with their own objectives to pursue. If what the customer wants does not match the needs of the corporation, the latter's long-term viability may be at stake. Positive matching of the needs and objectives of customer and corporation is required for a lasting good relationship. But such matching is relative and if the competition is able to offer a better match, the corporation will be at a disadvantage over time. In other words, the matching of needs between customer and corporation must not only be positive, it must be better or stronger than the match between the customer and the competitor. When the corporation's approach to the customer is identical to that of the competition, the customer cannot differentiate between them. The result could be a price war that may satisfy the customer's but not the corporation's needs.

Marketing strategy, in terms of these three key constituents, must be defined as an endeavor by a corporation to differentiate itself positively from its competitors, using its relative corporate strengths to better satisfy customer needs in a given environmental setting.

Based on the interplay of the strategic three Cs, formation of marketing strategy requires the following three decisions:

1. Where to compete; that is, it requires a definition of the market (for example, competing across an entire market or in one or more segments).
2. How to compete; that is, it requires a means for competing (for example, introducing a new product to meet a customer need or establishing a new position for an existing product).
3. When to compete; that is, it requires timing of market entry (for example, being first the market or waiting until primary demand is established).

EXHIBIT 2.2

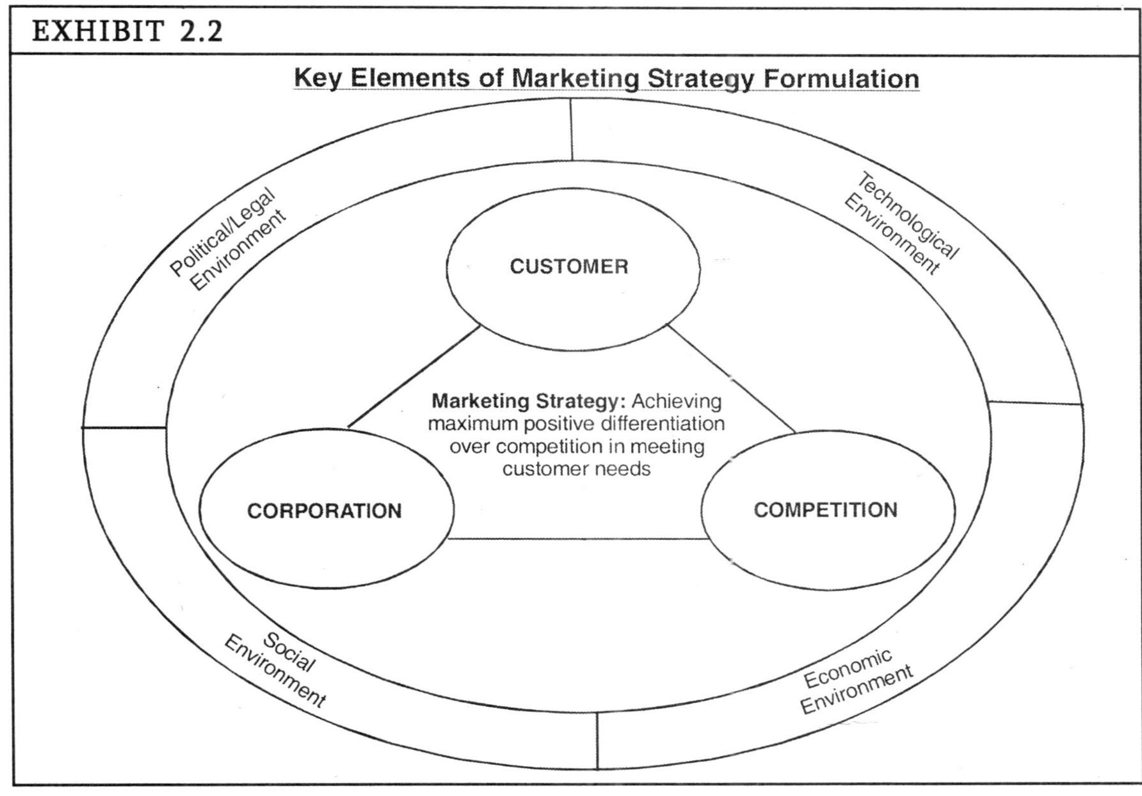

Thus, marketing strategy is the creation of a unique and valuable position, involving a different set of activities. Thus, development of marketing strategy requires choosing activities that are different from rivals.

The concept of strategic marketing may be illustrated with reference to the introduction by Gillette Company of a new shaving product, Mach 3, in April 1998. For some time, Gillette had faced slow growth in its razor's division, partly because Schick, its smaller rival, had recently launched a new razor of its own. Investors had begun to fret about slowing growth and lackluster sales at Gillette. This threatened its basic business, that is, razor and blades market, in which it had 71% of the North American and European market. Apparently, Gillette needed a marketing strategy to protect its razor and blades territory. Looking around, Gillette decided to introduce a new razor that its research laboratory had been developing and that was ready to be launched. Gillette had an unusual approach to innovation. Most companies tweaked their offerings in response to competition or demand. Gillette launched a new product only when it had made a genuine technical advance. To make the Mach 3, Gillette had found a way to bond diamond-hard carbon to slivers of steel. The time was on Gillette's side. It needed something revolutionary to strengthen its market position and its research laboratory had a unique product ready to be launched. Gillette delineated the following marketing strategy:

- Market (where to compete) - Gillette decided to introduce Mach 3 throughout the U.S. on the same day.
- Means (how to compete) - Gillette decided to offer Mach 3 as a premium product that was priced 3% more than Sensor Excel, which itself was 60% more expensive than Atra, its predecessor. Gillette reasoned: "People never remember what they used to pay. But they do want to feel they are getting value for money."
- Timing (when to compete) - Gillette decided to introduce the new product before its CEO, Mr. Al Zein retired. Mr. Zein's ability to communicate had been a hit on both Wall Street and in the company. Much of the Gillette's recent success was attributed to Mr. Zein and the company wanted Mach 3 to adequately settle in a dominant position before Mr. Zein retired.

Gillette's Mach 3 strategy emerged from a thorough consideration of the strategic three Cs. First, market entry was dictated by customer's willingness to adopt new products in the toiletry field. Eight years ago, Gillette was losing its grip on the razor market to cheap throwaways. Sensor, the decision to enter the market was based on full knowledge of the completion, which includes its own substitute products, such as Sensor and Atra shavers, as well as companies like Schick. The company was more concerned about its own products competing with Mach 23, launch and therefore it ran down stocks of its Sensor and Atra shavers ahead of Mach 3's launch. Third, Gillette's strength as an aggressive successful marketer of packaged goods with its vast experience in shaving products business and adequate financial resources (Gillette spent over $750 million in developing Mach 3) properly equipped it to enter the market. Finally, the environment (in this case, a trend towards acceptance of technologically advanced products; Mach 3 was covered by 35 patents) substantiated the opportunity.

This strategy seems to have worked well for Gillette. In nine months ending 1998, Gillette shaving products sales were up 28%. And yet, the company has to introduce the product in Europe (with 71% market) as well as in developing countries (Latin America, where the company has 91% market for blades and India with 69% of the market).

In as much as Gillette did not tailor its product to local peculiarities, it was able to achieve vast economies of scale in manufacturing. The economies of scale were mirrored on the distribution side as well. The company with razors then jumped into batteries, pens, and toiletries through the established sales channels.

ORIGIN OF STRATEGIC MARKETING

Strategic marketing did not originate systematically. As already noted, the difficult environment of the early 1970s forced managers to develop strategic plans for more centralized control of resources. It happened that these pioneering efforts at strategic planning had a financial focus. Certainly, it was recognized that marketing inputs were required, but they were gathered as needed or were simply assumed. For example, most strategic planning approaches emphasized cash flow and return on investment, which of course must be examined in relation to market share. Perspectives on such marketing matters as market share, however, were either obtained on an ad hoc basis or assumed as constant. Consequently, marketing inputs, such as market share, became the result instead of the cause: a typical conclusion that was drawn was that market share must be increased to meet cash flow targets. The financial bias of strategic planning systems demoted marketing to a necessary but not important role in the long-term perspective of the corporation.

In a few years time, as strategic planning became more firmly established, corporations began to realize that there was a missing link in the planning process. Without properly relating the strategic planning effort to marketing, the whole process tended to be static? Business exists in a dynamic setting and by and large, it is only through marketing inputs that perspectives of changing social, economic, political and technological environments can be brought into the strategic planning process.

In brief, while marketing initially got lost in the emphasis on strategic planning, currently the role of marketing is better understood and has emerged in the form of strategic marketing.

ASPECTS OF STRATEGIC MARKETING

Strategic thinking represents a new perspective in the area of marketing. In this section we will examine the importance, characteristics, origin and future of strategic marketing.

IMPORTANCE OF STRATEGIC MARKETING

Marketing plays a vital role in the strategic management process of a firm. The experience of companies well versed in strategic planning indicates that failure in marketing can block the way to goals established by the strategic plan. A prime example is provided by Texas Instruments, a pioneer in developing a system of strategic planning called the OST system. Marketing negligence forced Texas Instruments to withdraw from the digital watch business. When the external environment is stable, a company can successfully ride on its technology lead, manufacturing efficiency and financial acumen. As the environment shifts, however, lack of marketing perspective makes the best-planned strategies treacherous. With the intensification of competition in the watch business and the loss of uniqueness of the digital watch, Texas Instruments began to lose ground. Its experience can be summarized as follows:

The lack of marketing skills certainly was a major factor in the demise of its watch business. T.I. did not try to understand the consumer, nor would it listen to the marketplace. They had the engineer's attitude.

Philip Morris's success with Miller Beer illustrates how marketing's elevated strategic status can help in outperforming competitors. If Philip Morris had accepted the conventional marketing wisdom of the beer industry by basing its strategy on cost efficiencies of large breweries and competitive pricing, its Miller Beer subsidiary might still be in seventh place or lower. Instead, Miller Beer leapfrogged all competitors but Anheuser-Busch by emphasizing market and customer segmentation supported with large advertising and promotion budgets. A case of true strategic marketing, with the marketing function playing a crucial role in overall corporate strategy, Philip Morris relied on its corporate strengths and exploited its competitor's weaknesses to gain a leadership position in the brewing industry.

Indeed, marketing strategy is the most significant challenge that companies of all types and sizes face. As a study by Coopers & Lybrand and Yankelovich, Skelly and White notes, "American corporations are beginning to answer a new call to strategic marketing, as many of them shift their business planning priorities more towards strategic marketing and the market planning functions."

Strategic marketing holds different perspectives from those of marketing management. Its salient features are described in the paragraphs that follow.

Emphasis on Long-term implications. Strategic marketing decisions usually have far-reaching implications. In the words of one marketing strategies, strategic marketing is a commitment, not an act. For example, a strategic marketing decision would not be matter of simply providing an immediate delivery to a favorite customer but of offering 24-hour delivery service to all customers.

In 1980 the Goodyear Tyre Company made a strategic decision to continue its focus on the tyre business. At a time when other members of the industry were deemphasizing, Goodyear opted for the opposite route. This decision had wide-ranging implications for the company over the years. Looking back, Goodyear's strategy worked. In 1990s, it continues to be a globally dominant force in the tyre industry.

The long-term orientation of strategic marketing requires greater concern for the environment. Environmental changes are more probable in the long run than in the short run. In other words, in the short run, one may assume that the environment will remain stable, but this assumption is not at all likely in the long run.

Proper monitoring of the environment requires strategic intelligence inputs. Strategic intelligence differs from traditional marketing research in requiring much deeper probing. For example, simply knowing that a competitor has a cost advantage is not enough. Strategically, one ought to find out how much flexibility the competitor has in further reducing price.

Corporate Inputs. Strategic marketing decisions require inputs from three corporate aspects: corporate culture, corporate publics and corporate resources. **Corporate culture** refers to the style, whims, fancies, traits, taboos, customs and rituals of top management that over time have come to be accepted as intrinsic to the corporation. **Corporate publics** are the various stakeholders with an interest in the organization. Customers, employees, vendors, governments and society typically constitute an organization's stakeholders. **Corporate resources** include the human, financial, physical and technology assets/experience of the company. Corporate inputs set the degree of freedom a marketing strategist has in deciding which market to enter, which business to divest, which business to invest in, etc., the use of corporate-wide inputs in formulating marketing strategy also helps to maximize overall benefits for the organization.

Varying Roles for Different Products/Markets. Traditionally it has been held that all products exert effort to maximize profitability. Strategic marketing starts from the premise that different products may be in the growth stage of the product life cycle, some in the maturity stage, others in the introduction stage. Each position in the life cycle requires a different strategy and affords different expectations. Products in the growth stage need extra investment; those in the maturity stage should generate a cash surplus. Although conceptually this concept - different products serving different purposes - has been understood for many years, it has been articulated for real world application in recent years. This lead in this regard was provided by the Boston Consulting Group, which developed a portfolio matrix in which products are positioned on a two-dimensional matrix of market share and growth rate, both measured on a continuous scale from high to low.

The portfolio matrix essentially has two properties: (a) it ranks diverse businesses according to uniform criteria, and (b) it provides a tool to balance a company's resources by showing which businesses are likely to be resource providers and which are resource users.

The practice of strategic marketing seeks first to examine each product/market before determining its appropriate role. Further, different products/markets are synergistically related to maximize total marketing effort. Finally, each product/market is paired with a manager who has the proper background and experience to it.

Organizational Level. Strategic marketing is conducted primarily at the business unit level in the organization. At General Electric, for example, major appliances are organized into separate business units for which strategy is separately formulated. At Gillette Company, strategy for the Duracell batteries is developed at the batteries business unit level.

Relationship to Finance. Strategic marketing decision-making is closely related to the finance function. The importance of maintaining a close relationship between marketing and finance and for that matter, with other functional areas of a business is nothing new. But in recent years, frameworks have been developed that make it convenient to simultaneously relate marketing to finance in making strategic decisions.

STRATEGIC MARKETING PLANNING PROCESS

Let us understand the formal process of planning marketing strategies in today's competitive age. Plans should be short term and long term. Most firms make annual plans, which are divided into quarterly plans. To be market proactive, the plans should be kept flexible to enable firms to alter them to dovetail the changing market environment. The following steps are needed for making the plans:

- Customer behaviour analysis
- Analysis of external environment
- Study of the firm's internal strengths and weakness
- Idea generation for planning
- Brainstorming for prioritizing the ideas generated
- Customer behavior analysis
- Analysis of competitors
- Market analysis
- Drafting annual and Short-term plans
- Drawing up final plans with sales and cash flow forecasts.

Customer's Behaviour Analysis

We have discussed earlier why, where, when and how much customers buy, which can be ascertained with a degree of accuracy through market research. Let us take a simple customer behaviour pattern. It includes the following elements of internal information processing, guided by external information and stimuli:

- **Belief:** It is the customer's conviction and firm opinion of a product/brand.
- **Perception:** it comes from a customer's recognition of a product as desirable based on intuition and information gathered at the sensory plane.

- **Attitude:** It is the customer's way of thinking about the product, his opinion about it.
- **Preference:** Out of his belief, perception and attitude the customer makes his preference of one product over other products and tries to buy it.

Thus, we can define the multi-attribute decision-making process as one 'based on concepts Beliefs, Attitudes, Perceptions and Preferences from the basis of multi-attribute decision-making. It is the notion that objects in a choice-set (product attributes and related benefit) can lead to external behavior purchase or no purchase. Each object in the set has a value on each attribute used to define the choice-set.

Let us take an example to illustrate the point. The purchase of a car in a family is a major event and the decision-making process is multi-dimensional one. While the affluent buy cars as status symbols, the middle class person buys it as a means of transport. Let us take three symbols; the middle class person buys it as a means of transport. Let us take three cars in the economy segment and plot their benefits to customers. The figures given in Exhibit 2.3 are only arbitrary and not conclusive. The figures are based on a scale of 0-10.

EXHIBIT 2.3 ***Comparative Benefits of three economy cars***

Benefits	*Zen*	*Santro*	*Matiz*
Comfort	7.5	8	8.5
Economy	4	5	6
Safety	3.8	4.5	5
Brand equity	4	7	6
Service facilities	9	6	5

On a different plane another matrix can be made with benefits on one axis and decision-making concepts for each car separately, before the final decision is taken as per Exhibit 2.4.

The decision-making process, therefore, calls for a three-dimensional matrix. This is done in the following way:

1. What attributes are used to define the product? (for example, for a car it could be brand name, comfort or economy. For a house it could be location, construction and area).

2. How much of the attribute is present in the product? (Is the car more economical than other cars in the same category)? This is really the value of the attribute and its perception in the customer's mind. Another example could be airlines, where passenger safety is of prime concern. However, airlines never talk about this aspect as it is taken for granted. They prefer to talk about ease of getting their tickets, food, in-flight service and entertainment and easy check-in and customers form attitudes on the basis of these attributes.
3. What is the relative importance of each attribute in the overall product performance? For instance, in the airline business is in-flight service more important than ease of getting tickets?
4. Do customers weigh each of the attributes to reinforce their perception of overall product performance? How much weightage is given to each of the attributes and does it differ from customer to customer, or is it product specific?

EXHIBIT 2.4 ***Purchase Decision Matrix***

Decision concepts/Benefits	*Comfort*	*Economy*	*Safety*	*Brand equity*
Beliefs				
Attitudes				
Perceptions				
Preferences				

Note: An Attributes-Perception study for different products is to be done to find out how customer's perceptions and preferences are formed.

It will be found that different customers have different yardsticks for measuring the various attributes. They trade off one against the other while making purchase decisions, as can be seen from the following example. Some people buy a car for its brand name, e.g. Mercedes. Some buy car for speed and power, and some due to fuel efficiency. Many look for several of the attributes in some order of importance. This is called the Dictionary Rule.

According to this rule, if a customer finds the first or the most important attribute to the equality present in two products, and then he looks for disparity in the next level attribute. He keeps doing so till he finds on attribute where there is a difference in the two products. (When you look for a word in a dictionary you first match the first letter then the next and so on, till you find the exact word, hence the name).

Multi-attribute analysis helps sellers understand customers who represent identifiable segments in terms of their perceptions and preferences.

Let us consider the levels of competition or competitor's hierarchy. A competitor can be defined as the seller who competes for the same customer rupee in the widest competition level. Narrowing it down competitors are those who sell the same products from the same industry. Further narrowing the definition would be the market segment competitors.

To clarify the above let us take the banking business. At the first level would be the banking system, which would include banks, financial institutions, non-banking financial institutions, merchant bankers and moneylenders. At the second level would be banks that cater to customers with a few banking products. At the third level would be banks in the same town or the same street.

That competition is becoming diversified can be seen from the following:

1. Banking services have competition from software companies now, as a lot of online Internet banking is being done with the help of software.
2. Used cars compete with new cars.

It is therefore possible to define competition by analyzing customer's data. It can be done as given below:

- Define the product.
- Let the prospective customers decide the possible uses and benefits, as many as they can imagine the product to be possessing. Can they think of other ways of getting the same benefits? This way firms can get differential competitive analysis from the customer's viewpoint.
- The customers should determine the products, whose performance is satisfaction, and the benefits which they accrue from the product's use.
- The data thus obtained can be listed as per the priority given by the customers.

The data will provide the firm with information on the competitors for each product in the same range as the firm itself.

Summarizing it can be said that, Competitors analysis requires the prudent use of secondary and primary information to determine current and likely strategies. Customers can be used to classify uses and benefits of products and to rank competitors.

Let us see the assets and skills grid for competitors. These can be divided into two parts:

1. Primary: Product development, product quality, product manufacturing cost, product differentiation, customer satisfaction and market share.
2. Secondary: Flexi-production, financial muscle, sales force, distribution network, brand image/equity, advertising and promotion, quality of service and growth of the market for the product.

MARKET ANALYSIS

The following aspects need to be understood while analyzing the market:

- Market size - actual and potential
- Market growth prospects
- Product-wise profitability
- Cost structure
- Distribution pattern
- Success parameters

Market size and its growth can be assessed by knowing the demographic changes taking place in the market, income and salary growth of people in the market and changes in government policies relating to business of the products. In the maturity and decline stage of the product life cycle (PLC), the firm has to identify the following points:

- Price wars start if there is no product differentiation and there is production over-capacity.
- Level of buyer's sophistication.
- Availability of substitution products.
- It there is no growth, is there a new competitive product in the market?

To analyse the profit picture of a market the following points need to be seen:

- Competition in the market - is it a monopoly, an oligopoly or a fragmented market with a vast number of sellers. What is the market share of competitors and how are they safeguarding it - through price-cutting or brand management?
- How many new players are likely to join the competition? How serious are they and what is their potential threat as a competitor?
- How strong are the substitute products vying for the customer's money?
- What is the bargaining power of the suppliers?
- What is the bargaining power of the buyers?
- The firm should know the number of competitors, their size, similarity of product, level of fixed costs and exit barriers. It should know keep track of the capital requirements of new entrants economies of scale, availability of distribution channels, raw materials and product differentiations.

It can be seen that high-growth markets can suffer from severe competition with overcrowding of players, penetrating prices, technology changes and resources crunch.

Environment analysis helps the firm know the effects of changes in technology, macro-economics, government policies, culture, demography and global.

THE PROCESS OF STRATEGIC MARKETING: AN EXAMPLE

The process of strategic marketing planning, charted in Exhibit 2.5, may be illustrated with an SBU (health-related remedies) of the New England Products Company (a fictional name). Headquarters in Hartford, Connecticut, NEPC is a worldwide manufacturer and marketer of a variety of food and nonfood products, including coffee, orange juice, cake mixes, toothpaste, diapers, detergents and health-related remedies. The company conducts its business in more than 100 countries, employs approximately 110,000 people, operates more than 147 manufacturing facilities and maintains three major research centers. In 1998 (year ending June 30), the company's worldwide sales amounted to $37.3 billion.

EXHIBIT 2.5 The Process of Strategic Management

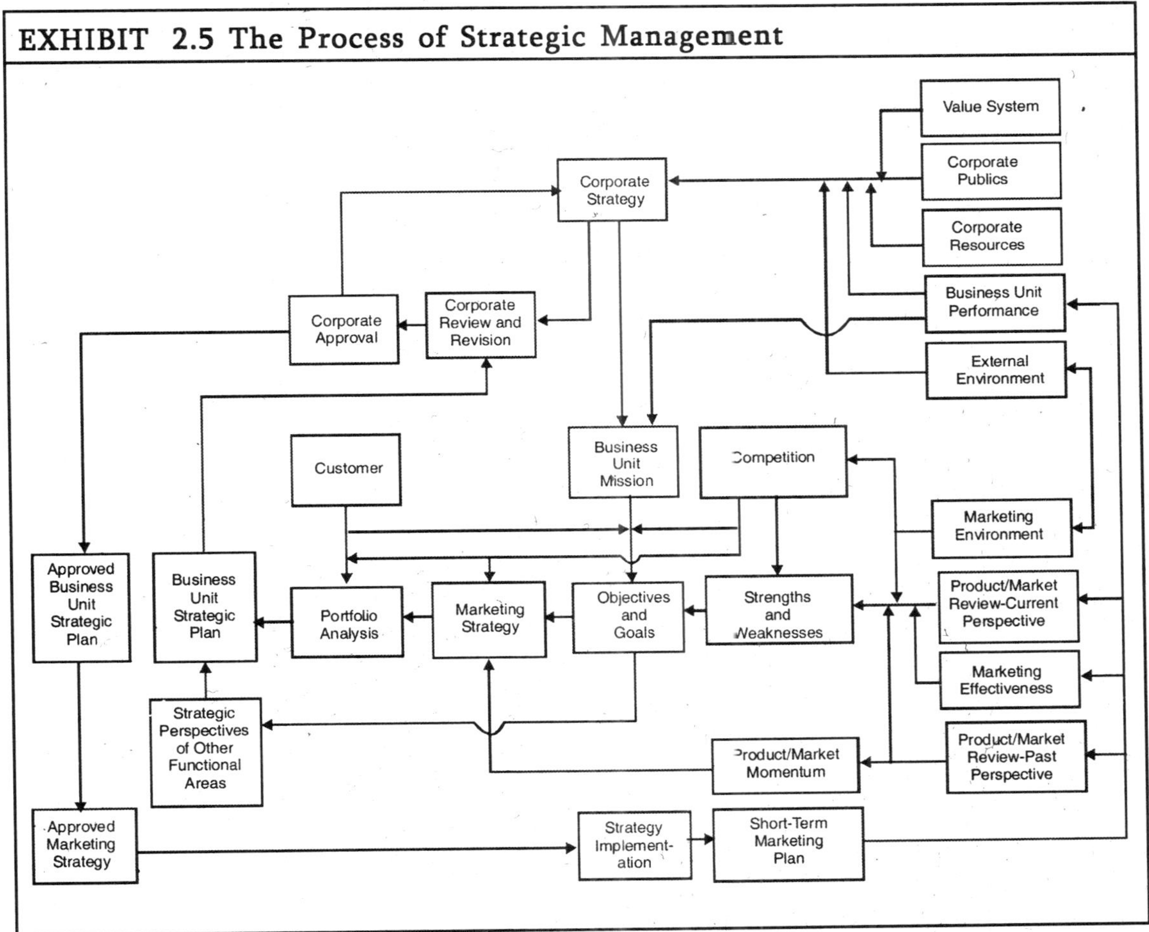

Corporate Strategy

In 1991, the company's strategies plan established the following goals:

- To strengthen significantly, the company's core business (i.e., toothpaste, diapers and detergents).

- To view health care products as a critical engine of growth.
- To boost the share of profits from health-related products from 20 percent to 30 percent over the next decade.
- To drive those businesses not meeting the company's criteria for profitability and growth, thus providing additional resources to achieve other objectives.
- To make an 18 percent return on total capital invested.
- To a great extent, to depend on retained earnings for financing growth.

This above strategy rested on the five factors, shown in Exhibit 2.5 that feed into corporate strategy:

- Value system - always to be strong and influential in marketing, achieving growth through developing and acquiring new products for specific niches.
- Corporate publics - the willingness of NEPC stockholders to forgo short-term profits and dividends in the interest of long-term growth and profitability.
- Corporate resources - strong financial position, high brand recognition, marketing powerhouse.
- Business unit performance - health-related remedies sales, for example, were higher worldwide despite recessionary conditions.
- External environment - increased health consciousness among consumers.

The mission for one of NEPC's 36 business units, health-related remedies, emerged from a simultaneous review of corporate strategy, competitive conditions, customer's perspectives, past performance of the business unit and marketing environment, as charted in Exhibit 2.5. The business unit mission for health-related remedies was delineated as follows:

- To consolidate operations by combining recent acquisitions and newly developed products and by revamping old products.
- To accelerate business by proper positioning of products.
- To expand the product line to cover the entire human anatomy.

The mission for the business unit was translated into the following objectives and goals:

- To invest heavily to achieve $5.3 billion in sales by 2003, an increase of 110 percent over $2.8 billion in 1998.
- To achieve a leadership position in the United States.
- To introduce new products overseas as early as possible to preempt completion.

Marketing objectives for different products/markets emerged from these overall business unit objectives. For example, the marketing objectives for a product to combat indigestion were identified as follows:

- To accelerate research to seek new uses for the product.
- To develop new improvements in the product.

Marketing Strategy

Marketing objectives, customer and competitive perspectives and product/market momentum (i.e., extrapolation of past performance to the future) form the basis of marketing strategy. In the case of NEPC, the major emphasis of marketing strategy for health-related remedies was on positioning through advertising and on new product development. Thus, the company decided to increase advertising support throughout the planning period and to broaden research and development efforts.

NEPC's strategy was based on the following rationale. Consumers are extremely loyal to health products that deliver, as shown by their willingness to resume buying Johnson & Johnson's Tylenol after two poisoning episodes. But while brand loyalty makes consumers harder to lure away, it also makes them easier to keep and good marketing can go a long way in this endeavor. The company was able to enlarge the market for its indigestion remedy, which experts thought had hit maturity, through savvy marketing. NEPC used television advertising to sell it as a cure for overindulgence, which led to a 30 percent increase in business during 1993-98.

As NEPC pushes further into health products, its vast research and technological resources will be a major asset. NEPC spends nearly $1 billion a year on research and product improvements have always been an important key to the company's marketing process.

The overall strategy of the health-related remedies business unit was determined by industry maturity and the unit's competitive position. The industry was found to be growing, while the competitive position was deemed strong.

With insurers and the government trying to drive health care costs down, consumers are buying more and more over-the-counter nostrums. Advertisers are making health claims for products from cereal to chewing gum. As the fitness craze exemplifies, interest in health is higher than ever and the ageing of the population accentuates these trends: people are going to be older, but they are not going to want to feel older. Thus the health-related remedies industry has a significant potential for growth. NEPC is the largest over-the-counter remedies marketer. As shown in the list below, it has products for different ailments. The company's combined strength in marketing and research puts it in an enviable position in the market.

- Skin - NEPC produces the leading facial moisturizer. NEPC also leads the teenage acne treatment market. Work is now underway on a possible breakthrough anti-ageing product.

- Mouth - After being on the market for 28 years, NEPC's mouthwash is the market leader. Another NEPC product, a prescription plaque-fighting mouthwash, may go over the counter or it may become an important ingredient in other NEPC oral hygiene products.
- Head - An NEPC weak spot, its aspirin, holds in insignificant share of the analgesic market. NEPC may decide to compete with an ibuprofen-caffeine combination painkiller.
- Chest - NEPC's medicated chest rub is an original brand in a stable that now includes cough syrup, cough drops, a nighttime cold remedy and nasal spray. Other line extensions and new products are coming, but at a fairly slow pace.
- Abdomen - The market share for NEPC's indigestion remedy is up 22 percent in the last three years. Already being sold to prevent traveler's diarrhoea, it may be marketed as an ulcer treatment. NEPC also dominates the over-the-counter bulk laxative market. New clinical research shows that its laxative may reduce serum cholesterol.
- Bones - NEPC orange juice has a 10 percent share of the market. Orange juice with calcium is now being expanded nationwide and could be combined with a low-calorie version.

Briefly, these inputs, along with the business unit's goal, led to the following business unit strategy: to attempt to improve position, to push for share.

Portfolio Analysis: - The marketing strategy for each product/market was reviewed using the portfolio technique .By positioning different products/markets on a multifactor portfolio matrix (high/medium/low business strength and high/medium/low industry attractiveness), strategy for each product/market was examined and approved from the viewpoint of meeting business unit missions and goals. Following the portfolio analysis, the approved marketing strategy became a part of the business unit's strategic plan, which, when approved by top management, was ready to be implemented. As a part of implementation, an annual marketing plan was formulated and became the basis for operations managers to pursue their objectives.

Implementation of the Strategic Plan: - A few highlights of the activities of the health-related remedies business unit during 1998-2003 show how the strategic plan was implemented.

- Steps were taken to sell its laxative as an anti-cholesterol agent.
- The company won FDA permission to promote its indigestion remedy to doctors as a preventive for traveler's diarrhoea.

- Company research has shown that its indigestion remedy helps treat ulcers. Although some researchers have disputed this claim, the prospect of cracking the multibillion dollar ulcer treatment market is tantalizing.
- The company introduced its orange juice brand with calcium. The company sought and won the approval of the American Medical Women's Association for the product and put the group's seal on its containers.

STRATEGIC MARKETING IMPLEMENTATION

Strategic marketing has evolved by trial and error. In the 1980s, companies developed unique strategic-marketing procedures, systems and models. Experience shows, however, that most companies marketing strategies are burdened with undue complexity. They are bogged down in principles that produce similar response to competition. Changes are needed to put speed and freshness into marketing strategy.

The following are the common problems associated with marketing strategy formulation and implementation.

1. Too much emphasis on "where to compete and not enough on "how" to compete. Experience shows that companies have devoted much more attention to identifying markets in which to compete than to means to compete in these markets. Information on where to compete is easy to obtain but seldom brings about sustainable competitive advantage. Further, "where" information is usually easy for competitors to copy. "How" information, on the other hand, is tough to get and tough to copy. It concerns the fundamental workings of the business and the company. For example, McDonald's motto, QSC & V, is a how-to-compete strategy - it translates into quality food products; fast, friendly service, restaurant cleanliness; and a menu that provides value. It is much more difficult to copy the "how" of McDonald's strategy than the "where".

In the next era of marketing strategy, companies will need to focus on how to compete in entirely new ways. In this endeavor, creativity will play a crucial role. For example, a large insurance company substantially improved its business by making improvements in underwriting, claim processing and customer service, a "how" strategy that could not be replicated by competitors forthwith.

2. Too little focus on uniqueness and adaptability in strategy. Most marketing strategies lack uniqueness. For example, specialty stores increasingly look alike because they use the same layout and stock the same merchandise. In the 1980s, when market information was scarce, companies pursued new and different approaches. But today's easy access to information often leads companies to follow identical strategies to the detriment of all.

Ideas for uniqueness and adaptability may flow from unknown sources. Companies should, therefore, be sensitive and explore all possibilities. The point may be illustrated with reference to Arm and Hammer's advertising campaign that encouraged people to place baking soda in their refrigerators to reduce odors. The idea was suggested in a letter from a consumer. The introduction of that unique application for the product in the early 1970s caused sales of Arm and Hammer baking soda to double within two years.

3. Inadequate emphasis on 'When" to compete. Because of the heavy emphasis on where and how to compete, many marketing strategies give inadequate attention to "when" to compete. Any move in the marketplace should be adequately timed. The optimum time is one that minimizes or eliminates competition and creates the desired impact on the market, in other words, the optimum time makes it easier for the firm to achieve its objectives. Timing also has strategy implementation significance. It serves as a guide for different managers in the firm to schedule their activities to meet the timing requirement.

Decisions on timing should be guided by the following:

a. Market knowledge. If you have adequate information, it is desirable to market readily; otherwise you must wait until additional information has been gathered.

b. Competition. A firm may decide on an early entry to beat minor competition. If you face major competition, you may delay entry if necessary; for example, to seek additional information.

c. Company readiness. For a variety of reasons, the company may not be ready to complete. These reasons could be lack of financial resources, labor problems, inability to meet existing commitment and others.

Having the ability to do all the right things, however, is no guarantee that planned objectives will be realized. Any number of pitfalls may render the best strategies inappropriate. To counter the pitfalls, the following concerns should be addressed.

1. Develop attainable goals and objectives.
2. Involve key operating personnel.
3. Avoid becoming so engrossed in current problems that strategic marketing is neglected and thus becomes discredited in the eyes of others.
4. Don't keep marketing strategy separate from the rest of the management process.

5. Avoid formality in marketing strategy formulation that restrains flexibility and inhibits creativity.
6. Avoid creating a climate that is resistant to strategic marketing.
7. Don't assume that marketing strategy development can be delegated to a planner.
8. Don't overturn the strategy formulation mechanism with intuitive, conflicting decisions.

MANAGING ACROSS THE PRODUCT LIFE CYCLE

With a lot of effort going into new product development, firms have the benefit of introducing new products. Care should be taken in managing the new introduction to ensure profits and volume business. Later on during the growth, maturity and decline stages of the product life cycle proper management is required. Figure 2.1 gives the different stages of a PLC.

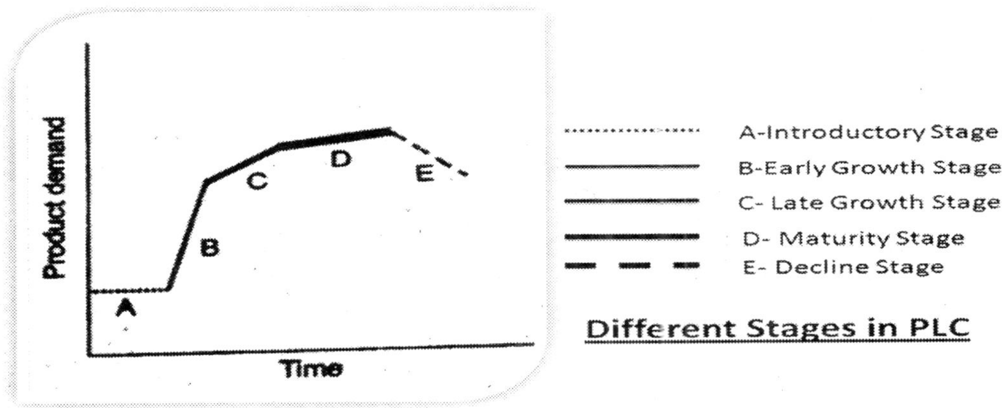

FIGURE 2.1

Introductory Stage

This stage is fast gaining importance as due to faster rate of obsolescence the life cycle of most products is shrinking. New technologies are emerging in several products to make earlier products obsolete. Firms need to capture maximum market in this stage and often as there is little competition they can charge skimming prices to get the maximum revenue. The main characteristics of the introductory stage are as follows:

1. Growth is slow as customers are not aware of the product and its concept. A lot of concept selling is therefore required before actual volume business starts. (i) The product itself is not well defined. (ii) Channels of distribution are new, but since the channel member has customers coming to item for other products, they hold the

key to business and have the power over the manufacturers. (iii) Price - the rule of the game has not yet been finalized. (iv)Advertising gives most of the information to competitors about the product, price, channels of distribution and market segment sought out by the firm.

2. Firms introducing a new product have advantage during this phase and other leaders and followers are not significant.
3. Penetrating price is adopted for gaining and maintaining market share. Along with low price, the firms spend money on advertising and promotion as they depend on volume business and economics of scale for profits.
4. Skimming price is used when competition is yet far away. Customer base is narrow and firms prefer not to spend a lot of money on advertising and promotion. Firms depend on high prices and low expenses for profits.
5. In case of skimming prices, competition comes in fast as other companies see the large margins of profit.
6. Penetrating price keeps competition away for some time.

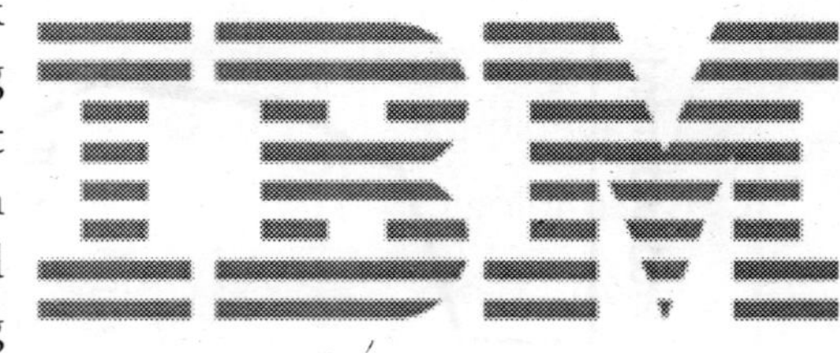

As can be seen, pioneering firms have the task of developing the market through concept selling and advertising and the later firms who follow get the benefit of these efforts. For example, if a firm introduces the computer in a virgin underdeveloped market it will be doing concept selling telling customers the advantages of using a computer. It will not be able to talk about its brand say, IBM. Later sellers like Compaq will be able to build on the concept acceptance of the customers and can advertise their brands and generate brand awareness, during brand loyalty and brand equity.

Summarizing, market pioneers the introductory stage of PLC can pursue strategies to capture a narrow customer base with skimming price for extra profits or they plan on a broad market base with penetrating pricing.

In early growth stage, market size increases as does the distinction between leaders and followers. Product quality stabilizes and firms dependence on channels reduces; hence the power of channels also reduces giving way to advertising and promotions besides personal selling by salespersons.

Hence it can be concluded that PLCs are identifiable and require distinct marketing skills at each stage, especially the introductory stage when failure risk and product costs are both high, quality often uneven and market acceptance is not fully assured. Second, marketers have a choice in pricing the product in the introductory stage. They can either have widespread business with penetrating prices and market share, or gain high unit profits with skimming prices.

Costs, Volumes and Experience Curve

Marketing strategies are needed to adapt the core competencies of firms according to changes in the business environment. This is essential for the long-term well-being and growth of the firm. The prerequisites of good strategy are analysis of the firm, competition and customers in a dynamically changing business environment.

Let us discuss the market leadership position a firm can enjoy. For getting volumes needed for leadership, a firm has to have penetrating prices. Hence, the cost of leadership, is reduced profit on unit product. In order to reduce the loss in profit the following is required to be done:

- Integrating marketing and production plans.
- Making an objective of high volume and low cost production as a result using Economies of scale of manufacture; Experience Curve and Bellir Technology.
- Focus on market share.
- Gain cost leadership.

Cost leadership is gained through the following methods:

1. Technological advancements.
2. Inputs from suppliers and customers for streamlining the cost element in manufacture, by being high quantity manufacturer.
3. Economies of scale, which help in reducing the unit fixed costs. For instance, in larger productions, rentals, salaries and other overheads do not change and hence unit fixed cost gets reduced.
4. Experience curve which helps in reducing variable costs, as with passage of time, workers get to know the working better and wastage gets reduced. Production time also shortens. With increase in cumulative experience, workers do better. This is most valid in high labour cost industries, Complex assembly line operations and production of high numbers of standard products.

Experience curve cost reduction comes from the following areas:

- Labour efficiency.
- Work specialization and improvement of methods.
- New production processes.

It helps in product standardization and redesign. Experience effect results from the firms attempt to achieve lower relative costs than competitors. Low cost production gives higher profit margins.

Market Share Strategy

Firms are constantly striving to improve their market share. For this purpose the following strategies are adopted:

- Plan large capacity production, which will help in achieving economies of scale of production and thereby reduce fixed costs.
- Penetrating or aggressive pricing policy helps in getting larger market share as more price-conscious customers buy the product. Initially, to gain a foothold in the market sellers resort to selling on marginal costs where the price is equal to the fixed cost plus a little element of variable cost. Once the planned market share is reached and some amount of brand loyalty gained, the price is increased to cover both fixed and variable costs and also some profit margin. This is especially true for price-sensitive segments of the market. The idea is to keep the price low initially and in a way invest in the future growth of the market. However, this strategy can rebound if the market does not grow at all.

Let us now discuss some successful cases of experience curve effect.

- Manufacture of semiconductor devices, including Integrated Circuits: initially the rejection rate was as high as 50 percent. As the firms got experience in manufacturing, the workers could reduce rejections and today the rejection rate is less than 1 per cent. This has resulted in price reduction of not only components, but also of the final electronic equipments.
- Honda motorcycles reduced prices substantially (in seven years price came down by US$ 100 due to experience effect.)

However, there also risks involved with gaining cost reduction through experience curve:

- Manufacturers base their production plan as per the market forecasts. In case the demand projections prove to be wrong and demand fails to come to the anticipated levels, the cost reductions become void as then the production is tailored to the real demand only.
- Customer tastes keep changing, especially in fashion garments where the rate of obsolescence is high.
- Induction of new technology in manufacturing also reduces the effect of the experience curve.
- Ego or fixation on old manufacturing process can also affect gains from the experience curve. Firms can argue that they have spent a lot of money in the old technology and cannot abandon it so soon. Such mindsets harm the growth of the firm and also reduces the benefits of experience as the new technology may help lower the cost of manufacture.

Summarizing it can be said that:

- Cost leadership is a powerful strategic tool where learning curve and economies of scale provide higher profits and better market share than that of competitors.
- Economies of scale and experience curve effects must fulfill market needs. A firm also generates extra profits that can be used to finance the more effective operations and also go for new projects.

Marketing strategies are needed at every stage of the PLC to combat market realities and use the options available, as the firm's and the competitor's relationship keep changing with the customers all the time. We will now look at the other stages of the PLC.

Growth Stage Strategy

Early growth involves large increases in volumes and an increasing number of competitors. Market players use advertising to build brand equity to elevate their market share and position. The following changes take place:

1. Sales volumes increase rapidly.
2. Competition rises.
3. Product design and specifications get standardized
4. Firms plan their advertising and sales efforts to gain brand superiority.
5. Prices may start their downward slide.
6. Distribution network gets into place and power over customers begins to move towards manufactures from the channel members.
7. Demand shifts from primary, say any PC or car to secondary, as for a Wipro PC or a Honda City car, as people/customers become brand conscious.
8. At times pioneers, who started the sale of the product and did the initial concept selling lose their lead in the growth stage to other players. For instance, Philips pioneered the audio cassettes and did the concept selling against competition from LPs EPs and 8 tracks. It gave its technology to Sony which did better than Philips during the growth stage.

Growth stage involves increase in demand which has to be met by the manufacturers. Their strategic options depend on the position they enjoy in the market as can be seen from below.

Let us take the firm's position as that of a market leader first and then or that of market follower.

Options as a Market Leader

- Flight - Maintain - or Enhance
- Flight - Exit - or Fortify
- For maintaining market share the firm increase its business as per the market growth and invest in advertising and selling on that basis.
- For enhancing market share the firm should increase its market share faster than the market growth.
- In reality, if the firm plans only to maintain its market share, it may end up losing its position. If it plans to enhance it may just be able to maintain its market share as competitors are also implementing their plans.
- The second option for firms could be that of flight, or giving up their leadership position. They can either exit or fortify, i.e., get into a niche market. At times the expenditure in maintaining leadership position is so high that it eats into all the profit. Firms in such situations to leave the leadership position. For instance HP Calculators gave its leadership to Texas Instruments and went into a niche market with low advertising costs. It also raised prices after relinquishing the position of market leader.

Options for Market Followers

Followers can either take up leadership position or remain as followers. For each the choices are given below:

- Assume leadership by copying the leader or by leapfrogging using latest techniques or radical innovations.

In case of copying, the follower can do better by learning from the leader's mistakes. He thus challenges the leader by tracking the latter's mistakes and turning them into opportunities. If the leader is not making mistakes then the follower has to overtake the leader by using new technology, new plans and policies. A good example of leapfrogging is the leadership position now being enjoyed by Japanese automobile manufacturers, which were once the virtual monopoly of the Americans. In the area consumer electronics too Japanese firms have leapfrogging to leadership position. Their success is largely due to improvements in process technology, offering better products, re-engineering in production technology an innovative distribution. They have gone for high volumes and economies of scale of manufacture. The customers do not see the new process; they see only better and economically priced products.

- The second option for the followers is to settle for being number two. The second place helps in remaining focused (the firm can advertise that it tries harder to please the customer it is number two.) It can cater to customers who are not with the leader. The leader could be in the mass market spending large sums of money in advertising and promotion to say number one. The second number could get into a niche market or target all customers except those with number one, like those with number three or four.

Late Growth Stage Strategy

Segmentation is a useful strategy in the late growth stage to satisfy knowledgeable customers. Strategically, firms need to either defend their position or find out unexplored niche markets.

The salient features of the late growth stage are:

- Slow growth in sales volume.
- Many competitors.
- Beginning of price war.
- Possibility of excess capacity.
- Channel members play one against the other to gain advantage.
- Customers become intelligent and demand a lot as specific benefits.
- Marketing efforts focus on specified segments.

Computer industry the world over has suffered as the growth in the last ten years has reduced from a healthy 50 per cent to only 25 per cent. This has resulted in excess capacity and the sellers are resorting to promotional plans. They bundle a lot of software with the hardware as a sales promotion strategy. With low demand and reduced production, the fixed costs per unit go up.

In the later growth stage, customers demands are more specific and market segmentation becomes critical. The strategies which leaders and followers can pursue, include:

Leaders - target many segments

Followers - target a few segments only.

Each segment needs a different type of at least one of the 4Ps. (Product, Price, Place and Promotion)

Due to excess production capacity and price pressures a firm could decide to exit from the business altogether. It could need money for some other business or a follower may have leapfrogged to leadership and the leader may decide/to exit.

Summarizing it can be concluded that:

1. Early and late growth stages of the PLC have different increases in sales volumes which require different strategic initiatives.

2. Leaders and followers have separate strategic requirements in all stages of the life cycle.

Maturity Stage Strategy

When products reach the maturity stage, growth in demand reaches a plateau. Firms need to manage the sales in this stage either for cash or plan product differentiation or geographic extension of markets within, the country or through exports. However, if opportunity costs exceed present value benefits, it is better to exit from the product sales.

Mature markets are known for sophisticated buyers, well-organized segments reduced differences in products from competition and stable sales volumes. Its two main characteristics are:

- Constant sales volumes year to year and little.
- Product differentiation vanishes as competition makes 'Me Too' products.

It is however not necessary that all models in a product range may be in the same stage of life cycle, e.g., in cars one model may have reached maturity and another may be in the introductory stage. Sustainable competitive advantage (SCA) can be achieved by differentiating one or more of the following in the maturity stage:

- Service.
- Distribution.
- Advertising of intangible benefits like brand equity or service.
- Product differentiation does not make much of an impact in the maturity stage.
- Pricing takes a toll and has to be competitive - as new car models entered the Indian market; Maruti had to reduce its price.
- Buyers are knowledgeable, know about firms and competitive products, are discerning and have bargaining power.
- There are relatively few new buyers. Firms, when they want to increase sales, either lure customers away from competitors or fight for the small number of new buyers. In most cases some old buyers quit and new ones replace them.

Let it be understood that for most products other than MCGs taking customers from competition is a difficult task as price reduction can lead to price war. The lower price can in any case be met by competition leaving the market share status-quo.

In the maturity stage, leaders and followers have different strategic options available to them. Leaders may treat mature products as cash cows or they may harvest the profits. Followers may try to keep the market share at the existing level, grow or even exit.

Leaders - manage for cash/or harvest, i.e., reduce market share by going for niche market.

Followers - maintain market share/grow/exit.

Maintaining or increasing market share needs investment and therefore reduces profit. Market share cases to be of any importance in the maturity stage. Followers can take the leadership position if the leader's quitting or is taking a follower's position. However, the followers must find out why the leader is leaving the top spot. Is there a new technology available now? Market segmentation is the key to success in this stage. It is necessary to offer specific benefits to a group of customers or to a segment. This is especially important if the switching costs of customers for changing products are low.

Let us see how a firm can keep prices high in the maturity stage. It can have distinct product differentiation to keep the switching costs high. It can build its brand equity and offer superior service. These intangible benefits will lodge the product in the customer's minds, keep competition away and the firm can enjoy high profit margins.

Summarizing, mature markets are stable with few major players and reduced product differences among competitors. These markets also provide cash for invigorating newer product concepts. Automobile major Ford was losing market share in the 1980s. Its new president Don Peterson told his management team, 'Get the best features of the cars worldwide, without omitting any feature, including door handles and glove compartment size.' Ford was back on its feet in less time than was envisaged.

Decline Stage Market Strategies

Decline stage in a PLC is characterized by decrease in sales volume as a result of low product demand, demographic changes and technological changes over a period of time. Cheaper substitute products and changes in customers' tastes also account for the decline demand.

The characteristics of the decline stage are:

- Production over capacity
- Severe price competition
- Several competitors.

The marketing strategies for the decline stage are given in Exhibit 2.6

EXHIBIT 2.6 ***Decline Stage Marketing Strategies***

	Hospitable Market	Inhospitable Market
Leaders	Maintain lead	Harvest
Followers	Harvest	Divest

Hospitable market in the decline stage is when the rate of decline is slow; otherwise it becomes an inhospitable market. Leaders in a hospitable market can balance their rate of decline to the rate the market is declining. For harvesting firms bring down their market share and try to get into a niche market. In an inhospitable market the best strategy followers is to exit. Marketing wars begin in the decline stage, starting with price wars. It should however be understood that the players are all fighting over a shrinking pie. Penetrating prices and higher investments in advertising and promotion mark the decline stage. It becomes a vicious circle, like the arms race between the USA and erstwhile USSR in the twentieth century and hence should be avoided by firms. Most firms decide to get out of the market. However, the firm which decides to stay enjoying a monopoly and can reap skimming price benefits till the market remains.

When radio manufacturers started using semiconductor devices most radio valve manufacturers around the world stopped making valves. However, one firm in India confirmed production of valves resulting in a monopoly situation. As there was some market in Africa the firm could skim price for a few years before the demand dwindled to zero. Similarly in case of some product being reintroduced in the market, the last survivor gets the benefit.

Summarizing, a life cycle audit helps firms in determining where their products are placed in the life cycle so that their marketing can be strategically planned. A life cycle audit table as given in Exhibit 2.7.

EXHIBIT 2.7 ***Life Cycle Audit***

Competitive Position: Leaders/Followers	Introductory Stage	Growth Stage	Maturity Stage	Decline Stage
Objectives				
Target customers				
Product				
Price				
Distribution				
Advertising				
Promotion				

The audit summarizes the entire life cycle. It is possible to plan strategies for the entire life cycle with built-in contingencies.

PORTFOLIO MANAGEMENT ANALYSIS

Portfolio analysis takes into account the fact that large multi-product firms have synergies within and that they need to provide resources for growing their profitable businesses and divesting poor performers with unattractive profits or losses. They need to divert resources from mature and stable businesses into promising new businesses.

Portfolio analysis empowers managers to balance current and future opportunities by assessing business attractiveness and competitive position in a two-dimensional matrix.

Firms have a life of their own. A single-product firm will die if that product fails. Managers of a multi-product firm want to ensure that some of their products remain in growth stage always. Portfolio analysis helps:

- Focus on two major dimensions of marketing strategy.
- Look for business attractiveness to assess how good is the business opportunity and relative competitive position to understand if the firm can be a winner.
- Understand different resources needs - some business need resources and others have excess resources.

Resources can be finance, human, technology and information. So far our discussion has been on getting the competitive advantage for an individual product. However, in case of a multi-product firm, emphasis should be on managing the products together and not separately. For making an analysis of a firm's strength the Boston Consultancy Group (BCG) has developed a matrix (see Exhibit 2.8).

EXHIBIT 2.8 ***The BCG Matrix***

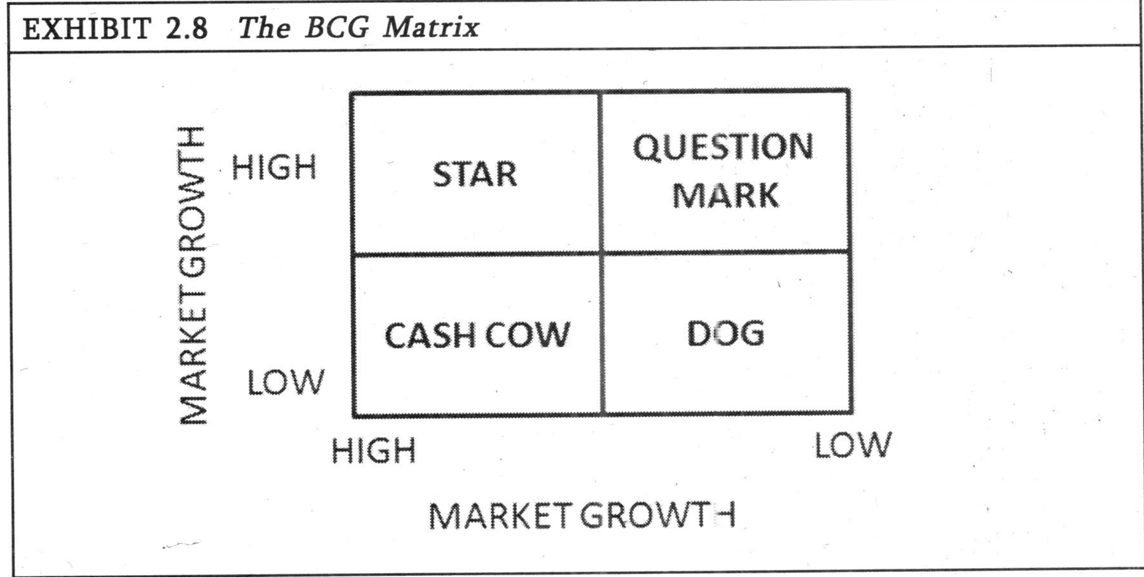

In the BCG Matrix, the horizontal axis shows the market share of the product and the vertical axis shows the market growth. Let us see the position of products in different quadrants.

Quadrant Star

In this quadrant the market growth is high and the firm's product enjoys high market share. The following are the quadrants characteristics:

- The product enjoys the position of a market leader.
- Market growth is high and attractive.
- Competitors' better technology and superior market acceptance can make the firm's business risky, if it currently enjoys leadership position.
- Profit is low, as the leader has to spend large amount on marketing including advertising to maintain leadership.
- High expenditure is required for marketing mix factors.

The strategic options in the Star Quadrant are as follows:

1. Increase share: Invest in anticipation of higher market growth; put entry barriers for newcomers through low pricing, innovative distribution and advertising.
2. Maintain share: Have good market intelligence to be able to counter competitors actions; invest in marketing mix selectively.

Quadrant Question Mark

In this quadrant, the market share is low although the growth of the market is high. The position of the product is as follows:

- The product is in the growth stage and has low market share.
- The firm has the opportunity to increase its market share by investing in advertising promotion and other marketing areas like higher commissions to channel members, training of sales staff.
- The firm is often a new entrant. All players could be new or one could have assumed leadership in the market.
- Risks are high as technology and product acceptance in the market are not fully established.
- Negative profits due to huge expense in marketing for either concept selling or for increasing market share.
- Long-term commitment of the management is needed for the product to reach the Star Quadrant.
- The firm must find out how many of its products are in this quadrant and how many of them it can support on a long-range basis.
- The firm could get into some niche market segment.
- If the firm has several products in this quadrant, it is in a strategic trap, because it cannot place proper resources for them and is in danger of losing all.

Quadrant Cash Cow

Here the firm enjoys high market share but market growth is low. The firm can reduce its marketing expenses as it is in a domain position and can become low-cost supplier. The firm's market situation can be described as follows:

- Dominant market position
- Slow market growth
- Low-cost supplier
- Good profit and cash generation
- Low market risk.

Strategies for cash low quadrant are:

1. Manage for cash, maintain market share.
2. Invest cautiously as market growth is slow.
3. Cash generation can be used for products in Question Mark Quadrant.
4. Harvest: Go for niche market if future prospects are unattractive.
5. Divest if product demand is decreasing rapidly because of new technology products in the market or because customers' tastes are changing.

Quadrant Dog

In this quadrant the market growth is weak and the firm has low market share. The market situation can be described as given below:

- Weak market position
- Slow market growth
- High-cost supplier
- Poor or no profit and cash generation. However, by managing carefully using the niche market route, profit can be increased.
- Several times the product could be based on management ego, as once it was a star product.
- High management support, as the product is not doing well, 'customers know us because of this product'.
- The product takes a lot of management time in planning its strategies for hardly any gain.

Strategies for Dog Quadrant are given below:

1. Maintain market share for whatever cash the product generates.

2. Plan for changing or adding some market segments.
3. Stop all new investments in the product.
4. Divest: Sell and use the funds for other products in the Question Mark Quadrant.
5. Keep the product for any goodwill it may have or if there are strong exit barriers.
6. Turn around by innovating, product differentiation and downsizing.
7. Get into niche market.

Investment cycle for the BCG Matrix is therefore as given in Exhibit 2.9

The extra cash generated in the cash cow stage is invested in the question mark stage to bring the product to the star stage. Over time market growth of the star product slows when it reaches the maturity stage of its life cycle the cash quadrant, and it starts having extra cash, which is invested in the question mark stage to complete the cycle.

EXHIBIT 2.9 ***BCG Matrix Investment Cycle***

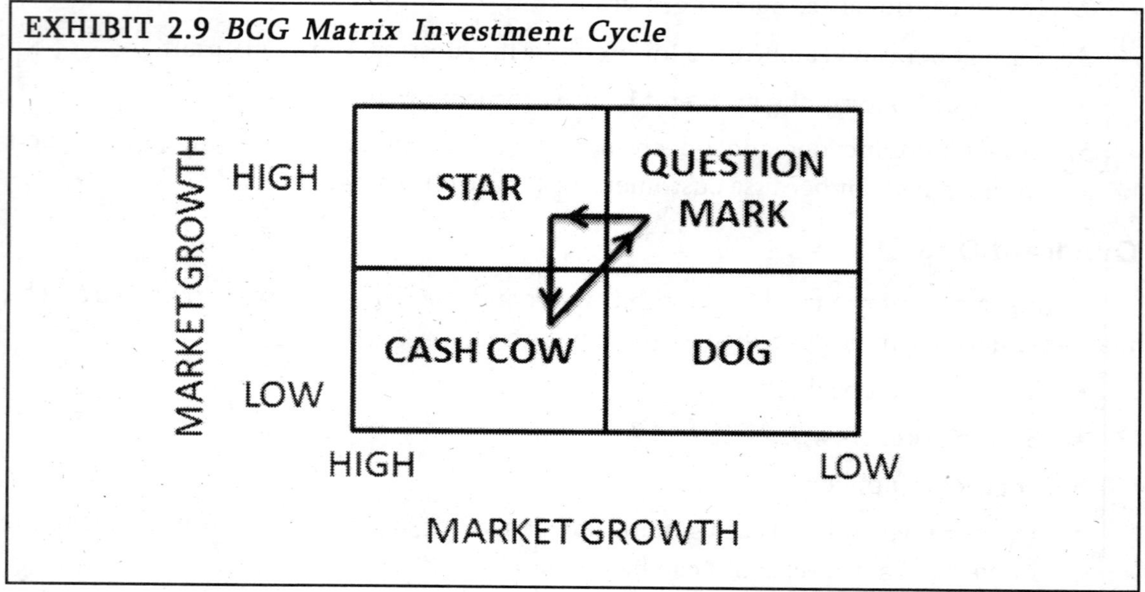

Summarizing, market share and market potential are mapped in a portfolio analysis to provide a visual understanding of the industry players and the attractiveness and competitive position of a firm's products. Portfolio analysis can be used to find out where resources should be deployed and to determine the firm's position among competitors.

CUSTOMER, COMPETITION AND THE FIRM

In a competitive field firms have to keep track of customers' mindsets, changes in demographic profiles of the customers and increase or decrease in demand in the market segment that the firm is targeting. After considering these factors and market dynamics the marketing plans are made. The best of the plans can become ineffective unless they are implemented in the correct manner and are kept on the rolling mode, i.e., with facility to alter the plan with speed and efficiency.

The firm's marketing department must work towards an objective; without an objective the firm is like a rudderless boat; it has no direction in which to go. Marketing objectives are finalized after discussions between the CEO, the marketing manager, production head and the finance manager. As the marketing brings profits to the firm, the importance of marketing objectives can never be overrated. The objectives should be made keeping in mind the opportunities available in the business environment and the resources available with the firm. If a firm can produce only 3,000 scooters in a month it would be unwise to set the objective of selling 10,000 scooters per month, unless the firm is planning partial outsourcing of production. In case the marketing department is given multiple objectives like selling a certain number of units and improvement in brand equity by a certain percentage, there could be a possibility of direct assistance between the objectives or there could also be conflict over say resource allocation. Salesman may want bigger allocation of funds for travelling and increase in dealer commission and advertising managers may ask for funds for advertising. Objectives must be acceptable and marketing departments must be committed to the achievement of these objectives; the objectives must also be challenging, achievable but with a stretch.

Firms need to implement their marketing plans in the following manner:

- Convert marketing plans into action tasks and procedures.
- Convey the firm's objective; which drives the plan, to the marketing team and obtain full commitment of all the members on the objectives.
- Give sufficient authority for implementing the plan.
- Assign tasks to the marketing team members, both individually and as a team.
- Monitor the progress of the implementation through unobtrusive checks.
- Get the team's commitment on the time needed for the implementation.

Firms need to quickly evaluate the causes of loss in sales. Is it the plan's failure or that of people implementing the plan? Have the people assigning the implementation to the team gone wrong or is the fault of the objectives? The other causes of failure could be incorrect budget allocations for the implementation, ineffective training given to the team members or limitations of coordination between the team members, which could be due to ignorance or ego of some of the members. The firm's management must be aware of the process of evaluating the effectiveness of plan implementation.

Most implementation problems arise because of lack of clarity in setting up the marketing goals and objectives and the provision of tools for evaluating the success of the plan.

Product portfolio management is possible only if the firm knows the profit picture of each product it sells. Besides, it is important to understand the marketing and support expenses needed or made for each product. Several firms find to their dismay that they are spending far too much on the products in maturity or decline stage of the PLC. Firms are known to have kept loss making products in their ranger either due to lack of knowledge about its profitability or due to ego problems, 'this was our first product launched ten years ago and it gave us lot of profits earlier.'

Firms need to look at some of the other areas as well:

- Keep their current assets under control by tracking the inventory levels, using push sales technique by passing on the inventories to the distribution channel members.
- Keep track of competitive pricing. Does the firm want to be price leader or merely price follower? At times firms increase prices and find that the competition was just waiting to follow suit.
- Keep a track of customer complaints and their redressal.
- Keep a track on customer complaints and improvement or deterioration in customer satisfaction level for the product.
- Carry out a technical audit of all technology-related complaints and keep the production, quality and R&D people aware of the same, with a time-bound correction of the faults levels.
- If the product has failed, then no amount of marketing or advertising can help it. The management must decide quickly to withdraw it from the market as soon as possible.
- An audit of advertising and promotions must be made periodically to ensure that these expensive efforts do not go in vain. The single variable technique, where the firm imposes a ban on other promotional activities for a period can give most precise results in this complicated issue.
- How good are the salesmen - are they properly trained, motivated and committed to the firm and their own tasks? Is the rivalry among them healthy or destructive? They can be assessed by obtaining and studying the daily or weekly reports sent in by the salesman. These control points and implementation plans must be announced well in advance and told to the concerned people with total transparency to get the best out of the team members.

Firms should keep a grip on things all the time because it would be futile to cry over spilt milk. Timely corrective actions like counseling of the erring persons, change in plans and altering time schedules can become the guiding factors in the success of firms.

Is the firm exploiting the marketing opportunities fully, product-wise, market-wise and distribution-wise? The management team comprising the CEO, marketing director and finance director should be involved in understanding the market position of the firm, its ethical approach and societal responsibilities. The marketing director should use sales analysis, product-wise, area-wise salesman-wise and distribution-wise, to know the growth of the market, the firm's market share, percentage of market expense in each area's sales, and compare these with the objectives. Financial market analysis should look at the profit or loss situation for each product, area salesman and distributor network and compare the same with the objectives. The marketing managers should evaluate the efficacy of advertising, promotion, distribution channels and salesman to help in modifying the plans to make them more effective, as shown in Exhibit 2.10

EXHIBIT 2.10 ***Marketing Plan Assessment***

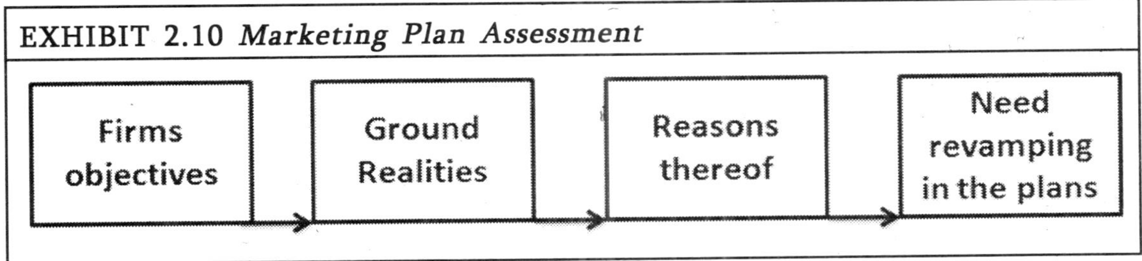

The decline in sales revenue and profits could be attributed to decline in the total market, decline in the firm's market share, a decline due to reduced prices or increase in selling expenses.

A motorcycle firm had planned to sell 1,00,000 bikes annually at a price of Rs. 30,000 each, with the total revenue being Rs. 300 crore. It was targeting a total of 25 per cent of the country's market. However, it could sell only 80,000 bikes at a net price of Rs. 25,000 each, totaling revenue of Rs. 200 crore; the market leaders got the balance of the sale. A price revision had to be done to reduce the onslaught of competitive forces.

Also the market grew by 10 per cent the same year. By virtue of this the firm should have sold 1,10,000 bikes. The firm therefore lost the sale of 30,000 bikes and revenue of Rs. 90 crore.

Audit of various branches can be an eye opener as at times when the firm is making profits, a few loss-making branches can be carried as extra baggage. The moment the tide turns against the firm these loss-making branches become the first victim. The profit picture should be analyzed in terms of each branch, profit centre, Strategic Business Unit (SBU) and market segment. There are times when each sale is loss making and increase in sales only adds to the losses. These could be for products in the Dog Quadrant of the BCG Matrix. Firms must decide the proper strategy to get out of the loss making situation at the earliest. Even in case of distributor channels making profits also, the firm could be spending too much on helping them make profits, for instance giving high commissions. It is worthwhile to evaluate brand equity and dealers' reputation to accurately determine the level of dealer commission to be paid. When it comes to new products dealers do have an upper hand as they are in touch with the customers selling them other products. Later, however, when the product itself develops brand equity, which helps in selling the product to a large extent, the dealer commission can be downsized; while ensuring that channel members remain loyal, like by asking them to participate in promotional plans, joint advertising efforts.

At times firms take the decision of selling a product on the basis of marginal costing. This usually is restored to when there is locked inventory or a new competitive market has to be entered. However, in such cases the loss in profit must be self-evident and the sales team should not be pressured into bringing back the profits in the rest of the sales. However, attempts by the sales team should be praised.

Similarly, there is an age-old rivalry between the production unit and the sales force. When orders are not received in time and there is an inventory build up, the production team starts blaming the sales force. Conversely when there are delays in meeting orders, the blame is borne by the production department. Situations like these cannot be eliminated, but they can be reduced in intensity by establishing coordination teams between the two departments and enforcing transparency in the operations of the two departments. It is therefore to know if the firm's increase or decrease in market share is in consonance with increase or decrease of the total market demand, else the firm can become complacent about its achievements.

Market share thus assumes great importance in a firm's marketing plans. Most CEOs consider market share and brand equity as two of the most important assets of a firm. While the growth of the market is dependent on factors outside of the firm, it affects the entire firm. Firms should therefore realize the factors which are responsible for increase or decline of market at any point of time.

The general business environment, including factors like legal issues affect business but they do not have the same effect on all the competitive firms. The 9/11 incidents did shrink the tourism business but the affect was different on different firms.

Firms should benchmark their operating results against the best in the industry. However if the firm is a market leader then it should compare with it's own past performance or with that of the nearest competitor.

Market share loss could be due to the firm leaving unprofitable areas and may in fact lade to better bottom line. Entry of new firms would also lead to loss of share, but the percentage loss may not be the same for all the competitors.

Market share depends on the number of customers with the firm, their buying patterns and buying quantities, the ratio of the firm's buyers in the market and the purchase average of the firm's customer's vis-à-vis competitive customers. It also depends on the price differential between firms, especially for products aimed at the low and middle income groups where price sensitivity is a major issue.

The effect of marketing expense needs to be monitored and it should be major criteria for the way marketing plans are developed, as can be seen from Figure 2.2.

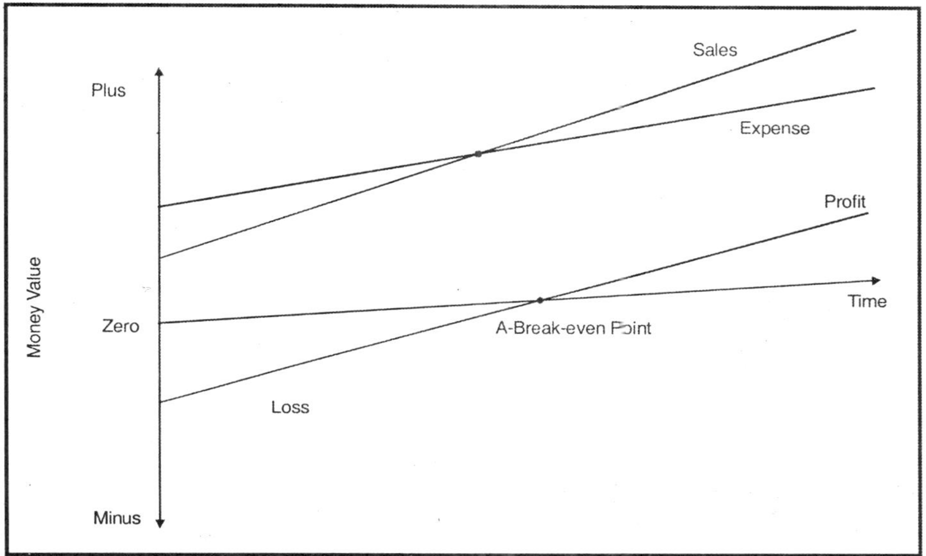

Figure 2.2: P&L Graph

As can be seen from the graph in Fig. 2.2 if the marketing expenses go up, the profit may decline and there may even be a loss. Marketing expenses can be divided into:

- Salaries and travel expenses of salesmen
- Advertising
- Sales promotion
- Distribution channel commission (unless channel members are allowed to have a mark-up on prices)
- Sales overheads like administrative expenses, rentals, telephones and other correspondence.
- Marketing research.
- Training of sales persons including those of channel members.

Depending on the firm these costs vary a lot. Soft drink companies spend 25 to 30 per cent of their sales revenue on advertising and promotion, while some industrial goods manufacturers may not spend more than 5 per cent of the sales revenue on the same. Firms need to benchmark these expenses and keep a checklist at the end of the year it is found that the expenses have skyrocketed without a resultant increase in sales and profits. There of course can be regional and seasonal fluctuations in these expenses, but firms could do well to provide guidelines to the sales teams about the possible upper limits on each of the expenses. The back-up given below provides an idea of the prevalent expenses as percentages of sales turnover in most industries (it would be better to go by industry norms in most cases, unless the situation is unusual like a product launch).

- Sales team salaries and travel 10-15 per cent
- Advertising 5-25 per cent
- Promotion 3-10 per cent
- Distribution channel commission 7-15 per cent
- Sales overheads 2-5 per cent
- Marketing Research 0.5-1 per cent.

The variation seen above into consideration the product type - consumer durables, FMCGs, industrial goods and services. Individual firms need to take their historical norms into consideration. New firms can benchmark against the most efficient firm in the same business and almost equal in size.

Firms can also build Marketing Score Cards (MSCs) for soft numbers as against hard facts like sales. These can then be modulated for each sales team and each salesman. The MSCs should focus on the following:

- Master list of all the customers and prospective customers for industrial products.
- Master list of the distribution channel members and their major clients for FMCGs and consumer durables.
- Master cards of all new customers giving their full particulars.
- List of customer complaints and the delay in their redressal and similar study of competition.
- Rating points on customer service as compared to competitor's service.
- Current market segment being catered to and new segments which can be targeted in the future.
- Product awareness levels in the target market segment.
- Product acceptance level in the target segment.

The two hidden costs of the marketing team - they are a cost of inefficiency and cost of unethical practices must be unearthed so that they can be reduced if not completely eliminated.

Cost of inefficiency: This can be seen from the low number of sales calls by the salesman, low call effectiveness, increase in cost per call, increase in entertainment expense without relative increase in sales, decrease in number and value of orders received and customers lost.

Cost of unethical practices: This can be seen in the undue lowering of rates for low volumes of orders, unmatched inventories of accessories, unauthorized commitment by salesmen to customers causing losses to the firm.

In a nutshell, the marketing team should be given freedom of action within the framework of authority, but must also be accountable to achieving the firm's marketing objectives. Controls in the area of marketing should be instituted more as a help to the sales team until they prove to be going totally off the track.

STRATEGIC MARKETING AND MARKETING MANAGEMENT

Strategic marketing focuses on choosing the right products for the right growth markets at the right time. It may be argued that these decisions are no different from those emphasized in marketing management. However, the two disciplines approach these decisions from different angles. For example, in marketing management, market segments are defined by grouping customers according to marketing mix variables. In the strategic marketing approach, market segments are formed to identify the group(s) that can provide the company with a sustainable economic advantage over the competition. To clarify the matter, Henderson labels the latter grouping a **strategic sector**. Henderson notes:

A strategic sector is one in which you can obtain a competitive advantage and exploit it. Strategic sectors are the key to strategy because each sector's frame of reference is competition. The largest competitor in an industry can be unprofitable in that the individual strategic sectors are dominated by smaller competitors.

A further difference between strategic marketing and marketing management is that in marketing management the resources and objectives of the firm, however defined, are viewed as uncontrollable variables in developing a marketing mix. In strategic, objectives are systematically defined at different levels after a thorough examination of necessary inputs. Resources are allocated to maximize overall corporate performance and the resulting strategies are formulated with a more inclusive view. As Abel and Hammond have stated:

A strategic market plan is not the same as a marketing plan; it is a plan of all aspects of an organization's strategy in the market place. A marketing plan, in contrast, deals primarily with the delineation of target segments and the product, communication, channel and pricing policies for reaching and servicing those segments - the so-called marketing mix.

Marketing management deals with developing a marketing mix to serve designated markets. The development of a marketing mix should be preceded by a definition of the market. Traditionally, however, market has been loosely defined. In an environment of expansion, even marginal operations could be profitable; therefore, there was no reason to be precise, especially when considering that the task of defining a market is at best difficult. Besides, corporate culture emphasized short-term orientation, which by implication stressed a winning marketing mix rather than an accurate definition of the market.

To illustrate how problematic it can be to define a market, consider the laundry product Wisk. The market for Wisk can be defined in many different ways: the laundry detergent market, the liquid laundry detergent market or the prewash-treatment detergent market. In each market, the product would have a different market share and would be challenged by a different set of competitors, which definition of the market is most viable for long-term healthy performance is a question that strategic marketing addresses.

A market can be viewed in many different ways and a product can be used in many different ways. Each time the product-market pairing is varied, the relative competitive strength is varied, too. Many businesspeople do not recognize that a key element in strategy is choosing the competitor whom you wish to challenge, as well as choosing the marketing segment and product characteristics with which you will compete.

Exhibit 2.11 summarizes the differences between strategic marketing and marketing management. Strategic marketing differs from marketing management in many respects: orientation, philosophy, approach, relationship with the environment and other parts of the organization and the management style required. For example, strategic marketing requires a manager to forgo short-term performance in the interest of long-term results. Strategic marketing deals with the business to be in; marketing management stresses running a delineated business.

EXHIBIT 2.11 Major differences between strategic marketing and marketing management*

Point of difference	*Strategic Marketing*	*Marketing Management*
Time frame	Long range; i.e., decisions have long-term implications	Day-to-day; i.e., decisions have relevance in a given Financial year
Orientation	Inductive and intuitive	Deductive and analytical
Decision process	Primarily bottom up	Mainly top-down
Relationship with Environment	Environment considered every changing & dynamic	Environment considered constant with occasional disturbances
Opportunity sensitivity	Ongoing to seek new opportunities	Ad hoc search for a new opportunity
Organizational behavior	Achieve synergy between different components of the organization,both horizontally and vertically	Pursue interests of the decentralized unit
Nature of job	Requires high degree of creativity and originality	Requires maturity, experience and control orientation
Leadership style	Requires proactive perspective	Requires reactive perspective
Mission	Deals with what business to emphasize	Deals with running a delineated business

*These differences are relative, not opposite ends of a continuum.

For a marketing manager, the question is: Given the array of environmental forces affecting my business, the past and the projected performance of the industry or market and my current position in it, which kind of investments am I justified in making in this business? In strategic marketing, on the other hand, the question is rather: What are my options for upsetting the equilibrium of the marketplace and reestablishing it in my favor? Marketing management takes market projections and competitive position as a given and seeks to optimize within those constraints. Strategic marketing, by contrast, seeks to throw off those constraints wherever possible. Marketing management is deterministic; strategic marketing is opportunistic. Marketing management is deductive and analytical; strategic marketing is inductive and intuitive.

CLOSING CASE: BHARAT HEAVY ELECTRICALS LIMITED (BHEL)

Bharat Heavy Electricals Limited (BHEL) is India's largest public sector engineering company and one of its kinds in this part of hemisphere. It manufactures a wide range of state of the art power generation equipments and systems, besides equipment for industry, transmission, transportation, defence, telecommunications and the oil business. The first plant of BHEL was set up in Bhopal in 1956, which signaled the drawn of heavy electrical industry in India. In the early sixties three major plants were set up in Hardwar, Hyderabad and Triuchirapalli , which formed the core of the diversified product range ,systems and services that BHEL offers now. The company has 14 manufacturing divisions, 9 service centres and power sector regional centres besides projects sites spread all over India and also abroad to provide prompt and effective service to customers.

BHEL's business broadly covers conversation, transmission, utilization and conservation of energy in the core sectors of the economy that fulfils vital infrastructural needs of the country. Its products have established an enviable reputation for high quality and reliability, which is largely due to the emphasis placed all along on contemporary technology. BHEL has constantly upgraded its design and manufacturing facilities to international standards by acquiring and assembling some of the best technologies in the world from leading companies in the USA, Europe and Japan, together with the technologies from its own R&D centres.Having attained ISO 9001 certification ,BHEL is now embarking upon Total Quality Management (TQM) for its operations.

Business Mission

a. Maintain a leading position as suppliers of quality equipment, systems and services in the field of conversation, transmission utilization and conservation of energy, for applications in the area of electric power, transportation, oil and gas exploration and industries.

b. Utilize company's capabilities and resources to expand business into allied areas and other priority sectors of the economy like defence, communications and electronics.

Objectives

Growth: To ensure a steady growth by enhancing the competitive edge of BHEL in existing business, new areas and international operations so as to fulfill national expectations from BHEL.

Profitability: To provide a reasonable and adequate return on capital employed, primarily through improvements in operational efficiency, capacity utilization and productivity and to generate adequate internal resources to finance the company growth.

Customer focus: To build a high degree of customer confidence by providing increased value for his money through international standards of product quality, performance and superior customer service.

People orientation: To enable each employee to achieve his potential, improve its capabilities, perceive his role and responsibilities and participate and contribute positively to growth and success of the company. To invest in human resources continuously and be alive to their needs.

Technology: To achieve technological excellence in operations by development of indigenous technologies and efficient absorption and adaptation of imported technologies to suit business needs and priorities and provide a competitive advantage to the company.

Image: To fulfill the expectations which stakeholders like government (as owner), employees, customers and the country at large have from BHEL.

BUSINESS SECTOR

BHEL's operations are organized around three business sectors, namely power, industry and international operations. This enables the company to have a strong customer orientation, to be sensitive to needs and respond quickly to changes in the market.

PERFORMANCE

Figure 2.3 gives the corporate structure of BHEL. Figure 2.4 - 2.7 gives the turnover capital employed, EPS and PAT of BHEL respectively. Figure 2.8 gives the sector-wise turnover for the year 1999-2000.Figure 2.9 provides the debt/equity ratio trends and Fig.2.10 gives the value added vs. capital employed for the year 1999-2000.Inspite of several odds, BHEL has done reasonably well. This is mainly due to strategic marketing employed by the company.

STRATEGIC MARKETING @ BHEL

1. Concentrate on technology and R&D. The thrust areas are :
    a. Large size gas turbines
    b. HVDC technology

   c. Gas-insulated substations
   d. 5000 hp locomotives with thyristorised controls
   e. Defence equipments / electronics.
2. Focus on non-conventional energy (NCE) resources. The thrust areas are:
   a. Eco-friendly energy generators
   b. Economic Models
3. Continue to develop defence equipment
4. Consolidate international operations. Develop a niche for non-conventional energy products in neighboring countries and compete or collaborate or co-exist on business sharing basis. In the present context, however, the appropriateness of some of these strategies is causing concern to the company.

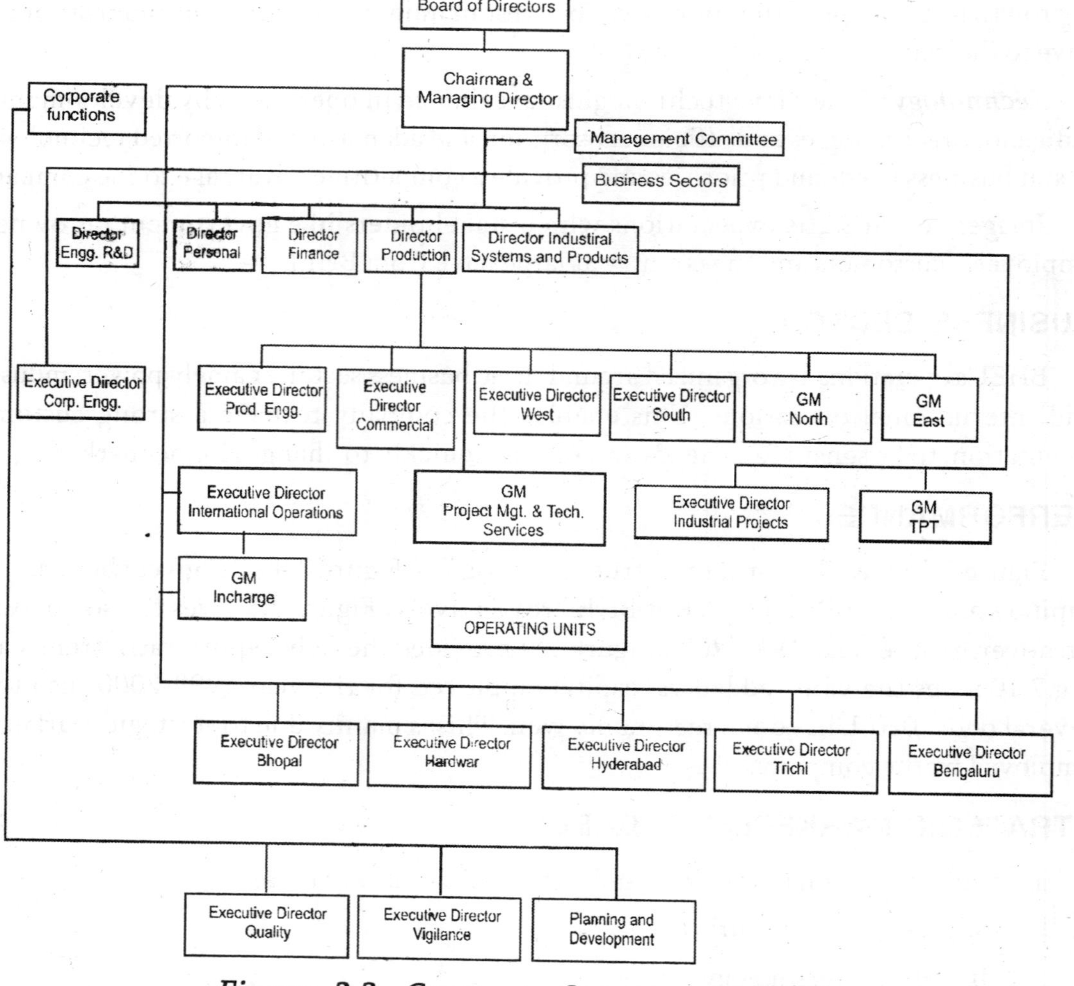

Figure 2.3 Corporate Structure of BHEL

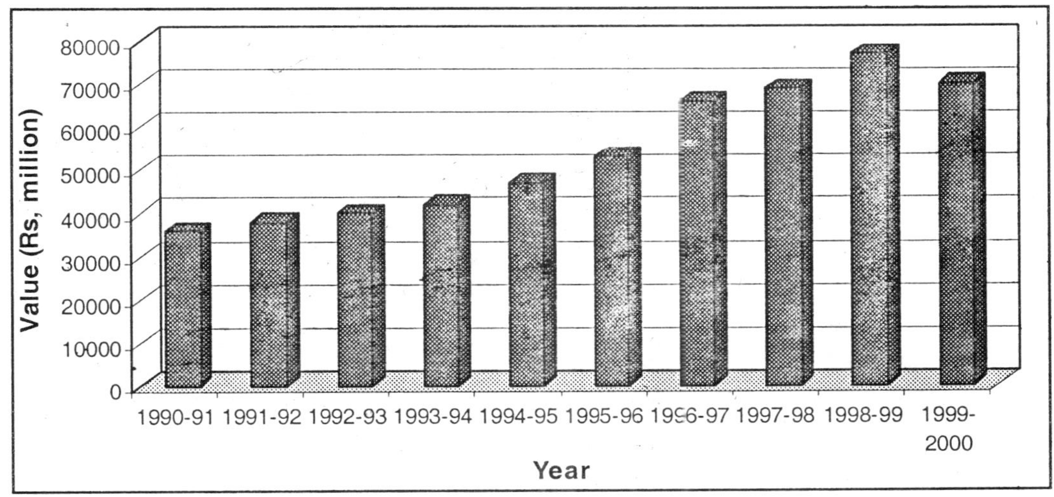

Figure 2.4 Turnover of BHEL from 1990-91 to 1999-2000

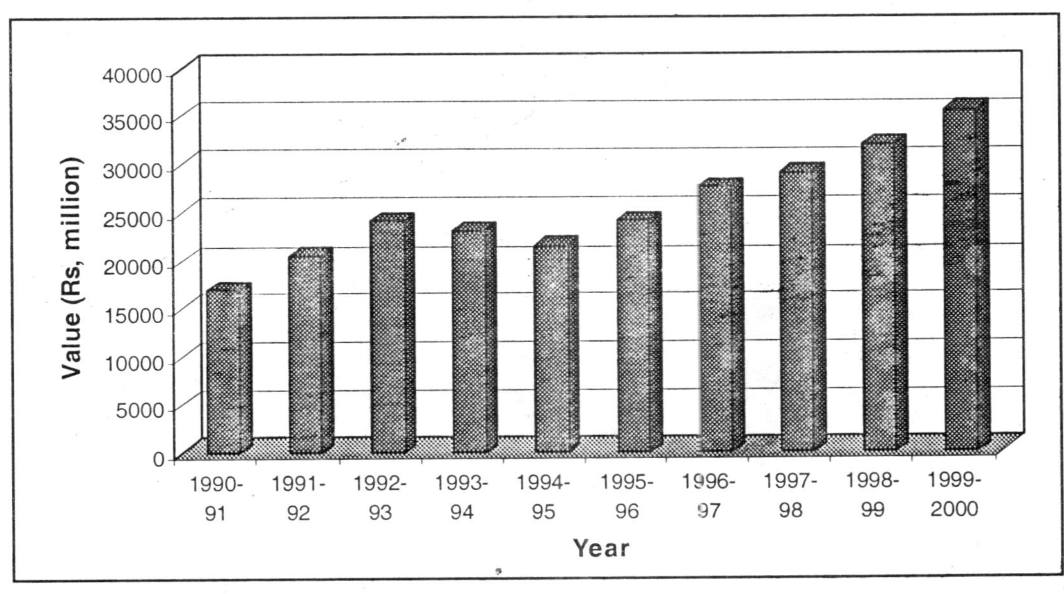

Figure 2.5 Capital Employed

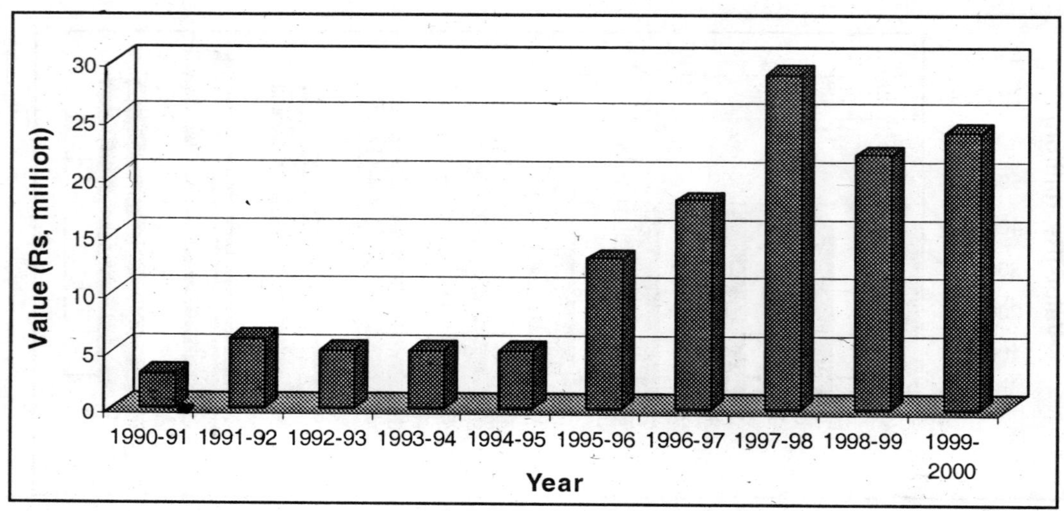

Figure 2.6 Earnings per share (EPS)

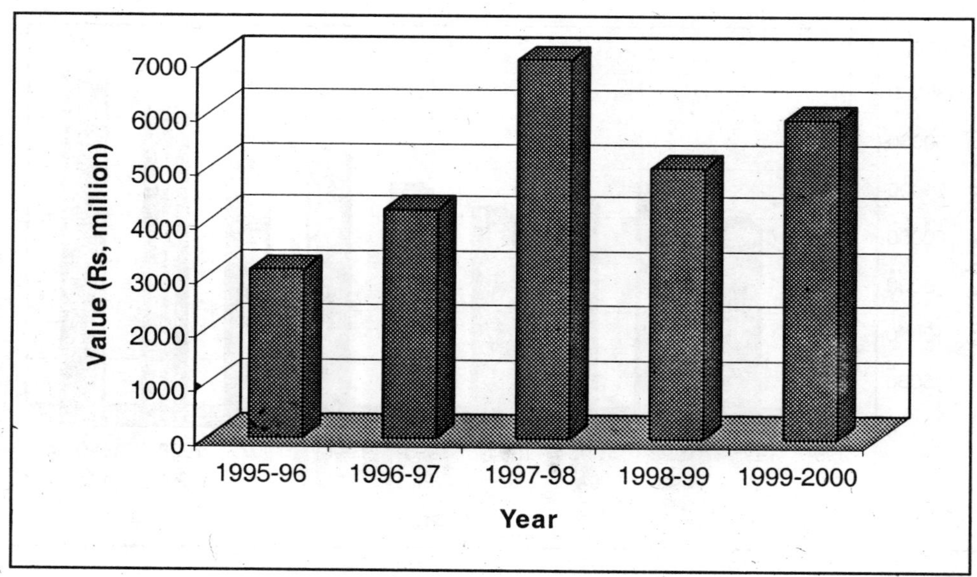

Figure 2.7 Profit after tax

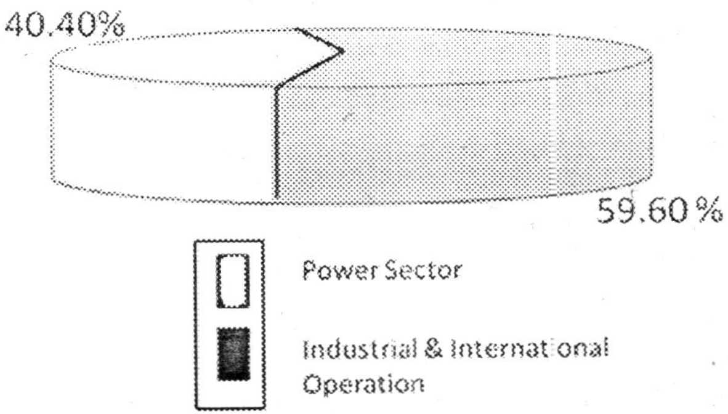

Figure 2.8: Sector-wise Turnover

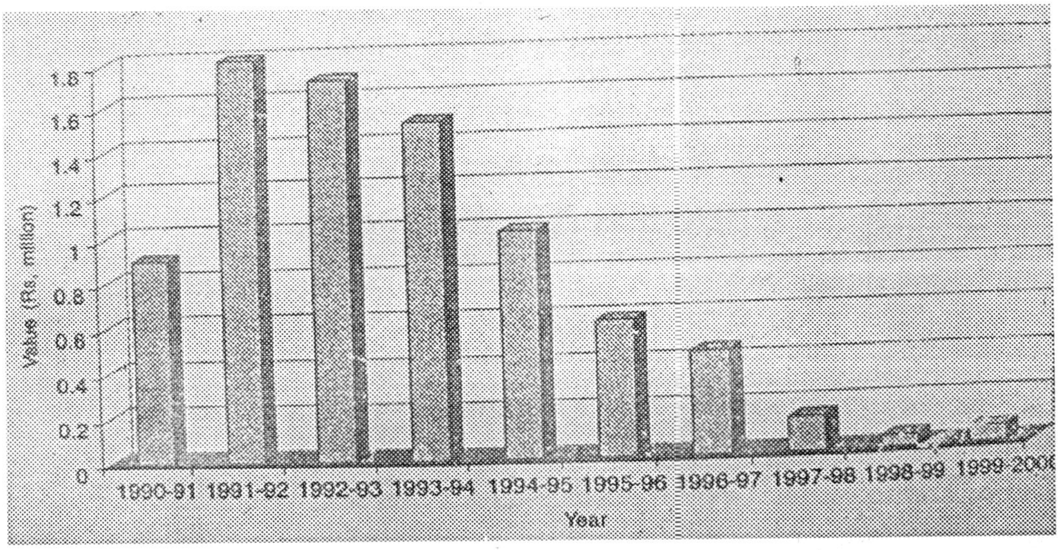

Figure 2.9: Debt/Equity Ratio

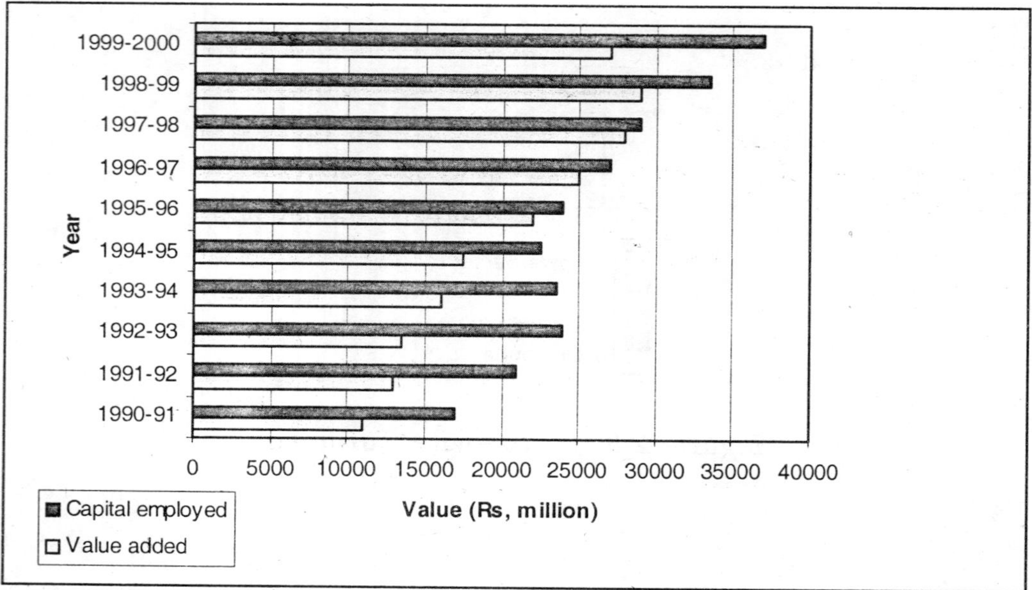

Figure 2.10 Value added Vs capital employed

SUMMARY & KEY TERMS

This chapter introduced the concept of strategic marketing and differentiated it from marketing management. Strategic marketing focuses on marketing strategy, which is achieved by identifying markets to serve, competition to be tackled, and the timing of market entry/ exit. Marketing management deals with developing a marketing mix to serve a designated market.

The complex process of marketing strategy formulation was described. Marketing strategy, which is developed at the SBU level, essentially emerges from the interplay of three forces - customer, competition, and corporation - in a given environment.

A variety of internal and external information is needed to formulate marketing strategy. Internal information flows both down from top management (e.g., corporate strategy) and up from operations management (e.g., past performance of products/markets). External information pertains to social, economic, political, and technologies trends and product/ market environment. The effectiveness of marketing perspectives of the economy is another input in strategy formulation.

The importance of strategic marketing revealed the facts that marketing plays a vital role in strategic management process of a firm. Marketing strategy is the most significant challenge that companies of all types and sizes face. Strategic marketing decisions usually have far reaching implications. In other words strategic marketing is a commitment and not an act.

Traditionally it has been held that all products exert effort to maximize profitability. Strategic marketing starts from the premise that different products may be in the growth stage of the product life cycle, some in the maturity stage and others in the introduction stage. Each position in the life cycle requires a different strategy and affords different expectations.

Portfolio analysis takes into account the fact that large multi-product firms have synergies within and that they need to provide resources for growing their profitable businesses and divesting poor performers with unattractive profits or losses. They need to divert resources from mature and stable businesses into promising new businesses. For making an analysis of a firm's strength, the Boston Consultancy Group (BCG) has developed a matrix .In the BCG Matrix, the horizontal axis shows the market share of the product and the vertical axis shows the market growth.

The market share and market potential are mapped in a portfolio analysis to provide a visual understanding of the industry players and the attractiveness and competitive position of a firm's products. Portfolio analysis can be used to find out where resources should be deployed and to determine the firm's position among competitors.

KEY TERMS

- BCG Matrix
- Corporate culture
- Corporate publics
- Marketing Strategy
- Product Life Cycle-PLC
- Strategic sector

DISCUSSION QUESTIONS

1. What is strategic competitive advantage? Explain it with reference to the core competencies of a firm.
2. Explain the key elements of marketing strategy formulation.
3. Elucidate the process of strategic marketing by taking an example.
4. What do you mean by Strategic Marketing Planning Process (SMPP)?
5. Differentiate between strategic marketing and marketing management.

OPENING CASE: KODAK VS FUJI

In the fall of 1997, Mr. George Fisher, CEO of Eastman Kodak Company, was meeting his top marketing executives to formulate the strategy to contain Fuji Photo film Co. from making further inroads in the U.S. film market.

For some years now, Fuji and Kodak have been battling it out in overseas film markets. But in the United States the picture was quite different. Kodak and Fuji treated that market like a cozy, mutually profitable duopoly. Both enjoyed fat margins. Kodak controlled over 80 percent of the American film market and distant No.2 Fuji always priced its film just a little bit lower.

Then, in the spring of 1997, Fuji began slashing prices by as much as 25 percent. Fuji's explanation was that Costco, one of its five largest distributors in the United States, ditched Fuji for Kodak and the company got stuck with 2.5 million rolls of film. Fuji unloaded the film at a steep discount to other distributors. When consumers saw that the familiar red, white and green boxes were a dollar or two cheaper, they snapped them up. Over the past year Fuji increased its share of the U.S. film market to nearly 16 percent from 10 percent, while Kodak's share took an unprecedented tumble from 80 percent to just under 75 percent.

Fuji executives deny that they intended to start a price war. Yet Fuji's prices were still kept low even after the excess inventory had been worked off. Whatever the case, for the first time in its long history, Kodak can no longer take its home market for granted.

EASTMAN KODAK COMPANY

The Eastman Kodak Company was established in 1884 in Rochester, New York and still overwhelmingly dominates the $2.7 billion U.S. amateur film market. Until recently, the Kodak brand remained solid gold and its quality was never in dispute. But Fuji's gains in the United States were ominous, especially because the Japanese film company was already poised to surpass Kodak on a global basis, particularly in Asia, where film sales were growing at 20 percent a year or more. (Worldwide, Fuji and Kodak were neck-and-neck, with about a third of the market each.) Alex Henderson, managing director of technology research at Prudential Securities Inc. in New York, who had been watching the two companies for twelve years, believes that if current trends hold, Fuji will overtake Kodak by 1999.

"When that happens," says Henderson, "Kodak will go from being Coke to being Pepsi. That's a very damning thing." Worse yet, he expected that in the United States, Fuji would continue to creep up on Kodak by a rate of about 2 percent a year.

FUJI PHOTO FILM COMPANY

The Fuji Photo Film Company was established in Japan in 1909. In 1997, financially, Fuji was a very strong company, giving it more flexibility to cut prices. Fuji's sales in 1996 were a record $11 billion and profits were a near-record $757 million; at the same time, Fuji had a net cash position of about $4.5 billion and access to incredibly cheap borrowing-around 2.5 percent interest-thanks to Japan's record-low interest rates. Kodak had more than $1 billion in short and long-term debt and was in the midst of a sales and profit slide, in addition to impending restructuring write-offs likely to run $1 billion or more. Also, Kodak could not borrow at much under a 7 percent rate of interest. Fuji could afford a show-down, but Kodak could not.

MARKETPLACE

Kodak and Fuji have been slugging it out for three equally important parts of the consumer photo business. Those little yellow and green film boxes are the most obvious to the man in the street, but Fuji and Kodak also manufacture photographic paper, mostly for sale to big photo-processing laboratories and small retail developers. To ensure a market for their paper, both companies have invested heavily in the third line of business-developing-by buying up big film-processing companies across the United States. Fuji's deep pockets had enabled it to make acquisitions like the estimated $400 million purchase of Wal-Mart's six wholesale photo labs in 1996, a move that in one swoop gave it about 15 percent of the U.S. photo-processing market.

Fuji's long-term strategy was to transplant as much film and paper production as possible on to U.S. soil. That kept costs down, reduced nettlesome trade disputes and made Fuji's factories more responsive to local market demands. In 1987, just 3.5 percent of Fuji's production was outside Japan; now the figure was 31 percent and the move off-shore was accelerating. In April 1997, Fuji opened a highly automated, $300 million photographic paper plant in Greenwood, South Carolina, which was already producing about 20 percent of the photo paper consumed in North America. Later that year, Fuji is scheduled to open an equally high-tech, $200 million film plant in Greenwood. According to industry sources, it would not take much time or investment to double the plants capacities should Fuji need it.

COMPETITION

Fuji was one of the leanest and meanest of Japans' big companies. Led for the past 17 years by no-nonsense Chairman and CEO Minoru Ohnishi, Fuji was cutting white-collar overhead long before it started to become fashionable in Japan. In the past ten years the company's sales nearly doubled worldwide, but its staffing in Japan remained almost flat. Ohnishi tried to maintain a sense of crisis by reminding staff that Kodak was still out front. "He likes to constantly cut costs in order to anticipate a rainy day," says a consultant, "so that there will be less pain down the road." Or, more likely greater market share.

Fuji's aggressive tactics had sometimes earned its charges of unfair trading practices. In the early 1990s, the U.S. Commerce department investigated charges that the Japanese company dumped photo-graphic paper in the U.S. market. Fuji managed to dodge import duties by agreeing to raise prices to levels just above the going rate. (Fuji subsequently lost most of its 20 percent market share but bounced back when it opened its paper plant in Greenwood and bought out Wal-Mart's processing labs.) Also, the World Trade Organization is expected to rule soon on U.S. allegations that the government of Japan worked with Fuji to exclude competitors from the Japanese market, which Fuji dominated with a 70 percent market share. A decision is expected in the spring of 1998, though it was not likely to affect either company's business.

Ironically, Fuji got its big break in the American market, thanks to Kodak. The company opened its first office in the United States in 1958 in the Empire State Building, but it only began selling film there in 1970, when it was one of several relative minnow-among them GAF, Agfa and 3M-swimming in Kodak's pond. Then, in 1984, the Olympics came to Los Angeles. Olympic czar Peter Ueberroth believed that Kodak was the natural choice to be the exclusive film sponsor, but Kodak wouldn't bite. Even after Ueberroth visited Rochester to make his pitch, Kodak refused to pay $1 million, far below the $4 million floor for sponsorships that Ueberroth had established. So he approached Fuji, which in those days was still barely known in the U.S. market. Ohnishi agreed on the spot and eventually committed around $7 million. No marketing investment ever brought better returns. Within months of becoming a sponsor, Fuji landed 50,000 new distribution outlets. "Salespeople said that accounts that didn't used to return their calls were suddenly calling them," says

Tom Shay, head of corporate communications for Fuji USA and a 26-year Fuji veteran. "The Olympics completely changed the way people looked at us."

Since then, Fuji has built a reputation for price, quality and sharp marketing. It has won a strong following among professional photographs, some of whom rave over the film's luminous blues and greens. Its acceptance in the professional world has given Fuji a lot of cachet with amateur shutter bugs. Fuji also adopted a hipper, more technologically oriented marketing image to differentiate itself from the sentimental Kodak style. In 1993, Fuji ran a highly successful, award-winning TV campaign obliquely directed at Kodak. The killer line; "Pictures should be nostalgic; your film shouldn't. "Fuji's current slogan also painted the company as forward looking: "You can see the future from here."

In technology too, Fuji has shown that it could set the pace by consistently spending about 7 percent of sales on R&D. In 1986, Fuji was the first to introduce the disposable camera, a product that has been a huge born for both Kodak and Fuji. Fuji also worked with Kodak and other companies to introduce a new 24mm "advanced photo system" film, which uses a new generation camera, a hybrid of digital and traditional systems. In Japan, the launch was a great success, thanks to Fuji's ensuring that the cameras and processing were readily available. Advanced Photo System film already accounts for about 10 percent of the color-negative film market in Japan. "Fuji's greatest strength is that they always make sure that consumers are ready to buy their new products and they actually get the products to the consumers, "remarked Toby Williams, an analyst at SBC Warburg in Tokyo. By contrast, Kodak flubbed the U.S. introduction of its advanced photo system, called Advantix.

If Kodak and Fuji have one thing in common, it is their vulnerability as photography moves into the digital age. In 1997 alone, market watchers expect to see 1.8 million digital cameras sold world-wide and that number will grow sharply as quality improved and prices drop. That poses three big issues for film companies: One was the danger- still much in dispute- that film sales will soften as digital cameras made by companies like Sony, Canon and Casio take up a bigger share of the market. Another was a challenge on the photographic paper and processing front from Canon, Epson and Hewlett-Packard. Their latest generation ink-jet printers produce high quality prints of digital images on plain and coated paper. (Fuji just launched a printer of its own.) Both Kodak and Fuji are working on ways to add value to digital photography, such as a service that lets customers order prints directly over the Internet, but those ideas are untested.

Finally, Kodak and Fuji have jumped into the digital camera business themselves. But they are in a mob of nearly two dozen camera, computer and consumer electronics companies trying to get into the same space. One thing is sure: The companies that win in digital photography will need marketing and product smarts, technology and not the least, money. Fuji, it seems, has them all.

Chapter: 3

Product and Services Strategies

Learning Objectives

In this chapter the main stress is given on :

- The concept of product and its constituents
- Understanding product modification
- To study the various strategies related to products and new product strategies
- To understand product diversification strategies
- To understand Portfolio models
- The emergence of marketing thought in services sector
- The specific characteristics of services
- The importance of strategic planning
- The components of services marketing mix
- The issues involved in strategy implementation, evaluation and control.

So long as a product is not bought and consumed, it remains a raw material or at best an intermediate – Peter Drucker

PRODUCT- KEY CONCEPTS

The product is a bundle of satisfaction that a customer buys. It represents a solution to a customer's problems. It is in this context that the marketing definition of a product is more than just what the manufacturer understands it to be. As Peter Drucker puts it, so long as a product is not bought and consumed. It remains a raw material or at best an intermediate the product is almost always a combination of tangible and intangible benefits. For example a refrigerator is not just merely steel, plastic, Freon gas, brand name, number of doors and so on, but also involves factors like after sales service, delivery and installation assistance in purchase of the product, dealer network and service. It also connotes status in developing countries. It is the same with products like TV, music systems, automobiles, personal products and services like banks, airlines, telephone, courier and so forth.

What Constitutes a Product?

To understand and appreciate it, we need to perceive it as a four layer item. At the heart of it is the "core" or "generic" part. As Levitt puts it, this is the table stakes of business or what is needed to play the game of market participation. For a refrigerator manufacturer is the compressor, steel, Freon gas, condenser and various other electrical or electronic components that need to be assembled. To a five star hotel management it is the number of rooms, restaurants and swimming pools. To an airline operator, it is the aircraft. But in today's competitive world, there is hardly any difference between firms on the generic component of the product. Also, because of the standardization of technology, customers are never able to perceive any significant difference among "core" or "generic" products of competing firms in the industry.

Formal product and Augmented Product

To differentiate its product from all others, the firm names it (branding), packs it , puts additional features-like laminated top, a stand or a water tap on the door of the refrigerator-uses colors and aesthetics to give a distinctive appeal. This makes a "core" product a "formal product" or the expectant Product. But as inter-firm rivalry intensifies, differentiation on the basis of the formal product ceases to exist. Consider the example of ceiling fans. Today, there is no difference in the fans marketed by Crompton and others. All look like in terms of attributes, style and color. Besides, all have identical warranties making the task of fan marketer difficult. It is here that the marketer searches for possible differentiation. When technology ceases to give one and it becomes a price and promotion wars, the marketer looks for the intangibles. Intangibles are services like after sales service, delivery and installation schedules and helping buyers purchase the product through low cost financing options.

There is no fixed range of services that a marketer may offer. It is based on customer needs and the marketer's creative strategy to serve it. This intangible component of the product along with formal and core components is called "augmented product". Levitt believes that further competition will be in the augmented product. The marketer keeps expanding the service component, thus enhancing the product value. Not all customers for all products and under all circumstances can be attracted by this ongoing process of value enhancement. They may prefer a low priced product to an augmented product. Some customers may not be able to use the extra services offered by the marketer. Nonetheless, it is an irony in marketing that as customers get more enlightened about the product (through marketer's communication about the use of the product), the more vulnerable the marketer becomes to losing them. And this is precisely when the customer shops for a price. "At this point, it makes sense to embark on systematic programmed of customer benefiting and therefore customer keeping, product augmentation."

The firm should also undertake cost reduction programmers so that it can compete on the price front too. According to Levitt the augmented product is a condition of market maturity or of relatively experienced or sophisticated customers. The potential product consists of everything that might be done to attract and hood customers. These offerings differ from one market to another because of varying economic and competitive conditions. The driving force in developing these offerings is the prime goal of any firm-retains competitive advantage Figure 3.1 explains these product concepts. Thus, the product is the total concept that a customer buys. As competition intensifies, markets open up, telecommunication and information networks improve and exposures of Indian families improve, firms will have to re-examine their product concepts. For an important fact to be kept in mind is that these concepts keep changing as customers become more aware and sophisticated.

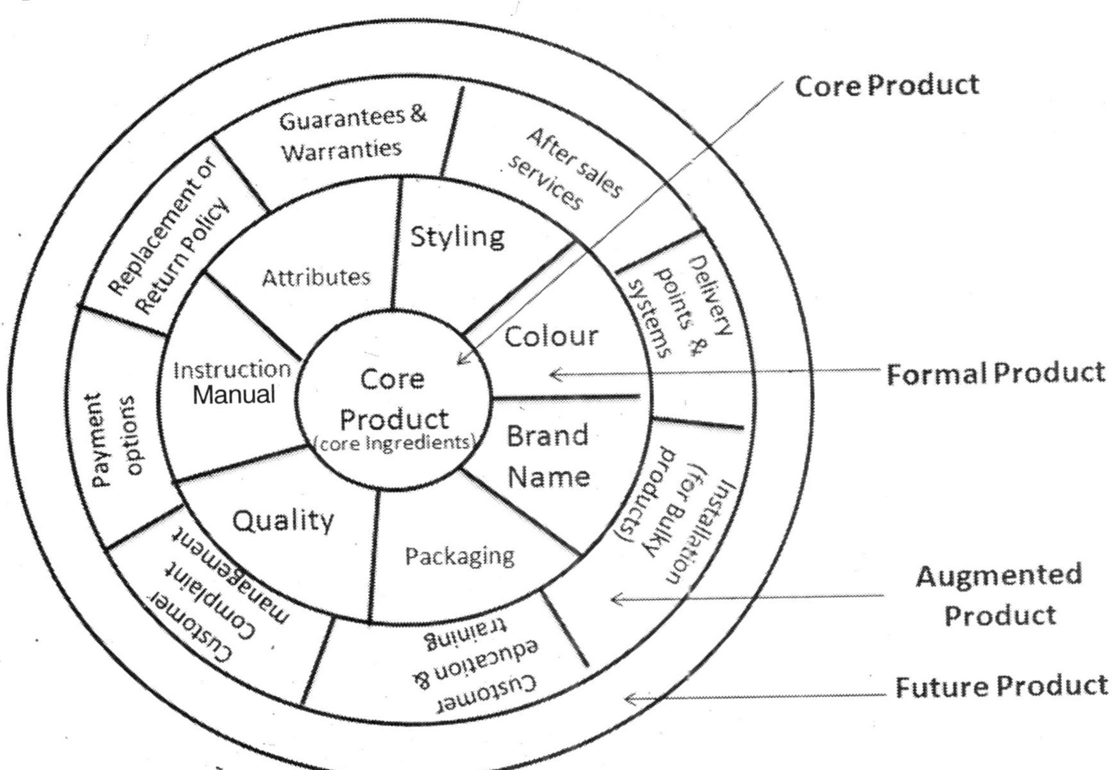

Figure 3.1 The Total Product Concept

(**Source:** Adapted from Theodore Levitt, Ibid.)

Product Mix

One of the realities of business is that most firms deal with multiple products. This helps a firm diffuse its risks across different product groups. Also, it enables the firm to appeal to a much larger group of customers or to different needs of the same customer group. So when a company like Samsung entered India with a diversified product portfolio consisting of television, music systems, washing machines, refrigerators, microwave ovens and call phones, it sought to satisfy the aspirations of the middle and upper middle income group of consumers. Likewise, Bajaj Electricals a household name in India has almost ninety products in its portfolio ranging from low value items like bulbs to high priced consumer durables like mixers, luminaries and lighting projects. The number of products carried by a firm at a given point of time is called its product mix. This product mix contains product lines and product items. In other words it's a composite of products offered for sale by a firm.

Product Line

This consists of different products that are closely related to each other by virtue of satisfying a particular class of needs, being used together, being distributed through the same channels or possessing common physical of technical characteristics. In other words, a product line refers to a group of products clubbed together because they have one of the above described characteristics in common. The number of product lines carried by a firm at a given point of time is a function of its resources and competitive position.

The Change "TELCO" has gone through

Telco continued to be a single product line firm until the mid 1980s, when its competitive position was threatened in the heavy motor vehicles market by the low cost, more efficient Japanese light commercial vehicles (LCVS). TELCO responded by developing its own LCV and also by diversifying into the passenger car segment. This was a new product line as it catered to a different customer group deferent need and also required different distribution. In the late 1990s, TELCO launched its passenger car, Indica. Faced with the failure of the product, the company realized that it needed a different orientation; passenger car marketing required an understanding of lifestyle marketing, customer service, and development of a channel which was customer friendly. The company modified the Indica after their research on failures and customer lifestyle. No more did the company market it as an engineering feat. It was marketed as a 'large small car' for the Indian family and available in diesel and petrol versions. The company launched its mid-size car Indigo in 2003 and in one year's time it became one of the most successful mid-size cars- competing with Esteem, Hyundai Accent, Ford Ikon, etc. The company's name. Tata Motors reflects the change TELCO has gone through. Thus a market savvy company's product line is generally in line with changing market conditions.

In many cases, a firm may start as a single product line company, emerge a winner, "harvest the crop", and then add other product lines. Nirma , T-Series, Reliance, and many other new generation entrepreneurs have followed this route. Associated with product mix are issues like breadth, depth and consistency. **Breadth** in product mix refers to the number of product lines marketed by a firm. **Depth** refers to the number of product items and variations (like size, packaging, colors, etc.) offered in each product line. **Consistency** in product mix is the degree of similarity between product lines with respect to end use, technology, production techniques, and distribution channels. This element of consistency is based on the firm's long- term objectives, its competitive position in the industry, strengths, and resource position. Some firms prefer diversity and hence inconsistency is visible in their product mix. An example of this is the engineering giant Larsen and Turbo (L&T), which has diversified into cement and medical diagnostics. Likewise, ITC Ltd diversified into hotels, vegetable oils, exports (sea food), financial services agrotech, and detail and now in e-business. Some firms, on the other hand, have product lines that consistent with their main business.

The ideal product mix is an issue that varies from firm to firm and may be hard to define and come by. The following situations may suggest that the firm has a sub-optimal product mix:

(a) Excess capacity in a firm's manufacturing, warehousing or transportation facilities

(b) High proportion of profits from a small percentage of product items

(c) Insufficient use of sales force contacts and skills

(d) Steadily declining sales or profits

Product Mix Decisions

Often firms decide to change their product mix. These decisions are dictated by the above factors and also by the changes occurring in the market place. Just like changing lifestyles of Indian consumers BPL-Sanyo to launch an entire range of white goods like refrigerators, washing machines, and micro wave ovens, it also motivated the firm to launch other entertainment electronics products. Rahejas well-known construction firm in Mumbai, took a major decision to convert one of its theatre building in the western suburbs of Mumbai into a large garments and accessories stores for men, women and children-perhaps the first of its kind in India to have almost all products required by these custom groups. Competition from low priced washing powders forced Hindustan Lever to launch different brands of detergent at different price levels and positioned them at different market segments. Customer preferences for herbal products motivated Lever to launch the black Sunsilk shampoo was Shikakai. Furthermore, low purchasing power and a cultural bias against the shampoo market made Hindustan Lever consider smaller packs, mainly sachets, for single use. So, it is the change or antedated change in the market-place that motivates a firm to consider changes in its product mix. The change takes the following forms:

Product Line Addition/Deletion:

A firm may add new products or delete existing ones or both in its existing product lines. Further, a firm may upgrade its technology and use state of-the-technology or decide to stretch the product line downwards towards a more simple technology. Consider the example of a consumer product company like Bajaj Electricals. When the firm decided to launch a state-of -the-art washing machine in collaboration with a major international firm, it was moving up in technology. This is termed as stretching the product line upwards. It was not only in technology that Bajaj Electricals moved up but also in the customer group that it now attracted. Its washing machines customer was no more a low income housewife but an upper-middle and high income house wife. The need served by this washing machine was much more than just washing, cleaning, rinsing and drying. It was now a status symbol and perhaps visualized as representing a "progressive and liberated" woman. But when Bajaj Electricals decided to launch a manual washing machine at a price equivalent to 40 percent of the top-end model prices, it was stretching its product line downwards. Now reached out to the low income consumer who may not be very educated. But perhaps, within the segment, she may be perceived as an opinion leader. She buys it for washing her clothes and also demonstrate her "being superior" to her neighbors, friends and peer group.

Likewise, when publishing houses like Times of India group offered web editions of its publications, it entered a new market segment, viz., customers who are tech savvy and overseas Indians who wanted to keep in touch with developments in India. Adding or stretching a product line upwards or downwards is done due to structural changes in the market-place- the most important being customer lifestyles and demo-graphic characteristics like rising incomes and lower proportion of consumer income being spent on toad and other essential items. Developments in media, contributing to increased awareness, may also motivate a firm to stretch its product line. Today we are seeing the expending role of television, with more channels and programmers and internet in creating an increased awareness of new products and ideas. This awareness also exists in rural markets now. It is no wonder that more companies are now jumping on to the consumer goods bandwagon. They are also now developing real-time delivery modules to enhance the value of their products. Competitive pressure may also drive a firm to extend its product line to include hi-tech products. Cutthroat competition and imitation forced firms like Bajaj Electricals, Blue Star and Voltas and many others to take to hi-tech products and vacate the low tech product areas. Besides, a firm's strength in the market-place, brand image, distribution network and sales force strengthens its resolve to stretch product lines upwards. The decision to stretch the product line downwards is often dictated by a firm's desire to be present in all market segments. Marketing capabilities, strengths in the distribution channel and a gap in the market-place are some of the key factors that drive firms to do so.

Many a time competition and customer preferences can in combination, driving the firm to launch low priced or less sophisticated products. This is precisely what happened when Hindustan Lever decided to launch Surf Ultra, Rin (blue colored), Wheel (green) and Sunlight (yellow) detergent powder to counter the threat from Nirma. While Surf Ultra and Rin were positioned at the middle or upper middle and high income housewife, the other two were targeted at a low income and price sensitive housewife. The move to launch low priced detergent powders was fuelled by declining sales and market share of Hindustan Lever in the detergent market.

But at times a firm may stretch its product line downwards because it has a brand image in a particular market segment and would now like to expand its market share in the target market. Taj Hotels is a big name in India's tourism industry. It perhaps represents the finest and the best service in the hotel industry. Invariably, all its hotels, countrywide or internationally, are in the five star or five star deluxe categories. With a boom in domestic tourism and also a large number of middle-rung executives travelling on business, Taj saw an opportunity and launched its new line of hotels called Taj Gateway. These hotels had all the comforts of a five star hotel, but without the frills. They were, therefore, priced lower too. A downward stretch may also be undertaken to take advantage of a brand name and market opportunity created by changing consumer lifestyles and/or needs.

Product Abandonment: This involves discontinuing or deleting either an individual product or an entire product line.

The rejection of on-line shopping facility
Shopper's stop abandoned its on-line shopping facility when it found that there were not many takers for it. So was the case of LG Electronics which started their on-line shop with a big fanfare. Today it's a moot question if it is a profitable venture. This is because Indians rarely buy on-line consumer durables, garments and accessories. Likewise, Bajaj Electricals abandoned the entertainment electronics line in 1985 and with it came the end of an era of Bajaj transistors and TV. Parle (Exports) had to withdraw from the fast food market twice- once when they had to withdraw Big Bite and later when they withdrew Bisca (cup-a-noodle). Generally, products that are abandoned are those for which demand is low leading to uneconomical short production runs or frequent and uneconomical price and inventory adjustments. These products could also be consuming excessive management time not justified by their profit contribution. Sometimes these products may be outdated and therefore detract from the company's image. In brief, these products have either lived their life or are unprofitable.

Product Modification:

Sometimes just a cosmetic modification may be required the existing product line or product item. These changes may be tangible or intangible and may be achieved by reformulation, redesign, changing unit sizes and adding or removing features. Pan Parag, the famous pan masala, introduced new sachet packs of different size and at different prices. This helped it to penetrate and expand-the market. When the firm decided to add tobacco (zarda) to the pan masala the effect was a manifold increase in its market share. Most often these changes are dictated by a firm's long-term goals, customer preferences and competitive developments in a particular product market. It is apparent that product mix decisions are strategic in nature and often aimed at enhancing a firm's competitive advantage in the market-place. But how can a firm take decision to add or delete product lines and items? In other words, what analysis does a firm need to do and what tools are available to a firm to conduct this exercise?

Product modification is achieved by reformulation, redesign, changing unit sizes and adding/removing features are dictated by a firm's long-term goals, customer preferences and competitive developments in the particular product market.

Criteria that Decides Product Addition/Deletion:

(A) Portfolio Analysis: One of the tools used in analyzing market scenarios and strategic decisions concerning product mix is the portfolio analysis. We referred to this and the two major models, BCG and GE approach, in the chapter or market Opportunity Analysis. We shall again revert to these two models and examine their strategic implications.

(B) BCG Model: This model, called Boston Consulting Group (BCG), categorizes products into four group's question marks, stars, cash cows and dogs-based on their market share in relation to competition and the market growth rate. An important assumption made by BCG is that products can be treated as strategic business units (SBUs), provided they fulfilled the following conditions.

1. The product (s) /SBU must have a clear, well defined and identifiable competito which is trying to outsmart the firm
2. The product(s) /SBUs can be planned separately from the rest of the firm
3. It has an independent manager responsible for its sales, profits and strategic planning.

Further, the BCG model assumes a market growth rate of 10 percent as the cutoff point. All SBUs growing at a rate higher than 10 percent are in the high growth segment and those growing at a rate lower than this are perceived to be in the low growth segment. Market growth rate is represented on the vertical axis. The horizontal axis represents the SBU's market share relative to its largest competitor. The market share is expressed in a log scale and 1.0 is taken as a cutoff point. Based on these two factors, a firm's product items or product lines can be categorized as:

I. Problem Child or Question mark: This is a product growing at a rate of more than 10 percent and hence is in the high growth market. But, as its relative market share is low (lower than 1.0) the firm has to decide either to-

(i) build, or

(ii) withdraw

The strategy to build a question mark or problem child is based on competitive forecasts, market trends and corporate objectives. Many a times, a firm may decide to build a product not because it is getting good profits but purely for maintaining an image. These products/ SBUs require huge cash resources since the firm has to keep acquiring plant and machinery and personnel to keep pace with the high growth market. Further, these are generally new products and consequently the firm's learning cost is high compared to the sales revenue generated by these products.

At times, some existing of a firm may also be in this segment. The strategy of withdrawal is mainly based on a strategist's perception of a firm's strengths and competitive position. For example, if the strategist perceives a high level of inter firm rivalry and the firm does not have the ability to stay out, the product may be withdrawn. A large number of electronic companies have withdrawn from consumer markets because of their inability to survive in a competitive market.

II. Star: A star is an SBU which is a market leader in a high growth market. Mostly, question marks go on to become stars. Just because it is a market leader does not mean that the star generates surplus of profits. On the contrary, a star requires cash to maintain its leader status. These resources are ploughed in as on-going process for market development fighting off competition. The strategist will have to examine which SBUs are stars and plan a strategy of maintenance or hold for them.

III. Cash Cows: The irony of the market-place is that after some time it stops growing at rates higher than 10 percent. This happens when the market reaches a saturation point. Once a star has been the market leader and has deployed strategies to build customer loyalties, it usually becomes a cash cow. A cash cow is an SBU that generates cash surplus. The stronger the cash cow, the higher the cash generation. The strategy here is to harvest or milk these cash cows, particularly those that are soon going to be losing their relevance by becoming "dogs". Strong cash cows may be maintained but the strategist must not forget that these SBUs are fast becoming obsolete and customer preferences are changing towards newer or more efficient products. Hence in the long term they may not be viable.

IV. Dogs: Dogs are SBUs or products that have lost their position of leadership and are in the low growth markets. These are also weak cash cows. These SBUs need to be killed or divested. Otherwise they will consume management time and scarce resources which could otherwise be more effectively utilized elsewhere. Figures 3.2 and 3.3 illustrate the BCG model cash situation and strategy in different quadrants. It is important for the market to appreciate that SBUs change their positions in the growth share matrix over a period of time. This change may be brought about by environmental factors like customer preference, competitive activity, government policy and so on. It should also be understood that a good product portfolio consists of many stars and question marks and several cash cows of varying strengths. The success route is to modify cash cows and give them a fresh lease of life before they become dogs. In fact, the marketer needs to continuously evaluate the product mix every year and examine the product's growth rate vis-à-vis the industry and the largest competitor. Further the marketer must also examine market share data. In case the performance of any product is not satisfactory, the marketer should re-examine the strategy and make appropriate modifications. The most important contribution of this model is that it helps a firm to effectively plan its product mix.

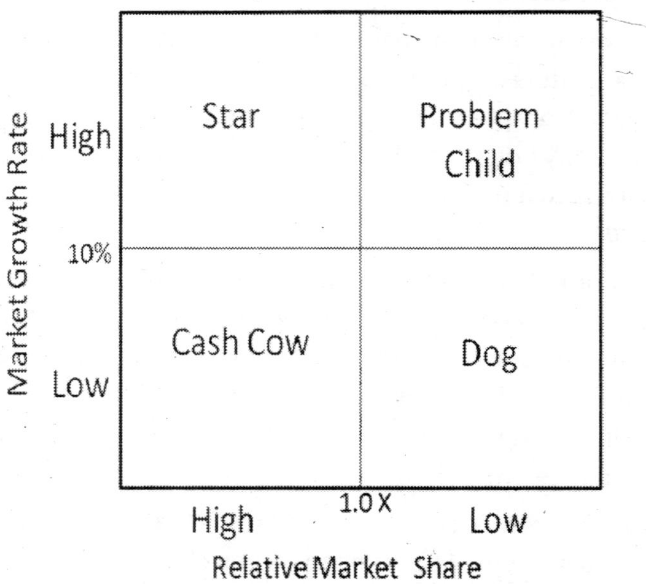

Figure 3.2 The BCG Model

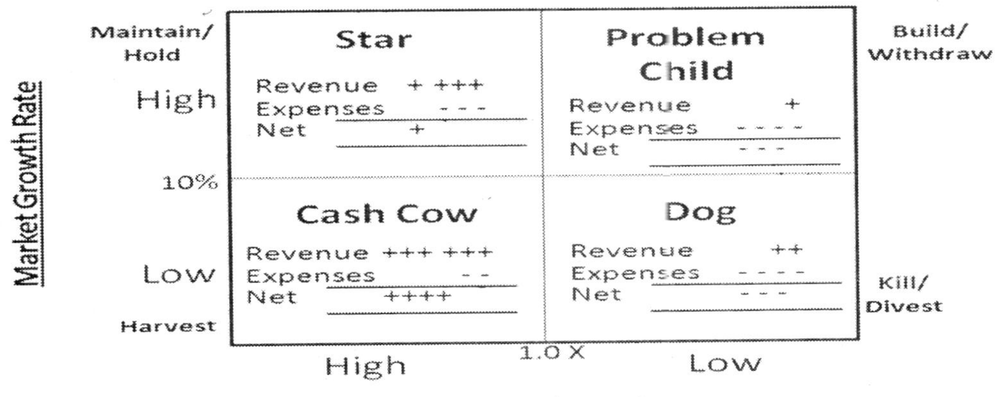

Figure 3.3 The BCG Model: Cash Position and Strategy

(C) The GE Approach: The problem with the BCG model is that the cutoff point in market growth rate classifying high growth and low growth markets is arbitrary; and in most cases 10 percent is too high a growth rate. To overcome this problem and also to consider factors contributing to market growth and share the GE (General Electric) approach comes in handy. The two axes in the GE matrix are market attractiveness and a firm's strengths or competitive position. Market attractiveness is measured by factors like market size, annual growth rate and competitive intensity rate of technological development, government policy and influence of other interest groups.

Competitive position is assessed by factor like market share, annual growth in market share, customer brand loyalty, product quality, brand image, distribution network, productivity, R&D and financial position. Figure 3.4 once again illustrates the GE matrix.

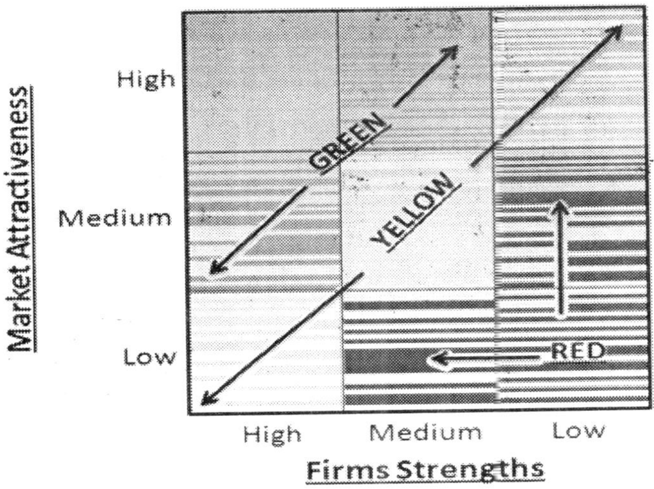

Figure 3.4 The GE MATRIX

On examining the product portfolio of a firm, one may find that some SBUs may fall in the green segment, some in the yellow and some in the red segment. SBUs in green need to be developed and supported. The strategies are those of protecting strategic positions and investing in these SBUs to gain a higher strategic leverage in the market-place. SBUs in the yellow segment require to be mentored carefully and wherever required, refocusing or selective investing and building should be done. However, SBUs in the red segment are to be harvested or divested for obvious reasons of moderate to weak competitive position in an unattractive market.

Thus, in evaluating the product mix of a firm, we need to examine each product line from the point of view of market attractiveness and its competitive position. Unfortunately, in many of the product groups, a firm may not be able to correctly estimate its market share or even the market growth rate. This is evident in Industrial sectors which have a large number of small-scale firms. Most often their sales data are not available, particularly, on a unit to unit basis. Market share is also difficult to estimate in industries with a high possibility of counterfeit or duplicate products, as in the case of the automobile components industry. In such cases the best approach is to consider market share and sales of firms in the organized sector (or the corporate sector) and estimate the total market demand for the product at a given time. The difference the demand and sales of organized sector firms can tell on a tough basis, the sales of the small or unorganized sector. This is based on the assumption that gap exists between demand and supply. However, there is still the problem of knowing who, among the small firms, is a leader or is likely to pose a threat to a firm's product. The only way to resolve this to conduct an opinion poll of dealers and retailers which can help the marketer know the ratio of sales of the firm to that of other smaller units.

Notwithstanding these and other data related limitations of the Indian marketer, these two models help a marketer plan the firm's product portfolio.

PRODUCT LIFE CYCLE (PLC)

Another approach to examining product mix is to look at the life cycle phase of each product. Each product goes through a life cycle. It shows the introduction, growth, maturity decline during its period of existence. The product life cycle reflects sales and profits on product over a period of time. Generally, most products follow an established and when their sales are plotted against time, one gets an S-shaped curve as shown figure 3.5.

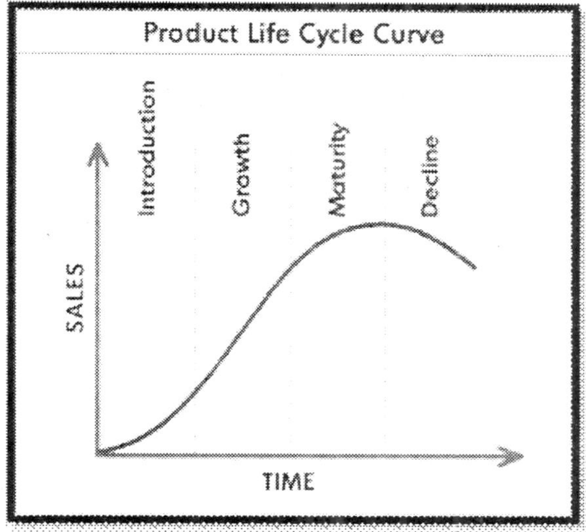

Figure 3.5 The Product Life Cycle(PLC)

However, there are exceptions when the product may not follow this path. There are products that either show a sharp growth and then a sharp decline, or remain in the maturity phase for a long time and in fact may never face a decline. While fads and fashions can be grouped in the first category, products in a closed and sheltered market or in a monopolistic mark represent the second type. One may also have commodities like steel, cement and food product where the demand remains inelastic, relative to other manufactured products.

In India, Premier Ambassador Cars, refrigerators and many other products sales did not experience a decline competition set in following liberalization and the opening up of the economy in 1980s and more specifically after 1991.

Another factor that has to be borne in mind is that profits form a product peak before its sales profits never or rarely appear in the introduction phase. The growth phase brings profits and by the time a product enters the later part of growth or early maturity, profits start declining. Figure 3.5 shows the relationship between sales, profit and time.

PRODUCT STRATEGIES

Product strategies specify market needs that may be served by different product offerings. It is a company's product strategies, duty related to market strategies that eventually come to dominate both overall strategy and the spirit of the company. Product strategies deal with such matters as number and diversity of products, product innovations, product scope and product design. In this chapter, different dimensions of product strategies are examined for their essence, their significance, there limitations, if any, their contributions to objectives and goals. Each strategy will be exemplified with illustrations from marketing literature.

The implementation of product strategies requires cooperation among different groups: finance, research and development, the corporate staff and marketing. This level of integration makes product strategies difficult to develop and implement. In many companies, to achieve proper coordination among diverse business units, product strategy decisions are made by top management. At Gould, for example, the top management decides what kind of business Gould is and what type it wants to be. The company pursues products in the areas of electro-mechanics, electrochemistry, metallurgy and electronics. The company works to dispose of products that do not fall strictly into its areas of interest.

In some companies, the overall scope of product strategy is laid out at the corporate level, whereas actual design is left to business units. These companies contend that this alternative is more desirable than other arrangements because it is difficult for top management to deal with the details of product strategy in a diverse company. In this chapter, the following product strategies are recognized:

(a) Product-positioning strategy
(b) Product-repositioning strategy
(c) Product-overlap strategy
(d) Product-scope strategy
(e) Product-design strategy
(f) Product-elimination strategy
(g) New-Product strategy
(h) Diversification strategy
(i) Value-marketing strategy

Each strategy is examined from the point of view of an SBU.

PRODUCT-POSITIONING STRATEGY

The term positioning refers to placing a brand in that part of the market when it will receive a favorable reception compared to competing products. Because the market is heterogeneous, one brand cannot make an impact on the entire market. As a matter of strategy, therefore, a product should be matched with that segment of the market in which it is most likely to succeed. The product should be positioned so that it stands apart from competing brands. Positioning tells what the product stands for, what it is and how customers should evaluate it.

Positioning is achieved by using marketing mix variables, especially design and communication. Although differentiation through positioning is more visible in consumer goods, it is equally true of industrial goods. With some products, positioning can be achieved on the basis of tangible differences (e.g., product features); with many others, intangibles are used to differentiate and position products. As Levitt has observed:

> *Fabricators of consumer and industrial goods seek competitive distinction via product features some visually or measurably identifiable, some cosmetically implied and some rhetorically claimed by reference to real or suggested hidden attributes that promise results or values different from those of competitors products. So too with consumer and industrial services what I call, to be accurate, "intangibles." On the commodities exchanges, for example, dealers in metals, grains and pork bellies trade in totally undifferentiated generic products. But what they "sell" is the claimed distinction of their execution-the efficiency of their transactions on their client's behalf, their responsiveness to inquiries, the clarity and speed of their confirmations and the like. In short, the offered product is differentiated, though the generic product is identical.*

The desired position for a product may be determined using the following procedure (Exhibit 3.1):

EXHIBIT 3.1 Steps to choose an overall position for the product

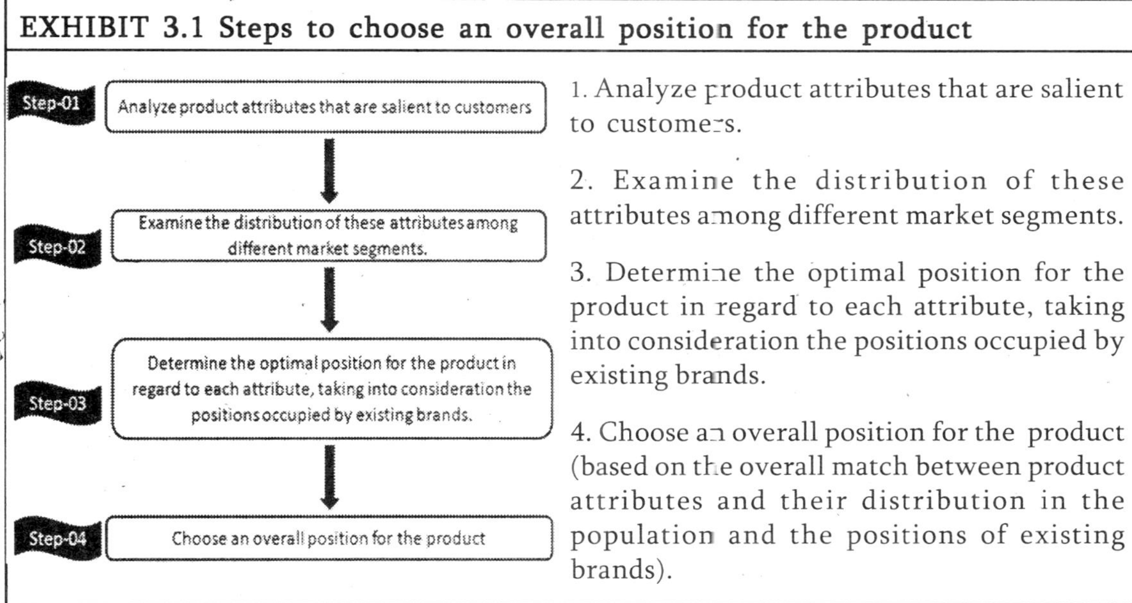

1. Analyze product attributes that are salient to customers.
2. Examine the distribution of these attributes among different market segments.
3. Determine the optimal position for the product in regard to each attribute, taking into consideration the positions occupied by existing brands.
4. Choose an overall position for the product (based on the overall match between product attributes and their distribution in the population and the positions of existing brands).

For example, cosmetics for the career woman may be positioned as "natural" cosmetics that supposedly make the user appear as if she were wearing no makeup at all. An alternate position could be "fast" cosmetics, cosmetics to give the user a mysterious aura in the evenings. A third position might be "light" cosmetics, cosmetics to be worn for tennis and other leisure activities.

Consider the positioning of beer. Two positioning decisions for beer are light versus heavy and bitter versus mild. The desired position for a new brand of beer can be determined by discovering its rating on these attributes and by considering the size of the beer market. The beer market is divided into segment according to these attributes and the position of other brands. It may be found that the heavy and mild beer market is large and that Stroh and Budweiser compete in the light and mild beer market, another big segment, Miller and Anheuse Busch are the dominant competitors. Management may decide to position a new brand in competition with Miller Lite and Bud Light.

Disney stores demonstrate how adequate positioning can lead to instant success. Disney stores earn more than three times what other specialty stores earn every square foot of floor space. Disney has created retail environments with entertainment as their chief motif. As a customer enters the store, he/she sees the Magic Kingdom, a land of bright light and merry sounds packed full of Mickey Mouse merchandise. From a phone at the front of each store, a customer can get down on their hands and knees when they laid the stores to be sure that their sight lines would work for a three-year-old. The back wall, normally a prime display area, is given over to a large video screen that continuously plays clips from Disney's animated movies and cartoons. Below the screen, at kid level, sit tiers of stuffed animals that toddlers are encouraged to play with. Adult apparel hangs at the front of the stores to announce that they are for shoppers of all ages. Floor fixtures that hold the merchandise angle inward to steer shoppers deeper into this flashy money trap. Managers spend six weeks in intensive preparatory classes and training before being assigned to a store. Garnished with theatrical lighting and elaborate ceiling displays, the stores have relatively high start-up and fixed costs, but once up and running, they earn high margins.

Six different to positioning may be distinguished:

1. Positioning by attribute (i.e., associating a product with an attribute, feature or customer benefit).
2. Positioning by price/quality (i.e., the price/ quality attribute is so pervasive that it can be considered a separate approach to promotion).
3. Positioning with respect to use or application (i.e., associating the product with a use or application).
4. Positioning by the product user (i.e., associating a product with a user or a class of users).
5. Positioning with respect to a product class (e.g., positioning Caress soap as a bath oil product rather than as soap).
6. Positioning with respect to a competitor (i.e., making a reference to competition, as in Avis's now-famous campaign: "we're number two, so we try harder.").

Two types positioning strategy are discussed here: single-brand strategy and multiple-brand strategy. A company may have just one brand that it may place in one or more chosen market segment, or alternatively, it may have several brands positioning in different segments.

How to Position a single Brand?

To maximize its benefits with a single brand, a company must try to associate itself with a core segment in a market where it can play a dominate role. In addition, it may attract customers from other segment outside its core as a fringe benefit. BMW does very well, for example, positioning its cars mainly in a limited segment to high income young professionals. An alternative single-brand strategy is to consider the market undifferentiated and to cover it with a single brand. Several years ago, for example, the Coca-Cola Company followed a strategy that proclaimed that Coke quenched the thirst of the total market. Such a policy, however, can work only in the short run. To seek entry into a market, competitions segment and challenge the dominance of the single brand by positioning themselves in small, viable niches. Even the Coca-Cola Company now has a number of brands to serve different segments: Classic Coke, Diet Coke, Fanta, Sprite, Tab, Fresca and even orange juice.

Consider the case of beer. Traditionally, brewers operated as if there were one homogeneous market for beer that could be served by one product in one package. Miller, in order to seek growth, took the initiative to segment the market and positioning its High Life brand to younger customers. Thereafter, it introduced a seven-ounce pony bottle that turned out to be a favorite among women and older people who thought that the standard 12-ounce size was simply too much beer to drink. But Miller's big success came in 1975 with the introduction of another brand, low-calorie Lite. Lite now stands to become the most successful new beer introduced in the United States in this century.

To protect the position of a single brand, sometimes a company may be forced to introduce other brands. Kotler reports that Heublein's Smirnoff brand had a 23 percent share of the vodka market when its position was challenged by Wolfschmidt, priced at $1 less a bottle. Instead of cutting the price of its Smirnoff brand to meet the competition, Heublein raised the price by one dollar and used the increased revenues for advertising. At the same time, it introduced a new brand, Relska, positioning it against Wolfschmidt and also marketed Popov, a low-price vodka. This strategy effectively met Wolfschmidt's challenge and gave Smirnoff an even higher status. Heublein resorted to multiple to protect a single brand that had been challenged by a competitor.

Anheuser-Busch has been dependent on Bud and Bud Light for more than two-thirds of its brewery volume and for over half of its sales revenues. It was this dependence on as single brand that led the company to introduce Michelob. This brand, however, is not doing as well as expected and at the same time, rivals are showing signs of fresh energy and determination, making it urgent for the company to diversify.

Whether a single brand should be positioned in direct competition with a dominant brand already on the market or be placed in a secondary position is another strategic issue. The head-on route is usually risky, but some variation of this type of strategy is quite common. Avis seemingly accepted a number two position in the market next to Hertz. Gillette, on the other hand, positioned Silkience Shampoo directly against Johnson's Baby Shampoo and Procter & Gamble's Prell. Generally, a single - brand strategy is a desirable choice in the short run, particularly when the task of managing multiple brands is beyond the managerial and financial capability of company. Supposedly, this strategy is more conductive to achieving higher profitability because a single brand permits better control of operations than do multiple brands.

There are two requisites to managing a single brand successfully: a single brand must be so positioned that it can stand competition from the toughest rival and its unique position should be maintained by creating an aura of a distinctive product. Consider the case of Cover Girl. The cosmetics field is a crowded and highly competitive industry. The segment Cover Girl picked out-sales in super markets and discount stores-is one that large companies, such as Revlon, Avon and Estee Lauder, have not tapped. Cover Girl products are sold at a freestanding display without sales help or demonstration. As far as the second requisite is concerned, creating an aura of a distinctive product, an example is Perrier. It continues to protect its position through the mystique attached to its name. In other words, a single brand must have some advantage to protect it from competitive inroads.

Positioning Multiple Brands

Business units introduce multiple brands to a market for two major reasons: (a) to seek growth by offering varied products in different segments of the market and (b) to avoid competitive threats to a single brand. General Motors has a car to sell in all conceivable segments of the market. Coca- Cola has a soft drink for each different taste. IBM sells computers for different customer needs. Procter & Gamble offers a laundry detergent for each laundering need. Offering multiple brands to different segments of the same market is an accepted route to growth.

To realize desired growth, multiple brands should be diligently positioned in the market so that they do not compete with each other and create cannibalism. For example, 20 to 25 percent of sales of Anheuser-Busch's Michelob Light are to customers who previously bought regular Michelob but switched because of the Light brand's low-calorie appeal. The introduction of Maxim by General Foods took sales away from its established Maxwell House brand. About 20 percent of sales of Miller's Genuine Draft beer come from Miller High Life. Thus, it is necessary to be careful in segmenting the market and to position the product, through design and promotion, as uniquely suited to a particular segment.

Of course, some cannibalism is unavoidable. But the question is how much cannibalism is acceptable when introducing another brand. It has been said that 70 percent of Mustang sales in its introductory year to buyers who would have purchased another Ford had the Mustang not been introduced; the remaining 30 percent of its sales came from new customers. Cadbury's experience with the introduction of a chocolate bar in England indicates that more than 50 percent of its volume came from market expansion, with remaining volume coming from the company's existing products. Both the Mustang and the chocolate bar ware rated as successful introductions by their companies. The apparent difference in cannibalism rates shows that cost structure, of market maturity and the competitive appeal of alternative offerings affect cannibalism sales and their importance to the sales and profitability of a product line to individual items.

An additional factor to consider in determining actual cannibalism is the vulnerability of an existing to a competitor's entry into a presumably open spot in the market. For example, suppose that a company's new brand derives 50 percent of its sales from customers who would have bought its existing brand. However, if 20 percent of the sales of this existing brand were susceptible to a competitor's entry (assuming a fairly high probability that the competitor would have indeed positioned its new brand in that open spot), the actual level of cannibalism should be set at 30 percent. This is because 20 percent of the revenue from sales of the existing brand would have been lost to a competitive brand had there been no new brand.

Multiple brands can be positioned in the market either head-on with the leading brand or with an idea. The relative strengths of the new entry and the established brand dictate which of the two positioning routes is more desirable. Although head-on positioning usually appears risky, some companies have successfully carried it out. IBM's personal computer was positioned in head-on competition with Apple's Datril, a Bristol-Myers painkiller was introduced to compete directly with Tylenol. Positioning with an idea, however, can prove to be a better alternative, especially when the leading brand is well established. Positioning with an idea was attempted by Kraft when it positioned three brands (Brayers and Seal test ice cream and Light 'n' Lively ice milk) as complements rather than as competitors. Vick Chemical positioned Nyquil, a cold remedy, with the idea that Nyquil assured a good night's sleep. Seagram successful introduced its line of cocktail mixes, Party Tyme, against heavy odds in favor of Holland House, a National Distillers brand, by promoting it with the Snowbird winter drink.

Positioning of multiple brands and their management in a dynamic environment call for ample managerial resources. When these resources are lacking, a company is better off with a single brand. In addition, if a company already has a dominant position, its attempt to increase its share of the market by introducing an additional brand may invite antitrust action. Such an eventuality should be guarded against. On the other hand, there is also a defensive or share maintenance, issue to be considered here even if one has the dominant entry. A product with high market share may not remain in this position forever if competitors are permitted to chip away at its lead with unchallenged positions. As a strategy, the positioning of multiple brands, if properly implemented, can lead to increases in growth, market share and profitability.

PRODUCT-REPOSITIONING STRATEGY

Often, a product may require repositioning. This can happen if (a) a competitive entry is positioned next to the brand, creating an adverse effect on its share of the market; (b) consumer preferences change; (c) new customer preference clusters with promoting opportunities are discovered; or (d) a mistake is made in the original positioning.

Citations from the marketing literature serve to illustrate how repositioning becomes desirable under different circumstances. When A & W went national in 1989 showed that consumers perceived cream soda as an extension of the root beer family. To correct this, the company repositioned the brand as a separate soda category by emphasizing the vanilla through advertising and packaging. Following the repositioning, cream soda's sales increased rapidly. Over the years, Coca-Cola's position has shifted to keep up with the changing mood of the market. In recent years, the theme of Coca-Cola's advertising has evolved from "Things go better with Coke" to "It's the real thing" to "Coke is it to "Can't beat the feeling" to "Catch the Wave" to "Always new, always real always you, always Coke". The current perspective of Coca-Cola's positioning is to reach a generation of young people and those young at heart.

The risks involved in positioning or repositioning a product or service are high. The technique of perceptual may be used gainfully to substantially reduce those risks. Perceptual mapping helps in examining the position of a product relative to competing products. It helps marketing strategists

- Understand how competing products or services are perceived by various consumer groups in terms of strengths and weakness.
- Understand the similarities and dissimilarities between competing products and services.
- Understand how to reposition a current product in the perceptual space of consumer segments.
- Position a new product or service in an established marketplace.
- Track the progress of a promotional or marketing campaign on the perceptions of targeted consumer segments.

EXHIBIT 3.2 A Perceptual Map of Brand Images

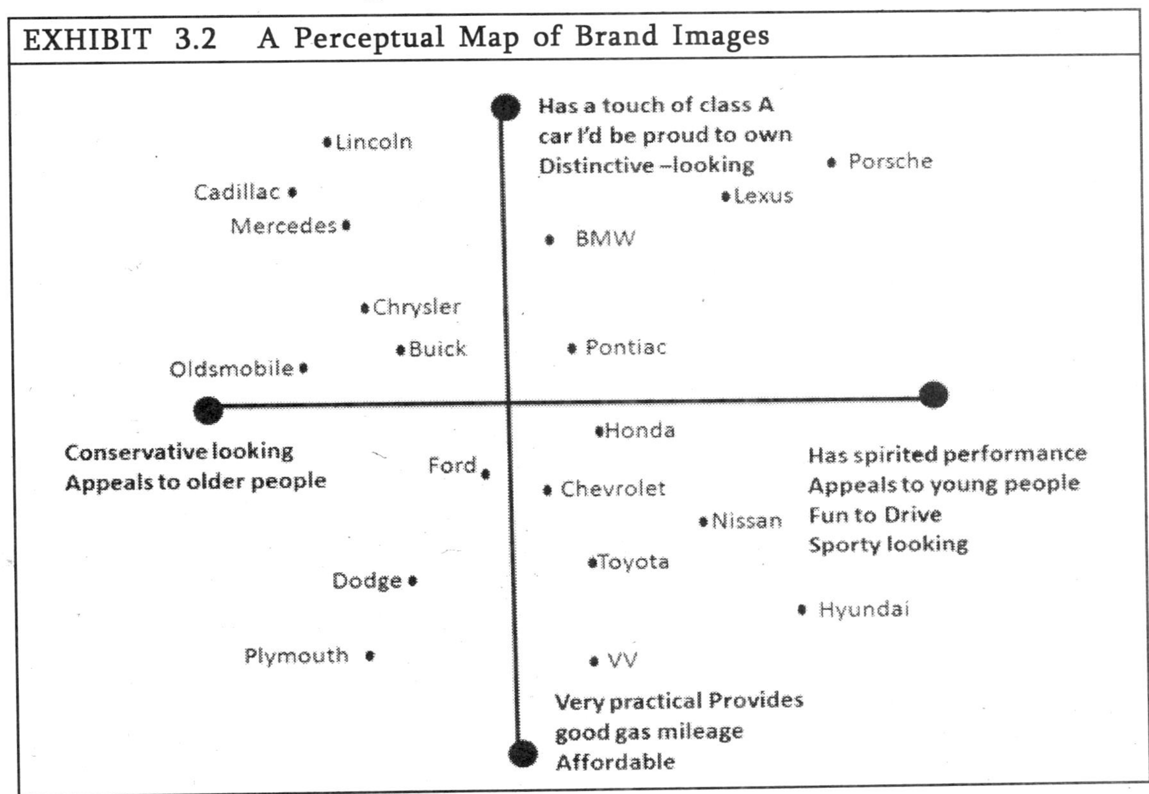

The use of perceptual mapping may be illustrated with reference to the automobile industry. Exhibit 3.2 shows how different cars are positioned on a perceptual map. The map helps the marketing strategist in calculating whether a company's cars are on target. The concentration of dots, which represent competing models, shows how much opposition there is likely to be in a specific territory on the map. Presumably, cars higher up on the graph fetch a higher price than models ranked towards the bottom where the stresses on economy and practicality. After looking at the map, General Motors might find that its Chevrolet division, traditionally geared to entry-level buyers, ought to move down in practicality and more to the right in youthfulness. Another problem for General Motors, which the map so clearly demonstrates, is the close proximity of its Buick and Olds mobile divisions. This close proximity suggests that the two divisions are waging a marketing war more against each other than against the competition.

Basically, there are three ways to reposition a product: among existing users, among new users, and for new uses. The discussion that follows will elaborate on these repositioning alternatives.

Repositioning among Existing Customers

Repositioning a product among existing customers can be accomplished by promoting alternative uses for it. To revitalize its stocking business, Du Pont adopted a repositioning strategy by promoting the "fashion smartness" of tinted hose. Efforts were directed towards expanding women's collections of hosiery by creating a new fashion image for hosiery: hosiery was not simply a neutral accessory; rather, a suitable tint and pattern could complement each garment in a woman's wardrobe. General Foods Corporation repositioned Jell-O to boost its sales by promoting it as a base for salads. To encourage this usage, the company introduced a variety of vegetable-flavored Jell-Os. A similar strategy was adopted by 3M Company, which introduced a line of colored, patterned, waterproof, invisible and write-on Scotch tapes for different types of gift wrapping.

The purpose of repositioning among current users is to revitalize a product's life by giving it a new character as something needed not merely as a staple product but as a product able to keep up with new trends and new ideas. Repositioning among users should help the brand in its sales growth as well as increasing its profitability.

Repositioning among the new users

Repositioning among new users requires that the product be presented with a different twist to people who have not hitherto been favorably inclined towards it. In so doing, care must be taken to see that, in the process of enticing new customers, current customers are not alienated. Miller's attempt to win over new customers for Miller High Life beer is noteworthy. Approximately 15 percent of the population consumes 85 percent of all the beer sold in the United States. Miller's slogan "the champagne of bottled beer "had more appeal for light users than for heavy users. Also, the image projected too much elegance for a product like beer, Miller decided to reposition the product slightly to appeal to a wider range of beer drinkers without weakening its current franchise: "Put another way, the need was to take Miller High Life out of the champagne bucket, but not to put it in the bathtub. "After conducting a variety of studies, Miller came up with a new promotional campaign built around this slogan: "If you've got the time, we've got the beer." The campaign proved to be highly successful. Through its new slogan the brand communicated three things: that it was a quality product worth taking time out for; that it was friendly, low-key and informal: and that it offered relax action and reward after the pressures of the workday.

At Du Pont, new users of stockings were created by legitimizing the wearing of history among early teenagers and sub teenagers. This was achieved by working out a new ad campaign with an emphasis on the merchandising of youthful product and style to temp young consumers. Similarly, Jell-O attempted to develop new users among consumers who did not perceive Jell-O as a dessert or salad product. Jell-O was advertised with a new concept-a fashion-oriented weight-control appeal.

The addition of new users to a product's customer base helps enlarge the overall market and thus puts the product on growth route. Repositioning among new users also helps increase profitability because very few new investments, except for promotional costs, need to be made.

Repositioning for new users

Repositioning for new uses requires searching for latent uses of the product. The case of Arm and Hammer's baking soda is a classic example of an unexplored use of a product. Today this product is popular as a deodorizer, yet deodorizing was not the use originally conceived for the product. Although new uses for a product can be discovered in a variety of ways, the best way to discover them is to gain insights into the customer's way of using a product. If it is found that a large number of customers are using the product for a purpose other than the one originally intended, this other use could be developed with whatever modifications are necessary.

Repositioning for new uses may be illustrated with reference to Disney World's efforts to expand its business. In 1991, it opened a Disney Fairy Tale Weddings Department, which puts on more than 200 full-service weddings a year, each costing about $10,000.

At Du Pont, new uses for nylon sprang up in varied types of hosiery (stretch stockings and stretch socks), tires, bearings, etc., its new uses have kept nylon on the growth path: wrap knits in 1945, tire cord in 1948, textured yarns in 1955, carpet yarns in 1959 and so on. Without these new uses, nylon would have hit the saturation level as far back as 1962. General Foods found that women used powdered gelatin dissolved in liquid to strengthen their fingernails. Working on this clue, General Foods introduced a flavorless Jell-O as a nail-building agent. The new-use strategy is directed towards revamping the sales of a product whose growth, based on its original conceived use, has slowed down. This strategy has the potential to increase sales growth, market share and profitability.

PRODUCT-OVERLAP STRATEGY

The product-overlap strategy refers to a situation where a company decides to compete against its own brand. May factors lead companies to adopt such a strategic posture? For example, A&P stores alone cannot keep the company's 42 manufacturing operations working at full capacity. Therefore, A&P decided to distribute Many of its products through independent food retailers. A&P's Eight O' Clock coffee, for example, is sold through 7-Eleven stores. Procter & Gamble has different brands of detergents virtually competing in the same market. Each brand has its own organization for marketing research, product development, merchandising and promotion. Although sharing the same sales force, each brand behaves aggressively to outdo others in the marketplace. Sears' large appliance brands are actually manufactured by the Whirlpool Corporation. Thus, Whirlpool's branded appliance competes against those that it sells to Sears.

There are alternative ways in which the product-overlap strategy may be operational zed. Principal among them are having competing lines, doing private labeling and dealing with original-equipment manufacturers.

Competing Brands

In order to a gain.a larger share of the total market, many companies introduce competing products to the market. When a market is not neatly delineated, a single brand of a product may not be able to make an adequate impact. If a second brand is placed to compete with the first one, overall sales of the two brands should increase substantially, although there will be some cannibalism. In other words, two competing brands provide a more aggressive front against competitors.

Often the competing-brands strategy works out to be short-term phenomenon. When a new version of a product is introduced, the previous version is allowed to continue until the new one has fully established itself. In this way, the competition is prevented from stealing sales during the time that the new product is coming into its own. In 1989, Gillette introduced the Sensor razor, a revolutionary new product that featured flexible blades that adjusted to follow the unique contours of the face. At the same time, its previous razor, Atra, continued to be promoted as before. It is claimed that together the two brands were very effective in the market. It is estimated that 36 percent of Sensor users converted from Atra. If Atra had not been promoted, this figure would have been much more and Sensor would have been more vulnerable to the Schick Tracer and other rigid Atra look-alikes. Interestingly, however, when Gillette introduced the Mach 3 razor in 1998, it decided to run down stocks of its Sensor and Atra shavers ahead of the new product's launch.

To expand its overall coffee market, Procter & Gamble introduced a more economical form of ground coffee under the Folgers label. A more efficient milling process that refines coffee into flakes allows hot water to come into contact with. Coca -Cola, for example, supplies to A&P stores both its own brand of orange juice, Minute Maid and the brand it produces with the A&P label. At one time, many companies equated supplying private brands with lowering their brands images. But the business swings of the 1980s changed attitudes on this issue. Frigidaire appliances at one time were not offered under a private label. However, in the 1980s Frigidaire began offering them under Montgomery Ward's name. An interesting question that can be raised about private branding is whether cars can be sold under a distributor's own label. The idea has surfaced at Auto Nation, the country's biggest car retailer, who might one day buy a car manufactured in, say, South Korea and sell it under its own label.

A retailer's interest in selling goods under its own brand name is also motivated by economic considerations. The retailer buys goods with its brand name at low cost, then offers the goods to customers at a slightly lower price than the price of a manufacturer's brand (also referred to as a national brand). The assumption is that the customer, motivated by the lower price, will buy a private brand assuming that its quality is on par with that of the national brand. This assumption is, of course, based on the premise that a reputable retailer will not offer something under its name if it is not high quality. Consider the save-A-Lot chain, a unit of Minneapolis food distribution super Value Inc. whose 85% of sales come from private-label items. With a total of 706 stores in 31 states, with sales amounting to $3 billion, it is one of the nation's fastest growing grocery chains.

Dealing with Original-Equipment Manufacturers (OEMs)

Following the strategy of dealing with an OEM, a company may sell to competitors the components used in its own product. This enables competitors to compete with the company in the market. For example, in the initial stages of color television, RCA was the only company that manufactured picture tubes. It sold these picture tubes to GE and to other competitors, enabling them to compete with RCA color television sets in the market.

The relevance of this strategy may be discussed from the viewpoint of both the seller and the OEM. The motivation for the seller comes from two sources: the desire to work at near-capacity level and the desire to have help in promoting primary demand. Working at full capacity is essential for capitalizing on the experience effect. Thus, by selling a component to competitors, a company may reduce the across-the-board costs of the component for itself, and it well have the price leverage to compete with those manufacturers to whom it sold the component. Besides, the company will always have the option of refusing to do business with a competitor who becomes a problem.

The second source of motivation is the support competitors can provide in stimulating primary Demand for a new product. Many companies may be working on a new-product idea. When one of them successfully introduces the product, the others may be unable to do so because they lack an essential component or the technology that the farmer has. Since the product is new, the innovator may find the task of developing primary demand by itself tedious. It may make a strategic decision to share the essential-component technology with other competitors, thus encouraging them to enter the market and share the burden of stimulating primary demand.

A number of companies follow the OEM strategy. Auto manufactures sell parts to each other. Texas Instruments sold electronic chips to its competitors during the initial stages of the calculator's development. In the 1950s, Polaroid bought certain essential ingredients from Kodak to manufacture film. IBM has shared a variety of technological components with other computer producers. In many situations, however, the OEM strategy may be forced upon companies by the justice Department in its efforts to promote competition in an industry. Both Kodak and Xerox shared the products of their technology with competitors at the behest of the government. Thus, as a matter of strategy, when government interference may be expected, a company will gain more by sharing its components with others and assuming industry leadership. From the standpoint of results, this strategy is useful in seeking increased profitability, though it may not have much effect on market share or growth.

As for as the OEMs are concerned, the strategy of depending upon a competitor for an essential component only works in the short run because the supplier may at some point refuse entirely to sell the component or may make it difficult for the buyer to purchase it by delaying deliveries or by increasing prices enormously.

PRODUCT-SCOPE STRATEGY

The product-scope strategy deals with the perspective of the product mix of a company (i.e., the number of product lines and items in each line that the company may offer). The product-scope strategy is determined by making reference to the business unit mission. Presumably, the mission defines what sort of business it is going to be, which helps in selecting the products and services that are to become a part of the product mix.

The product-scope strategy must be finalized after a careful review of all facets of the business because it involves long-term commitment. In addition, the strategy must be reviewed from time to time to make any changes called for because of shifts in the environment. The point may be elaborated with reference to Eastman Kodak Company's decision to enter the instant photography market in the early 1970s. Traditionally, Polaroid bought negatives for its films, worth $50 million, from Kodak. In 1969, Polaroid built its own negative plant. This meant that Kodak would lose some $50 million of Polaroid's business and be left with idle machinery that had been dedicated to filling Polaroid's needs. Further, by producing its own film, Polaroid could lower its costs; if it then cut prices, instant photography might become more competitive with Kodak's business. Alternatively, if Polaroid held prices high, it would realize high margins and would soon be very rich indeed. Encouraged by such achievements, Polaroid could even develop a marketing organization rivaling Kodak's and threaten it in every sphere. In brief Kodak was convinced that it would be shut out of the instant photography market forever if it delayed its entry any longer. Subsequently, however, a variety of reasons led Kodak to change its decision to go ahead with instant photography. Its pocket instamatic cameras turned out to be highly successful and some of the machinery and equipment allocated to instant photography had to be switched over to pocket instamatics. A capital shortage also occurred and Kodak, as a matter of financial policy, did not want to borrow to support the instant photography project. In 1976 Kodak again revised its position and did enter the field of instant photography.

In brief, commitment to the product-scope strategy requires a thorough review of a large number of factors both inside and outside the organization. The three variants of product-scope strategy that will be discussed in this section are single-product strategy, multiple-products strategy and system-of-product strategy. It will be recalled that in the previous chapter, three alternatives were discussed under market-scope strategy: single-market strategy, multimarket strategy and total-market strategy. These market strategies may be related to the three variants of product-scope strategy, providing nine different product/market-scope alternatives.

Single Product

A business unit may have just one product in its line and must try to live on the success of this one product. There are several advantages to this strategy. First, concentration on a single product leads to specialization, which helps achieve scale and productivity gains. Second, management of operations is much more efficient when a single product is the focus. Third, in today's environment, where growth leads most companies to offer multiple products, a single-product company may become so specialized in its field that it can stand any competition.

A narrow product focus, for example, cancer insurance, has given American Family Life Assurance Company of Columbus, Georgia, a fast track record. Cancer is probably more feared than any other disease in the United States today. Although it kills fewer people than heart ailments, suffering is often lingering and severe. Cashing in on this fear, American Family Life became the nation's first marketer of insurance policies that cover the expenses of treating cancer.

Despite its obvious advantages, the single-product company has two drawbacks: First, if changes in the environment make the product obsolete, the single-product company can be in deep trouble. American history is full of instances where entire industries were out. The disposable diaper, initially introduced by Procter & Gamble via its brand Pampers, pushed the cloth diaper business of the market. The Baldwin Locomotive Company's steam locomotives were made obsolete by General Motors diesel locomotives.

Second, the single-product strategy is not conductive to growth or market share. Its main advantage is profitability. If a company with a single-product focus is not able to earn high margins, it is better to seek a new posture. Companies interested in growth or market share will find the single-product strategy of limited value.

Multiple Products

The multiple-product strategy amounts to offering two or more products. A variety of factors lead companies to choose this strategic posture. A company with a single product has nowhere to go if that product gets into trouble; with multiple products, however, poor performance by one product can be balanced out. In addition, it is essential for a company seeking growth to have multiple product offering.

In 1970, when Philip Morris bought the Miller Brewing Company, it was a one-product business ranking seventh in beer sales. Growth prospects led the company to offer a number of other products. By 1978, Miller had acquired the number two position in the industry with 15 percent of the market. Miller continues to maintain its position (market share in 1998 was 18.2 percent), although Anheuser-Busch, the industry leader, has taken many steps to dislodge it. As another example, consider Chicago-based Dean Foods Company, which traditionally has been a dairy concern. Over the years, diet-conscious and aging consumers have increasingly shunned high-fat dairy products in favor of low-calorie foods, and competition for the business that remains is increasingly fierce.

To successfully operate in such an environment, the company decided to add other faster-growing, higher-margin refrigerated foods, such as party dips and cranberry drink, to the company's traditional dairy business. Dean's moves have been so successful that, although milk processors were looking to sell out, Dean was concerned that it might be bought out. Similarly, Nike began with a shoe solely for serious athletes. Over the years, the company has added a number of new products to its line. It now makes shoes, for both males and females, for running, jogging, tennis, aerobics, soccer, basketball and walking. Lately, it has expanded its offerings to include children.

Multiple products can be either related or unrelated. Unrelated products will be discussed later in the section on diversification. Related products consist of different product lines and items. A food company may have a frozen vegetable line, a yogurt line, a cheese line and a pizza line. In each line, the company may produce different items (e.g., strawberry, pineapple, apricot, peach, plain and blueberry yogurt). Note, in this example, the consistency among the different food lines:

(a) They are sold through grocery stores

(b) They must be refrigerated

(c) They are meant for the same target market

These underpinnings make them related products. Although not all products may be fast moving, they must complement each other in a portfolio of products. Suffice it to say, the multiple-products strategy is directed towards achieving growth, market share and profitability. Not all companies get rich simply by having multiple products: growth, market share and profitability are functions of a large number of variables, only one of which is having multiple products.

System of Products

The word *system* as applied to products is a post-World War II phenomenon. Two related forces were responsible for the emergence of this phenomenon:

(a) The popularity of the marketing concept that business sells satisfaction, not products.

(b) The complexities of products themselves often call for the use of complementary products and after-sale services.

A cosmetics company does not sell lipstick, it sells the hope of looking pretty; an airline should not sell plane tickets, it should sell pleasurable vacations. However, vacationers need more than an air line ticket. Vacationers also need hotel accommodations, ground transportation and sightseeing arrangements. Following the systems concept, an airline may define itself as a vacation packager that sells air transportation, hotel reservations, meals, sightseeing and so on. IBM is a single source for hardware, operating systems, packaged software, maintenance, emergency repairs and consulting services. Thus, IBM offers its customers a system of different products and services to solve data management problems.

Offering a system of products rather than a single product is a viable strategy for a number of reasons. It makes the customer fully dependent, thus allowing the company to gain monopolistic control over the market. The system-of-products strategy also blocks the way for the competition to move in. With such benefits, this strategy is extremely useful in meeting growth, profitability and market share objectives. If this strategy is stretched beyond its limits, however, a company can get into legal problems. Several years ago, IBM was charged by the justice department with monopolizing the computer market. In the aftermath of this charge, IBM has had to make changes in its strategy.

The successful implementation of the system of products strategy requires a thorough understanding of customer requirements, including the processes and functions the consumer must perform when using the product. Effective implementation of this strategy broadens both the company's concept of its product and market opportunities for it, which in turn supports product market objectives of growth, profitability and market share.

PRODUCT-DESIGN STRATEGY

A Business unit may offer a standard or a custom-designed product to each individual customer. The decision about whether to offer a standard or a customized product can be simplified by asking questions, among others: what are our capabilities? What business are we in? With respect to the first question, there is a danger of over identification of capabilities for a specific product. If capabilities are over identified, the business unit may be in trouble. When the need for the product declines, the business unit will have difficulty in relating its product's capabilities to other products.

It is, therefore, desirable for a business unit to have a clear perspective about its capabilities. The answer to the second question determines the limits within which customizing may be pursued. Between the two extremes of standard and custom products, a business unit may also offer standard products with modifications. These three strategic alternatives, which come under the product-design strategy, are discussed below.

Standard Products

Offering standard products leads to two benefits. First, standard products are more amenable to the experience effect than are customized products; consequently, they yield cost benefits. Second, standard products can be merchandised nationally much more efficiently. Ford's Model T is a classic example of a successful standard product. The standard product has one major problem; however it orients management thinking towards the realization of per-unit cost savings to such an extent that even the need for small changes in product design may be ignored.

There is considerable evidence to suggest that larger firms derive greater profits from standardization by taking advantage of economies of scale and long production runs to produce at a low price. Small companies, on the other hand, must use the major advantage they have over the giants, that is, flexibility. Hence, the standard-product strategy is generally more suitable for large companies. Small companies are better off as job shops, doing customize work at a higher margin.

A standard product is usually offered in different grades and styles with varying prices. In this manner, ever though a product is standard, customers have broader choices. Likewise, distribution channels get the product in different price ranges. The result; standard-product strategy helps achieve the product/market objectives or growth, market share and profitability.

Customized Products

Customized products are sold on the basis of the quality of the finished product, that is, on the extent to which the product meets the customer's specifications. The Producer usually works closely with the customer, reviewing the progress of the product until completion. Unlike standard products, price is not a factor for customized products. A customer expects to pay a premium for a customized product. As mentioned above, a customized product is more suitable for small companies to offer. This broad statement should not be interpreted to mean that large companies cannot successfully offer customized products. The ability to sell customized products successfully actually depends on the nature of the product. A small men's clothing is in a better position to offer custom suits than a large men's suit manufacture. On the other hand, GE is better suited to manufacture a custom-designed engine for military aircraft than a smaller business.

An innovative aspect of this product strategy is mass customization, making goods to each customer's requirements. One company that practice mass customization is customer Foot. It makes shoes that meet individual tastes and size requirements, yet does so on a mass-production basis, at slightly lower prices than many premium brands sold off the shelf. This requires a flexible manufacturing system that anticipates a wide range of options.

Many companies can find an important competitive edge in mass customization. If company X offers a one-size-fits-all product and company Y can tailor the same product to individual tastes without charging much more, the latter will be more successful. It is a powerful tool for building relationships with customers, since it requires a company to gather information, often of a very personal nature, about customer's tastes and needs.

Over and above price flexibility, dealing in customized products provides a company with useful experience in developing new standard products. A number of companies have been able to develop mass market products out of their custom work for NASA projects. The microwave oven, for example, is an offshoot of the experience gained from government contracts. Customized products also provide opportunities for inventing new products to meet other specific needs. In terms of results, this strategy is directed more towards realizing higher profitability than are other product-design strategies.

Standard Products with Modifications

The strategy of modifying standard products represents a compromise between the two strategies already discussed. With this strategy, a customer may be given the option to specify a limited number of desired modifications to a standard product. A familiar example of this strategy derives from the auto industry. The buyer of a new car can choose type of shift (standard or automatic), air conditioning, power brakes, power steering, size of engine, type of tires and color. Although some modifications may be free, for the most part the customer is expected to pay extra for modifications.

This strategy is directed towards realizing the benefits of both a standard and a customized product. By manufacturing a standard product, the business unit seeks economics of scale; at the same time, by offering modifications, the product is individualized to meet the specific requirements of the customer. The experience of a small water pump manufacturer that sold its products nationally through distributors provides some insights into this phenomenon. The company manufactured the basic pump in its facilities in Ohio and then shipped it to its four branches in different parts of the country. At each branch, the pumps were finished according to specifications requested by distributors. Following this strategy the company lowered its transportation costs (because the standard pump could be shipped in quantity) even while it provides customized pumps to its distributors.

Among other benefits, this strategy permits the business unit to keep in close contact with market needs that may be satisfied through product improvements and modifications. It also enhances the organization's reputation for flexibility in products other things equal; this strategy can be useful in achieving growth, market share and profitability.

PRODUCT-ELIMINATION STRATEGY

Marketers have believed for a long time that sick products should be eliminated. It is only in recent years that this belief has become a matter of strategy. A business unit's various products represent a portfolio, with each product playing unique role in making the business viable. If a product's role diminishes or if it does not fit into the portfolio, it ceases to be important.

When a product reaches the stage where continued support is no longer justified because performance is falling short of expectations, it is desirable to pull the product out of the marketplace. Poor performance is easy to spot. It may be characterized by any of the following:

i. Low profitability.
ii. Stagnant or declining sales volume or market share that is too costly to rebuild.
iii. Risk of technological obsolescence.
iv. Entry into a mature or declining phase of the product life cycle.
v. Poor fit with the business unit's strengths or declared mission.

Products that are able to limp along must be eliminated. They drain a business unit's financial and managerial resources that could be used more profitably elsewhere. Hise, Parasuraman and Viswanathan cite examples of a number of companies, among them Hunt Foods, Standard Brand's and crown Zellerbach, that have reported substantial positive results from eliminating products.The three alternatives in the product-elimination strategy are harvesting, line simplification and total-line divestment.

Harvesting

Harvesting refers to getting the most from a product while it lasts. It is a controlled divestment whereby the business unit seeks to get the most cash flow it can from the product. The harvesting strategy is usually applied to a product or business whose sales volume or market share is slowly declining. An effort is made to cut the costs associated with the business to improve cash flow. Alternatively, price is increased without simultaneous increase in costs. Harvesting leads to a slow decline in sales. When the business ceases to provide a positive cash flow, it is divested.

Du Pont followed the harvesting strategy in the case of its rayon business. Similarly, BASF Wyandotte applied harvesting to soda ash. As another example, GE harvested its artillery business a few years ago. Even without making any investments or raising prices, the business continued to provide GE with positive cash flow and substantial profits. Lever Brothers applied this strategy to its Lifebuoy soap. The company continued to distribute this product for a long time because, despite higher price and virtually no promotional support, it continued to be in popular demand.

Implementation of the harvesting strategy requires severely curtailing new investment, reducing maintenance of facilities, slicing advertising and research budgets, reducing the number of models produced. Curtailing the number of distribution channels, eliminating small customer and cutting service in terms of delivery time, speed of repair and sales assistance. Ideally, harvesting strategy should be pursued when the following conditions are present:

1. The business entity is in a stable or declining market.
2. The business entity has small market share, but building it up would be too costly; or it has a respectable market share that is becoming increasingly costly to defend or maintain.
3. The business entity is not producing especially good profits or may even be producing losses.
4. Sales would not decline too rapidly as a result of reduced investment.
5. The company has better uses for the freed- up resources.
6. The business entity is not a major component of the company's business portfolio.
7. The business entity does not contribute other desired features to the business portfolio, such as sales stability or prestige.

Line Simplification

Line-simplification strategy refers to a situation where a product line is trimmed to a manageable size by pruning the number and variety of products or services offered. This is a defensive strategy that is adopted to keep a falling line stable. It is hoped that the simplification effort will restore the health of the line. This strategy becomes especially relevant during times of rising costs and resource shortages.

The application of this strategy in practice may be illustrated with an example from GE's house wares business. In the early 1970s, the house wares industry faced soaring costs and stiff competition from Japan. GE took a hard look at its house wares business and raised such questions as: Is this product segment mature? Is it one we should be harvesting? Is it one we should be investing money in and expanding? Analysis showed that there was a demand for house wares, but demand was just not attractive enough for GE at that time. The company ended production of blenders, fans, heaters and vacuum cleaners because they were found to be on the downside of the growth curve and did not fit in with GE's strategy for growth.

Similarly, Sears, Roebuck & Co. overhauled its retail business in 1993, dropping its famous catalog business, which contributed over $3 billion in annual sales. Sears's huge catalog operations had been losing money for nearly a decade (about $175 million in 1992), as specialty catalogs and specialty stores grabbed market share from the country's once-supreme mail-order house. Kodak discovered that more than 80% of all its sales are achieved by less than 20% of the product line. Therefore, the company eliminated 27% of call sales items. Procter & Gamble got rid of marginal brands such as Bain de Soleil sun-care products. In addition, the company cut product items by axing extraneous size, flavors and other variants.

The implementation of a line-simplification strategy can lead to a variety of benefits: potential cost savings from longer production runs; reduced inventories; and a more forceful concentration of marketing, research and development and other efforts behind a shorter list of products. However, despite obvious merits, simplification efforts may sometimes be sabotaged. Those who have been closely involved with a product may sincerely feel either that the line as it is will revive when appropriate changes are made in the marketing mix or that sales and profits will turn up once temporary conditions in the marketplace turn around. Thus, careful maneuvering is needed on the part of management to simplify a line unhindered by corporate rivalries and intergroup pressures.

The decision to drop a product is more difficult if it is a core product that has saved as a foundation for the company. Such a product achieves the status of motherhood and a company may like to keep it for nostalgic reasons. For example, the decision by General Motors to drop the Cadillac convertible was probably a difficult one to make in light of the prestige attached to the vehicle. Despite the emotional aspects of a product-deletion, the need to be objective in this matter cannot be overemphasized. Companies establish their own criteria to screen different products for elimination.

In finalizing the decision, attention should be given to honoring prior commitments. For example, replacement parts must be provided even though an item is dropped. A well-implemented program of product simplification can lead to both growth and profitability. It may, however, be done at the cost of market share.

Total-Line Divestment

Divestment is a situation of reserve acquisition. It may also be a dimension of market strategy. But to the extent that the decision is approached from the product's perspective (i.e., to get rid of product that is not doing well even in a growing market), it is an aspect of product strategy. Traditionally, companies resisted divestment for the following reasons, which are principally either economic or psychological in nature:

1) Divestment means negative growth in sales and assets, which runs counter to the business ethic of expansion.
2) Divestment suggests defeat.

3) Divestment requires changes in personnel, which can be painful and can result in perceived or real changes in status or have an adverse effect on the entire organization.
4) Divestment may need to be effected at a price below book and thus may have an adverse effect on the year's earnings.
5) The candidate for divestment may be carrying overhead, buying from other business units of the company or contributing to earnings.

With the advent of strategic planning in the 1970s, divestment became an accepted option for seeking faster growth. More and more companies are now willing to sell a business if the company will be better off strategically. These companies feel that divestment should not be regarded solely as a means of ridding the company of an unprofitable division or plan; rather, there are some persuasive reasons supporting the divestment of even a profitable and growing business. Business that no longer fit the corporate strategic plan can be divested for a number of reasons:

- There is no longer a strategic connection between the base business and the part to be divested.
- The business experiences a permanent downturn, resulting in excess capacity for which no profitable alternative use can be identified.
- There may be inadequate capital to support the natural growth and development of the business.
- It may be dictated in the estate planning of the owner that a business is not to remain in the family.
- Selling a part of the business may release assets for use in other parts of the business where opportunities are growing.
- Divestment can improve the return on investment and growth rate both by ridding the company of units growing more slowly than the basic business and by providing cash for investment in faster-growing, higher-return operations.

Whatever the reason, a business that may have once fit well into the overall corporate plan can suddenly find itself in an environment that causes it to become a drain on the corporation, either financially, managerially or opportunistically. Such circumstances suggest divestment.

Divestment helps restore balance to a business portfolio. If the company has too many high-growth businesses, particularly those at an early stage of development, its resources may be inadequate to fund growth. On the other hand, if a company has too many low-growth businesses, it will often generate more cash than is required for investment and will build up redundant equity. For a business to grow evenly over time while showing regular increments in earnings, a portfolio of fast-and slow-growth business is necessary. Divestment can help achieve this kind of balance. Finally, divestment helps restore a business to a size that will not lead to an antitrust action.

The use of this strategy is reflected in GE's decision to divest its consumer electronics business in the early 1980s. In order to realize a return that GE considered adequate, the company would have had to make additional heavy investments in this business. GE figured that it could use the money to greater advantage in an area other than consumer electronics. Hence, it divested the business by selling it to Thomson, a French company.

Essentially following the same reasoning, Olin Corporation divested its aluminum business on the grounds that maintaining its small 4 percent share required big capital expenditures that could be employed more usefully elsewhere in the company. Westinghouse sold its major appliance line because it needed at least an additional 3 percent beyond the 5 percent share it held before it could compete effectively against industry leaders GE and Whirlpool. GE and Whirlpool divided about half the total market between them. Between 1986 and 1988, Beatrice sold two-thirds of its business, including such well-known names as Playtex, Avis, Tropicana, and Meadow Gold. The company considered these divestments necessary to transform itself into a manageable organization.

It is difficult to prescribe generalized criteria to determine whether to divest a business. However, the following questions may be raised, the answers to which should provide a starting point for considering divestment:

1. ***What is the earnings pattern of the unit?*** A key questions is whether the unit is acting as a drag on corporate growth. If so, then management must determine whether there are any offsetting values. For example, are earnings stable compared to the fluctuation in other parts of the company? If so, is the low-growth unit a substantial contributor to the overall debt capacity of the business? Management should also a whole series of "what-if" questions relating to earnings: what if we borrowed additional funds? What if we brought in new management? What if we made a change in location? Etc.
2. ***Does the business generate any cash?*** In many situations, a part of a company may be showing a profit but may not be generating any discretionary cash. That is, every dime of cash flow must be pumped right back into the operation just to keep it going at existing levels. Does this operation make any real contribution to the company? Will it eventually? What could the unit be sold for? What would be done with the cash from this scale?
3. ***Is there any tie-in value-financial or operating-with existing business?*** Are there any synergies in marketing, production or research and development? Is the business countercyclical? Does it represent a platform for growth internally bases or through acquisitions?

4. ***Will selling the unit help or hurt the acquisitions effort?*** What will be the immediate impact on earnings (write-offs, operating expenses)? What effect, if any, will the sale have on the company's image in the stock market? Will the sale have any effect on potential acquisitions? (Will I, too, be sold down the river?) will the divestment be functional in terms of the new size achieved? Will a smaller size facilitate acquisitions by broadening the "market" of acceptable candidates or, by contrast, will the company become less credible because of the smaller size?

In conclusion, a company should undertake continual in-depth analysis of the market share; growth prospects, profitability and cash-generating power of each business. As a result of such reviews, a business may need to be divested to maintain balance in the company's total business. This, however, is feasible only when the company develops enough self-discipline to avoid increasing sales volume beyond a desirable size and instead buys and sells business with the sole objective of enhancing overall corporate performance.

NEW-PRODUCT STRATEGY

New-product development is an essential activity for companies seeking growth. By adopting the new-product strategy as their posture, companies are better able to sustain competitive pressures on their existing products and make headway .The implementation of his strategy has become easier because of technological innovations and the willingness of customers to accept new ways of doing things.

Despite their importance in strategy determination, however,.implementation of new-product programs is far from easy. Too many products never make it in the marketplace. The risks and penalties of product failure require that companies move judiciously in adopting new-product strategies.

Interestingly, however, the mortality rate of new product ideas has declined considerably since the 1960s. In 1968, on average, 58 new-product ideas were considered for every successful new product. In 1981, only seven ideas were required to generate one successful new product. However, these statistics vary by industry. Consumer nondurable companies consider more than twice as many new product ideas in order to generate one successful new product, compared to industrial or consumer durable manufactures.

Top management can affect the implementation of new-product strategy; firstly, by establishing policies and broad strategic directions for the kind of new products the company should seek; secondly, by providing the kind of leadership that creates the environmental climate needed to simulate innovation in the organization; and thirdly, by instituting review and monitoring procedures so that managers are involved at the right decision points and can know whether or not work schedules are being met in ways that are consistent with broad policy directions.

The turn new product is used in different senses. For our purpose, the new-product strategy will be split into three alternatives:

(a) Product improvement/ modification

(b) Product imitation

(c) Product innovation

Product improvement/ modification is the introduction of a new version or an improved model of an existing product, such as "new, improved Crest". Improvements and modifications are usually achieved by adding new features or styles, changing processing requirements or altering product ingredients. When a company introduces a product that is already on the market but new to the company, it is following a product-imitation strategy. For example, Schick was imitating when it introduced its Tracer razor to compete with Gillette's Sensor. For our purposes, a product innovation will be defined as a strategy with a completely new approach in fulfilling customer desires (e.g., Polaroid camera, television, typewriter) or one that replaces existing ways of satisfying customer desires (e.g., the replacement of slide rules by pocket calculators). About 90% of new products are simply line extensions, such as Frito-lay's Doritos Flamin, Hot Tortilla Chips in snack-size bags. This is despite the fact that truly original products-the remaining 10% posses the real profit potential.

New product development follows the experience curve concept; that is, the more you do something, the more efficient you become at doing it .Experience in introducing products enables companies to improve new-product performance. Specifically, with increased new-product experience, companies improve new-product profitability by reducing the cost per introduction. More precisely, with each doubling of the number of new-product introductions, the cost of each introduction declines at a predictable and constant rate. For example, among the 13000 new products introduced by 700 companies surveyed by Booz, Allen and Hamilton between 1976 and 1981, the experience effect yielded a 71 percent cost curve. At each doubling of the number of new products introduced the cost of each introduction declined by 29 percent.

Product Improvement Modification

An existing product may reach a stage that requires that something be done to keep it viable. The product may have reached the maturity stage of the product life cycle because of shifts in the environment and thus has ceased to provide an adequate return. Or product, pricing, distributions and promotion strategies employed by competitors may have reduced the product to the me-too category. At this stage, management has two options: either eliminate the product or revitalize it by making improvements or modifications. Improvements or modifications are achieved by redesigning or reformulating the product so that it satisfies customer needs more fully. This strategy seeks not only to restore the health of the product but sometimes seeks to help distinguish it from competitors' products as well. For example, it has become fashionable these days to target an upscale or premium, version of product at the upper end of the price performance pyramid. Fortune's description of Kodak's strategy is relevant here:

On the one hand, the longer a particular generation of cameras can be sold, the more profitable it will become. On the other hand, amateur photographers tend to use less film as their cameras age and lose their novelty; hence, it is critical that Kodak keep the camera production eternally young by bringing on new generations form time to time. In each successive generation, Kodak tries to increase convenience and reliability in order to encourage even greater film consumption per camera- a high "burn rate" as the company calls it. In general, the idea is to introduce as few major new models as possible while ringing in frequent minor changes powerful enough to stimulate new purchases.

Kodak has become a master of this marketing strategy. Amateur film sales took off with a rush after 1963. That year the company brought out the first cartridge-loading, easy-to-use instamatic, which converted many people to photography and doubled film usage per camera. A succession of new features and variously priced models followed to help stimulate film consumption for a decade. Then Kodak introduced the pocket instamatic, which once again boosted film use both because of its novelty and because of its convenience. Seven models of that generation have since appeared.

Kodak's strategy points out that it is never enough just to introduce a new product. The real payoff comes if the product is managed in such a way that it continues to flourish year after year in a changing and competitive market place. In the 1990s, the company continued to pursue the strategy with yet another new product, the throwaway camera. Fun, cheap and easy to use are the features that have turned the disposable camera (basically a roll of film with a cheap plastic case and lens) into a substantial business. In 1992, the sales at retail reached over $200 million with Kodak holding over 65% of the market.

There is no magic formula for restoring the health of product. Occasionally, it is the ingenuity of the manager that may bring to light a desired cure. Generally, however, a complete review of the product from marketing perspectives is needed to analyze underlying causes and to come up with the modifications and improvements necessary to restore the product to health. For example, General Mills continues to realize greater profits by rejuvenating its old products-cake mixes, Cheerios and Hamburger Helper. The company successfully builds excitement for old products better than anyone else in the food business by periodically improving them. Compared with Kellogg, which tends not to fiddle with its core products, General Mills takes much greater risks with established brands. For instance, the company introduced two varieties of cheerios-Honey, Nut in 1979 and Apple Cinnamon in 1988-and successfully created a megabrand.

To identify options for restoring a damaged product to health, it may be necessary to tear down competing products and make detailed comparative analysis of quality and price. One framework for such an analysis is illustrated in Exhibit 3.3

EXHIBIT 3.3

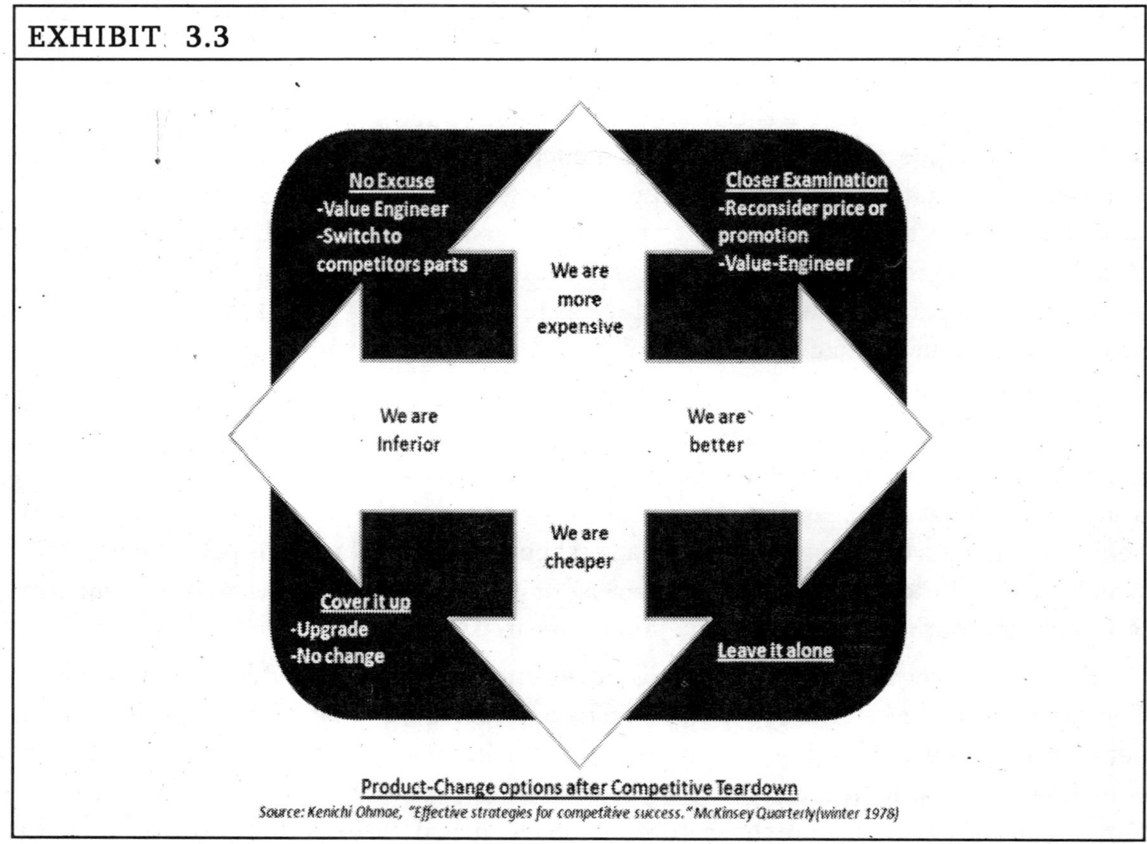

Product-Change options after Competitive Teardown

Source: Kenichi Ohmae, "Effective strategies for competitive success." McKinsey Quarterly(winter 1978)

The basic premise of Exhibit 3.3 is that by comparing its product with that of its competitors, a company is able to identify unique product strengths on which to pursue modifications and improvements. The use of the analysis suggested by Exhibit 3.3 may be illustrated with reference to a Japanese manufacturer. In 1978, Japan's amateur color film market was dominated by Kodak, Fuji and Sakura, the last two being Japanese companies. For the previous 15 years, Fuji had been gaining market share, whereas Sakura, the market leader in the early 1950s with over half the market, was losing ground to both its competitors. By 1976, Sakura had only about a 16 percent market share. Marketing research showed that, more than anything else, Sakura was the victim of an unfortunate word association. Its name in Japanese means "cherry blossom", suggesting a soft, blurry, pinkish image. The name Fuji, however, was associated with the blue skies and white snow of Japan's sacred mountain. Being in no position to change perceptions, the company decided to analyze the market from structural, economic and customer points of view. Sakura found a growing

Cost consciousness among film customers: to wit, amateur photographers commonly left one or two frames unexposed in a 36-exposure roll, but they almost invariably tried to squeeze extra exposures onto 20-exposure rolls. Here Sakura saw an opportunity. It decided to introduce a 24-exposure film. Its marginal costs would be trivial, but its big competitors would face significant penalties in following suit. Sakura was prepared to cut its price if the competition lowered the price of their 20-frame rolls. Its aim was twofold. First, it would exploit the growing number of cost minded users. Second and more important, it would be drawing attention to the issue of economics, where it had a relative advantage and away from the image issue, where it could not win. Sakura's strategy paid off. Its market share increased from 16 percent to more than 30 percent. Pepsi Co. has developed a new product, Pepsi One, to fulfill the unmet needs of young men. The company launched the product with about $100 million promotion and hoped to generate $1 billion in annual retail sales. Overall, the product-improvement strategy is conducive to achieving growth, market share and profitability alike.

Product Imitation

Not all companies like to be first in the market with a new product. Some let others take the initiative. If the innovation is successful, they ride the bandwagon of the successful innovation by imitating it. In the case of innovations protected by patents, imitators must wait until patents expire. In the absence of a patent, however, the imitators work diligently to design and produce products not very different from the innovator's product to compete vigorously with the innovator. The imitation strategy can be justified in that it transfers the risk of introducing an unproven idea/product to someone else. It also saves investment in research and development. This strategy particularly suits companies with limited resources. Many companies, as a matter of fact, develop such talent that they can imitate any product, no matter how complicated. With a limited investment in research and development, the imitator may sometimes have a lower cost, giving it a price advantage in the market over the leader.

Another important reason for pursing an imitation strategy may be to gainfully transfer the special talent a company may have for one product to other similar products. For example, the Bick Pen corporation decided to enter the razor business because it thought it could successfully use its aggressive marketing posture in that market. In the early 1970s, Corporation gained resounding success with L'eggs, an inexpensive pantyhose that it sold from freestanding racks in food and drugstore outlets.

The imitation strategy may also be adopted on defensive grounds. Being sure of its existing products(s), a company may initially ignore new developments in the field. If new developments become overhearing, however, they may cut into the share held by an existing product. In this situation, a company may be forced to imitate the new development as a matter of survival. Colorado's Adolph Coors company conveniently ignored the introduction of light beer and dismissed Miller Lite as a fad. Many years later, however, the company was getting bludgeoned by Miller Lite. Also, Anheuser-Busch began to challenge the supremacy of cross in the California market with its light beer. The matter became so serious that Coors decided to abandon its one-product tradition and introduced a low-calorie light beer.

Another example of product imitation is the introduction of specialty beers by major brewers. While the U.S. beer industry has been stagnating throughout the 1990s, the specialty brews have been growing at better than a 40 percent annual rate. This has led the four major beer companies that control 80 percent of the market to offer their own brands of specialty beers: Anheuser (Red hook Ale, Red Wolf, Elk Mountain, Crossroads); Miller (Red Dog, Icehouse, Celis); Coors (Sandlot, George, Kill man); and Stroh (Steeman, Red River Valley).

Imitation also works well for companies that want to enter new markets without resorting to expensive acquisitions or special new-product development programs. For example, Owens-Illinois adapted heavy-duty laboratory glassware into novelty drinking glasses for home use.

Although imitation does avoid the risks involved in innovation, it is wrong to assume that every imitation of a successful product will succeed. The marketing program of a limitation should be as carefully chalked out and implemented as that of an innovation. Limitation strategy is most useful for achieving increases in market share and growth.

Product Innovation

Product innovation strategy includes introducing a new product to replace an existing product in order to satisfy a need in an entirely different way or to provide a new approach to satisfy an existing of latent need. This strategy suggests that the entrant is the first firm to develop and introduce the product. The ballpoint pen is an example of a new product; it replaced the fountain pen. The VCR was a new product introduced to answer home entertainment needs.

Product innovation is an important characteristic of U.S. industry. Year after year companies spend billions of dollars on research and development to innovate. In 1997, for example, American industry spent almost $100 billion on research and development. Research and development expenditures are expected to continue rising at an average of 10 percent annually as we enter the next century. This shows that industry takes a purposeful attitude towards new-product and new-process development.

Product innovation, however, does not come easy. Besides involving major financial commitments, it requires heavy doses of managerial time to cut across organizational lines.

And still the innovation may fail to make a mark in the market. A number of companies have discovered the risks of this game. Among them is Taxes Instruments, which lost $660 million before withdrawing from the home computer market. RCA lost $500 million on ill-fated videodisc players. RCA, GE and Sylvania, leaders in vacuum-tube technology, lost out when transistor technology revolutionized the radio business. RJR Nabisco abandoned the "smoke less" cigarette, Premier, after a 10-year struggle and after spending over $500 million.

Most innovative products are produced by large organizations. Initially, an individual or a group of individuals may be behind it, but a stage is eventually reached where individual efforts require corporate support to finally develop and launch the product. To encourage innovation and creativity, many large companies are spinning off companies. For example, Colgate-Palmolive Co. launched Colgate Venture Co. to support entrepreneurship and risk taking. In this way, a congenial environment within the large corporation is maintained for generating and following creative pursuits.

In essence, innovation flourishes where divisions are kept small (permitting better interaction among managers and staffers), where there is willingness to tolerate failure (encouraging plenty of experimentation and risk taking), where champions are motivated (through encouragement, salaries and promotions), where close liaison is maintained with the customer (visiting customers routinely; inviting them to brainstorm product ideas), where technology is shared corporate wide (technology, wherever it is developed, belongs to everyone), and where projects are sustained, even if initial results are discouraging.

The development of a product innovation typically passes through various stages: idea generation, screening, business analysis, development of a prototype, test market, and commercialization. The idea may emerge from different sources: customers, private researchers, university researchers, employees, or research labs. An idea may be generated by recognizing a consumer need or just by pursing a scientific endeavor, hoping that it may lead to a viable product. Companies follow different procedures to screen ideas and to choose a few for further study. If an idea appears, it may be carried to the stage of business analysis, which may consist of investment requirements, revenue and expenditure projections, and financial analysis of return on investment, pay-back period, and cash flow. Thereafter, a few prototype products may be produced to examine engineering and manufacturing aspects of the product. A few sample products based on the prototype may be produced for market testing. After changes suggested in market testing have been incorporated, the innovation may be commercially launched.

Procter & Gamble's development of Pringles is a classic case of recognizing a need in a consumer market and then painstakingly hammering away to meet it. Americans consume about one billion dollars' worth of potato chips annually, but manufactures of potato chips face a variety of problems. Chips made in the traditional way are so fragile that they can rarely be shipped for more than 200 miles; even then a quarter of the chips get broken. They also spoil quickly; their shelf life is barely two months. These characteristics have kept potato chip manufacturers split into many small regional operations. Nobody, before Procter & Gamble, had applied much technology to the product since it was invented in 1853.

Procter & Gamble knew these problems because it sold edible oils to the potato chip industry and it set out to solve them. Instead of slicing potato and flying them in the traditional way, Procter & Gamble's engineers developed a process somewhat akin to paper making. They dehydrated and mashed potatoes and pressed them for flying into a precise shape, which permitted the chips to be stacked neatly on top of one another in hermetically sealed containers that resemble tennis ball cans. Pringles potato chips stay whole and have a shelf life of at least a year.

After a new product is screened through the lab, the division that will manufacture it takes over and finances all further development and testing. In some companies, division managers show little interest in taking on new products because the costs of introduction are heavy and hold down short-term profits. At Procter & Gamble, executives ensure that a manager's short-term record is not marred by the cost of a new introduction.

Before a new Procter & Gamble product is actually introduced to the market, it must prove that it has a demonstrable margin of superiority over its prospective competitors. A development team begins refining the product by trying variations of the basic formula, testing its performance under almost any conceivable condition and altering its appearance. Eventually, a few alternative versions of the product are produced and tested among a large number of Procter & Gamble employees. If the product gets the approval of employees, the company presents it to panels of consumers for further testing. Procter & Gamble feels satisfied if a proposed product is chosen by fifty-five out of one hundred consumers tested. Though Pringles potato chips passed all these tests, they only recently started showing any profits for Procter & Gamble.

There is hardly any doubt that, if an innovation is successful, it pays off lavishly. For example, nylon still makes so much money for Du Pont that company would qualify for the Fortune 500 list even if it made nothing else. However, developing a new product is a high-risk strategy requiring heavy commitment and having a low probability of achieving a breakthrough. Thus, the choice of this strategy should be dictated by a company's financial and managerial strengths and by its willingness to take risks. Consider the case of Kevlar, a super-tough fiber (lightweight but five times stronger than steel) invented by Du Pont. It took the company 25 years and $900 million to come out with this product, more time and money than the company had ever spent on a single product. Starting in 1985, however, the payoff began: annual sales reached $300 million. Du Pont forecasts Kevlar's annual sales growth at 10 percent during the 1990s. Meanwhile, company continues its quest for new applications that it hopes will make Kevlar a blockbuster.

Exhibit 3.4 suggests an approach that may be used to manage innovations successfully. As a company grows more complex and decentralized, its new-product development efforts may fail to keep pace with change, weakening vital lines between marketing and technical people and leaving key decisions to be made by default. The possible result is the ultimate loss to competitive edge. To solve the problem, as shown in Exhibit 3.4(a), both technical and market opportunity may be plotted on a grid. From this grid, innovations may be grouped into three classes: heavy emphasis (deserving full support, including basic research and development); selective opportunistic development (i.e., may be good or may be bad; may require a careful approach and top management attention); and limited defence support (i.e., merits only minimum support). Exhibit 3.4(b) lists the relevant kinds of programs for each area. This approach helps gear research efforts to priority strategic projects.

EXHIBIT 3.4 Managing Innovations

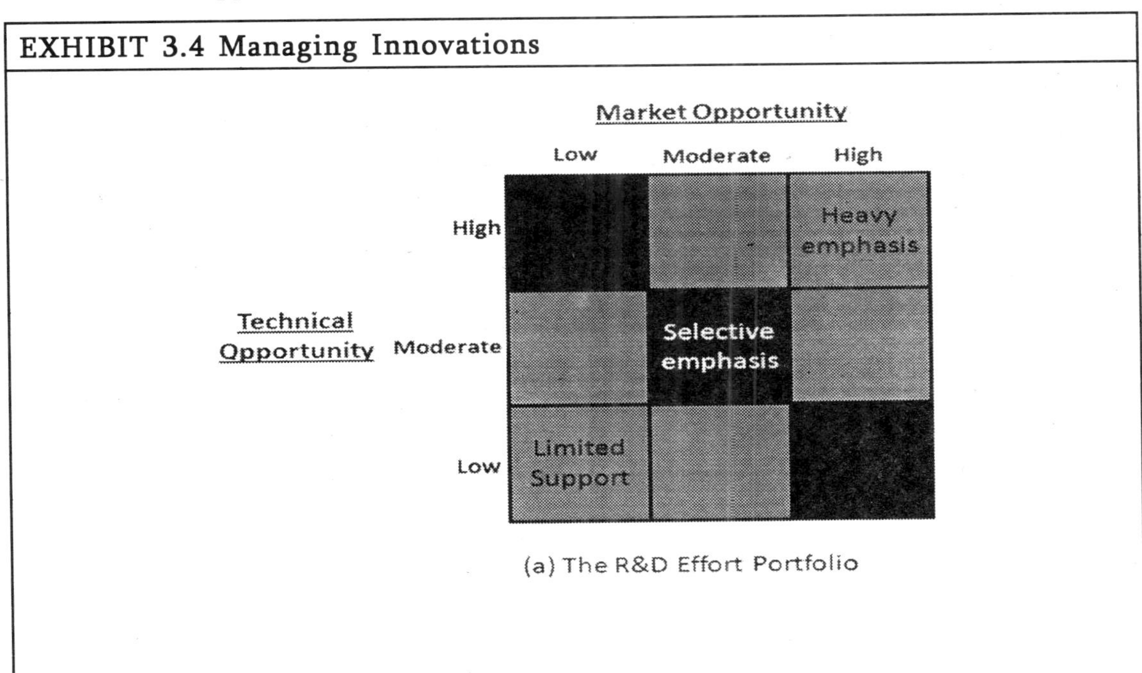

(a) The R&D Effort Portfolio

R&D Program Elements						
R&D Emphasis	Primary Level of Funding	Focus of work	Level of Basic Research	Technical Risk	Acceptable Time for payoff	Projects to exceed or Maintain Competitive Parity
Heavy	High	Balance between new and existing produces	High	High	Long	Many
Selective	Medium	Mainly existing products	Low	Medium	Medium	Few
Limited	Low	Existing processes	Very Low	Low	Short	Very Few

(b) Implied Nature of R& D Effort

Source: Richard N. Foster, "Linking R&D to strategy," Business Horizons, December 1980 © 1980 by the Foundation for the School of Business at Indiana University.

DIVERSIFICATION STRATEGY

Diversification refers to seeking unfamiliar products or markets or both in the pursuit of growth. Every company is best at certain products; diversification requires substantially different knowledge, thinking, skills and processes. Thus, diversification is at best a risky strategy and a company should choose this path only when current product/market orientation does not seem to provide further opportunities for growth. A few examples will illustrate the point that diversification does not automatically bring success. CAN financial Corporation faced catastrophe when it expanded the scope of its business from insurance to real estate and mutual funds: it ended up being acquired by Loews Corporation. Schrafft's restaurant did little for Pet Incorporated. Pacific Southwest Airlines acquired rental cars and hotels, only to see its stock decline quickly. Diversification into the wine business (by acquiring Taylor Wines) did not work for the Coca-Cola Company.

The diversification decision is a major step that must be taken carefully. On the basis of a sample from 200 firms and the PIMS database, Biggadike notes that it takes an average of 10 to 12 years before the return on investment from diversification equals that of mature business.

The term diversification must be distinguished from integration and merger. Integration refers to the accumulation of additional business in a field through participation in more of the stages between raw materials and the ultimate market or through more intensive coverage of a single stage. Merger implies a combination of corporate entities that may or may not result in integration. Diversification is a strategic alternative that implies deriving revenues and profits from different products and markets. The following factors usually lead companies to seek diversification:

1. Firms diversify when their objects can no longer be met within the product/market scope defined by expansion.
2. A firm may diversify because retained cash exceeds total expansion needs.
3. A firm may diversify when diversification opportunities promise greater profitability than expansion opportunities.
4. Films may continue to explore diversification when the available information is not reliable enough to permit a conclusive comparison between expansion and diversification.

Diversification can take place at either the corporate or the business unit level. At the corporate level, it typically entails entering a promising business outside the scope of existing business units. At the business unit level, it is more likely to invoice expanding into a new segment of the industry in which the business presently participates. The problems encountered at both levels are similar and may differ only in magnitude. Diversification strategies include internal development of new products of markets (including development of international markets for current products), acquisition of an appropriate firm of firms, a strategic alliance with a complementary organization, licensing of new product technologies and importing or distributing a line of products manufactured by another company. The final choice of an entry strategy involves a combination of these alternatives in most cases. This combination is determined on the basis of available opportunities and of consistency with the company's objectives and available resources.

Caterpillar Tractor Company's entry into the field of diesel engines is a case of internal diversification. Since 1972, the company has poured more than $1 billion into developing new diesel engines "in what must rank as one of the largest internal diversifications by a U.S. corporation." Hershey Foods ventured into the restaurant business by using the Friendly Ice Cream Corporation, illustrating diversification by acquisition. Hershey adopted the diversification strategy for growth because its traditional business, chocolate and candy, was stagnant because of a decline in candy consumption, sharp increases in cocoa prices, and changes in customer habits. Hershey subsequently sold Friendly in 1988 to a private company, Tennessee Restaurant Co.

An empirical study of entry strategy shows that higher barriers are more likely to be associated with question than with entry through internal development. Thus, in choosing between these two entry modes, business unit managers should take into account, among other factors, the entry barriers surrounding the market and the cost of breaching them. Despite high apparent barriers, the entrant's relatedness to the new entry may make entry financially more desirable.

Essentially, there are three different forms of diversification a company may propose: concentric diversification, horizontal diversification and conglomerate diversification. No matter what of diversification a company seeks, the three essential tests of success are

1. **The attractiveness test**- The industries chosen for diversification must be structurally attractive or capable of being made attractive.
2. **The cost-of-entry test** - The cost of entry must not capitalize all future profits.
3. **The better-off test**- The new unit must either gain competitive advantage from its link with the corporation or vice versa.

Concentric Diversification

Concentric diversification bears a close synergistic relationship to either the company's marketing or its technology or both. Thus, new products that are introduced share a common thread with the firm's existing products, either through marketing or production. Usually, the new products are directed to a new group of customers. Texas Instruments venture into pocket calculators illustrates this type of diversification. Using its expertise in integrated circus, the company developed a new product that appealed to a new set of customers. On the other hand, PepsiCo's venture into the fast-food business through the acquisition of Pizza Hut is a case of concentric diversification in which the new product bears a synergistic relationship to the company's existing marketing experience.

Toys "R" Us branched into children's clothing on the ground that is marketing as well as technological skills (purchasing power, brand name, storage facilities, retail outlets and sophisticated information system) would give it an edge in the new business. Similar logic persuaded Honda to diversify from motorcycles to lawn mowers and cars; and Black & Decker from power tools to home appliances.

Although a diversification move per se is risky, concentric diversification does not lead a company into an entirely new world because in one of two major fields (technology or marketing), the company will operate in familiar territory. The relationship of the new product to the firm's existing product(s), however, may or may not mean much. All that the realization of synergy does is make the task easier; it does not necessarily make it successful. For example, Gillette entered the market for pocket calculators in 1974 and for digital watches in 1976. Later it abandoned both businesses. Both pocket calculators and digital watches were sold to mass markets where Gillette had expertise and experience. Despite this marketing synergy, it failed to sell either calculators or digital watches successfully.

Gillette found that these lines of business called for strategies totally different from those it followed in selling its existing products. Two lessons can be drawn from Gillette's experience. One, there may be other strategic reasons for successfully launching a new product in the market besides commonality of markets or technology. Two, the commonality should be analyzed in breadth and depth before drawing conclusions about the transferability or current strengths to the new product. Philip Morris's acquisition of Miller Brewing Company illustrates how a company may achieve marketing synergies through concentric diversification. Cigarettes and beer are distributed through many of the same retail outlets, and Philip Morris had been dealing with them for years. In addition, both products serve hedonistic consumer markets. Small wonder, therefore, that the marketing research techniques and emotional promotion appeals of cigarette merchandising worked equally well for beer. Miller moved from seventh to second place in the beer industry in the short span of six years.

Horizontal Diversification

Horizontal diversification refers to new products that technologically are unrelated to a company's existing products but that can be sold to the same group of customers to whom existing products are sold. A classic case of this form of diversification is Procter & Gamble's entry into potato chips (Pringles), toothpaste (Crest and Gleem), coffee (Folgers), and orange juice (Citrus Hill). Traditionally a soap company, Procter & Gamble diversified into these products, which were aimed at the same customers who bought soap. Similarly, Maytag's entry into the medium-priced mass market to sell refrigerators and ranges, in addition to selling its traditional line of premium-priced dishwashers, washers and dryers, is a form of horizontal diversification. Mattel's introduction of clothing items (skirts, shoes, jeans, shirts and pajamas) for little girls, sizes 4 to 6x, under the Barbie brand name is another example of horizontal diversification. Using the Barbie phenomenon, the company has successfully launched the new business. As a company executive puts it, "Barbie is a designer brand for the little customers, their Calvin Klein." Note that in the case of concentric diversification, the new production may have certain common ties with the marketing of a company's existing product except that it is sold to a new set of customers.

In horizontal diversification, by contrast, the customers for the new product are drawn from the same ranks as those for an existing product. Other things being equal, in a competitive environment horizontal diversification is more desirable if present customers are favorably disposed towards the company and if one can expect this loyalty to carry over to the new product; in the long run, however, a new product must stand on its own.

For example, it product quality is lacking, if promotion is not effective, or if the price is not right, a new product will flop despite customer loyalty to the company's other products. Thus, while Crest and Folgers made it for Procter & Gamble, Citrus Hill has been struggling and Pringles has been disappointing, even though all these products are sold to the same "loyal" customers. In other words, horizontal diversification should not be regarded as a route to success in all cases.

An important limitation of horizontal diversification is that the new product is introduced and marketed in the same economic environment as the existing products, which can lead to rigidity and instability. Stated differently, horizontal diversification tends to increase the company's dependence on a few market segments.

Conglomerate Diversification

In conglomerate diversification, the new product bears no relationship to either the marketing or the technology of the existing product(s). In other words, through Conglomerate diversification, a company launches itself into an entirely new product/market arena. ITT's ventures into bakery products (Continental Baking Company), insurance (Hartford Insurance Group), car rentals (Avis Rent-A-Car system, Inc.), and the hotel business (Sheraton Corporation) illustrate the implementation of conglomerate diversification. (ITT divested its car rental business a few years ago.)Dover Corp. provides another example of conglomerate diversification. The company, with annual sales of over $3 billion, is a manufacturer with 54 operating companies engaged in more than 70 diverse businesses, from elevators and garbage trucks to values and welding torches. It is necessary to remember here that companies do not flirt with unknown products in unknown markets without having some hidden strengths to handle conglomerate diversification. For example, the managerial style required for a new product to prosper may be just the same as the style the company already has.

Thus, managerial style becomes the basis of synergy between the new product and an existing product. By the same token, another single element may serve as a dominant factor in marketing a business attractive for diversification. In as much as conglomerate diversification does not beer an obvious relationship to a company's existing business, there is some questions as to why companies adopt it. There are two major advantages of conglomerate diversification. One, it can improve the profitability and flexibility of a firm by venturing into business that have better economic prospects than those of the firm's existing business. Two, a conglomerate firm, because of its size, gets a better reception in capital markets. Overall, this type of diversification, if successful, has the potential of providing increased growth and profitability.

VALUE-MARKETING STRATEGY

In the 1990s, value has become the marketer's watchword. Today, customers are demanding something different than they did in the past. They want the right combination of product quality, good service and timely delivery. These are the keys to performing well in the next century. It is for this reason that we examine this new strategic focus.

Value marketing strategy stresses real product performance and delivering on promises. Value marketing doesn't mean high quality if it is only available at ever-higher prices. It doesn't necessarily mean cheap, if cheap means bare bones or low grade. It doesn't mean high prestige, if the prestige is viewed as snobbish or self-indulgent. At the same time, value is not about positioning and image mongering. It simply means providing a product that works as claimed, is accompanied by decent service and is delivered on time.

The emphasis on value is part atmospherics, part economics and part demographics. Consumers are repudiating the wretched excess of the 1980s and are searching for more traditional rewards of home and family. They are concerned about the seemingly non-ending economic ups and down. The growing focus on value also stems from profound changes in the American consumer marketplace.

For example, real income growth for families got a boost when women entered the work force. But now, with many women already working and many baby boomers assuming new family responsibilities, the growth in disposable income is scarily. Aging baby boomers whose debt burden is already high realize that they must worry about their children's college tuitions and their own retirement. At the same time, the new generation of consumers is both savvier and more cynical than were its predecessors. Briefly, consumers want products that perform, sold by advertising that informs. They are concerned about intrinsic value, not simply buying to impress others.

Quality Strategy

Traditionally, quality has been viewed as a manufacturing concern. Strategically, however, the idea of total quality is perceived in the market; that is quality must exude from the offering itself and from all the services that come with it. The important point is that quality perspective should be based on customer preferences, not on internal evaluations. The ultimate objective of quality should be to delight the customer in every way possible, providing levels of service, product quality, product performance and support that are beyond his/her expectations, ultimately, quality may mean striving for excellence throughout the entire organization. For assessing perceived quality, the step-by-step procedure used by the Strategic planning Institute may be followed:

1. A meeting is held, in which a multifunctional team of managers and staff specialists identify the non price product and service attributes that affect customer buying

decisions. For an office equipment product, these might include durability, maintenance costs, flexibility, credit terms and appearance.

2. The team is then asked to assign "importance weights" for each attribute representing their relative decisions. These relative importance weights sum to 100. (For markets in which there are important segments with different importance weights, separate weights are assigned to each segment.)
3. The management team creates its business unit's product line and those of leading competitors, on each of the performance dimensions identified in step 1. From these attribute-by-attribute ratings, each weighted by its respective importance weight, an overall relative quality score is constructed.
4. The overall relative quality score and other measures of competitive position (relative price and market share) and financial performance (ROI, ROS, and ROE) are validated against benchmarks based on the experience of "look-alike" business in similar strategic positions in order to check the internal consistency of strategic and financial data and confirm the business and market definition.
5. Finally, the management team tests its plans and budgets for reality, develops a blueprint for improving market perceived quality, relative to competitors and calibrates the financial payoff. In many cases, the judgmental ratings assigned by the management team are tested (and, when appropriate, modified) by collecting from customers via field interviews.

This approach to assessing relative quality is similar to the multi-attribute methods used in marketing research. These research methods are, however, employed primarily for evaluating or comparing individual products (actual or prospective), whereas the scores here apply to a business unit's entire product line.

Attaining adequate levels of excellence and customer satisfaction often requires significant cultural change; that is, change in decision-making processes, inter-functional relationships and the attitudes of each member of the company. In other words, achieving total quality objectives requires teamwork and cooperation. People are encouraged and rewarded for doing their jobs right the first time rather than for their success in resolving crises. People are empowered to make decisions and instilled with the feeling that quality is everyone's responsibility. The following are the keys to success in achieving world-class total quality. First the program requires unequivocal support of top management. The second key to success is understanding customer need. The third key is to fix the business process, if there are gaps in meeting customer needs. The fourth key is to compress cycle time to avoid bureaucratic hassles and delays. The next is empowering people so that they are able to exert their best talents. Further, measurement and reward systems must be reassessed and revamped to recognize people. Finally, the total quality program should be a continuous concern, a constant focus on identifying and eliminating waste and inefficiency throughout the organization.

Organizationally, the single most important aspect of implementing a quality strategy is to maintain a close liaison with the customer. Honda's experience in this matter in designing the new Accord is noteworthy:

When Honda's engineers to design the third-generation (or 1986) Accord in the early 1980s, they did not state with a sketch of a car. The engineers started with a concept-"man maximum, machine minimum" that captured in a short, evocative phrase the way they wanted customers to feel about the car. The concept and the car have been remarkably successful: since 1982, the Accord has been one of the best-selling cars in the United States; in 1989, it was the top-selling car. Yet when it was time to design the 1990 Accord, Honda listened to the market, not to its own success. Market trends were indicating a shift away from sporty sedans towards family models. To satisfy future customer's expectations and to reposition the Accord, moving it up-market just a bit, the 1990 model would have to send a new set of product messages-"an adult sense of reliability". The ideal family car would allow the driver to transport family and friends with confidence, whatever the weather or road conditions; passengers would always feel safe and secure.

This message was still too abstract to guide the engineers who would later be making concrete choices about the new Accord's specifications, parts and manufacturing processes. So the next step was finding an image that would personify the car's message to consumers. The image that managers emerged with was "a rugby player in a business suit." It evoked rugged physical contact, sportsmanship and gentlemanly behavior-disparate qualities the new car would have to convey. The image was also concrete enough to translate clearly into design details. The decision to replace the old Accord's retractable head lamps with headlights made with a pioneering technology developed by Honda's supplier, Stanley, is a good example.

To the designers and engineers, the new lights totally transport cover glass symbolized the will of a rugby player looking into the future calmly, with clear eyes. The next and last step in creating the Accord's product concept was to break down the rugby player image into specific attributes the new car would have to possess. Five sets of key words captured what the product leader envisioned: "open minded", "friendly communication", "tough sprit", "stress-free" and "love forever." Individually and as a whole, these key words reinforced the car's message to consumers. "Tough sprit" in the car, for example, meant maneuverability, power and sure handling in extreme driving conditions, while "love forever" translated into long-term reliability and customer satisfaction. Throughout the course of the project, these phrases provided a kind of shorthand to help people make coherent design and hardware choices in the face of competing demands.

There are three generic approaches to improving quality approaches to improving quality performance: catching up pulling ahead and leapfrogging. Catching up involves restoring those aspects about which the firm has been behind to standard. Catching up is a defensive strategy where the emphasis is either to be as good as the competition or to barely meeting market requirements. Pulling ahead, going further than the customer asks or achieving superiority over the competition, provides a firm competitive advantage that may lead to greater profitability, thus, it makes sense to resist the temptation to focus on just catching up and to find a way to make a sustainable move to pull ahead. Finally, leapfrogging involves negating competitive disadvantage that is, creating a sustainable competitive advantage through different vantage that is, creating a sustainable competitive advantage through differentiation. In other words, leapfrogging comprises coming from behind and getting ahead of the competition through providing a quality product in keeping with customer demands. For example, by leapfrogging Detroit on several key attributes, Japanese companies rolled further up the "quality-for-price curve"; that is, they shifted into better value positions.

Several benefits accrue to business that offer superior perceived quality, including stronger customer loyalty, more repeat purchase, less vulnerability to price wars, ability to command higher relative price without affecting share, lower marketing costs and share improvements.

Customer-Service Strategy

Customer service has come to occupy an important place in today's competitive market. Invariably, customers want personal service, the kind of service delivered by live bodies behind a sales counter, a human voice at the other end of a telephone or people in the teller's cage at the bank. Paying attention to the customer is not a new concept. In the 1950s, General Motors went all the way towards consumer satisfaction by designing cars for every lifestyle and pocketbook, a breakthrough for an industry that had been largely driven by production needs ever since Henry Ford promised to deliver any color car as long as it was black. General Motors rode its insights into customers needs to a 52 percent share of the U.S. car market in 1962. But with a booming economy, a rising population and virtually no foreign competition, many U.S. companies had it too easy. Through the 1960s and into the 1970s, many U.S. car markets could sell just about anything they could produce. With customers seemingly satisfied, management concentrated on cutting production costs and making splashy acquisitions. To manage these growing behemoths, CEOs turned to strategic planning, which focused on winning market share, not on getting in touch with remote customers. Markets came to be defined as aggregations of competitors, not as customers.

In recent times, Japanese companies were the first to recognize a problem. They started to rescue customers from the limbo of so-so merchandise and take it-or-leave-it service. They built loyalty among U.S. car buyers by assiduously uncovering and accommodating customer needs. The growing influence of Japanese firms as well as demographics and hard economic times have forced American companies to realize the need to listen to customers.

Creative changes in service can make the difference. For example, companies offering better service can charge 10 percent more for their products than competitors. Even smaller companies with fewer management layers are finding that personal relationships between senior executives and customers can help in various ways. Many companies attach so much importance to service that they require their senior managers to put in time at the front lines. For example, Xerox requires that its executives spend one day a month taking complaints from customers. About machines, bills and service. Similarly, at Hyatt Hotels, senior executives put in time as bellhops.

Briefly, a company must decide who it wants to serve, discover what those customers want and set a strategy that single-mindedly provides that service to those customers. With such clearly articulated goals, top management can give frontline employees responsibility for responding instantly to customer needs in those crucial moments that determine the company's success of failure. The following episode, which underlines Scandinavian Airline's emphasis on service, shows how far a company can go to stand by the customer.

Rudy Peterson was an American businessman staying at the Grand Hotel in Stock-Holm. Arriving at Stockholm's Arlanda airport for an important day trip with a colleague to Corporation on a Scandinavian Airlines (SAS) flight, he realized he'd left his ticket in his hotel room.

Everyone knows you can't board an airplane without a ticket, so Rudy Peterson resigned himself to missing the flight and his business meeting in Copenhagen. But when he explained his dilemma to the ticket agent, he got a pleasant surprise. "Don't worry, Mr. Peterson, "she said with a smile. "Here's your boarding card. I'll insert a temporary ticket in here. If you just tell me your room number at the Grand Hotel and your destination in Copenhagen, I'll take care of the rest." While Rudy and his colleague waited in the passenger lounge, the ticket agent dialed the hotel. A bellhop checked the room and found the ticket. The ticket agent then sent an SAS limo to retrieve it from the hotel and bring it directly to her. They moved so quickly that the ticket arrived before the Copenhagen flight departed. No one was more surprised than Rudy Peterson when the flight attendant approached him and said calmly, "Mr. Peterson? Here's your ticket."

What would have happened at a more traditional airline? Most airline manuals are clear. "No ticket, no flight." At best, the ticket agent would have informed her supervisor of the problem, but Rudy Peterson almost certainly would have missed his flight. Instead, because of the way SAS handled his situation, he was both impressed and on time for his meeting.

The SAS experience shows how far a business must be willing to go to become a truly customer-driven company, a company that recognizes that its only true assets are satisfied customers, all of whom expect to be treated as individuals.

Many firms argue that service by definition is difficult to guarantee. Services are generally delivered by human beings, who are less predictable than machines. Services are also usually produced at the same time that they are consumed. Although there can be exceptions to the rule, service can be guaranteed in any field. Consider the guarantee offered by "Bugs" Burger Bug killer (BBBK), a Miami-based pest extermination company, a division of S.C. Johnson and Sons:

Most of BBBK's competitors claim that they will reduce pests to "acceptable levels"; BBBK promises to eliminate them entirely. Its service guarantee to hotel and restaurant clients promises:

- You don't owe one penny until all pests on your premises have been eradicated.
- If you are ever dissatisfied with BBBK's service, you will receive a refund for up to 12 months of the company's services plus fees for another exterminator of your choice for the next year.
- If a guest a pest on your premises, BBBK will pay for the guest's meal or room, send a letter of apology, and pay for a future meal or stay.
- If your facility is closed down due to the presence of roaches or rodents, BBBK will pay any fines, as well as all lost profits plus $5,000. In short, BBBK says, "If we don't satisfy you 100%, we don't take your money.

The company's service program has been extremely successful. It charges up to 10 times more than its competitors and yet has a disproportionately high market share in its operating areas. In designing a good service program, a company should be conversant with a number of important trends. First, customers don't read (e.g., customers don't read assembly and operation instructions). Second, customers don't understand ownership responsibilities (e.g., some hotels require customers to program their own wake-up calls into a confusing computerized system). Third, high technology and product complexity make product differentiation difficult (i.e., with like products, better service can become an important differentiating factor). Fourth, consumers have lower confidence and expectations for products and services (i.e., customer service can have an enormous impact on consumer confidence). Fifth, high-quality service has become a product attribute (i.e., consumer's rate qualitative service factors as more important than product cost and features). Sixth, consumer attention is drawn to negative publicity (i.e., negative word of mouth is extremely detrimental). Seventh, consumers believe they are not getting their money's worth.

Improved customer service can play a major role in changing customer service can play a major role in changing customer perceptions about a product and its value and can directly affect a company's success and profitability. The quality of service accompany provides depends largely on people, not only those with direct customer responsibility but also with managers, supervisors and support staff. Thus, success in providing adequate service largely depends on preparing employees for it.

Time-Based Strategy

When a product market changes quickly, companies must respond quickly if they want to preserve their positions. In today's changing markets, time-based strategy that aims to beat the competition has assumed new dimensions.

GE has cut the time to deliver a custom-made industrial circuit breaker box from three weeks to three days. In the past, AT&-T needed two years to design a new phone; now it needs only one year. Motorola used to take three weeks to turn out electronic pagers after the factory received the order; now it takes two hours.

Time-based strategy brings about important competitive benefits. Market share grows because customers love getting their orders now. Inventories of finished goods shrink because they are not necessary to ensure quick delivery; the fastest manufacturers can make and ship an order the day it is received. For this and other reasons, costs fall. Many employees become satisfied because they are working for a more responsive, more successful company and because speeding operations require giving them more flexibility and responsibility. Quality also improves. Briefly, doing it fast forces a firm to do it right the first time.

Speed can also pay off in product development even if it means going over budget by as much as 50 percent. For example, a model development by Mc Kinsey and company shows that high-tech products that come to market on budget but six months late earn 33 percent less profit over five years. In contrast, coming out 50 percent over budget but on time cuts profits only by 4 percent.

To implement a time-based strategy, the entire production process must be redesigned for speed. GE's experience is relevant here. Its circuit breaker business was old and stagnant. Market growth was slow and Siemens and Westinghouse were strong competitors. GE assembled a team of manufacturing, design and marketing experts to focus on overhauling the entire process. The goal was to cut the time between order and delivery from three weeks to three days. Six plants around the United States were producing circuit breaker boxes. The team consolidated production into one plant and automated its facilities. But the team did not automate operations as they were. In the old system, engineers custom-designed each box, a task that took about a week. Engineers chose from 28000 unique parts to create a box. To set up an automated system to handle that many parts would have been a nightmare. The design team reduced the number of parts to 1,275, making most parts interchangeable. Even with this drastic reduction in parts, customers were still given 40,000 different sizes, shapes and configurations from which to choose.

The team also devised a way to phase out the engineers, by replacing them with computers. Now a salesperson enters the specification for a circuit breaker into a computer at GE's main office and the order flows to a computer at the plant, which automatically programs factory machines to custom-make the order with minimum waste.

Although these advances are indeed impressive, the team still had to conquer another source of delay-solving problems and making decisions on the factory floor. The solution was to eliminate all line supervisors and quality inspectors, reducing the organizational layers between worker and plant manager from three to one. Everything middle managers used to handle-vacation scheduling, quality, work rules-became the responsibility of the 129 workers on the floor, who were divided into teams of 15 to 20. It worked. The more responsibility GE gave the workers, the faster problems were solved and decisions were made.

The results: The plant that used to have a two-month backlog of order now works with a two-day backlog. Productivity has increased 20 percent over the past year. Manufacturing costs have dropped 30 percent or $5.5 million a year and return on investment is running at over 20 percent. The speed of delivery for a higher-quality product with more features has shrunk from three weeks to three days. And GE is gaining share in a flat market.

Another area ripe for time-based strategy is the administrative/approval area. According to the Thomas Group, a Dallas-based consulting firm specializing in speed, manufacturing typically takes only 5 to 20 percent of the total time that is needed to get an order for a given product to market; the rest is administrative. For example, at Adca Bank, a subsidiary of West Germany's Reebobank (with assets of $90 billion), an application for a loan used to go through numerous layers of bureaucracy. A branch would send a loan application to a loan officer at headquarters, which would look at it and change it. Then the loan officer's manager would look at the application and change it, and so on. The bank eventually got rid of five layers of management and gave officers in all branches more authority to make loans. It used to take 24 managers to approve a loan. Now it takes 12.

Teamwork seems to be the key ingredient among the fastest companies. Nearly all of them form multidepartment teams. AT&-T formed teams of six to twelve members, including engineers, manufacturers and marketers, with complete authority to make every decision about how a product would look, work be made and cost. At AT&-T the key was setting rigid speed requirements, such as six weeks and leaving the rest to the team. Teams could meet these strict deadlines because they did not need to send each decision up the line for approval with this new approach, AT&T cut development time for its new 4200 phone from two years to just a year while lowering costs and increasing quality.

Application of time-based strategy to distribution is equally important. Even the world's fastest factory cannot provide much of a competitive advantage if everything it products gets snagged in the distribution chain. For example, Benetton takes its distribution very seriously and has created an electronic loop that links sales agent, factory and warehouse. If a saleswoman in one of Benetton's Los Angeles shops finds that is starting to run out of a best-selling sweater, she calls of Benetton's 80 sales agents, who enter the order in a personal computer, which sends it to a mainframe in Italy. The mainframe computer, which has all of the measurements for the sweater, sets the knitting machines in motion. Once the sweaters are finished, workers box them up and label the box with a bar code containing the Los Angeles address. The box then goes into the warehouse. The computer next sends a robot flying. The robot finds the box and any others going to Los Angeles, picks them up, and loads them onto a truck. Including manufacturing time, Benetton can get an order to Los Angeles in four weeks.

Implementation of time-based strategy requires a number of steps. First, start from scratch (i.e., set a time goal and revamp entire operations to meet this goal rather than simply improving efficiency in current operations). Second, wipe out approvals (i.e., cut down bureaucratic layers of control and let people make decisions on the stop). Third, emphasize teamwork (i.e., nothing short of disaster should be a valid excuse for delay). Fourth, develop time-effective distribution (i.e., snags in distribution must be simultaneously worked out). Fifth, put speed in the culture (i.e., train people in the company at all levels to understand and appreciate the significance of speed).

The advantages of speed are undeniably impressive. Although it is a common precept that time is money, in practice, companies have paid only lip service to it. The time it took to do a job, whatever the amount, was considered a necessity to meet organizational requirements, system, procedures and hierarchical relationships. Now, however, there is a new realization that time saved is a strategic factor for gaining competitive advantage. Companies that grasp and appreciate the unprecedented advantages of getting new products to market sooner and orders to customers faster hold the key for achieving competitive preeminence in the 1990s and beyond.

HOPE IS NOT A STRATEGY

The truth is we shouldn't engage a sales team until we have a repeatable sales process for all the buyer persons in a well-defined market segment. Place is the fourth P, not the first. Summarizing product management is a game of the future. Product managers, who know the market, identify and quantify problems in a market segment. They assess the risk and financials so the company can run as a business. They communicate this knowledge to the departments in the company that need the information, allowing products and services to be built which solve a known problem and expand the customer base profitability. And they show their expertise to the outside world by engaging the market with smart ideas.

Companies fail when employing market without marketing, when worrying more about promotion than problem, when focusing more on selling than solving. That is, failure is likely when delivering products without market knowledge. We should rely on product management to focus on next year and the year after. To be thinking many moves ahead in the roadmap instead of only on the current release.

Many CEOs realize product management brings process and business savvy to the creation and delivery of products. Perhaps that's why we've seen a shift over the years of where product managers report in the organization. Many organizations put the job within another department.

Traditional consumer product companies have always considered product management to be a marketing role, which is why it seems to make sense to put product management there. And it does make sense-if the marketing department is defining and delivering products and not just promoting theme. Alas, as we explored earlier, many technology companies consider the term "marketing" to be synonymous with "marketing communications." So if the marketing department is only about delivering products but not defining them, product managers should be elsewhere.

For technology companies, particularly those with enterprise or B2B products, the product management job is very technical. This is why we see many product managers reporting to Development or Engineering. However, we've seen a shift away from this in recent years, from 19% in 2001 to 12% in 2008. The problem appears to be that technical product managers spend so much time writing requirements that they don't have time to visit the market to better understand the problems their products are designed to solve. They spend so much time building products that they're not equipped to help deliver them to the market.

Very few product managers find themselves in a sales (or sales & marketing) department. From 10% in 2001, the percentage of product managers in sales has slipped to 6% in 2008. It seems clear that product managers in sales will spend all of their time supporting sales people with demos and presentations. The product manager becomes the sales engineer.

In effect, subordinating product management relegates it to a support role for the primary goal of the department. Vice presidents and department heads have a natural inclination to support their primary department's role. The VP of Development, primarily responsible for delivering products, tends to use product managers as project managers and Development gofers. The VP of marketing owns collateral, sales tools, lead generation, and awareness programmes. So this VP often uses product managers as content providers to marketing communications. And the VP of sales, focused on new sales revenue, uses product managers to achieve that goal; product managers become "demo boys and demo girls" who support sales people one deal at a time.

In management challengers for the 21st century, peter Drucker tells us that organization charts really don't fix problems; process and personnel problems are never solved by a re-org. The truth is, it doesn't matter where product management reports. What matters is how the head of the organization holds product management accountable. In other words, what does "success" look like for a product manager?

As companies grow larger and become more mature, the company president needs someone thinking about the product we ought to be offering and new markets we could serve. In other words, the company needs someone thinking about the future of the product. We already have people focused on product, promotion and place. Who-if anyone-is identifying market problems for the next round of products? Who is the VP of market problems? And what result does the company president want from product Management?

Increasingly we see companies creating a VP of product Management, a department at the same level in the company as the other major departments. This VP focuses the product management group on the business of the product. The product management group interviews existing and potential customers, articulates and quantifies market problems in the business case and market requirements, defines standard procedures for product delivery and launch, supports the creation of collateral and sales tools by Marketing communications and trains the sales teams on the market and product. Product Management looks at the needs of the entire business and the entire market.

Recognizing that existing and future products need different levels of attention, some companies split the product management job into smaller bits: one group is responsible for next year's products while another group provides sales and marketing support for existing products. These companies often add a product marketing component to the marketing communications effort, supporting them with market information and product content. As we grow ever larger, the product marketing role expands further: we still need a group defining our go-to-market strategy and providing content to marketing communications, but now we also need more marketing assistance in the field. So field marketing is born: product marketing people in the sales regions that create specific programmers for all of the sales people in a given geographic area.

In summary, product management needs to focus on market problems. Subordinating the role to other departments usually forces product management to support the primary needs of that department, to the detriment of spending time looking forward beyond the next cycle of activity. In a product management department focus can remain on market problem and future opportunities.

Some product managers have a natural affinity for working with Development, others for sales and Marketing Communications and others prefer to work on business issues. Finding these three orientations in one person is an almost impossible task. Instead, perhaps we should find three different people with these skills and have them work as a team.

NEW PRODUCT STRATEGIES-INNOVATION, MARKET ENTRY, PRODUCT LINE EXTENSION

For a marketing plan to be successful it is essential that all elements of the marketing mix should support each other. Marketing mixes will change between products, services and market situations and indeed this is what makes marketing dynamic; it is the skill of the individual marketing person in manipulating the individual mixes that can make a product or service a success or a failure. Different emphases to individual elements in the marketing mix are often called for. However, the product or service is particularly important in this calculation for this is the tangible element that will appeal to customers and it is upon this that customer' purchases and repeat purchases are based. This is what must provide the end satisfaction for this, after all, is the practical application of the marketing concept.

A study of products and services is concerned with, amongst other things, design, appearance, length of time it will last and how is perceived by customers and non-customers alike.

Meaning of Product

As per the marketing practitioners term People purchase a 'bundle of satisfactions'. This includes obvious things like the physical product itself or a less tangible service offering. If asked to state what they have purchased most customers will simply mention the product or service in its simplest terms. However, there is much more to a purchase than simply this.

It is the task of marketing to take a more expansive view of what constitutes an augmented product or service and then combine the marketing mix in such a way as to present consumers with the 'bundle of satisfactions' that marketing research has identified as being most pertinent to their requirements. This augmented product concept is sometimes called the extended product and this definition includes the total marketing effort. Thus a view of the product or service is rather broader than the mere object or service offering; it is the utility or a 'bundle of satisfactions' that provides satisfaction.

Categories of products

Given the background that has been presented, we are now in a position to present a formal classification system for products and services. This is needed in order that marketing planners can more easily formulate and design their strategies and tactics.

Industrial goods are separated from consumer goods as the first part of this categorization.

Industrial goods

The mention of industrial goods conjures images of components and raw materials, but not all industrial goods are as tangible as this. A number of additional items and services are important to ensure the smooth running of a factory. A classification exists to describe categories of industrial goods and services:

- ***Installations*** include the plant and machinery required for a company's manufacturing processes. These are very critical purchases and usually involve complex purchasing decision making processes with price not necessarily being the deciding factor when making such purchases.
- ***Accessories*** are also capital items but are less critical and depreciated over a shorter period of time. They include items like office equipment and materials handling equipment.
- ***Raw materials*** are the most obvious of industrial goods and this is the major task in a modern purchasing department. Here, buyers are specifically looking for a keen price coupled with quality and reliability of delivery.
- ***Component parts and materials*** are items that are required in the production process, but are not part of the finished product. It includes such items as packaging, greases and oils.
- ***Supplies*** include items like cleaning and maintenance materials and stationery. Buying here tends to be more routine and it is often a matter of simply reordering with price being the major criterion consistent with a standard specification of quality.

This classification is linked to organizational buying behavior where the fact that buyers are dealing with larger sums of money and larger quantities tends to make it a more professional and organized process than in consumer goods purchasing.

Consumer goods

These are the types of products and services with which we, as individuals, are familiar. Unlike industrial products, more irrational and emotional motives tend to be connected with their purchase and it is upon this factor that many manufacturers base much of their marketing effort. As with industrial goods, they also lend themselves to a number of sub-categories.

- ***Convenience goods*** are everyday items whose purchase takes little effort on the buyer's part. They can be classed as everyday necessities, purchased on a regular basis. Advertising plays an important role in terms of attempting to persuade the consumer to take a particular brand. Staple convenience goods are purchased routinely for consumption and it is more difficult to differentiate one product from another and no pre-planning goes into their purchase. Many such products are delivered to the door like milk and newspapers.
- ***Shopping goods*** is the term used to describe durable products and their purchase tends to be at infrequent intervals. More planning goes into their purchase on the part of buyers and buyer behavior is more complex. The purchasing cycle is much longer and more complex models of buyer behavior apply. Further classifications relate to homogeneous shopping goods that are standard items like toasters and kettles and heterogeneous shopping goods that are non-standard and where personal choice plays a more important role.
- ***Specialty goods*** are major purchases made at infrequent intervals. Here, much probing in the market-place is undertaken by customers. Many more purchasing motivations are involved in the final decision and quite often the final purchase is a compromise decision between a number of purchasing criteria. Examples of such purchases are motor cars and a major item of relatively expensive clothing.
- ***Unsought goods*** are ones that the purchaser has not actively considered buying. Techniques used in their marketing are often rather dubious and this has led to much criticism of marketing. Consumers usually have to be persuaded that they need such products, as it would never occur to them to go out and actively purchase. Insurance typifies such a service - particularly life assurance, where the potential customer does not necessarily see an immediate need for this service. Methods of selling such goods and services tend to use more directly targeted approaches like direct mail, telephone selling and door-to-door.

Product management

Larger organizations, especially those that produce consumer durables and fast moving consumer goods (FMCG) often have what is termed a 'product management' system of managing single products or a line of similar products. In FMCG companies, the term used tends to be 'Brand Manager' whose responsibility it is to manage the image and the marketing (but not the selling) of a single product line. This person acts as a liaison between the advertising agency and the company and is responsible for the 'image' of the product and will commission marketing research when it is needed.

This kind of system has been criticized on the grounds that product managers have to rely upon others, especially the sales force, to carry out their ideas. This has the potential for conflict, particularly on the part of the field sales force who have to be sold the promotional idea with which they may or may not agree.

Where a system of product management is in operation, the typical organization of the marketing function is that the marketing manager is in overall control and is directly under the managing director. Under the marketing manager is the overall products manager and under the products manager come individual brand managers. Alongside the products manager comes the sales manager and under the sales manager comes the sales team organized by various kinds of geographical or functional split.

Strategic considerations

Under this heading of product management it is appropriate to discuss the strategies that are open to product managers when devising strategies for their product portfolios. Igor Ansoff first introduced his idea of a simple matrix in 1957 and it is described in Figure 3.6:

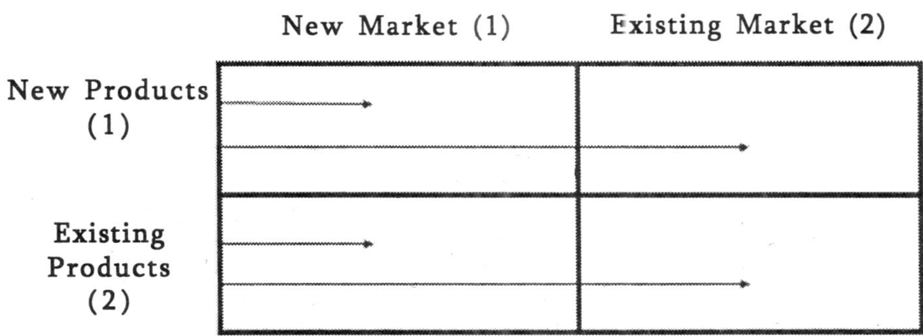

Figure 3.6 Ansoffs matrix

Each of the decisions is looked at in turn under their respective headings:

- **1/1 decision** takers are the true innovators, but the strategy is perhaps rather risky in terms of expenditure costs and the high failure rate of new products. This strategy is referred to as 'diversification'.
- **1/2 decisions** (new products into existing markets) comprise producers who like to stay ahead of their competitors or are able to provide some sustainable advantage that makes their product unique in the minds of consumers. This is a strategy of 'product development'.
- **2/1 decisions** (existing products into new markets) relate to manufacturers who are seeking to expand their total sales volume by moving into an entirely new (to them) marketplace. An example might be an industrial adhesives manufacturer who decides to target the office stationery market by modifying the existing range of industrial adhesives. This strategy is known as 'market development'.
- **2/2 decisions** are taken by manufacturers who play safe. Arguably, it lacks imagination and there is a possibility of such manufacturers being left exposed if their particular market hits recessionary times. This is a strategy of 'market penetration'.

New products

Different companies have different policies in relation to this subject. Many let others taking risks and follow when new products are launched and proved. They are, however, very important for the thrusting innovative company, but there are risks attached in terms of damage to the company's reputation if the new product fails plus the attendant costs of development and launch. The product or service is the main component of marketing as it provides revenue. Before the formal development programme is discussed, a listing of the types of new product categorization used by marketing people is now described:

- ***Innovative products*** are completely new to the marketplace.
- ***Replacement products*** are ones that provide a different slant on a traditional theme and might include well-known items, but with a new design and functions.
- ***Imitative products*** are quite common once an innovative product has become successfully established. Marketing slang refers to them as 'me too' products. There is, of course, less risk involved in their launch.
- ***Relaunched products*** happen when an original product has gone into decline, but the company anticipates that there is sufficient potential sale if the image of the product is altered through manipulation of the marketing mix.

How new product development is managed is a critical factor in relation to potential success or failure. There are a number of different organizational alternatives in this respect:

- ***New product managers*** are given the sole task of developing new products. Sometimes this task is part of the duty of a product manager or brand manager in a smaller organization.
- ***New product committees*** receive new product ideas from marketing or research and development or indeed from any other source within the organization and assess their viability in terms of potential success.
- ***New product departments*** exist in large innovative companies and their work cuts across a number of departments. When a new product idea looks to be viable they appoint a 'product (or project) champion' to see the development through from its design and development to its market launch.
- ***New product venture*** teams comprise people from different parts of the organization who are brought together on an ad hoc basis in order that different views can be incorporated in new product decision making. Their task is to develop products within predetermined budget and time constraint parameters.

The process of new product development

The process of new product development goes through a logical series of seven steps from the inception of the idea to the actual launch of the product. These steps are explained below:

STEP-01: ***Idea generation can*** come from a variety of sources. In innovative companies, such ideas tend to be research driven. The notion of marketing orientation tells us that we should look to our customers first (through marketing research) before embarking upon new product development. In the case of companies producing 'breakthrough' products this might be difficult as customers will not necessarily be able to envisage what they require. However, as we shall see later in this section, ideas are not simply generated and made into products that are then marketed. Marketing research does come into the equation, but more through procedures like product testing come later in the process. A culture should exist within the organization that encourages new product ideas amongst more than simply the Research & Development function. The sales force should be a regular source of new product ideas and such data can be gathered from the company's marketing information system. Brainstorming is a good method of producing new product ideas as long as it is chaired competently, but regular meetings of planning committees should have this at the head of their agenda. Venture teams can then be set up to progress likely ideas.

STEP-02: ***Screening*** is the first stage of sifting viable ideas from less viable ones and obvious issues are addressed at this stage in terms of potential demand, the company's capability in terms of development and production and the profit potential. This is an important stage at which 'Go' or 'Drop' decisions are made. This screening process should have due regard to whether or not the new product will fit into range of products that the company markets. To start a completely new venture might mean expensive investment in not only production capacity and skills, but a completely new marketing team might be required.

STEP-03: ***Business analysis*** is where the new product idea's financial viability is appraised. By this phase only 'serious' contenders will remain and here a critical stage has been reached. Such analysis needs to take into consideration total costs rather than simply development and production costs.

STEP-04: ***Product development*** is the point at which the company has committed itself and indeed this is when costs start to increase sharply. Where appropriate, prototypes will be developed and these can be assessed by marketing research through product appraisal tests. It is also here that product refinement and modification will be possible through feedback from marketing research. It might also be the point at which the product is abandoned if expectations do not match up to reality, rather than risk a 'high exposure' failure in the marketplace.

STEP-05: ***Test marketing*** is the last but one stage. This might be appropriate where the product is a fast moving consumer good when it can be tested in test towns or a television test areas before going 'national', but this is not always appropriate for more durable products. Here, product placement tests with members of the general public are probably more appropriate. The only problem with full scale test marketing is that it allows your competitors to see what you are doing, so clearly this disadvantage must be weighed against the advantages of simulating a National launch before full scale commitment. This indeed is why product testing, rather than higher profile test marketing, is better in terms of confidentiality.

STEP-06: ***Commercialization*** is where the product is to be launched on the market. All of the various filters have taken place, but even at this stage success is not guaranteed. However, there is a far greater likelihood of success if the procedure just described has been undertaken.

An American firm of consultants, Booz, Allen and Hamilton first put forward the notion of the decay curve of new product ideas which is illustrated in Figure 3.7:

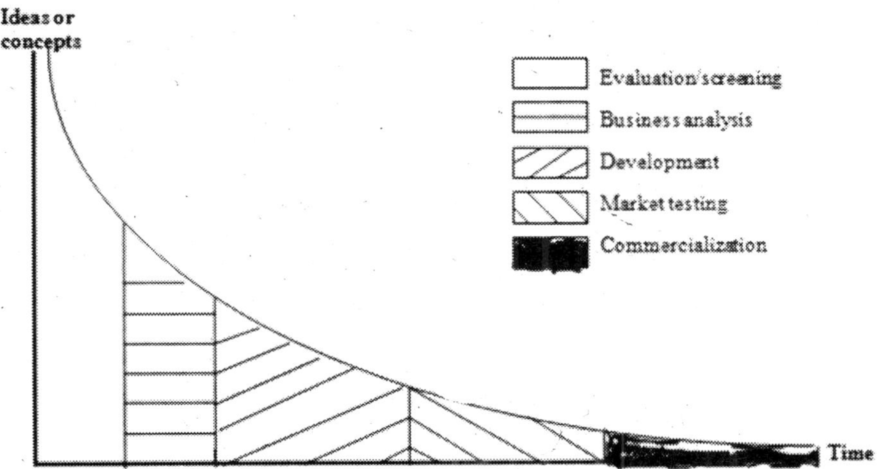

Fig. 3.7 Decay curves of new product ideas

In their original research Booz, Allen and Hamilton found that it took 58 new product ideas to produce one potentially successful product. However, even during the 'commercialization' stage there was still a 50/50 chance that the product would not be successful. Later research that they undertook suggested that it took considerably fewer new product ideas to produce a successful product.

Factors for successful innovation

McKinsey & Co conducted research in 1980 that investigated a number of large multinational organizations. The research examined factors that were deemed to be essential in their successful operation and eight factors were highlighted:

I. a bias towards action
II. simple line and team staff organization
III. continued contact with customers
IV. productivity improvement via people
V. operational autonomy and the encouragement of entrepreneurship
VI. simultaneous loose and tight controls
VII. stress on one key business value
VIII. an emphasis on sticking to what it knows best

This research has stood the test of time and it is still cited today as being the critical success formula for successful international enterprise.

Product mix and product line

The above terms are used a lot within product management in addition to the terms 'depth' and 'width' of the product mix (or product assortment). This latter description means all of the product lines and items that a company offers for sale. Basically, the product line is a group of closely related product items. The width of the product mix denotes the number of product lines carried. The depth of the mix denotes the range of items within each line and is calculated by dividing the total number of items carried by the number of lines. There is another term that is 'consistency', and this relates to the closeness of items in the range in terms of product and marketing characteristics. By attempting this analysis, product management can look more objectively at its overall product mix and decide whether or not certain lines should be lengthened, shortened or deleted.

Product life cycle

The notion of the product life cycle is almost as old as the subject of marketing. Various stages are proposed which show that a product passes through a number of stages in its life from the time it is conceived (the development phase) to the time it is deleted during the decline stage. Marketing people have found it to be a useful planning tool and this point is expanded shortly.

The principal problem with this theory is that it is so neat as to be totally 'believable' and some product managers tend to expect that every product will fit this neat curve. Marketing academics (notably, Dallah and Yuspeh) have, therefore, criticised the concept on the basis that when a product is launched it is often killed off prematurely because sales suggest that it has gone into a quick decline, whereas the reality is that what they are is probably only a slight hiccup in the growth curve of the product.

Figure 3.8 shows the theoretical curve of product life cycle. On this diagram is superimposed the revenue curve which shows the product recovering its costs of development and launch and then moving into profitability. Naturally, all products will behave differently, but as a tool of planning this theory has much to commend it.

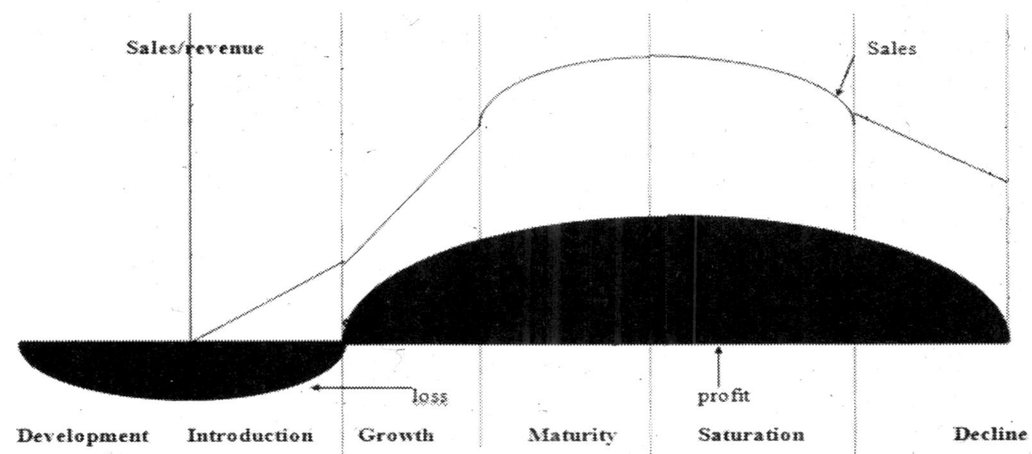

Figure 3.8 The product life cycle

The shape of the curve can alter and this is useful in illustrating the effect of different marketing conditions. Different patterns are suggested in Figure 3.9 with explanations, but more combinations are possible.

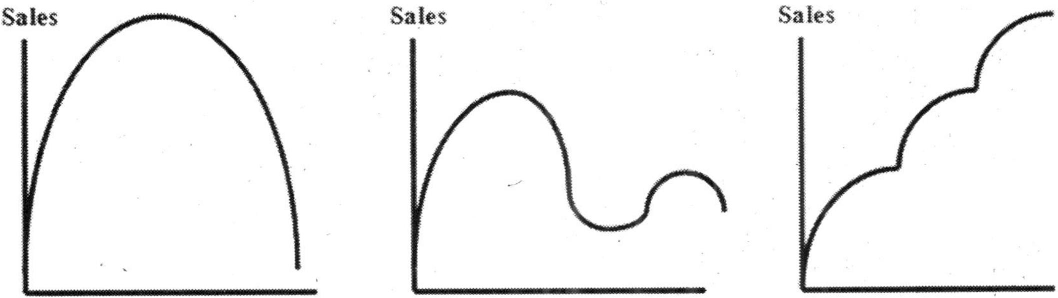

Figure 3.9 Different shapes of the product life cycle

In the above diagram the first diagram represents a 'fad' product which comes quickly into the marketplace and is never seen again. The second diagram represents a 'fashion' product whose sales might go in cycles. The third diagram represents a product that passes through a number of phases, but where the product manager does not allow the product to become 'stale' after it has entered maturity. This is done by introducing a modification that builds upon the success of the original product.

As has been mentioned, the concepts as outlined in Figure 3.9 can be used as planning tools and the shapes of curves can be hypothesized that can fit almost any marketing situation. It is useful as a tool of product planning.

The product life cycle is influenced by the nature of the product, changes in the competitive environment changes on the part of consumers who might display different preferences as the product moves through its life cycle. The shape of the curve, from an individual manufacturer's viewpoint, can also be altered as a result of competitive actions. The product life cycle can thus be applied to the industry as a whole (which will include a summation of all manufacturers' sales who are marketing that particular product) or it can apply only to the sales of a specific product for an individual company.

The time span of the product life cycle can range from say a fashion season to many years. In this latter case the maturity and saturation stages will be considerably lengthened. It is now acknowledged that different categories of life cycle exist. We have used soap and shoes as our illustrations, so the curve is applicable within one of the following groups:

Product category life cycles describe a generic product like soap or shoes. Life cycles here tend to be long or infinite.

Product form life cycles describe the type of product like perfumed soap or plastic shoes. Here the life cycle is shorter.

Brand life cycles describe the various manufacturers' brands of perfumed soap or plastic shoes. This might, in the case of plastic shoes, be linked to a single fashion season with a new brand coming out shortly afterwards, so this kind of life cycle is the shortest of all.

Strategies suggested by each life cycle stage

Successful use of the product life cycle concept is being able to identify the passage from one stage to another. This requires that the company makes use of marketing research and marketing intelligence which forms part of the company's marketing information system. The product life cycle can thus be used strategically and impart an anticipated course of product development for which strategies can be planned and which will ensure the company's long terms growth in the marketplace.

Marketing actions are now suggested which are normally appropriate to each of these separate stages.

- ***Development*** is of course the pre-launch phase and it is during this period that confidentiality will usually have to maintain in terms of keeping information away from competitors. In many larger organizations the research and development function is housed entirely separately from the main production unit. In fact, in a lot of cases research and development is on an entirely different site. As the research and development process progresses from experimentation to the tangible product, so, in a marketing orientated organization, the involvement of marketing research will tend to increase. This is not to say that marketing research should not be involved at the earlier stages. For instance, focus groups/group discussions would be appropriate in terms of testing out the concept on groups of the general public at an early stage in the process before too much has been committed in terms of research and development expenditure.

- ***Introduction*** is the launch period and the product is slowly gaining acceptance. There are few (indeed sometimes zero) competitors at this stage, but this are where a number of new products fail. Figure 3.8 indicated that even after a new product idea had gone through its various filter stages there is still an even chance that it might fail. The product is seen to be innovative at this stage and potential buyers must me informed as to what it will do, so advertising tends to be of an informative nature. Buyers tend to be what are known as 'innovators' and this is explained later in this chapter.

  The product is new and can normally sustain a high initial price (skimming) as there are few or no competitors. Indeed, the product will probably have been expensive to produce and the costs of creating awareness prior to and during, its launch might have been high, so this is an opportunity to recoup as many of those costs as the market will sustain. Distribution is not widespread at this stage and is often exclusive within a particular geographical location. Even now, the product may not be totally appropriate in the marketplace in terms of its performance or design features, so product modifications tend to be more frequent at this stage.

- ***Growth*** is the period during which competitors will start to appear with similar offerings. Indeed, they might well have been conducting parallel research and development, but have been slower in launching their innovative products. Even now, the product is still exposed to failure, perhaps through competitive activity, as competitors have been able to learn from your mistakes during your launch. They will know your price and might undercut, and they will know the perceived weaknesses of your product, so they can emphasize the strength of theirs. Although it might seem that being in the market first is a good policy, it is also a high risk policy. Unless the company is large enough to sustain a costly failure at this stage, or has other products to fall back upon, then such a policy is very high risk indeed.

  This growth phase is sometimes termed 'exponential' and it is during this period that sales begin to take off. If the company is small, then it might possibly be acquired by a large company. Such acquisitions are normally done on a mutually advantageous basis, but they can be aggressive if the company that has developed the new product is a public limited company, and a larger company seeks acquisition through direct offers to shareholders, whilst the management disagrees with the takeover terms.

  During this phase promotion tends to change from one of creating awareness to one of attempting to create an identifiable brand. Promotional expenditure is probably still quite high. Distribution too is important during this phase. There are two parallel forces at work here. The first is in terms of powerful retail buyers attempting to rationalize the total number of lines they sell. The second is in terms of manufacturers attempting to secure as many distribution outlet possibilities as possible, as the product has now lost its innovative appeal. In distribution terms they move from exclusive, then to selective and finally to intensive distribution. The philosophy of the latter is that maximum exposure at the point of sale is probably as important as brand awareness.

- ***Maturity and saturation*** are dealt with together, because the 'maturity' phase is the phase where the product's sales level off to a gradual peak over a longer period (often years or decades). The 'saturation' phase is from its peak, gradually downwards to the phase where sales start to decelerate towards the 'decline' phase. In fact, many marketing authors miss out the 'saturation' phase altogether and class all of this phase as 'maturity'.

  During this phase sales slowdown and repeat purchases are prevalent. There are attempts to 'differentiate' products through the addition of 'features'. Price competition is at its maximum as other manufacturers enter the market. These manufacturers come in with 'me too' products which have not had to sustain the heavy costs of research and development and promotional costs associated with their launch. Although their brands might not carry the same weight as the well-established brands, price is the main competitive weapon, and price 'wars' between the established brands and these newer competitors is now uncommon. By now, the 'mystique' surrounding the product has dissipated and consumers feel confident in purchasing a product that bears a relatively unknown brand label. There is an increasing trend among retailers to trim their inventories, so unless the product can offer a sustainable product, brand or price advantage then there will be reluctance to stock.

  As market growth has ceased, marketing management must attempt to at least retain market share in the face of increased competition and it is at this stage than a number of manufacturers withdraw from the marketplace. If the brand is a sustainable brand name then advertising will be necessary to keep this in the mind of consumers and to keep them loyal to the brand. Promotion to the trade is also important, as manufacturers will wish to retain their distribution outlets. Joint manufacturer/trade promotions are developed with costs being shared on an equitable basis. There is generally a move away from a 'pull' strategy of promotion towards a 'push' strategy.

- ***Decline*** is signaled by steadily and sustained falling sales after the 'saturation' phase. Marketing research should have told the company that this was due to happen in order that they could concentrate upon developing new product lines. However, company management quite often refuses to accept that its products are about to enter the decline phase and stay with it in the hope that the inevitable might not happen.

Such a decline might be a function of a change in customer preferences, but more likely it is a function of a new product or process supplanting the existing one. The phase is characterized by competitive intensity and price-cutting and sales falling continuously. Many producers decide to abandon the marketplace or are forced to abandon because of financial difficulties. Thus, the decision to abandon the marketplace is a critical one and as can be seen from Figure 3.8 (*The product life cycle*). This should theoretically come when the product moves from a positive to a negative revenue situation. However, a number of manufacturers do stay in business during the decline phase. It is only in relatively few cases that a product will decline completely and never appear again. There will usually be a residual or continued demand, but at far less volume than before.

A good example is solid fuel that has largely been supplanted by gas and electricity and to a lesser extent oil for home heating purposes. However, there is still demand for solid fuel and as most of the solid fuel processors have now departed from the marketplace there is a vibrant market left for those who have remained.

Product diffusion and adoption

The notion of product diffusion and adoption was first put forward by Everett Rogers. Diffusion processes relate to the speed and extent of take-up of a new product and it considers the people who are the ultimate target of marketing efforts, rather than the marketplace itself that is the function of the notion of the product life cycle. The diagram that forms the model suggested for the diffusion curve is very much like the model for the product life cycle and indeed there are similarities between them both. In the case of this theory, consumers do not necessarily fall into the same category for all purchases and the theory very much describes consumer behavior in relation to their individual needs and preferences. The theory is explained in Figure 3.10.

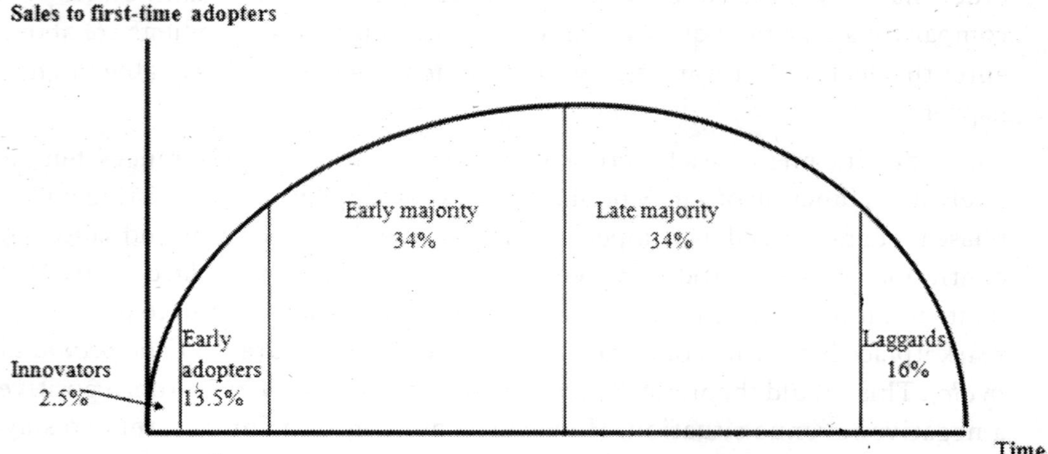

Figure 3.10 The product adoption process/diffusion of innovations

Figure 3.10 represents the rate at which the product is purchased for the first time by single individuals who are categorized into adopter categories, depending upon when in the cycle of time the purchase was made for the first time. The process is termed the 'diffusion of innovations'.

i. ***Innovators*** tend to be opinion leaders who are the first to purchase and these are basically the same purchasers as those who purchase at the introduction phase of the product life cycle. They are likely to be younger and better educated from reasonably affluent, high social status, family backgrounds. Their knowledge of the product tends to come more from their own feelings than from the efforts of marketing people. They represent the first 2.5% of the entire market - which is two standard deviations to the left of the mean.

ii. ***Early adopters*** possess similar characteristics to the innovators, but they are slightly more cautious and less gregarious. They tend to belong more to 'local' groups, but as opinion leaders they are influential. These comprise 13.5% of the entire market.

iii. ***Early majority*** purchasers tend to rate slightly above average in terms of their social class and now that the product has become more established, they rely principally upon marketing information before making their purchases. This group represents 34% of the market.

iv. ***Late majority*** purchasers tend to be more cautious, but are more prone to social pressures to adopt the product for the first time. This group comprises 34% of the total market.

v. ***Laggards*** are the final 16% category and they make up the cautious group. They tend to be older and more conservative, generally coming from a lower socio-economic class.

Diffusion is of course closely related to the adoption process of individual customers and it has been found that five particular facets of products will lead to a more rapid and wider adoption:

i. ***Relative advantage*** in terms of the greater the perceived advantage of the new product to customers the faster it will diffuse.

ii. ***Compatibility*** relates to the greater the extent to which the new product is compatible with existing products, the faster it will diffuse.

iii. ***Complexity*** is a disadvantage, because the more complex the new product is, the more difficult it will be to understand in the marketplace and the diffusion rate will thus be slower.

iv. ***Divisibility*** means the greater the ability of the new product to be used or tried on a limited scale before full commitment on the part of the purchaser, the faster it will diffuse.

v. ***Communicability*** means an ability of the new product to be demonstrated or communicated by early purchasers to later potential purchasers and then the quicker will be the rate of diffusion.

In the context of buyer behavior, the adoption process is very closely allied to the process that was cited in Figure 3.10. Indeed, it links in very neatly in terms of the decision-making processes that take place prior to making the purchase of a new innovatory product or service.

The adoption process can be described as:

Awareness → Interest → Evaluation → Trial → Adoption → Post-adoption confirmation

It is related to the diffusion of innovations in that this is typically the process through which purchasers must go before making a major new product purchasing decision; more so in this particular case as they have never tried the product before.

Although Figure 3.10 adds up to 100% this is not to say that everybody will ultimately purchase the product or service. If we consider home telephones as an example it could probably be said that the country has reached saturation in terms of new subscribers. However, a number are not subscribers because they like privacy and are not listed in the directory or have some other personal reasons for not wanting a telephone. A minority, of course, would like a telephone, but cannot afford one. In any case, the market for home telephones will never be 100% of all households. Those categories who never purchase are termed 'non-adopters'.

Innovative Strategies

Innovative Strategies deals with the firm rate of new product development and business model innovation. It asks whether the company is on the cutting edge of technology and business innovation. There are three types:

1. Pioneers
2. Close followers
3. Late followers

History shows that the companies that continue to invest in their innovative capabilities during tough economic times are those that fare best when growth returns. In a challenging business climate, focus is crucial. Open innovation can play an important part in the solution by breaking down the traditional corporate boundaries, open innovation allows intellectual property, ideas and people to flow freely both in and out of an organization. The five open-Innovation moves are listed below:

1. **Become a customer or supplier of your formal internal projects:** If your business is pursuing an important capability that it can neither afford to develop itself nor acquire on the open market and others in or beyond your industry. Then join with those others to fund, develop and launch it as an independent business and become its first customer.
2. **Let others develop your non-strategic initiatives:** If your business is reinforcing on its core activities and you have identified adjacent complimentary initiatives that drain too much attention, time and capital but that might attract outside interest and investment. Then spin them out to investors who can take over the development burden. Others will fund the progress and you can keep some equity in case they make it big.
3. **Make your intellectual property work harder for you and others:** If a lot of your company's intellectual property sits on a shelf and generates no direct financial benefit & you understand that its value, to you and to others, then let outside partners benefit from what you've created, continue its development and pay you licensing fees. Many businesses recover their R&D expenses spending in this way.
4. **Grow your ecosystem, even when you are not growing:** If your company is an active innovator, continually engaging with its customers, collaborators, industry expert's trade associations and others to identify future opportunities. Then build on your ecosystem of potential innovation partners. Be like a Major League baseball general managers, who always know which team will be interested in which player at what price

5. **Create open domains to reduce costs and expand participation:** If your internal ideas are likely to attract interest from valuable outside communities, potentially creating breakthrough advances or even changing the game within our industry. Then consider establishing open domains that either exchange information and ideas or provide shared facilities and services.

Taken together these are complicated activities that should be approached holistically, under the leadership of senior executives in strategic roles. Darwin taught us that it's neither the strongest nor the most intelligent species survive; it's those that adapt best to changes in the environment.

Market Entry

This is the most crucial decision by marketing managers because it involves the following points:

i. It involves cost to the maximum
ii. It is the beginning of a long journey of the product
iii. No mistake of even a minor nature is acceptable or admissible.

The process of commercialization is defined as a series of steps to be taken by the marketing management towards bringing this new product to the markets and to the consumers .Some of the major decisions have to be taken and strategies devised to launch and make product successful at the very outset. The decisions required are:

a. **WHEN** TO LAUNCH THE PRODUCT?
b. **WHERE** TO LAUNCH THE PRODUCT?
c. TO **WHOM** TO LAUNCH THE PRODUCT?
d. **HOW** TO LAUNCH THE PRODUCT?

Let us discuss each of these four decisions.

WHEN

In commercialization, the most important decision is to determine timing. If the product is seasonal in nature, the timing has to be in keeping with seasons. Secondly, the product has to be reviewed. Is it a replacement of an already existing product? If it's so, we must take into account the already existing stocks of old product. The firm has to take decisions on entry strategies too. Should the product be first to enter the market? Or should it have a parallel entry? or should it wait for late entry. The market will decide which timing is more suitable. The first entry advantage be taken or wait for competitors to enter and learn from the results. It all depends on the nature of the product. Is it new to the world type or new to the market or new to the firm or both or is very innovative or minor modification product. These features will determine our decision. But very careful study and review is important

WHERE

Is the product to be launched in a locality, region or several regions or nationally or even internationally. This geographical territory will decide the marketing approach. Advertisement, publicity and promotion, distribution, delivery modes, networking of systems and all other ingredients of marketing including cost of marketing will be decided on this crucial decision.

WHOM

It is yet another crucial decision. There are prime customers, heavy users, bulk customers, prestigious consumers, early adopters or opinion leaders. The approach in marketing has to be directed to some or all of such consumers. We must cover all possible customers and make sure that product has been accepted by them with more serious and strategic approach

HOW

Indeed, once the decision on timing and place and to whom has been taken, the decision on how becomes clear and easier. The marketing plan must be made on all aspects as covered before. Critical Path Scheduling (CPS) must be made to determine what needs to be done and after what.

Timing for each activity that needs to be done is worked out in CPS and proper planning is done and resources allocated already with clear responsibility.

Product Line Extension

A product line is a group of products that are closely related because they function in a similar manner, are sold to the same customer groups, are marketed through the same types of outlets or fall within given price ranges (Figure 3.11). For example, Nike produces several lines of athletic shoes and Motorola produces several lines of telecommunications products. In developing product line strategies, marketers face a number of tough decisions. The major product line decision involves product line length-the number of items in the product line. The line is too short if the manager can increase profits by adding items; the line is too long if the manager can increase profits by dropping items.

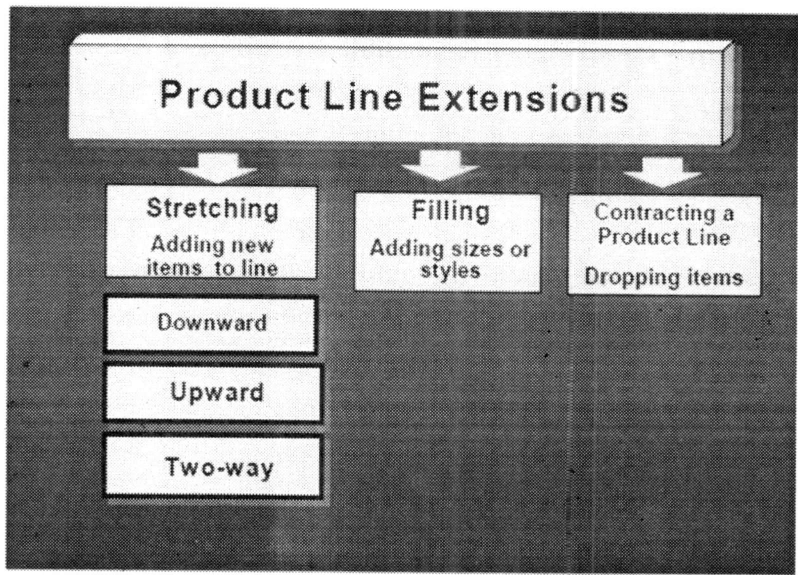

Figure 3.11 Product Line Extensions

Company objectives and resources influence product line length. Product lines tend to lengthen over time. The sales force and distributors may pressure the product manager for a more complete line to satisfy their customers or the manager may want to add items to the product line to create growth in sales and profits. However, as the manager adds items, several costs rise: design and engineering costs, inventory costs, manufacturing changeover costs, transportation costs and promotional costs to introduce new items. Eventually top management calls a halt to the mushrooming product line. Unnecessary or unprofitable items will be pruned from the line in a major effort to increase overall profitability. This pattern of uncontrolled product line growth followed by heavy pruning is typical and may repeat itself many times.

The company must manage its product lines carefully. It can systematically increase the length of its product line in two ways: by stretching its line and by filling its line. Product line stretching stretches its line downward, upward or both ways. Many companies initially locate at the upper end of the market and later stretch their lines downward. A company may stretch downward to plug a market hole that otherwise would attract a new competitor or to respond to a competitor's attack on the upper end. Or it may add low-end products because it finds faster growth taking place in the low-end segments.

PORTFOLIO MODELS-BCG AND GE MCKINSEY MATRIX

Boston Consulting Group Matrix (BCG)

The **BCG matrix** is a chart that had been created by Bruce Henderson for the Boston Consulting Group in 1968 to help corporations with analyzing their business units or product lines. This helps the company allocate resources and is used as an analytical tool in brand marketing, product management, strategic management and portfolio analysis (Fig-3.12).

This technique is particularly useful for multi-divisional or multiproduct companies. The divisions or products compromise the organizations "business portfolio". The composition of the portfolio can be critical to the growth and success of the company. The BCG matrix considers two variables, namely:

1. MARKET GROWTH RATE
2. RELATIVE MARKET SHARE

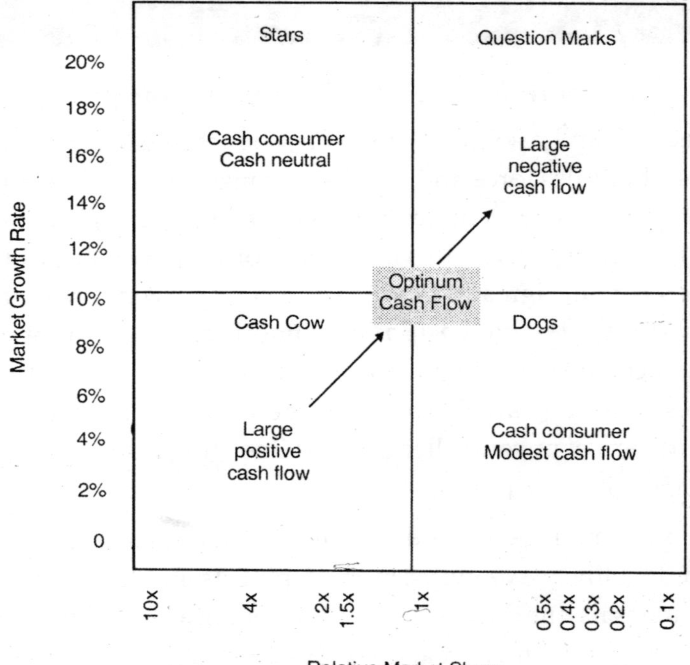

Fig. 3.12 The Boston Consulting Group's Growth Share Matrix

The market growth rate is shown on the vertical (y) axis and is expressed as a %. The range is set somewhat arbitrarily. The overhead shows a range of 0 to 20% with division between low and high growth at 10% (the original work by B Headley "Strategy and the business portfolio", Long Range Planning, Feb 1977 used these criteria). Inflation and/or Gross National Product have some impact on the range and thus the vertical axis can be modified to represent an index where the dividing line between low and high growth is at 1.0. Industries expanding faster than inflation or GNP would show above the line and those growing at less than inflation or GNP would be classed as low growth and show below the line. The horizontal (x) axis shows relative market share. The share is calculated by reference to the largest competitor in the market. Again the range and division between high and low shares is arbitrary. The original work used a scale of 0.1, i.e., market leadership occurs when the relative market share exceeds 1.0. The BCG growth/share matrix is divided into four cells or quadrants, each of which represents a particular type of business. Divisions or products are represented by circles. The size of the circle reflects the relative significance of the division/product to group sales. A development of the matrix is to reflect the relative profit contribution of each division and this is shown as a pie-segment within the circle.

QUESTION MARKS

These are products or businesses that compete in high growth markets but where the market share is relatively low. A new product launched into a high growth market and with an existing market leader would normally be considered as a question mark. Because of the high growth environment, they can be a "cash sink". Strategic options for question marks include.

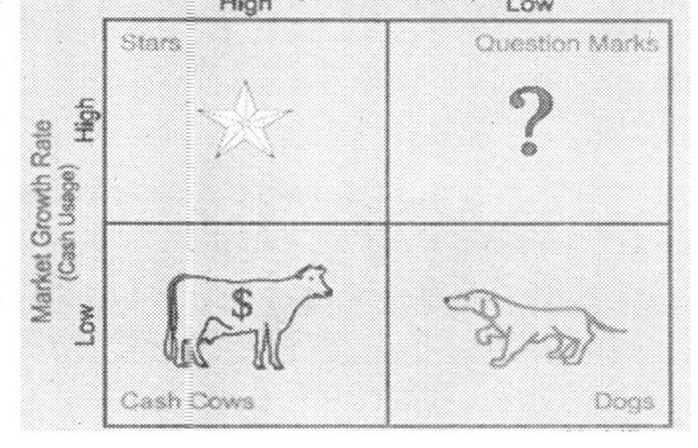

i. Market penetration
ii. Market development
iii. Product development

These are all intensive strategies or divestment.

STARS

Successful question marks become stars. i.e., market leaders in high growth industries. However, investment is normally still required to maintain growth and to defend the leadership position. Stars are frequently only marginally profitable but as they reach a more mature status in their life cycle and growth slows, returns become more attractive. The stars provide the basis for long term growth and profitability. Strategic options for stars include.

i. Integration - forward, backward and horizontal
ii. Market penetration
iii. Market development

iv. Product development

v. Joint ventures

CASH COWS

These are characterized by high relative market share in low growth industries. As the market matures the need for investment reduces. Cash Cows are the most profitable products in the portfolio. The situation is frequently boosted by economies of scale that may be present with market leaders. Cash Cows may be used to fund the businesses in the other three quadrants. It is desirable to maintain the strong position as long as possible and strategic options include-

i. Product development

ii. Concentric diversification

If the position weakens as a result of loss of market share or market contraction then options would include-

Retrenchment (or even divestment)

DOGS

These describe businesses that have low market shares in slow growth markets. They may well have been Cash Cows. Often they enjoy misguided loyalty from management although some Dogs can be revitalized. Profitability is, at best, marginal. Strategic options would include-

i. Retrenchment (if it is believed that it could be revitalized)

ii. Liquidation

iii. Divestment (if you can find someone to buy)

Success and Disaster Sequences in the Product Portfolio

Successful products may well move from question mark though star to Cash Cow and finally to Dog. Less successful products that never gain market position will move straight from question mark to Dog(Fig.3.13).

The BCG is simple and useful technique for strategic analysis. It is convenient for multi-product or multi-divisional companies. It focuses on cash flow and is useful for investment and marketing decisions.

One should not however, ignore the limitations of the technique. Definition (qualitative and quantitative) of the market is sometimes difficult. It assumes that market share and profitability are directly related. The use of high and low to form four categories is too simplistic. Growth rate is only one aspect of industry attractiveness and high growth markets are not always the most profitable. It considers the product or business in relation to the largest player only. It ignores the impact of small competitors whose market share is rising fast. Market share is only one aspect of overall competitive position. It ignores interdependence and synergy. Companies will frequently search for a balanced portfolio, since:-

i. Too many Stars may lead to a cash crisis
ii. Too many Cash Cows puts future profitability at risk
iii. And too many Question marks may affect current profitability.

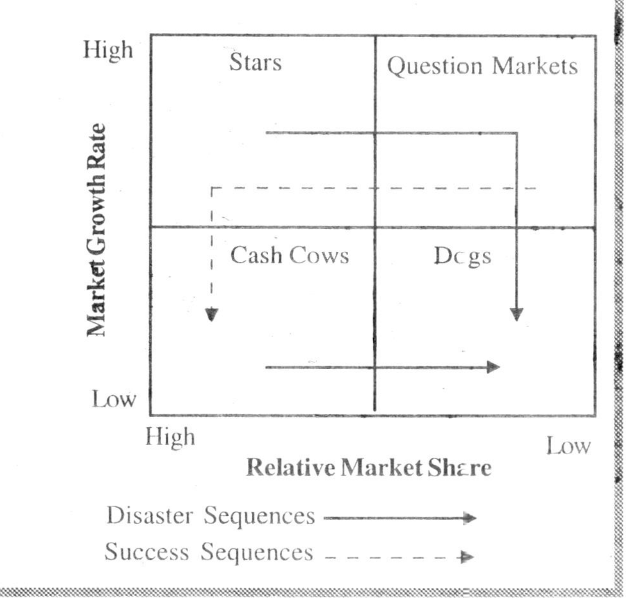

Fig. 3.13 Success and Disaster Sequences in the Product Portfolio

The GE-McKinsey Matrix

The GE/McKinsey Matrix was developed jointly by McKinsey and General Electric in the early 1970s as a derivation of the BCG Matrix. GE, by that time, had approximately 150 different business units and was disappointed with the profits derived from its investments. This raised internal concerns about the approach the organization had to investment decision making. While exploring new models to implement, GE started to be interested in visual strategic frameworks like the Growth-Share Matrix created by the Boston Consulting Group (BCG) a few years before. However, the BCG Matrix showed to have some limitations. It was considered not flexible enough to include all the broader issues that a company was facing while operating in a fast changing global environment.

The GE/McKinsey Matrix solves most of the issues of the BCG model and proposes a more sophisticated and comprehensive approach to investment decision making.

The GE-McKinsey Matrix is a nine-cell (3 by 3) matrix used to perform business portfolio analysis as a step in the strategic planning process. The GE/McKinsey Matrix identifies the optimum business portfolio as one that fits perfectly to the company's strengths and helps to exploit the most attractive industry sectors or markets.

Thus, the objective of the analysis is to position each SBU on the chart depending on the SBU's Strength and the Attractiveness of the Industry Sector or Market on which it is focused. Each axis is divided into Low, Medium and High, giving the nine-cell matrix as depicted below in Figure 3.14.

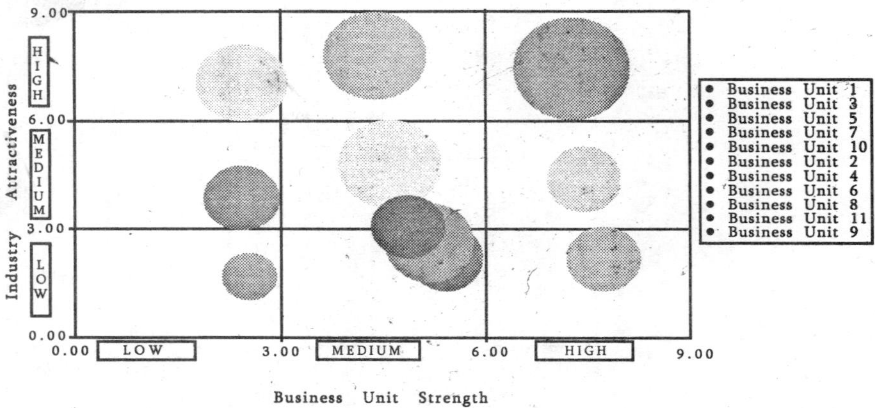

Figure 3.14 GE-McKinsey Matrix

SBUs are portrayed as a circle plotted on the GE/McKinsey Matrix, where the size of the circle represents a factor such as Market Size. The GE/McKinsey Matrix differs from other tools, like the Boston Consulting Group Matrix, in that multiple factors are used to define Industry Attractiveness and Business Unit Strength. Each factor can be given a different weighting in calculating the overall attractiveness of a particular industry.

Typically:

Industry Attractiveness = *Attractiveness Factor 1 Value by Factor 1 weighting + Attractiveness Factor 2 Value by Factor 2 weighting, etc.*

Business Unit Strength = *Strength Factor 1 Value by Factor 1 weighting + Strength Factor 2 Value by Factor 2 weighting, etc.*

The GE/McKinsey Matrix is a nine-cell (3 by 3) matrix and it is primarily used to perform business portfolio analysis on the strategic business units (SBU) of a corporation. A business portfolio is the collection of all the business units within a corporation and a large corporation has normally many SBUs. Each SBU is a distinctive and unique unit that falls under the same strategic hat. A well balanced portfolio is one of the top priorities of a large organization. The strategic business units are the basic blocks that compose a business portfolio. A unit can be a division or even a whole company owned by the parent organization. The nine-box matrix provides decision makers with a systematic and effective framework for a decentralized corporation to make better supported investment decisions and for developing strategies for future product development or new market segment entries. Instead of looking solely at each unit's future prospects, a corporation can adopt a multi-dimensional approach based on two components that will indicate how well the unit will perform in the future. The two components used to evaluate businesses, which also serve as the axes of the matrix, are the 'attractiveness' of the relevant industry and the unit's 'competitive strength' within the same industry. Each axis is then divided into Low, Medium and High(fig 3.15).

Market Attractiveness	low	medium	high
high	**Selectivity** Specialise niche Seek acqusition	**Selective Growth** Identify weakness Build on strengths	**Invest & Grow** Seek dominance Maximise investment
medium	**Harvest/Divest** Specialise niche Consider exit	**Selectivity** Specialise Invest selectively	**Selective Growth** Identify growth area Invest in growth
low	**Harvest/Divest** Attack rivals Time exit	**Harvest/Divest** Prue fines Minimise investments	**Selectivity** Maintain position Seek cash position
		Competitive Strength	

Figure 3.15 GE-McKinsey Matrix Portfolio Interpretation

Six steps are necessary to implement the GE/McKinsey analysis:

1. Determine which factors are relevant for the corporation in the industry where it operates
2. Assign a weight to each factor
3. Score each factor
4. Multiply the relative scores and weights
5. Sum up all and interpret the graph
6. Perform a review / sensitivity analysis

The plotted circles convey the information in the following way:

i. The size of the circle represents the market size of the SBU

ii. The share owned by the SBU is expressed as a pie slice with its relative percentage inside

iii. The expected future direction of the SBU is represented with an arrow

iv. The circles representing SBUs are then placed within the matrix. As a result, the executives of the corporation will have a clear and powerful analytic map for understanding and managing their entire multi-unit business.

v. The units that fall above the diagonal indicate the investment and growth to be pursued; the units along the diagonal require a thorough analysis and individual selection for investment;

vi. Finally the units below the diagonal might indicate divestments are necessary or otherwise that businesses can be kept only for cash reasons. The placement of the units within the matrix is a necessary first step before the analysis phase that requires human judgment can begin. For example, a strong unit in a weak industry is in a very different situation than a weak unit in a highly attractive industry.

Strengths and Weaknesses

The GE/McKinsey Matrix, as an extension of the BCG framework, shares the aforementioned advantages of the BCG model. Though the GE/McKinsey Matrix is more sophisticated than the BCG matrix and can provide higher value information for the executive management, it has several flaws and limitations:

- No proven relationship between market attractiveness and business position.
- The relationships between different units are not taken into account.
- The core-competencies that lead to value creation are not taken into consideration.
- The approach requires extensive data gathering.
- Scoring is personal and subjective (risk of bias)
- There is no hard and fast rule on how to weight elements.
- The GE/McKinsey Matrix offers a broad strategy and does not indicate how best to implement it.

For the above limitations and issues, the GE/McKinsey Matrix can serve more as a quick strategic visual framework rather than as a resource allocation tool.

Application to Competitive Intelligence: Apple Inc.

Apple Inc. is a large technology company with several business units operating in different markets, including desktop computers, laptops, tablet computers (iPads), portable music players (iPods), smartphones (iPhones) and software to support these products. A competitor wishing to gain competitive intelligence on the activities of Apple Inc. could do so by placing its business units into a GE/McKinsey Matrix. By analyzing this matrix, it could determine which business units Apple is likely to invest in heavily, develop selectively or divest.

The market attractiveness axis would be relatively easy for the competitor to assess if it is currently operating in that market, since this consists of factors external to Apple. This includes easily obtainable information such as the current market size and market growth rate. However, some factors would have to be assessed subjectively, such as barriers to entry and the state of technological development.

In contrast, the business unit strength axis would be more difficult to assess since it consists of factors internal to the company, such as customer loyalty, access to resources and management strength. However, a great deal of information could be obtained from secondary sources, such as the Internet, the media and shareholder reports **(Figure 3.16).**

Market Attractiveness / Business Unit Strength	High	Medium	Low
High	**Tables:** The iPad has first mover advantage and a dominant share in a fast-growing market. However, competitors are gaining strength. Release of the iPad 2 in spring 2011 reinforced Apple's position	**Smartphones:** The iPhone trails Nokia and RIM in market share, but this is a high-rwoth market. A new version of the iPhone will likely be released in summer 2011	
Medium	**iTunes:** Dispite the appeal of peer-to-peer sharing, Apple has the dominant position in paid online music purchases. **iPod:** Sales have flattened out, but Apple has the dominant market share	**Laptops:** Apple has strong revenue growth (Apple laptop sales have exceeded desktop sales since 2006)	
Low		**Desktops:** Apple has 8% market share, sales declined from 2008 to 2009 **Peripherals and Software:** Apple sales have been relatively flat; strength comes from custom products to support other Apple devices	

Figure 3.16 Assessment of Apple business units in the GE/McKinsey Matrix

From an assessment of the above GE/McKinsey Matrix, it becomes clear that Apple is at least moderately strong in each of its business units and it competes in a number of attractive and fast-growing segments, such as tablet computers and smart phones. A competitor performing this analysis would realize that Apple is unlikely to divest any of these business units and is likely using its personal computer and music products as cash cows in order to fund R&D and growth in the faster-growing markets. The barriers to entry in all of these markets are considerable, since entry would require a large amount of funding for either R&D or the acquisition of the necessary technology and expertise. If the company performing this analysis decides to compete with Apple, it should do so in the newest, fastest-growing markets (tablets and smart phones), as these represent the areas of greatest opportunity, despite Apple's early dominance.

BCG Matrix vs. GE/McKinsey Matrix

The BCG and the GE/McKinsey analytical models have been created and used for the last 40 years as portfolio analysis frameworks, with the main objective of supporting managers in taking more informed investment and/or divestment decisions. Both models adopt visual frameworks that map internal strategic business units versus predetermined external factors.

Although these models strongly focus on strategic decisions for large corporations, they can also be effectively used in the more comprehensive competitive intelligence environment. Competitive intelligence is often wrongly identified with marketing practices or competitive analysis. Competitive intelligence does not deal only with products and competitors, and it is a broader subject. It can be defined as the action of defining, gathering, analyzing and distributing intelligence about products, customers, competitors and any aspect of the environment needed to support executives and managers in making strategic decisions for an organization.

Going back to the models being analyzed, a few differences have to be considered. The GE/McKinsey Matrix is a far more sophisticated and powerful tool than the BCG Matrix because it takes into consideration more factors to measure the market attractiveness (external factors) and the strength of each SBU (internal factors). In the GE/McKinsey Matrix, market attractiveness and competitive strength substitute the BCG's market growth and market share, respectively.

Another difference is that GE/McKinsey is a 3*3 matrix while the BCG's is a 2*2. This allows for more sophistication. Being more complex, the framework takes a longer time to be implemented since the retrieval of all the necessary information could be lengthy. Because of that, in certain cases corporations can either lose the proper time to market or at the end of the collection process the data could be already old and thus not useful anymore.

Another drawback of the tool is that it could be misleading if not used properly. Assigning weights and scoring factors can be a very difficult work and has to be done by expert hands. When these are not done in the right way, results can lead executives in the wrong direction. Often companies need to rely on external consultant organizations to get the necessary professionalism.

The BCG Matrix's advantage is being a simple and effective tool. The market size of the business unit and the market share of the business under analysis are easily retrievable factors and the framework provides executives with a quick and valuable overview of the SBU's position. The GE/McKinsey and the BCG models can be effectively used in intelligence projects in different ways. Instead of considering only internal SBUs compared to the market, an effective approach would be to use the frameworks in analyzing the competitive landscape. This way, corporations can see where internal SBUs stand compared to competitors.

Ideally, the two tools can be used together in sequence to take advantage of each other's strengths. For example, initially when considering a large number of competitor's products, the BCG Matrix can be adopted as a first step The easy and quick approach that is the main advantage of this model, would let corporations perform a first skim, thus reducing the number of SBUs under analysis from many to just a few. The remaining competitors can be thoroughly analyzed with the GE/McKinsey Matrix, which provides a better and more inclusive framework.

When running intelligence projects, a particular attention should be given to the type and quality of data that is used with these tools. The data has to always be validated with a non-correlated secondary source of information and corporations should tap both into internal and external data to get a broader picture. Below is an example of internal and external sources that could be used:

i. Inside People (Internal to the organization)
ii. Inside Documents (Internal to the organization)
iii. Outside People (External to the organization)
iv. Outside Documents (External to the organization)

SERVICES CONCEPTS

Services have increasingly assumed an important role in the economic development of many countries, including India. Almost all developed countries and many developing countries are emerging as service economics or service. An economy is called a service economy when the contribution of the service sector to the GDP of the nation is more than 50 per cent. USA was the first economy to be declared as a service economy way back in 1948 with about 53 per cent contribution of the services sector to the GDP of the nation. There is an argument that the statistics of the service sector's contribution in many countries is a gross underestimation of the truth, since the value of the services produced by manufactures of goods in the industrial sector is not included in service output value. As such, there is a large 'hidden service sector' that is not classified under the service sector.

Services are becoming a critical source of wealth in many ways to the economics. Economics experienced increase in employment with the growth in service sector. While employment in the manufacturing sector is receding every year, employment in the service sector is rising. Even in times of economic recession, unlike in the manufacturing sector, the services sector has kept employment up.

All human beings are service producers as well as consumers. We cannot imagine our life in the absence of services. Transportation, education, communication, health care, hospitality, entertainment, banking, information technology, electricity and a host of services have become a part of our lives. In fact, the concept of service is as old and humankind and began when man started serving himself (self-servicing) when a part of the society became affluent, it started utilizing the services of others at a price. Then services became a business proposition over the years, services have grown in different ways throughout the world. However, until the beginning of the 20th century, the focus of the economics was to produce more and more tangible goods and sell agricultural and manufactured products. Services such as accounting banking, insurance and transportation were considered as support to the manufacturing units.

In the beginning throughout the world most services were in the public sector. Most organizations enjoyed the status of monopoly. The situations of excessive demand over supply and absence of competition on negligible competition led many service organizations to be insensitive to the marketing concept. The management and the marketing literature developed until the 1970s depicted manufacturing organizations and suggested that the same philosophies and technology be applied to the service organization also.

The deregulation of services in many parts of the world during the early 1980s, particularly in the areas of banking and insurance telecommunications, transportation and health care services, led to intensified competition among various organizations. The growth in size and volume of business and the growing demand made the organizations identify the gap between the available technical support and the support that is required to face the distinctive marketing challenges. The American Marketing Association took up the task of developing marketing technology and organized a series of marketing conferences on themes related to services marketing. One of the prominent works that appeared in the late 1970s was the writings of Lynn Shostack.

In 1977, Lynn Shostack, the then Vice President at Citi Bank, wrote an article "Breaking free from product marketing" in the Journal of marketing. This article influenced the course of thought related to services marketing. She asserted, "New concepts are necessary if service marketing is to succeed merely adopting product marketing's labels does not resolve the questions of whether product marketing can be overlaid on service business. Could marketing itself be 'myopic' in having failed to create relevant paradigms for the service sector?" Since then, efforts are on to develop new concepts, strategies and techniques for handling marketing problems of service organizations.

During the 1980s and later, there has been a huge growth in the number of publications and research reports with empirical base. Several keys issues and concepts were brought forth, including service quality, customer relationship marketing, internal marketing, designing of service packages, interactive marketing, moments of truth, service encounter management, customer evaluation process, customer perceived service quality, service failures and recovery strategies, losses of customer defections and so on.

Differentiating Goods from Services

It is very difficult to draw a clear, demarcating line between goods and services in a marketing offer. According to Theodore Levitt, a renowned marketing specialist, in almost every tangible pure physical product an intangible service component is associated. Therefore, everybody is in service. He classified products into two categories, namely, search goods and experience goods. Search goods are those which are packaged and the customers can see, evaluate and go for a trial before making a purchase. For example, scooters, fans, lock and so on. Experience goods are those which can be evaluated only after purchase and consumption. For example, a holiday, travel and so on. Philip Kotler, one of the world's leading authorities on marketing, classified products into the following five categories foe establishing goods-service relationship.

1. **Pure tangible goods:** These are like commodities that are identical or homogeneous. Differentiating these goods with supplier identity is difficult. Consumers do not attach any specific value to the little service that is associated. Agricultural produce and unbranded goods (mostly from the tiny and small scale sectors fall under this category.
2. **Tangible goods with accompanying services:** In this case consumers give greater weightage to the tangible part of the marketing offer. However, the services accompanying the tangible goods will also become part of the value assessment of the buyers. The buyers will get the title of the tangible goods transferred and get ownership over the goods. The accompanying services, though, accounting for a minor share in the total offer provides competitive advantage to the seller. In the light of significant developments that took place in technology development, most products are unable to find technical advantage on tangible factors and find enormous sources of differentiation in accompanying services. The vast majority of the manufacturing goods fall under this category. The role of services under this category is to support the tangible product. Services are identified and valued only in association with the tangible goods.

3. **Hybrid:** This is a typical marketing offer where the tangible goods and services may be given equal weightage by the consumers. For example, people patronize restaurants for both food and service. However, the proportion or weightage between the goods and service may not be equal in all restaurants though both are important for the consumers. In a five-star hotel, service takes a prominent place when compared to food items, whereas in ordinary restaurants the proportion may be more or less equal. In case of fast food centers, food may take domain position as compared to services. Therefore, there is a possibility of having a hybrid category of products, but it is uncommon to have a significant portion of such products in any economy.

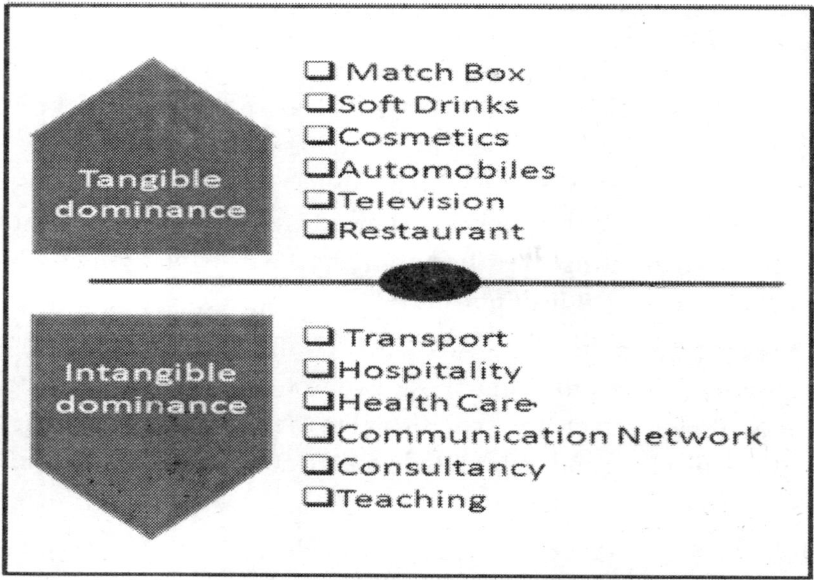

The tangibility spectrum

Figure 3.17

4. **Service with accompanying tangible goods:** This is a marketing offer, in which the intangible part is dominant. People buy service but not the tangible goods involved in the production of services. The accompanying goods play a major role in the value assessment of service by the customer. For example, people buy mobility service from a transport organization. To provide such service transport organizations really need tangibles like buses, trucks, trains, helicopters, aero planes and the like. Although consumers of the mobility service do not buy the tangibles, the condition and so on, will play a major role in assessing the value of the service. The vast majority of the service products fall under this category.

5. **Price service:** Pure service is a marketing offer, where consumers confirm themselves to valuing only the service they receive and nothing else. Service without any support of goods can serve the purpose of the users and is capable of giving satisfaction to the consumers. Teaching, consultancy, idea selling and the like fall under pure service category.

Figure 3.17 presents the tangibility spectrum. It illustrates the goods and services with varied proportion and intangibility

SERVICES DEFINED

The following definitions present the perception of various personalities and associations responsible for contributing significant work over the last four decades, that is, from 1960 onwards, in services management and marketing.

The American Marketing Association (1960) : The American Marketing Association has taken a lead in defining services as "activities, benefits or satisfactions which are offered for sale or provided in connection with the sale of goods "This definition provides a limited view of services. However, this was the first major attempt to identify services differently in valuing the output of a society. The definition does not provide for valuing services involved in producing the tangible goods.

Regan (1963): Regan in his definition classified services into two categories. According to him "services represent either tangibles, yielding satisfaction directly (transport, housing) or intangibles, yielding satisfaction jointly when purchased either with commodities or other services" "credit delivery". An attempt is made through this definition to give a distinctive focus for such services that are offered directly to the consumers as products.

Robert Judd (1964): According to Robert Judd, service is "a market transaction by an enterprise or entrepreneur where the object of the market transaction is other than the transfer of ownership of a tangible commodity". In this definition three broad areas of service are recognized. They are:

1. Right to possess and use a product (rented goods business).
2. The custom creation, repair or improvement of a product (owned product services).
3. No product element, but an experience (non-goods services)

An attempt was made through this definition to give an independent status to more and more services and to focus the attention of the researchers for further development.

William J. Stanton (1974): A comprehensive view of services was provided by Stanton. According to him services are "separately identifiable, activities which provide want satisfaction when marketed to consumers and/or industrial users and which are not necessarily tied to the sale of a product or another service." This definition focuses upon several issues for recognition. They are:

1. Services are those activities that are identifiable separately.
2. Services are intangibles that provide want satisfaction to consumers.
3. Services are marketed directly to consumers and also to the industrial users.
4. Services may or may not be tied with the sale of goods.
5. A service may be or may not be tied with the sale of another service.

Lehtinen (1983): According to Lehtinen a service product is "an activity or a series of activities which take place in interaction with a contact person or a physical machine and which provides consumer satisfaction. "This definition recognizes the services that are provided by machines such as vending machines and ATMs, besides the services provided by the contact persons.

Philip Kotler and Bloom (1984): Philip Kotler and Bloom defined service as "any activity or benefit that one party can offer to another that is successfully intangible and does not result in the ownership of anything its production may or may not be tied to a physical product." This definition more or less follows the earlier ones. The focus was given to the absence of ownership as a special feature of services, which has significant business implications.

Christian Gronroos (1990): According to Gronroos "a service is an activity or series of activities of more or less intangible nature that normally, not necessarily that place in interactions between the customer and service employees and/or physical resources or goods and/or systems of the service provider, which are provided as solutions to customer problems. "This is the definition in which an attempt was made to include all important issues relating to services management.

Zeithmal VA and Mary Jo Bitner (1996): Zeithmal and Bitner said "services are deeds, processes and performances". Although it seems that the definition is more precise, it provides marketing orientation to the services concept. This definition gives an understanding that the consumer is interested in deeds, processes and performances in perceiving the value of the service.

Services may be defined as intangible activities performed by persons or machines or both for the purpose of creating value perceptions among consumers. Since services are intangible activity (ies) or benefit(s) produced by the service provider, in association with the consumer, its quality results in perception and value assessment by the consumer.

SERVICES STRATEGY

Strategic planning entered business in the 1970s when the industry faced several shock waves in succession due to several crises such as energy crisis inflation, severe competition and changing government policy. A strategy is an integrated and coordinated set of commitments and actions designed to exploit core competencies and gain competitive advantage (Michael A. Hitt et. al). A strategy consists of a combination of competitive moves and business approaches that managers employ to please customers compare successfully and achieve organizational objectives (Thompson, Strickland). According to Philip Kotler, market-oriented strategic planning is a managerial process of developing and maintaining a viable fit between organizational objectives, skills and resources and its changing market opportunities. The aim of strategic planning is to shape the company's business and products in such a way that they yield target profit and growth. Thus, strategic planning is oriented to achieve two distinctive and most important objectives of an organization. They are growth in profits and growth in business.

The success or failure of a business mostly depends not only upon the management team's ability in setting a company's long term direction and developing competitively effective strategic moves and approaches, but also on effective execution of strategy. Excellent execution of excellent strategy is the best test of managerial excellence and the most reliable recipe for organizational success (Thompson, Strickland).

STRATEGIC PLANNING PROCESS

There are at least eleven questions that need to be answered accurately to formulate strategies. These are:

- What should be our business?
- What is our business?
- How should the business be developed?
- How should consumers be satisfied?
- How should competition be dealt with?
- What should be the response to the ever changing market conditions?
- How should strategic and financial results be achieved?
- How should the functional units in the organization be managed and coordinated?
- How should relationships with customers, suppliers and other influencers be managed?
- How can stakeholders be satisfied?
- What is value to customers?

It is difficult to answer these questions precisely. Even if satisfactory answers are found at a given point of time, the answers may lose their validity due to dynamic changes in the environment. Thus, organizations should redefine their business propositions and develop new strategies accordingly to achieve desired positions.

STEPS IN STRATEGIC PLANNING PROCESS

There are basically five steps in the strategic planning process of a business unit. They are:

- Business mission
- SWOT analysis
- Strategy formulation
- Strategy implementation
- Strategy evaluation and control

BUSINESS MISSION

The mission is a value statement around which the entire corporate strategy revolves. Peter F. Drucker said that defining the purpose and mission of a business is difficult, painful and risky. But this alone enables a business to set objectives, develop strategies, and concentrates its resources and goes to work. This alone enables a business to be managed by performance. A mission statement defines the scope of the business and long-term vision of an organization. Derek F. Abell has suggested that a company should define its business in terms of these dimensions: who is being satisfied (which consumer groups), what is being satisfied (what consumer needs) and how customers need being satisfied (distinctive competencies) (Derek F Abell) According to McGinnis a mission statement:

- Should define what the organization is and what the organization aspires to be
- Should be limited enough to exclude some ventures and broad enough to allow for creative growth
- Should distinguish a given organization from all others
- Should serve as a framework for evaluating both current and prospective activities
- Should be stated in terms sufficiently clear to be widely understand throughout the future

SWOT Analysis

The most popularly used analysis for relating organizational factors with an environmental factor in order to develop a strategic fit between them is SWOT analysis. The letters S and W represent 'strengths' and 'weaknesses' of the organization. The letters O and T reflect 'opportunities' and 'threats' that are existing or likely to emerge in the environment in relation to the organization.

A critical review of the strengths of the organization helps to identify its core competencies and define them in proper perspective. Strengths are internal competencies which may encompass company image, financial, personnel, marketing, production and R and D resources. The strengths of an organization are often measured against those of its competitors. Weaknesses are those competencies which the company lacks. Deficiencies in competitively important skills and technology, poorly organized functional areas and manpower, poor financial position, weak management and so on are some examples of weaknesses of and organization.

A business environment is a bundle of opportunities owing to the dynamic nature of the environment. The ability to identify and exploit an opportunity shapes the future of any company. The market opportunities most relevant to a company are those that offer important avenues for profitable growth, those where a company has the most potential for competitive advantage and those that match up well with the company's financial and organizational resource capabilities (Thompson and Strickland). Organizations should develop a mechanism to identify, evaluate and rank opportunities existing in the environment, in terms of business attractiveness and suitability to the core competencies.

A dynamic business environment may pose a threat to existing business. The emergence of cheaper or better technologies, the entry of new and better products, new government policy initiatives and changes may spell danger to the existing business.

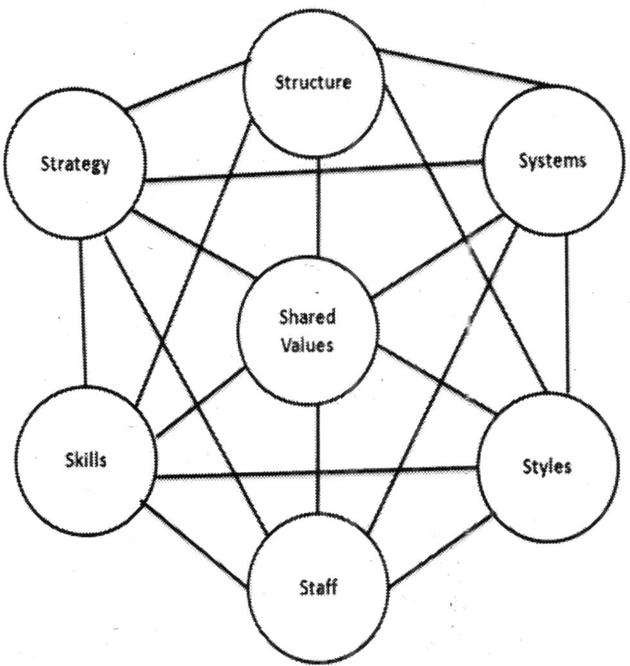

McKinsey 7S Framework

Source McKinsey 7S Framework from In search of Excellence: Lessons from American Best Run Companies

Figure 3.18

Every firm should develop a list of its strengths, weaknesses, opportunities and threats periodically and evaluate all of them in the light of the company's mission. The business unit should have an overall evaluation of opportunities and threats in the external environment and strengths and weaknesses of the internal environment so as to assess the core competencies and their adaptability to the changes in the external environment. Goal formulation for a specific period and listing the objectives in clear terms at various levels of the organization are the next steps to follow.

While goals indicate what a business unit to achieve, strategy is a game plan for the achievement of the goals. The kind of approach the organization pursues towards the achievement of the goal-whether it is the overall cost leadership, product differentiation or a business focus to an altogether new segment-needs to be decided. Besides, the company may also think of strategic alliances with respect to product or service, promotion, logistics and pricing, creative thinking and innovative approach. A specific action plan needs to be developed and executed. The McKinsey 7-S framework (fig. 3.18) suggests the combination of quality variables that ensure successful execution of the action program.

Strategy Formulation

In the formulation of a strategy, it is necessary to take tint consideration the full set of commitments, decisions and actions required for a firm to achieve strategic competitiveness. The SWOT analysis provides necessary strategic inputs for effective strategy formulation and implementation. A company's competitive strategy consists of the business approaches and initiatives it undertakes to attract customer and fulfill their expectations, to withstand competitive pressures and strengthen its market position (Thompson and Strickland).

In the words of Michael Porter, competitive strategy is about being different. It means deliberately choosing to perform activities different or to perform different activities than those of rivals to deliver a unique mix of value. Porter suggested five district competitive strategies which will benefit service organizations. These competitive strategies are (a) low cost provider strategy (b) differentiation strategy (c) best cost provider strategy (d) focused strategy (market niche) based on lower cost and (e) focused strategy (market niche) based on differentiation.

Low-cost provider strategy

Under this approach the company strikes to become a low-cost provider of service when compared to the competitors and appeals to the broad spectrum of customers. The strategy basically intends to attract many price sensitive buyers.

Differentiation strategy

Differentiation strategies are the most used strategies by the service organizations. One of the characteristics of the service, that is, variability, provides an opportunity to the service provider to pursue a differentiation strategy for each and every customer and thereby provide enhanced value perceptions. It is one of the most powerful competitive strategies for service firms. By pursing this they can move ahead of the competitions. The essence of a differentiation strategy is to be unique in ways that are valuable to customers (Thompson and Strickland). The service differentiating features are generally easy to copy for competitive firms. Therefore, service organizations are in a disadvantage position to achieve sustainable competitive advantage by way of differentiation. Innovation is the key for service differentiation. The most important way through which service firms can achieve differentiation advantage over competition is innovation. Peter F. Drucker said that most innovative business ideas come from methodically analyzing listing seven areas of opportunity, some of which lie within particular companies or industries and some of which lie in broader social or demographic trends. Astute managers will ensure that their organizations maintain a clear focus on all seven. But analysis will take you only so far. Once you have identified an attractive opportunity, you still need a leap of imagination to arrive at the right response called 'functional inspiration'. Innovations require knowledge, ingenuity and above all else, focus.

The seven sources of innovation are:

1. Unexpected occurrences
2. Incongruities
3. Process needs
4. Industry and market changes
5. Demographic changes
6. Changes in perception
7. New knowledge

New ideas are the first basic foundation for innovation. Theodore Levitt observed that a powerful new idea can lie around unused in a company for years, not because its merits are not recognized but because nobody has assumed the responsibility for converting it from words into action. What is often lacking is not creativity in the idea creating sense but innovation in the action producing sense that is, putting ideas to work. All in all, creation of ideas is relatively abundant; it is the implementation that is more scarce. Service firms need to search continuously for new ideas from the people within the organization and the sources outside such as customers, competitors and research institutes. Firms also need to design an institutional framework with an ability to transform an idea an innovative offer. Service firms are prone to competitive threats and surprising challenges owing to the dynamic environment they encounter. The right strategy therefore to reach the consumers, overtaking competitors, is to offer additional innovative value (AIV). When competitors are at par with the company in terms of financial, technological and human resources, it is innovation that provides the competitive edge. Thus, service firms must necessarily make innovation and institutional process on a continuous basis, in order to achieve profit as well as growth objectives.

Best cost provider strategy

Providing more value for the money customers pay for the service is the aim of this strategy. Service firms will focus on providing key service quality features and performance attributes in such a way that they exceed customer expectations, in relation to price. Organization should work for achieving cost efficiency in various service process attributes and strive to achieve excellent quality of service at a lower cost than competitors Christian Gronroos pointed out that improved productivity of resources-labour as well as capital- and better internal efficiency should always be an objective and new technology and production processes that save costs should be used. The main point here is that such internal developments have to be based on the characteristics of services, so that the relationships between the internal and external effects are taken into account. He emphasized that all costs are not equal. On the country, there is pivotal difference between various types of costs that have to be taken into account when strategic and operational decisions about efficiency, productivity and cost savings are considered.

John Carlson and his advisers classified costs into two categories-goods costs and evil costs, while initiating the turnaround process of the Scandinavian Airlines. Goods costs are such costs that are directly productive and improve the capabilities of a service organization to produce high quality services. The focus particularly is on improvement of buyer-seller interactions. Generally, in service organizations, the costs involved in maintaining frontline operations, support operations, training, physical goods required for service production and delivery and so on are considered as good costs. Goods costs are to be promoted in service organizations because the costs contribute for improved quality perceptions by the consumers and result in consumer satisfaction. Evil costs are non-productive costs that may not improve buyer-seller interactions but may affect adversely the quality of service to the customers. Costs involved in unnecessary operational and administrative routines, too many and too heavy management levels, unnecessary bureaucracy and supervision costs are example of evil costs in service organizations. The classification of costs by indentifying good costs and evil costs helps service organizations to initiate cost-saving action.

Focused (market niche) strategy based on low cost

Focused marketing or niche marketing is to identify subgroups within a broad market segment that has a distinctive set of traits and may seek a special combination of benefits. Niches are smaller and generally attract very few competitors. Service organizations focusing on niche markets find an opportunity to direct their limited resources for providing a relatively small group of consumers. Service firms may follow a strategy of serving the consumers in niche market at a cost lower than their competitors by providing comparable or better quality service.

Focused (market niche) strategy based on differentiation

The aim of this focused strategy is to do a better job serving buyers in the target market niche. When a company identifies a substantial group with well-defined desires, requiring special service attributes and quality levels, this strategy is capable of earning rich dividends.

MARKET-ORIENTED SERVICE STRATEGY

In designing strategy, service firms need to differentiate themselves from manufacturing organizations. They have to take market sensitivities in relation to service characteristics into consideration in deciding the strategic approach to achieve organizational goals. The conventional managerial thinking provides three thumb rules for strengthening the competitive edge of firm. The three rules are: decrease in the cost of production, enhancement of promotion budget and development of new products. Manufacturing firms believed and also achieved positive results by adopting the three distinctive strategies on the marketing front. However, if the three, time tested and proven, marketing strategies are applied to the services it is more likely the service organizations get into further trouble. Gronoors has described this as the 'strategic management trap'. Service firms need to watch for the conditions that lead to the strategic management trap and develop abilities to avoid the use of traditional arsenal and design a service-oriented marketing strategy.

Strategic Management Trap

When service firms choose to follow the traditional strategic approaches to face marketing problems, they may not be successful due to non applicability of such strategies to the specific and distinctive characteristics of services and their marketing. Fig. 3.19 illustrates the consequences of traditional strategies when used to solve services marketing problems let us assume that the service organizations is facing either financial problems or increased competition or both. The first option for the management of the service organization as per the traditional input is to focus upon cost control devices and through that, achieve internal efficiency. The decisions on internal efficiency often result in reduction of personnel, introduction of self service, increase in the work load of employees, automation (replacement of personnel by machines) and so on. In the manufacturing sector such decisions may improve productive efficiency, reduce the cost of production and may even improve the quality of goods. But in a service organization, the chances of such happenings are rare. Of course, such decisions definitely result in some marginal cost savings, but the consequences result in the deterioration of service quality. Let's suppose a person in an enquiry counter of an organization was required to attend to the calls of two telephones. He/she may have lot to freedom and comfort to attend to the calls and when a call is required, he/she may start with greetings, make enquiries for additional information from the caller, offer choices and suggestions and conclude with thanks. The employee will have ample time to clearly understand what the consumer wanted to communicate, to show empathy and to create an environment through which the consumer prefers to continue the relationship with the company.

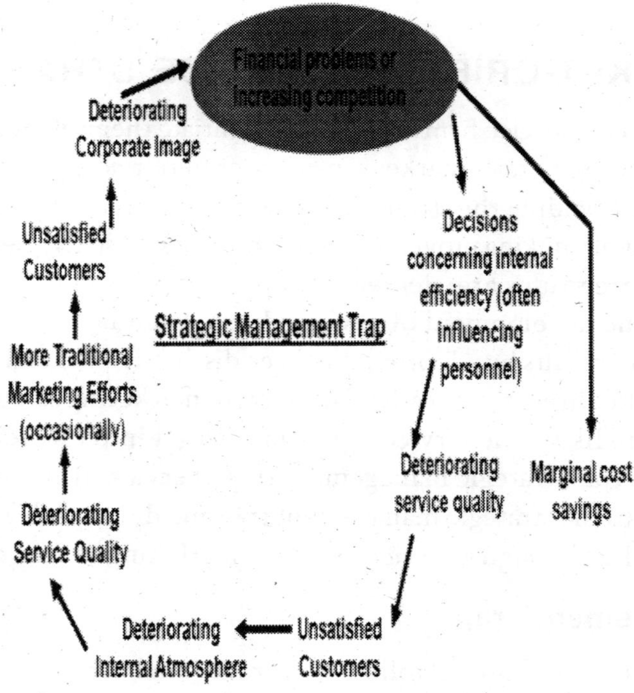

Figure 3.19

Consider, if as a cost reduction strategy the same employee is provided with five telephones to attend customer calls. The employee still has the capability of attending to the phones. But, the freedom and comfort enjoyed earlier disappears and the intention would be to reduce the call time. In the process insufficient information, miscommunication and many deficiencies in the interaction might result. Further, the quality of the service deteriorates and the customers get dissatisfied. The interactive personnel of a service firm who encounter comments, criticisms, aggression, irritation and unpleasant feeling of the customers due to deterioration in service quality become de-motivated. They cannot involve themselves in the service activity because of the unpleasant interactive environment. As a result, the internal atmosphere of the organization deteriorates, resulting in further deterioration of service quality.

When a service organization chooses the second strategy of spending heavily on promotion with an intention to attract the market, it may succeed in increasing the demand for services. However, the reduced internal efficiency dissatisfies the customers. As a result of all these activities, the corporate image of the organization weakens and the problems of the company multiply. When the image of the organization is low, even the introduction of a new product does not save the organization. A vicious circle gets formed when once the organization gets into the strategic management trap and it leads to multiple problems.

The basic question here is why do conventional wisdom and guidelines of the manufacturing sector not help in solving the marketing problems of service organizations? The reason is obvious: service organizations are different; they have certain characteristics of their own. The productivity of capital and labour and internal efficiency factors alone do not drive profit in a service organization. On the other hand, customer perceived service quality drives profit.

Service-oriented Approach

Service organization should develop a service-oriented strategic approach to tackle problems in marketing. The results of a service oriented strategic approach to handle the same problems illustrated earlier are shown in fig. 3.20. A service organization should focus on improving buyer-seller interactions, of course with cost control. As mentioned in the earlier paragraphs, necessary steps need to be initiated to control evil costs in the organization. The operations that influence or affect buyer-seller interactions need to be strengthened further. Such measures will lead to improved perceived service quality by the customers. Improvement in physical environment, infrastructure and systems and so on, will not only increase the level of satisfaction to the customer but also influence the contact employees positively. Employees show interest in interacting with the customers. At the same time the corporate image also improves. The more satisfied customers and the enhanced corporate image will result in increased sales volumes. The positive atmosphere, thus developed, will further improve buyer-seller interactions and the new cycle of growth continues.

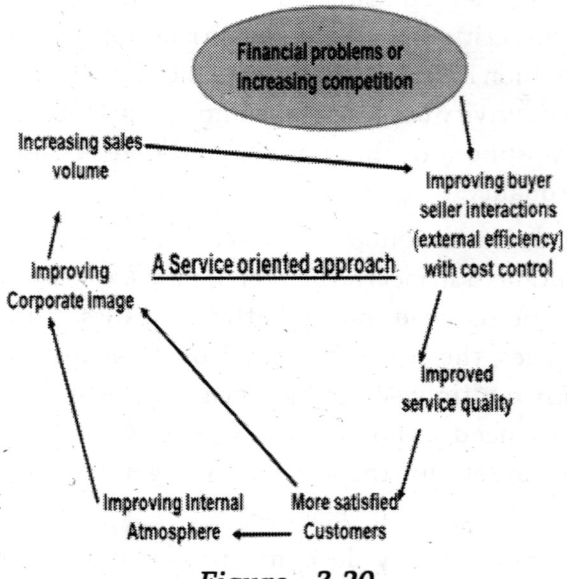

Figure 3.20

THE SERVICE TRIANGLE

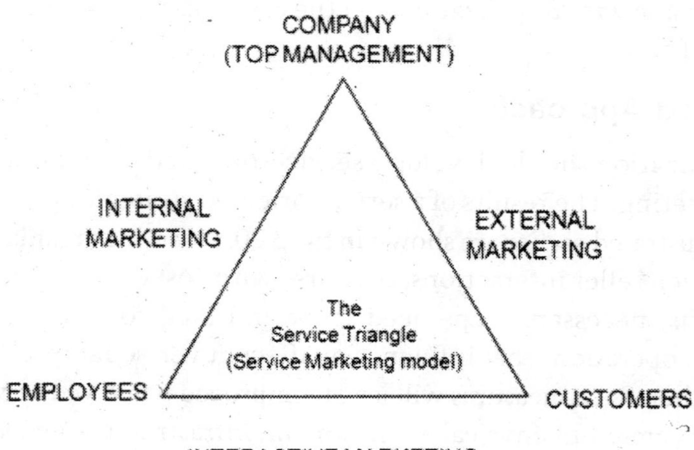

Figure 3.21

One of the most popular strategic models for services marketing was developed by Christian Gronroos. The model is called the service triangle Fig. 3.21 presents the services marketing model. Gronroos has identified three important groups that play critical roles in successfully accomplishing organizational goals. They are company (top management) employees and the customers. The model proposes a three-dimensional approach for the development of the overall marketing strategy. It suggests the design of three marketing programmers as the integral parts of the services marketing programme. The model calls for a special marketing programme between the company and its employees which is termed internal marketing. The second marketing programme is between the company and its customers and is termed external marketing. The third marketing programme is between employees and customers and is termed interactive is between employees and customers and is termed interactive marketing.

Internal Marketing

The role of employees in service marketing cannot be over-emphasized. An efficient and well motivated employee performs well even when there are some failures in the design systems and support services. On the other hand, an inefficient and de-motivated employee may not perform well in spite of support from all departments. The concept of internal marketing suggests that the philosophy of the management should be to satisfy its employees first. The employees shall be viewed as the first market for the service organization to serve. Proper pay, promotion and other benefit packages are to be designed to meet their expectations. Steps should also be initiated to motivate employees and promote their morale. The ultimate goal in internal marketing is to prepare the employee to serve the customers with motivation and commitment.

External Marketing

Customers are the co-products of service. Without their involvement, a service output cannot be qualitative. Therefore, it is the responsibility of the service firm to prepare the customer to receive the service in the right perspective. The major tasks are customer education about the features or the service, preparations required and the mindset and the kind of expectations to be developed. The limitations and other problems (or possible problems) if any, in the process of service production and consumption should also be mentioned. The customers need to play an active role in the service production process. If necessary, consumers should be given training so as to promote qualitative participation and high level of customer perceived quality. The ultimate aim of external marketing is to prepare the customer to participate in the service production and consumption, simultaneously and efficiently.

Interactive Marketing

Internal marketing and external marketing prepare the stage for actual interaction between employees and customers. The interaction between employees and service firms and their customers are also called 'service encounters'. This is an important phrase in services marketing. The service process needs to be facilitated between the two parties, with adequate support services, tangibles, systems, techniques and other support materials.

The goal of interactive is to facilitate efficient production and consumption process and to create positive and satisfactory experiences, if possible, for both customers and employees.

THREE DIMENSIONS OF MARKETING STRATEGY

Marketing is ultimately responsible for customer relationships. New organizational forms suggest that the role of marketing in the firm continues to evolve. Marketing managers no longer focus only on those activities that will facilitate a sale or on methods of achieving product differentiation, brand familiarity and loyalties for repeated sales. The new manager will negotiate a mutually beneficial relationship with customers, investing in projects that heighten the dependence of buyer and seller on each other, jointly exploring new technologies, sharing resources and developing new products and markets together.

The three dimensions of marketing, described by Webster-culture, strategy and tactics-aptly applies to services marketing (Fig.3.22).

The basic set of values and beliefs of the customers should guide an organization to formulate its corporate philosophy. An analysis of customer needs must be the basic input material for designing market attractiveness strategies. The culture thus evolved from the market feedback should reflect the overall value proposition of the company. A strategic orientation to divide the market into segment and to identify target markets is an absolute necessity. Market positioning of the service package is the other strategic proposition.

Three Dimensions of marketing

Figure 3.22

SERVICE-ORIENTED ORGANIZATION STRUCTURE

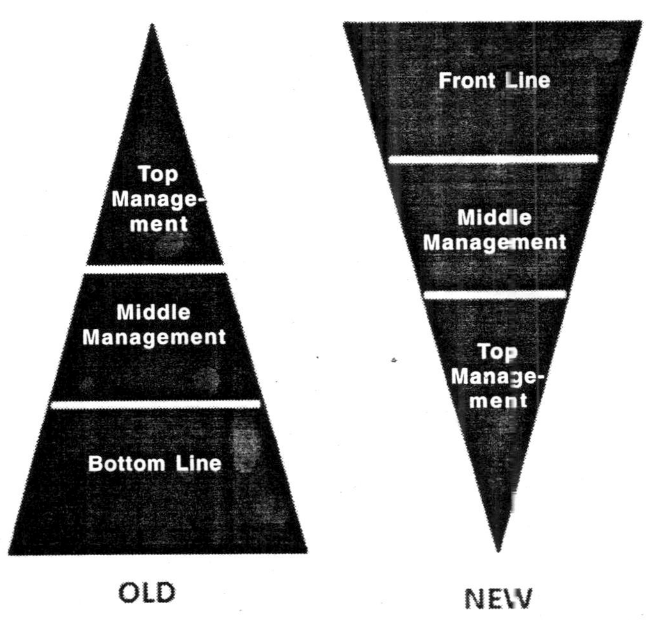

Figure 3.23

No service organization should have a large number of hierarchical levels or be unnecessarily bureaucratic. Market orientation requires more thoroughly understood and accepted responsibility for customers and the authority to take actions to serve them. The management should not be involved directly at the operational level decision-making. It should extend strategic support and resources necessary to pursue a service strategy. Fig. 3.23 shows the required shift in the organization structure of a service firm.

In a traditional military structure top management is far away from reality. Though the components of the pyramids are almost the same, the priorities are changed. Turning the pyramid upside down demonstrates the fact that the top management is not the apex level of the pyramid and the part of the organization structure that immediately determines whether the strategy of the firm will be a success or failure. It is the frontline, which includes personnel, physical resources and operational systems, interacting with the customers. The frontline people take most of the decisions relating to the basic service package (BSP) to be offered to each customer against the need patterns. The performance of the frontline decides the success or failure of the organization. The other managerial parts of the organization should facilitate the frontline, for efficient performance in buyer-seller interactions.

SERVICES MARKETING MIX

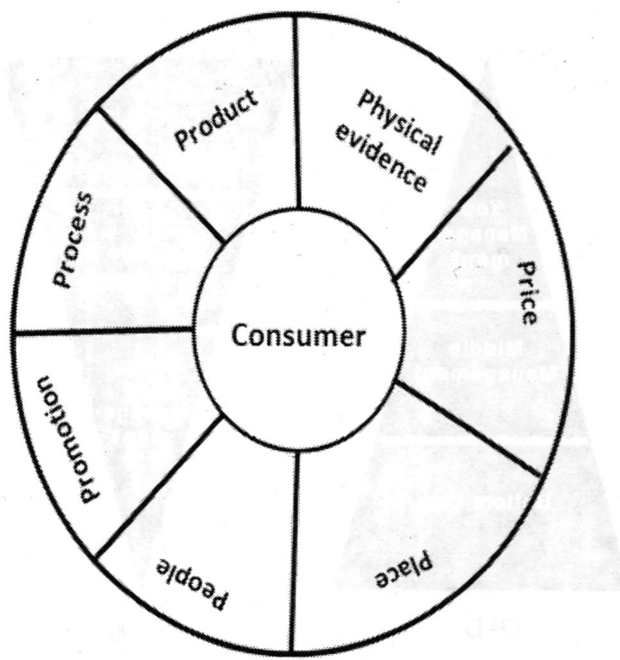

Figure 3.24

Service characteristics add too many challenges in the market place over goods marketing mix that was developed, keeping in view the goals of marketing, may also be adapted to services marketing. But the service organizations cannot satisfy themselves with the use of the traditional marketing mix as they are to stay at sub-optimal performance in marketing. Merely adopting marketing labels cannot resolve problems associated with the marketing of services. The four P's of traditional marketing mix (product, price, place and promotion) are controllable variables. It is believed that an effective combination of these four components will make an organization have a competitive edge in getting preference by the target market. Marketing researchers have well identified the limitations and insufficiencies of the traditional marketing mix if applied to services also, Booms and Bitner suggested in 1981, a seven P's marketing mix model to service firms. The seven P's were later supported by McGrath and other marketing specialists.

The marketing mixes for service organization are product, physical evidence, price, place, promotion and process. Fig. 3.24 exhibits the marketing mix of service. Thus, there are three additional components-physical evidence, people and process in the services marketing mix.

Components of the Services Marketing Mix

Product

Service is an intangible product. It consists of a bundle of features and benefits that have relevance to a specific target market. As such, there is a high level of flexibility and opportunity to be innovative in designing a product offer.

Physical evidence

Most services cannot be offered without the support of tangibles. Though customers cannot see the service, they can definitely see the tangibles associated, examine them and try to form an opinion on the service provider. Thus, a passenger transport organization's promise of a safe, comfortable and timely journey from one place to another will be examined by the transport vehicle's condition, seating facilities and other physical facilities, the personality of the driver and other personnel, the office furniture and equipment being used and also the way in which the employees are responding to customers. All these physical objects are used as evidence by the customer to assess and expert performance from the service provider. Hence, physical evidence plays a critical role in shaping consumer perceptions and also expectations.

Price

The pricing decision is a critical one in service too, as this firm consumer sensitivity to price would be higher in services than in goods. Though the basic methods of pricing are the same as in goods, the pricing strategies for services basically depends upon value perceptions of various groups of people that are targeted by the organization.

Place (distribution)

Services are intangible as well as inseparable. These two characteristics do not allow a service firm to follow the same channel options available for goods marketing. Due to the intangible character of service, traditional wholesalers and retailers cannot be used. As service cannot be stored and cannot be separated from producers, retailing cannot be an independent activity in services marketing. Production, distribution and consumption are simultaneous activities in services. However, services have an advantage of using a direct selling approach, through which services can be offered to the customer at a lower cost. This does not mean direct selling is the only way of selling the services. There are certainly other channels of distribution such as agents and brokers, franchisers and electronic channels that are used for distribution of services.

People

Service organizations are people-oriented and people-based organizations. Employees of a service firm constitute the major competency in undertaking business operations. Every employee of the service organization is a marketing person, who undertakes either fulltime or part-time marketing activity. Whether an employee is involved in direct contact with the customer or not, if he was placed on the line of visibility, his behavior, activities and performance will have a direct influence on consumers. Service employees are to be trained and motivated for better performance in marketing activities.

Promotion

Consumers are co-producers in the services business, the quality of services will not only depend upon the performance of the service provider but also on the performance of the service consumer. Very few service organization or service concepts can have readily available mature performers as consumers. It is the responsibility of service organizations to educate and if necessary, train customers so as to make them prepared to use the services efficiently. A well designed promotional programme is of immense help to organization to inform, persuade and train customers to better their experiences.

Process

Process is a functional activity that assures service availability and quality. The way the physical setting is designed technically and how the functions are scheduled and routed to provide promised services to the customers speaks of the efficiency of the process. In simple terms the management of process is to manage service encounters (the interaction between service employees and customers and service environment, systems and other facilities) effectively. Gronroos has described process as interactive marketing wherein moments of truth occur. The challenge of process management is to improve the moment of truth.

The seven P's of services marketing become the marketing offer of the organization to the target market. The marketing mix aims to achieve seven distinctive goals. They are matching the offer to the consumer needs and wants, consumer quality expectations, consumer perceptions, consumer satisfaction, consumer relationships, customer welfare and protection and societal well-being. The dynamic nature of the target market in all the seven distinctive areas offers to marketing organizations. Service firms can be successful only when they make all the marketing mix elements dynamic and adaptable to the changes in the market environment.

STRATEGY IMPLEMENTATION

The development of a good marketing of a good marketing strategy alone does not yield results. Implementation of the strategy is equally important. Strategies like a blue print indicate various courses of action to achieve desired objectives. Fred R. David rightly pointed out that strategy formulation is operational in character. Strategy formulation requires good conceptual, integrative and analytical skills but strategy implementation requires special skills in motivating and managing others. Strategy formulation occurs primarily at the corporate level of an organization, while strategy implementation permeates all hierarchical levels. Strategy formulation requires coordination among few individuals but strategy implementation requires coordination among many. Operational sing the strategy requires transcending various components of the strategy to different levels; mobilization and allocation of resources; structuring authority, responsibility, tasks and information flows; establishing policies; and evaluation and control (Francis Chernilam).

Effective implementation of strategies requires resource strengths and organizational capabilities. Service firms need to link the budget to the strategy and develop strategy and develop strategy support to policies and procedures. The best practices in internal management need to be initiated and a commitment among all the people for continuous improvements has to be promoted. For the purpose, whatever support systems are required have to be arranged to improve the performance of the people and reward system should be directed for the support of strategy implementation. Above all a right kind of corporate culture and strategic leadership need to be nurtured and develop for achieving the desired results.

STRATEGY EVALUATION AND CONTROL

Strategy evaluation at various levels of its implementation is essential to identify the deviators, if any, at an appropriate time and to initiate corrective action. There may be many hurdles in the process of strategy implementation, internally and externally. Some new problems may arise due to the implementation of the strategy and some problems may emerge to unexpected changes in the environment. Service firms have to exercise strategic surveillance for timely detection of such developments and take necessary corrective action. For the purpose of evaluation and control, an effective system that provides the following has to be designed:

- Establishment of evaluation criteria and standards
- Measuring and comparing performance
- Identification and analysis of performance gaps
- Initiating corrective measures

Service firms generally prefer preventive control rather than direct control of the system. Since service quality mostly depends upon the quality of the service personnel, the higher the quality of the personnel, the lesser will be the need for direct control. Preventive control systems aim at development of better personnel, capable of applying concepts, principles and techniques skillfully and with involvement. With the application of preventive control, support personnel and frontline employees know what is expected of them; they develop the ability to understand their levels of performance through measurement techniques and reorient themselves with the required changes in their approach.

CLOSING CASE: MARKETING OF EDUCATIONAL SERVICES

Sharada Educations institute is one of the few management institutes started early in the 1960s in India. The institute was regarded by many as one of the premier management institutes in the country. The old students of the institute occupied very important positions in the government and private enterprises within as well as outside the country. The strengths of the institute are: qualified teaching staff and infrastructure. The established image of the institution draws crowds for admission into the course. Mr. Parasuraman the newly appointed director of the institute was happy with the running of the institute. Demand management was not the problem. In spite of the mushrooming of a number of institutes at university and private levels, the number of candidates seeking admission was several times more than the seats available Mr. Parasuraman, however, recognized the number of applications was falling at a slow rate for the last five years.

When he pointed this out to some of the senior faculty, they discounted the factor as an effect of increased competition. Besides the demand issue, there are many more things that cause concern to the director.

1. Class work is not properly conducted.
2. Absenteeism among students is very high.
3. Teachers give more importance to research guidance, consultancy and extension services.
4. Placement cell is dormant.
5. Enthusiastic participation is absent, both from faculty and students.
6. Teacher-student relationships are neither positive nor negative.
7. The facilities offered by the institute are not used by the faculty and students to the optimum level.

Mr. Parasuraman certainly was not happy with these identifications. He wanted to rebuild the institute. He did not want to hang on to an image of the institute of yesteryears. He sensed that if something constructive was not done by him, the institute is certainly going to face some very serious problems in the future.

Mr. Parasuraman initiated the efforts. He talked to teachers, who expressed their wholehearted cooperation in this effort. He got the same promise of cooperation from the students, Mr. Parasuraman offered all supporting facilities liberally.

The director reasonably expected that there would be some improvement. He reviewed the condition after a month. There was no improvement at all. He talked informally again with both the students and the faculty. The teachers informally complained that students are not there though they are ready to take up the classes. On the other hand students complained that the teachers are not coming to the classes. Both the parents are not willing to give a formal complaint to the director on the issue.

Mr. Parasuraman realized that a serious attempt is required for the purpose. As a first step he started understanding the developments in the institute over a period of time. After a thorough analysis he found that the following factors are important:

1. Increase in the number of teaching faculty. Work load per teacher has reduced from 12 hours a week to 6 hours a week.
2. Increase in research, consultancy and extension services of the faculty.
3. Change in the qualification of the students-the percentage of engineering graduates getting admission has increased each year.
4. Promotion to a higher position at young age.

However, the director could not find anything about placement as there was no record available in this respect. Having gone through all these details, the director decided to refer this case to a marketing professional. This director thought that external consequences needed to be emphasized more to take corrective actions. Marketing orientation is required to strengthen and develop the institution.

Question:

1. Suppose this case is referred to you then how would you help Mr. Parasuraman?
2. How will you implement the services strategies in this institution to become competitive?
3. Organize a role play discussing the possible outcomes in the class.

SUMMARY & KEY TERMS

The mission of the business unit and the business is very much reflected by its Product strategies. The choice of product strategy should bear a close relationship to the market strategy of the company by following the marketing concept. The various product strategies and the alternatives under each strategy that were discussed in this chapter are outlined below:

1. Product-positioning strategy
2. Product-repositioning strategy
3. Product-overlap strategy
4. Product-scope strategy
5. Product-design strategy

6. Product-elimination strategy
7. New-product strategy
8. Diversification strategy
9. Value marketing strategy

In the above stated various product strategies the nature of different strategies was discussed and their relevance for different types of companies was examined. Service organization need to follow a strategic approach for the achievement of organizational goals. The traditional path followed by manufacturing organizations in strategic planning may not be suitable to service organizations as business parameters and consumer behavior are different in services and goods. When service companies follow the traditional thumb rule, there is a danger of getting into a strategic management trap. Services companies need to consider distinctive strategic options to face challenges in the market. Cost effectiveness is important but judicious categorization of good costs and evil costs is necessary to reduce or eliminate evil costs. Frontline employees should be empowered to take spot decisions accurately. Therefore, the organizational structure has to be changed suitably to facilitate frontline employees function efficiently. The service marketing triangle focusing on internal marketing, external marketing and interactive marketing provides a model for designing organizational policies and practices towards achievement of organizational objectives.

The marketing mix of services consists of seven P's In addition to the four P's of the traditional marketing mix; services marketing mix will have three additional components: physical evidence, people and process. Services firms should make the elements of marketing mix dynamic as well as adaptable to changes in the marketing environment. A marketing strategy formulated in accordance with the organizational goals need to be implemented with efficiency. Service firms should acquire resources and build organizational capabilities for effective implementation. Evaluation and control of the strategy is essential for effective execution and also for further development. Strategic surveillance is necessary for the purpose.

The BCG matrix is a chart that had been created by Bruce Henderson for the Boston Consulting Group in 1968 to help corporations with analyzing their business units or product lines. The BCG matrix considers two variables, namely:

1. Market growth rate
2. Relative market share

The GE/McKinsey Matrix was developed jointly by McKinsey and General Electric in the early 1970s as a derivation of the BCG Matrix. GE, by that time, had approximately 150 different business units and was disappointed with the profits derived from its investments. The GE-McKinsey Matrix is a nine-cell (3 by 3) matrix used to perform business portfolio analysis as a step in the strategic planning process. The GE/McKinsey Matrix identifies the optimum business portfolio as one that fits perfectly to the company's strengths and helps to exploit the most attractive industry sectors or markets.

For a marketing plan to be successful it is essential that all elements of the marketing mix should support each other. Marketing mixes will change between products, services and market situations and indeed this is what makes marketing dynamic; it is the skill of the individual marketing person in manipulating the individual mixes that can make a product or service a success or a failure. Different emphasis to individual elements in the marketing mix are often called for. However, the product or service is particularly important in this calculation for this is the tangible element that will appeal to customers and it is upon this that customer' purchases and repeat purchases are based.

The product line is a group of closely related product items. The width of the product mix denotes the number of product lines carried. The depth of the mix denotes the range of items within each line and is calculated by dividing the total number of items carried by the number of lines.

The notion of the product life cycle is almost as old as the subject of marketing. Various stages are proposed which show that a product passes through a number of stages in its life from the time it is conceived (the development phase) to the time it is deleted during the decline stage. Marketing people have found it to be a useful planning tool and this point is expanded shortly. Marketing academics (notably, Dallah and Yuspeh) have, therefore, criticized the concept on the basis that when a product is launched it is often killed off prematurely because sales suggest that it has gone into a quick decline, whereas the reality is that what they are is probably only a slight hiccup in the growth curve of the product.

Product category life cycles describe a generic product like soap or shoes. Life cycles here tend to be long or infinite. Product from life cycles describe the type of product like perfumed soap or plastic shoes. Here the life cycle is shorter. Brand life cycles describe the various manufacturers' brands of perfumed soap or plastic shoes. This might, in the case of plastic shoes, be linked to a single fashion season with a new brand coming out shortly afterwards, so this kind of life cycle is the shortest of all.

Innovative Strategies deals with the firm rate of new product development and business model innovation. A product line is a group of products that are closely related because they function in a similar manner, are sold to the same customer groups, are marketed through the same types of outlets, or fall within given price ranges.

KEY TERMS

- Product strategies
- OEMs
- Harvesting
- Divestment
- Competitive Teardown
- Product innovation
- Business portfolio
- Product strategies
- Fast Moving Consumer Goods (FMCG)
- SWOT analysis
- Good cost
- Internal marketing
- Business Mission
- Strategic management trap
- Boston Consulting Group Matrix (BCG)
- Market penetration
- Market Development
- Product Development
- GE-Mckinsey Matrix

DISCUSSION QUESTIONS

1. Conceptualize how a lagging brand (assume a grocery product) may be repositioned for new uses.
2. What conditions justify a company's dealing in multiple brands?
3. Explain the concept of product and also the strategies relevance for different types of companies.
4. Discuss the various steps in the strategic planning process. Explain its importance and process in a service company
5. How do service companies get into strategic management trap? What suggestions do you offer for getting out of the trap?
6. What is services marketing mix? Explain the components of the marketing mix

7. Illustrate strategic planning process by taking a service organization.
8. Explain the meaning of Product and categories of products.
9. Describe the process of new product development.
10. Differentiate between Product Mix and Product Line.
11. Explain in detail the Product Life Cycle (PLC).
12. Write short notes on :
    a. Innovation Strategies
    b. Product line extension
    c. Ansoff Matrix
13. Explain BCG and GE Mckinsey Matrix with examples.

OPENING CASE: EAST-WEST AIRLINES

The airlines industry in India is primarily for the transport of passengers though it has made some progress in airfreight too. The history of civil aviation in India dates back to 1929-1930 when the British, the Dutch and the French introduced international routes extending services in India. In 1932, J.R.D. Tata, father of Indian aviation, introduced the first Indian air service between Madras and Karachi once a week to transport mail. In 1934, the service increased to twice a week while a new company called Indian National Airways was set up by another group in 1933. In 1937, Tata sons started weekly services between Bombay and Delhi via Indore, Gwalior and Bhopal.

With the declaration of World War II, the above two air services came into the hands of the government and were used for defence services. After World War II, civil aviation got a boost and in 1946, the India Airways Act was amended to make it obligatory for new entrants to get permission and license to operate new services. Within two years eleven licenses were granted to various companies. In the International sector, Air India International was formed with the authorized capital of two crores, in which the government subscribed 49%, Air India International 10%, and the public the remaining capital.

Meanwhile, air companies started winding up due to poor performance, intense competition and deep financial crisis due to excess capacity. The Government appointed an inquiry committee in 1950. On the basis of its report, the government decided to bring air transport under its control. Accordingly, the Air Corporation Bill was placed before the Parliament on April 26, 1953. The Act was adopted on May 14, 1953. It provided for setting up of Indian Airlines and Air India by amalgamating the remaining private airlines.

OPEN SKY POLICY

Although there has never been a ban on operating air taxis, the big boom in this business has come only after the government announced the Open Sky Policy in April 1990. The year1993 has seen remarkable changes in civil aviation in India. The new policy permits air taxis to operate fromal 93 airports open to scheduled operations, which were restricted to only 55 earlier. The seating capacity ceiling of 50 has been removed. The restriction to operate flights two hours before or after flights of the national carriers has been removed. Under the new policy, use of multi-engine fixed wing aircraft is allowed for operation and NRIs allowed importing aircrafts using their own foreign exchange reserves, provided they set up 100% Indian companies. This policy has yielded rich dividends, with many NRIs starting new ventures.

The parliamentary committee on transport and tourism, consisting of 15 Rajya-Sabha members and 45 Lok-Sabha members submitted a report on the Government policy on private air taxis. The committee recommended changes in the government policies and amendment of Air Corporations Act 1953. The committee, while criticizing the government's confused civil aviation policy, alerted it to clearly define the role of DGCA, national and private air taxis, and enact a new law if necessary. The committee noted that the private air taxis are facing a number of problems, which are hampering their smooth functioning. They are not allowed to publish their departure schedules in the print media, discriminated against in providing space and adequate facilities in airports and not permitted to lift domestic air cargo. Private air taxi operates say a policy allowing utilization of the valuable Indian Airlines services and maintenance facilities by them would arrest outflow of foreign exchange. The committee recommended that Air India and Indian Airlines should have interlined agreement with air taxi operators to carry their passengers to their destinations. It also recommended credit facilities to private air taxis for aviation fuel against bank guarantee. However, the committee sounded an alert on overcrowding of trunk routes, as that may prove unhealthy for all.

While efforts are on by the government to deal with the issues, the private air taxis operators formed an association and started bringing pressure on the government to take necessary steps for the healthy growth of airline industry. Their demands, to quote a few, are: speedy repeal of Air Corporations Act 1953 to avail the passenger the full benefits of the government's liberalized aviation policies, lifting of the condition to fly 700 km of non-profitable routes for every 2500 km of flying and lifting the ban on advertising schedules.

The people or the customers are the key figures in the marketing of services. Sometimes service may be coupled with a product. For marketing purposes, four categories of offers can be distinguished. They are:

1. Tangible good - such as toothpaste, soap.
2. Tangible good with service - here service is an appeal to the customer, e.g., automobile.
3. A master service accompanied by a minor good - here service is accompanied by additional service and/or supporting good, e.g., airline travel.
4. A pure service - it is primarily a service, e.g., physiotherapy massages.

Services can be equipment based or people based. Airline is a mixture of both aircraft as an equipment and crew and ground staff as people that make the service effective. If either of the two fails, then the service fails. Similarly, one service may require client presence while another can be rendered without client presence, e.g., repair of an automobile can be done in the absence of the client, whereas air travel service needs client presence, which makes services marketing all the more crucial.

All the following characteristics of services apply to Airline Service Marketing:

1. **Intangibility:** Like all services, airline service is intangible, but passengers look for signs of evidence for better quality service. This may include, say, aircraft interiors, speedy grievance handling and hospitality,
2. **Inseparability:** The ground and in-flight service offered in an airline are typically produced and consumed at the same time. They cannot be kept in inventory and distributed later on. Since the client and service provider are present at the same time, the interaction of both is vital for efficient service in an airline.
3. **Personalized attention:** The service depends on the person who provides it and where it is provided.
4. **Perishability:** Timely service is very important to an airline.
5. **Irreplaceability:** A bad airline service, for that matter any service once offered, is offered and cannot be replaced by a good one. One may offer better service later on, but a bad service once offered cannot be replaced.
6. **Subjectivity:** Service offered by an airline can be tested only by experiencing the same.

GROWING COMPETITION IN DOMESTIC SECTOR

With the government liberalizing the air transport industry and declaring an open sky policy, in spite of many other problems, many entrepreneurs backed by NRIs entered the aviation scene. A comparatively large number of applicants were given No Objection Certificate and Permits. By 1994, four among the other private operators: East-West Airlines, Damania Airways, Jet Airways and Modiluft were strong in the arena and were offering the Indian travelling public the choice of airline, better services and value for money. Altogether, these four were lifting almost 12,000 passengers a day. In addition, other airways like Archana airways, Raj Air and Sahara Airlines with ambitious plans also entered the business. Understandably, the national air carrier, Indian Airlines, is facing increasing challenge and is gearing itself with defensive strategies. Recently, it started improved in-flight meal service and offering business class on A320 flights.

The existence of competition is so severe that within one year of their existence, the private air taxis had already chipped off 12,000 passengers daily from the Indian Airlines monopoly. The demand curve has not changed, the market shares have, Indian Airlines accuses private air taxis of undercutting measures like return air tickets for prolonged delay, free air ticket gifts, hotel discounts, lucky draws on-board, fashion shows and magic shows which are pampering passengers in all possible ways. The private air taxis describe complacency and inefficiency in Indian Airlines as the root causes for shifting of passenger loyalty.

Among private air taxi operators each one has its own strategy. While East-West Airlines claimed to offer a large network of efficient air service, Damania say they offer first class service at economy fare. Jet Airways boasted of international standards of service and Modiluft claimed to provide personalized service. Indian Airlines started complimentary tours for package travel, point-to-point fares and is trying desperately to improve in-flight services. Further, Indian Airlines is planning to induct six more aircrafts to its fleet size and to top it all, 11 more new air taxi operators are all set to enter the already crowded skies. With all this, it is inevitable that profit margins become thinner and thinner.

The signs of bitter competition are already there, wherein many air taxis are fast expanding their agent network and offering higher trade commissions. Introduction of frequent flier programs, wooing foreign tourists through interline arrangements are among other major strategies adopted by private airlines. But whether these measures are ethical or not, they seem to be of no concern to passengers, who after winters of discontent and monopoly, seem to be enjoying what is showered on them. Since aircraft interiors and seating arrangements are the same, the only real way to attract passengers is to keep them happy. With all this growing competition and dog-fights for the sides, opening of the economy to multinationals has started ringing the alarm bells, cautioning the air taxi operators.

❖ ❖ ❖

Chapter: 4

Competitive and Turnaround Strategies

Learning Objectives

In this chapter the main stress is given on :

- This chapter begins by examining the meaning of competition. The theory of competition is reviewed, and a scheme for classifying competitors is advanced.
- Porter's five forces model for competitive environment.
- Sustainable competitive advantage-Porters generic strategies.
- Various sources of competitive intelligence are mentioned and models for understanding competitive behavior are discussed.
- The impact of competition in formulating marketing strategy is analyzed.
- Understanding turnaround strategy

MEANING OF COMPETITION

In a free market economy, each company tries to outperform its competitors. A competitor is a rival. A company must know, therefore, how it stands up against each competitor with regard to "arms and ammunition" - skill in maneuvering opportunities, preparedness in reacting to threats and so on. To obtain adequate knowledge about the competition, a company needs an excellent intelligence network.

Typically, whenever one talks about competition, emphasis is placed on price, quality of product, delivery time and other marketing variables. For the purposes of strategy development, however, one needs to go far beyond these marketing tactics. Simply knowing that a competitor has been lowering prices, for example, is not sufficient. Over and above that, one must know how much flexibility the competitor has in further reducing the price. Implicit here is the need for information about the competitor's cost structure.

The term competition defies definition because the view of competition held by different groups (e.g., lawyers, economists, government officials and businesspeople) varies. Most firms define competition in crude, simplistic and unrealistic terms. Some firms fail to identify the true sources of competition; others underestimate the capabilities and reactions of their competitors. When the business climate is stable, a shallow outlook towards the competition might work, but in the current environment, business strategies must be competitively oriented.

NATURAL AND STRATEGIC COMPETITION

A useful way to define competition is to differentiate between natural and strategic competition. Natural competition refers to the survival of the fittest in a given environment. It is an evolutionary process that weeds out the weaker of two rivals. Applied to the business world, it means that no two firms doing business across the board the same way in the same market can coexist forever. To survive, each firm must have something uniquely superior to the other.

THEORY OF COMPETITION

Competition is basic to the free enterprise system. It is involved in all observable phenomena of the market - the prices at which products are exchanged, the kinds and qualities of products produced, the quantities exchanged, the methods of distribution employed and the emphasis placed on promotion. Over many decades, economics have contributed to the theory of competition. A well-recognized body of theoretical knowledge about competition has emerged and can be grouped broadly into two categories: (a) economic theory and (b) industrial organization perspective. These and certain other hypotheses on competition from the viewpoint of businesspeople will now be introduced.

ECONOMIC THEORY OF COMPETITION

Economists have worked with many different models of competition. Still central to much of their work is the model of perfect competition, which is based on the premise that, when a large number of buyers and sellers in the market are dealing in homogenous products, there is complete freedom to enter or exit the market and everyone has complete and accurate knowledge about everyone else.

INDUSTRIAL ORGANISATION PERSPECTIVE

The essence of the industrial organization (IO) perspective is that a firm's position in the marketplace depends critically on the characteristics of the industry environment in which it competes. The industry environment comprises structure, conduct and performance. Structure refers to the economic and technical perspectives of the industry in the context in which firms compete. It concludes (a) concentration in the industry (i.e., the number and size distribution of firms), (b) barriers to entry in the industry and (c) product differentiation among the offerings of different firms that make up the industry. Conduct, which is essentially strategy, refers to firms' behavior in such matters as pricing, advertising and distribution. Performance includes social performances, measured in terms of allocative efficiency (profitability), technical efficiency (cost minimization) and innovativeness.

Following the IO thesis, the structure of each industry vis-à-vis concentration, product differentiation and entry barriers varies. Structure plays an important role in the competitive behavior of different firms in the market.

Businesspeople must be continually aware of the structure of the markets they are presently in or of those they seek to enter. Their appraisal of their present and future competitive posture will be influenced substantially by the size and concentration of existing firms as well as by the extent of product differentiation and the presence or absence of significant barriers to entry.

If a manager has already introduced the firm's products into a market, the existence of certain structural features may provide the manager with a degree of insulation from the intrusion of firms not presently in that market. The absence or relative unimportance, of one or more entry barriers, for example, supplies the manager with insights into the direction from which potential competition might come. Conversely the presence or absence of entry barriers, for example, supplies the manager with insights into the direction from which potential competition might come. Conversely, the presence or absence of entry barriers indicates the relative degree of effort required and the success that might be enjoyed if the manager attempted to enter a specific market. In short, a fundamental purpose of marketing strategy involves the building of entry barriers to protect present markets and the overcoming of existing entry barriers around markets that have an attractive potential.

Business Viewpoint

From the businessperson's perspective, competition refers to rivalry among firms operating in a market to fill the same customer need. The businessperson's major interest is to keep the market to him or herself by adopting appropriate strategies. How and why competition occurs, its intensity and what escape routes are feasible have not been conceptualized. In other words, there does not exist a theory of competition from the business viewpoint.

In recent years, however, Henderson has developed the theory of strategic competition discussed above. Some of the hypothesis on which his theory rests derive from military warfare:

Competitors who persist and survive have a unique advantage over all others. If they did not have this advantage, then others would crowd them out of the market. If competitors are different and coexist, then each must have a distinct advantage over the other. Such an advantage can only exist if differences in a competitor's characteristics match differences in the environment that give those characteristics their relative value. Any change in the environment changes the factor weighting of environmental characteristics and therefore, shifts the boundaries of competitive equilibrium and "competitive segments." Competitors who adapt best or fastest gain an advantage from change in the environment.

Henderson presents an interesting new way of looking at the marketplace: as a battleground where opposing forces (competitors) devise ways (strategies) to outperform each other. Some of these hypothesis can be readily observed, tested and validated and could lead to a general theory of business competition. However, many of his interlocking hypothesis must still be revised and tested.

CLASSIFYING COMPETITORS

A business may face competition from various sources either within or outside its industry. Competition may come from essentially similar products or from substitutes. The competitor may be a small firm or a large multinational corporation. To gain an adequate perspective on the competition, a firm needs to identify all current and potential sources of competition.

Competition is triggered when different industries try to serve the same customer needs and demands. For example, a customer's entertainment needs may be filled by television, sports, publishing or travel. New industries may also enter the arena to satisfy entertainment needs. In the early 1980s, for example, the computer industry entered the entertainment field with video games.

Different industries position themselves to serve different customer demands - existing, latent and incipient. **Existing demand** occurs when a product is bought to satisfy a recognized need. An example is Swatch Watch to determine time. **Latent demand** refers to a situation where a particular need has been recognized, but no products have yet been offered to satisfy the need. Sony tapped the latent demand through Walkman for the attraction of "music on the move." **Incipient demand** occurs when certain trends lead to the emergence of a need of which the customer is not yet aware. A product that makes it feasible to read books while sleeping would illustrate the incipient demand.

A competitor may be an existing firm or a new entrant. The new entrant may enter the market with a product developed through research and development or through acquisition. For example, Texas instruments entered the educational toy business through research and development that led to the manufacture of their Speak and Spell product. Philip Morris entered the beer market by acquiring Miller Brewing Company.

Often an industry competes by producing different product lines. General Foods Corporation, for example, offers ground, regular instant, freeze-dried, decaffeinated and "international" coffee to the coffee market. Product lines can be grouped into three categories: a me-too product, an improved product, or a breakthrough product. A **me-too product** is similar to current offerings. One of many brands currently available in the market, its offers no special advantages over competing products. An **improved product** is one that, while not unique, is generally superior to many existing brands. A **breakthrough product** is an innovation and is usually technical in nature. The digital watch and the color television set were once breakthrough products.

In the watch business, companies have traditionally competed by offering me-too products. Occasionally, a competitor comes out with an improved product, as Seiko did in the 1970s by introducing quartz watches. Quartz watches were a little fancier and supposedly more accurate than other watches. Texas Instruments, however, entered the watch business via a breakthrough product, the digital watch.

Finally, the scope of a competing firm's activities may be limited or extensive. For example, General Mills may not worry if a regional chain of Italian eateries is established to compete against its Olive Garden chain of Italian restaurants. However, if McDonald's were to start offering Italian food, General Mills would be concerned at the entry of such a strong and seasoned competitor.

Exhibit 4.1 illustrates various sources of competition available to fulfill the liquid requirements of the human body. Let us analyze the competition here for a company that maintains an interest in this field. Currently, the thrust of the market is to satisfy existing demand. An example of a product to satisfy latent demand would be a liquid that promises weight loss; a liquid to prevent aging would be an example of a product to satisfy incipient demand.

The industries that currently offer products to quench customer thirst are the liquor, beer, wine, soft drink, milk, coffee, tea, drinking water, and fruit juice industries. A relatively new entrant is mineral and sparkling water. Looking just at the soft drink industry, assuming that this is the field that most interests our company; we see that the majority of competitors offer me-too products (e.g., regular cola, diet cola, lemonade, and other fruit-based drinks). However, caffeine-free cola has been introduced by two major competitors, Coca-Cola Company and PepsiCo. There has been a breakthrough in the form of low-calorie, caffeine-free drinks. A beverage containing a day's nutritional requirements is feasible in the future.

The companies that currently compete in the regular cola market are Coca-Cola, PepsiCo, Seven-Up, Dr. Pepper, and a few others. Among these, however, the first two have a major share of the cola market. Among new industry entrants, General Foods Corporation and Nestle Company are likely candidates (an assumption). The two principal competitors, Coca-Cola Company and PepsiCo, are large multinational, multi-business firms. This is the competitive arena where our company will have to fight if it enters the soft drink business.

INTENSITY, OR DEGREE, OF COMPETITION

The degree of competition in a market depends on the moves and countermoves of various firms active in the market. It usually starts with one firm trying to achieve a favorable position by pursuing appropriate strategies. Because what is good for one firm may be harmful to rival firms, rival firms respond with counter strategies to protect their interests.

Intense competitive activity may or may not be injurious to the industry as a whole. For example, while a price war may result in lower profits for all members of an industry, an advertising battle may increase demand and actually be mutually beneficial. Exhibit 4.2 lists the factors that affect the intensity of competition in the marketplace. In a given situation, a combination of factors determines the degree of competition

EXHIBIT 4.1

Factors Contributing to Competitive Rivalry
Opportunity potential
Ease of entry
Nature of product
Exit barriers
Homogeneity of market
Industry structure or competitive position of firms
Commitment to the industry
Feasibility of technology innovations
Scale economics
Economic climate
Diversity of firms

EXHIBIT 4.2	
Source of Competition	
Customer Need: Liquid for the Body	
Existing need	Thirst
Latent need	Liquid to reduce weight
Inciplent need	Liquid to prevent ageing
Industry Competition (How Can I Quench My Thirst?)	
Existing Industries	Hard Liquor
	Beer
	Wine
	Soft drink
	Milk
	Tea
	Water
New Indusry	Mineral Water
Product Line Competition (What Form of Product Do I Want?)	
Me-too products	Regular Cola
	Diet Cola
	Lemonade
	Fruit-based drink
Improved Product	Caffeine-free Cola
Breatthrough Product	Diet and Caffeine-free cola providing full nutrition
Organizational Competition (What Brand Do I Want?)	
Type of Firm	
Existing Firms	Coca-cola
	Pepsi Co
	Seven-Up
	Dr.Pepper
New entrants	General Foods
	Nestle
Scope of Business	
Geographic	Regional, national, multinational
Product/market	Single versus multiproduct industry

Opportunity Potential

A promising market is likely to attract firms seeking to capitalize on an available opportunity. As the matter of firms interested in sharing the pie increases, the degree of rivalry increases. Take, for example, the home computer market. In the early 1980s, everyone from mighty IBM to such unknowns in the field as Timex Watch Company wanted a piece of the personal computer pie. As firms started jockeying for position, the intensity of competition increased manifold. A number of firms, for example, Texas Instruments and Atari, were forced to quit the market. At the same time, new competitors such as Dell and Compaq entered the market, undermining even IBM.

Ease of Entry

When entry into an industry is relatively easy, many firms, including some marginal ones, are attracted to it. The long-standing, committed members of the industry, however, do not want "outsiders" to break into their territory. Therefore, existing firms discourage potential entrants by adopting strategies that enhance competition.

Nature of Product

When the products offered by different competitors are perceived by customers to be more or less similar, firms are forced into price and to a lesser degree, service competition. In such situations, competition can be really severe.

Exit Barriers

For a variety of reasons, it may be difficult for a firm to get out of a particular business. Possible reasons include the relationship of the business to other businesses of the firm, high investment in assets for which there may not be an advantageous alternative use, high cost of discharging commitments (e.g., fixed labor contracts and future purchasing agreements), top management's emotional attachment to the business and government regulations prohibiting exit (e.g., the legal requirement that a utility must serve all customers).

Homogeneity of the Market

When the entire market represents one large homogeneous unit, the intensity of competition is much greater than when the market is segmented. Even if the product sold is a commodity, segmentation of the market is possible. It is possible, for example, to identify frequent buyers of the commodity as one segment; and occasional buyers as another. But if a market is not suited to segmentation, firms must compete to serve it homogeneously, thus intensifying competition.

Industry Structure

When the number of firms active in a market is large, there is a good chance that one of the firms may aggressively seek an advantageous position. Such aggression leads to intense competitive activity as firms retaliate. On the other hand, if only a few firms constitute an industry, there is usually little doubt about industry leadership. In situations where there is a clear industry leader, care is often taken not to irritate the leader since a resulting fight could be very costly.

Commitment to the Industry

When a firm has wholeheartedly committed itself to a business, it will do everything to hang on, even becoming a maverick that fearlessly makes without worrying about the impact on either the industry or its own resources. Polaroid Corporation, for example, with its strong commitment to instant photography, must maintain its position in the field at any cost. Another example is Gillette's commitment to the shaving business. Such an attachment to an industry enhances competitive activity.

Feasibility of Technological Innovations

In industries where technological innovations are frequent, each firm likes to do its best to cash in while the technology lasts, thus triggering greater competitive activity.

Scale Economics

Where economies realizable through large-scale operations are substantial, a firm will do all it can to achieve scale economies. Attempts to capture scale economies may lead a firm to aggressively compete for market share, escalating pressures on other firms. A similar situation occurs when a business's fixed costs are high and the firm must spread them over a large volume. If capacity can only be added in large increments, the resulting excess capacity will also intensify competition.

Consider the airlines industry. Northwest Airlines commands 73% of the traffic at Detroit Metropolitan Wayne County Airport, and it wants to keep it that way by discouraging competitors. For example, a few years back, an upstart Spirit Airlines entered the Detroit-Philadelphia market with one-way fare of $49, while Northwest's average one-way fare was more than $170. Northwest soon slashed its fares to Philadelphia to $49 on virtually all seats at all times, and added 30% more seats. A few months later, Spirit abandoned the route and Northwest raised its fare to more than $220.

Economic Climate

During depressed economic conditions and otherwise slow growth, competition is much more volatile as each firm tries to make the best of a bad situation.

Diversity of Firms

Firms active in a field over a long period come to acquire a kind of industry standard of behavior. But new participants invading an industry do not necessarily like to play the old game. Forsaking industry patterns, newcomers may have different strategic perspectives and may be willing to go to any lengths to achieve their goals. The Miller Brewing Company's unconventional marketing practices are a case in point. Miller, nurtured and guided by its parent, Philip Morris, segmented the market by introducing a light beer to an industry that had hitherto considered beer a commodity-type product. When different cultures meet in the marketplace, competition can be fierce.

TYPES OF COMPETITION

There are several types of competition in the market.

- **Monopoly:** When there is only one supplier of a product in a given geographic area. In India, railways, power and some defence supplies are enjoying monopoly status so far. In such cases there is a tendency to adopt skimming prices, and giving less value for money. Only if there is a social commitment can price and service be in line with the rest of the market.
- **Oligopoly:** When the supplies are made by a small number of major firms. Firms making core raw materials like iron, steel and oil belong to this category.
- **Differentiated competition:** A phenomenon essentially of the Indian market. Here the industry is divided into large-scale organized players and small-scale assemblers and sellers of pirated goods.
- **Fragmented market:** There are several suppliers of similar products and hence pure and perfect competition rules the market.

COMPETITIVE ADVANTAGE

Firms can gain competitive advantage in the following ways:

- **Differentiation:** This can be made in either the product or any of the other marketing mix factors like price, promotion and placement.
- **Cost differential:** With the help of economies of scale, experience curve and better technology firms can achieve lower costs and strategies their pricing to suit the market conditions and gaining market leadership.
- **Response to market:** Understanding market needs and satisfying them at the appropriate time gives the firms an edge over competition.
- **Market focus:** This involves getting into a niche market and putting the marketing resources like advertising, promotion and personal selling in that market.
- **Service:** Differential in service is most difficult to copy, unlike product differential. Many Me too products join the fray no sooner than a successful product is launched in the market.
- **Vertical integration:** When a firm takes to manufacturing upstream products like raw materials and components and does its own retailing in the downstream area, it gains cost effectiveness due to better product availability, low or no

transaction cost, acceptable quality and better inventory management. It saves on cost, besides superior production planning as can be seen.

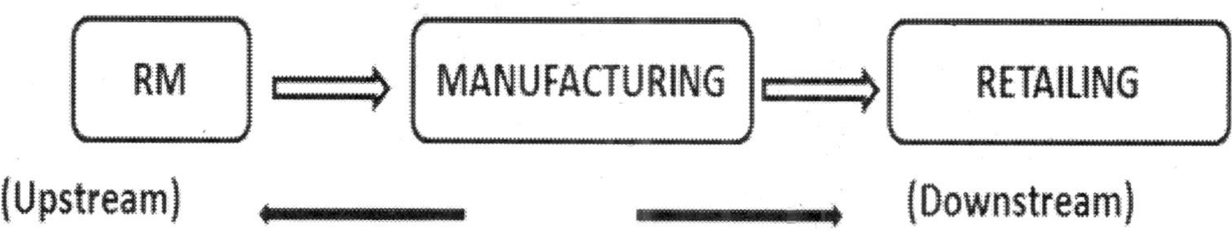

Understanding competition: Firms with same products, markets are the first level competition. (The middle part of Porter's five-force model). In order to compete with them one must know their strengths and weaknesses, core competencies, plans and policies and their keenness as a competitor.

Competitors' strengths could be in the following areas:

1. Product differentiation
2. Prices and discounts
3. Distribution channels
4. Cost of capital and ability to borrow funds at low interest rates
5. Loyal customers
6. Purchase
7. Manpower - committed and loyal
8. Research for new technology as per market demand
9. Government contacts
10. High brand equity and firm's image
11. Resource allocation.

To stay ahead, competitors keep modifying their plans, either as reaction to environment changes or as proactive approach to anticipated competitive moves. In either case a firm needs to continuously monitor competitors' plans. It will give the firm an insight into what the competitors are hoping to achieve by way of market share, geographic coverage and profits including cash flow situation of the competitors. Besides the mindset of competitive management, the size of the organization also should be known. A small manufacturer who is able to sell his product locally will not attempt to upset his market by any drastic strategic change unless he is setting up additional facilities for manufacturing larger volumes. A cash-rich competitor can sell at a loss to prevent new competitors from entering the market. Usually competitors' financial results of the last three years can give a good indication of their strengths and competencies. On the basis of their strengths and mindsets of their management, competitors can be classified as:

- **Market leaders:** With highest share of the market they spend a lot on retaining their position of leadership. As the market starts declining they reassess their options and strategies. They can hardly fight price wars.
- **Major competitors:** With a dominant market share they can afford a price war and take leadership position. They are price leaders in the market; others follow their pricing policy of increasing or decreasing prices.
- **Minor competitors:** They need additional resource and management efforts before they can take on leadership position.
- **Unsatisfactory competitors:** They have management problems and are directionless. They need a bold innovative manager who can turn the organization around. Such competitors should be monitored for their potential as major threats.
- **Problem competitors:** They are mostly on their ways out and with sensible planning you can convert their customers in to your own.

An assessment of competitors offers leverage in planning marketing strategies. Firms can plan resource allocation, management focus and benchmark their results with competitive knowledge. Cultural ethos also plays an important role in strategic planning. The following discussion gives an insight into different corporate cultures:

- **Dynamic culture:** Firms with this culture never lose sight of their objectives and are always on the move in pursuit of their goals. They relentlessly strive to increase their market share and brand equity. Coke and Pepsi are two such firms and they ensure that the other does not get even an inch of their ground. Firms dealing with these competitors should remain second or third players and want for a time in the future when the dominant player makes a mistake and slips down the ladder. Alternately, the firm could introduce a new concept product and invest heavily in marketing it to get the better of the dynamic competitor.
- **Mystery competitor:** This competitor keeps his cards close to his chest till his products are out in the market. New products and new packages are introduced to startle competition. Firms need to assess the viability of these competitive moves before taking any competitive action.
- **Follower competitor:** This firm tries to match others. Such a competitor should never be taken lightly, while copying he may improve on the original and avoid making the mistakes the innovator has made. Patenting designs and technology could save firms from loss of business to follower competitors.

Continuous market information about competitors from salespersons and channel members is the key to having an updated information bank. A firm's field force should therefore be its eyes and ears. The information should be analyzed and competitive firms categorized as weak or strong. The management must use the information to be a proactive player and avoid sudden market share jerks.

Customers' assessment of competitors is another effective way of categorizing competition. They can be asked to rate competitors a scale of 1 to 5 as given in Exhibit 4.3

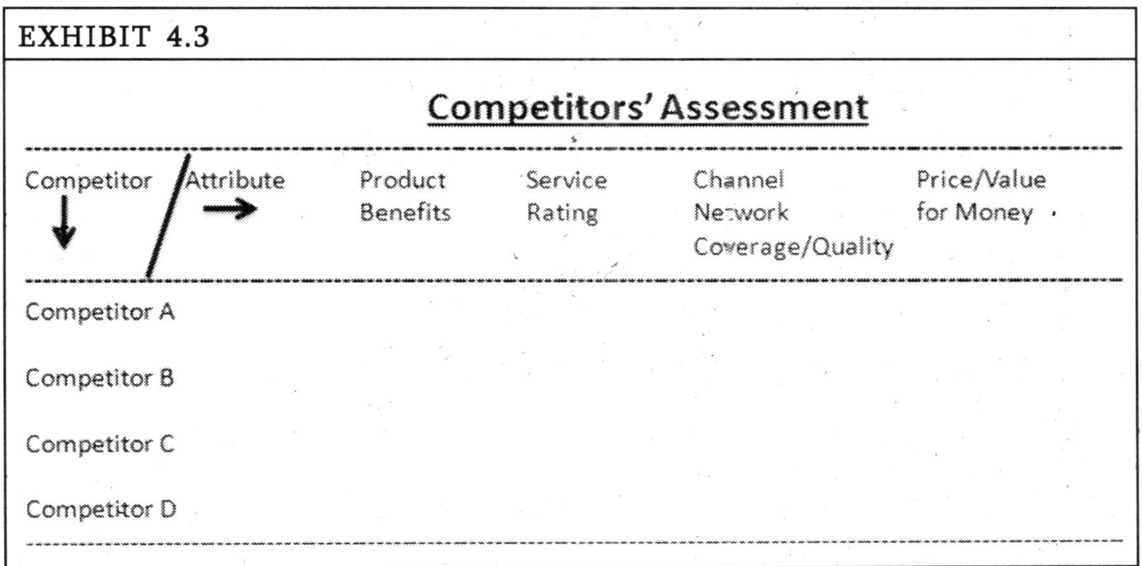

EXHIBIT 4.3

Competitors' Assessment

Competitor ↓ / Attribute →	Product Benefits	Service Rating	Channel Network Coverage/Quality	Price/Value for Money
Competitor A				
Competitor B				
Competitor C				
Competitor D				

Besides customer assessment, a firm should know competitors' market segment and their niche markets. This will help the firm in positioning its own products for optimum results.To outperform competitors and to grow despite them, a company must understand why competition prevails, why firms attack, and how firms respond. Insights into competitors' perspectives can be gained by undertaking two types of analysis: industry and comparative analysis. Industry analysis assesses the attractive of a market based on its economic structure. Comparative analysis indicates how every firm in a particular market is likely to perform, given the structure of the industry.

COMPETITIVE ANALYSIS - PORTER'S FIVE FORCES MODEL

The Porter's 5 Forces tool is a simple but powerful tool for understanding where power lies in a business situation. This is useful, because it helps to understand both the strength of the firm's current competitive position and the strength of a position the firm considering moving into. With a clear understanding of where power lies, a firm can take fair advantage of a situation of strength, improve a situation of weakness and avoid taking wrong steps. This makes it an important part of a firm planning toolkit.

Conventionally, the tool is used to identify whether new products, services or businesses have the potential to be profitable. However it can be very illuminating when used to understand the balance of power in other situations. This tool was created by Harvard Business School professor, Michael Porter, to analyze the attractiveness and likely-profitability of an industry. Since publication, it has become one of the most important business strategy tools. The classic article which introduces it is "How Competitive Forces Shape Strategy" in Harvard Business Review 57, March - April 1979, pages 86-93.

Understanding the Tool:

Five Forces Analysis assumes that there are five important forces that determine competitive power in a business situation. These are:

1. **Supplier Power:** Here you assess how easy it is for suppliers to drive up prices. This is driven by the number of suppliers of each key input, the uniqueness of their product or service, their strength and control over you, the cost of switching from one to another and so on. The fewer the supplier choices you have and the more you need suppliers' help, the more powerful your suppliers are.
2. **Buyer Power:** Here you ask yourself how easy it is for buyers to drive prices down. Again, this is driven by the number of buyers, the importance of each individual buyer to your business, the cost to them of switching from your products and services to those of someone else and so on. If you deal with few, powerful buyers, then they are often able to dictate terms to you.
3. **Competitive Rivalry:** What is important here is the number and capability of your competitors. If you have many competitors and they offer equally attractive products and services, then you'll most likely have little power in the situation, because suppliers and buyers will go elsewhere if they don't get a good deal from you. On the other hand, if no-one else can do what you do, then you can often have tremendous strength.
4. **Threat of Substitution:** This is affected by the ability of your customers to find a different way of doing what you do - for example, if you supply a unique software product that automates an important process, people may substitute by doing the process manually or by outsourcing it. If substitution is easy and substitution is viable, then this weakens your power.
5. **Threat of New Entry:** Power is also affected by the ability of people to enter your market. If it costs little in time or money to enter your market and compete effectively, if there are few economies of scale in place or if you have little protection for your key technologies, then new competitors can quickly enter your market and weaken your position. If you have strong and durable barriers to entry, then you can preserve a favorable position and take fair advantage of it.

These forces can be neatly brought together in a diagram like the one below (Figure 4.1):

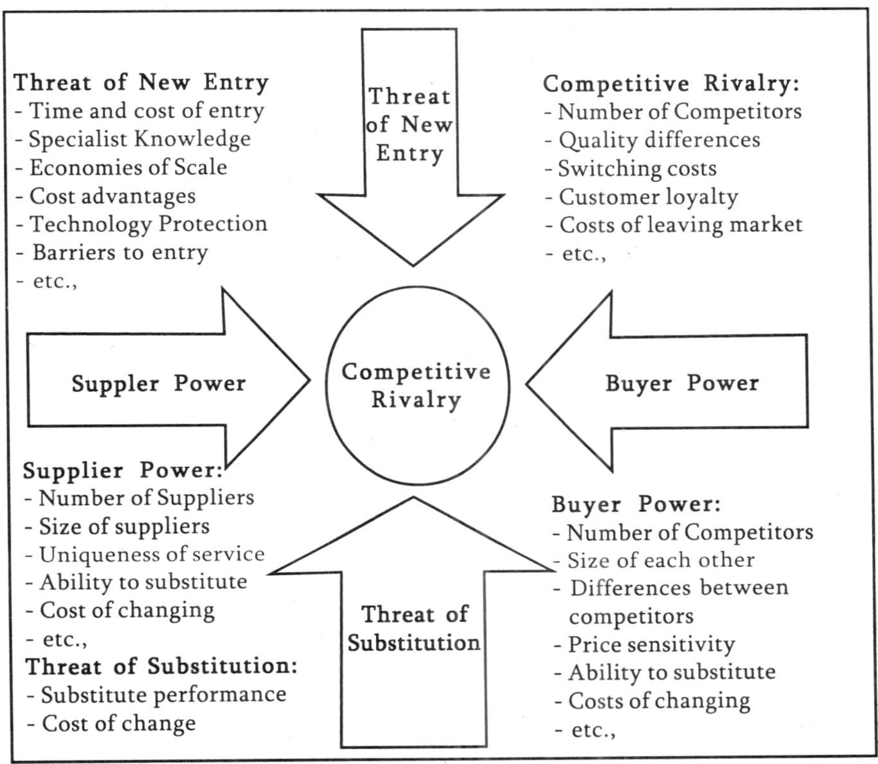

Figure 4.1 Porter's Five Forces Model

Porter's Five Forces Analysis is an important tool for assessing the potential for profitability in an industry. With a little adaptation, it is also useful as a way of assessing the balance of power in more general situations. It works by looking at the strength of five important forces that affect competition:

Supplier Power: The power of suppliers to drive up the prices of the inputs.

Buyer Power: The power of the customers to drive down your prices.

Competitive Rivalry: The strength of competition in the industry.

The Threat of Substitution: The extent to which different products and services can be used in place of your own.

The Threat of New Entry: The ease with which new competitors can enter the market if they see that you are making good profits (and then drive your prices down).

By thinking about how each force affects you and by identifying the strength and direction of each force, you can quickly assess the strength of your position and your ability to make a sustained profit in the industry. You can then look at how you can affect each of the forces to move the balance of power more in your favor.

SUSTAINABLE COMPETITIVE ADVANTAGE-PORTER'S GENERIC COMPETITIVE STRATEGIES

A competitive advantage is an advantage over competitors gained by offering consumers greater value, either by means of lower prices or by providing greater benefits and service that justifies higher prices. Following on from his work analyzing the competitive forces in an industry, Michael Porter suggested three "generic" business strategies that could be adopted in order to gain competitive advantage.

If the primary determinant of a firm's profitability is the attractiveness of the industry in which it operates, an important secondary determinant is its position within that industry. Even though an industry may have below average profitability, a firm that is optimally positioned can generate superior returns. A firm positions itself by leveraging its strengths. Michael Porter has argued that a firm's strengths ultimately fall into one of two headings: cost advantage and differentiation. By applying these strengths in either a broad or narrow scope, three generic strategies result: cost leadership, differentiation and focus. These strategies are applied at the business unit level. They are called generic strategies because they are not firm or industry dependent. The following figure 4.2 illustrates Porter's generic strategies:

Target Scope	Advantage	
	Low Cost	Product Uniqueness
Broad (Industry Wide)	Cost Leadership Strategy	Differentiation Strategy
Narrow (Market Segment)	Focus Strategy (low cost)	Focus Strategy (differentiation)

Figure 4.2 Porter's generic strategies

Cost Leadership Strategy

This generic strategy calls for being the low cost producer in an industry for a given level of quality. The firm sells its products either at average industry prices to earn a profit higher than that of rivals or below the average industry prices to gain market share. In the event of a price war, the firm can maintain some profitability while the competition suffers losses. Even without a price war, as the industry matures and prices decline, the firms that can produce more cheaply will remain profitable for a longer period of time. The cost leadership strategy usually targets a broad market. Some of the ways that firms acquire cost advantages are by improving process efficiencies, gaining unique access to a large source of lower cost materials, making optimal outsourcing and vertical integration decisions, or avoiding some costs altogether. If competing firms are unable to lower their costs by a similar amount, the firm may be able to sustain a competitive advantage based on cost leadership.

Firms that succeed in cost leadership often have the following internal strengths:

- Access to the capital required to make a significant investment in production assets; this investment represents a barrier to entry that many firms may not overcome.
- Skill in designing products for efficient manufacturing, for example, having a small component count to shorten the assembly process.
- High level of expertise in manufacturing process engineering.
- Efficient distribution channels.

Each generic strategy has its risks, including the low-cost strategy. For example, other firms may be able to lower their costs as well. As technology improves, the competition may be able to leapfrog the production capabilities, thus eliminating the competitive advantage. Additionally, several firms following a focus strategy and targeting various narrow markets may be able to achieve an even lower cost within their segments and as a group gain significant market share.

Differentiation Strategy

A differentiation strategy calls for the development of a product or service that offers unique attributes that are valued by customers and that customers perceive to be better than or different from the products of the competition.

The value added by the uniqueness of the product may allow the firm to charge a premium price for it. The firm hopes that the higher price will more than cover the extra costs incurred in offering the unique product. Because of the product's unique attributes, if suppliers increase their prices the firm may be able to pass along the costs to its customers who cannot find substitute products easily.

Firms that succeed in a differentiation strategy often have the following internal strengths:

- Access to leading scientific research.
- Highly skilled and creative product development team.
- Strong sales team with the ability to successfully communicate the perceived strengths of the product.
- Corporate reputation for quality and innovation.

The risks associated with a differentiation strategy include imitation by competitors and changes in customer tastes. Additionally, various firms pursuing focus strategies may be able to achieve even greater differentiation in their market segments.

e.g.,

- Coca-Cola - *brand image*
- Cadillac - *features*
- Intel microprocessors - *technology*

By using the differentiation strategy, a firm is able to influence the perception of customers that the product or the service is unique, rather than having to reduce its costs to attract customers

Focus Strategy

The focus strategy concentrates on a narrow segment and within that segment attempts to achieve either a cost advantage or differentiation. The premise is that the needs of the group can be better serviced by focus entirely on it. A firm using a focus strategy often enjoys a high degree of customer loyalty, and this entrenched loyalty discourages other firms from competing directly.

Because of their narrow market focus, firms pursuing a focus strategy have lower volumes and therefore less bargaining power with their suppliers. However, firms pursuing a differentiation-focused strategy may be able to pass higher costs on to customers since close substitute products do not exist. Firms that succeed in a focus strategy are able to tailor a broad range of product development strengths to a relatively narrow market segment that they know very well.

Some risks of focus strategies include imitation and changes in the target segments. Furthermore, it may be fairly easy for a broad-market cost leader to adapt its product in order to compete directly. Finally, other focusers may be able to carve out sub-segments that they can serve even better.

A Combination of Generic Strategies- Stuck in the Middle?

These generic strategies are not necessarily compatible with one another. If a firm attempts to achieve an advantage on all fronts, in this attempt it may achieve no advantage at all. For example, if a firm differentiates itself by supplying very high quality products, it risks undermining that quality if it seeks to become a cost leader. Even if the quality did not suffer, the firm would risk projecting a confusing image. For this reason, Michael Porter argued that to be successful over the long-term, a firm must select only one of these three generic strategies. Otherwise, with more than one single generic strategy the firm will be "stuck in the middle" and will not achieve a competitive advantage. Porter argued that firms that are able to succeed at multiple strategies often do so by creating separate business units for each strategy. By separating the strategies into different units having different policies and even different cultures, a corporation is less likely to become "stuck in the middle."

However, there exists a viewpoint that a single generic strategy is not always best because within the same product customers often seek multidimensional satisfactions such as a combination of quality, style, convenience, and price. There have been cases in which high quality producers faithfully followed a single strategy and then suffered greatly when another firm entered the market with a lower-quality product that better met the overall needs of the customers.

Generic Strategies and Industry Forces

These generic strategies each have attributes that can serve to defend against competitive forces. The following table compares some characteristics of the generic strategies in the context of the Porter's five forces as shown in fig 4.3.

Industry Force	Generic Strategies		
	Cost Leadership	Differentiation	Focus
Entry Barriers	Ability to cut price in retaliation deters potential entrants.	Customer loyalty can discourage potential entrants.	Focusing develops core competencies that can act as an entry barrier
Buyer Power	Ability to offer lower price to powerful buyers.	Large buyers have less power to negotiate because of few close alternatives.	Large buyers have less power to negotiate because of few alternatives.
Supplier Power	Better insulated from powerful suppliers.	Better able to pass on supplier price increases to customers.	Suppliers have power because of low volumes, but a differentiation-focused firm is better able to pass on supplier price increases.
Threat of Substitutes	Can use low price to defend against substitutes.	Customer's become attached to differentiating attributes, reducing threat of substitutes.	Specialized products & core competency protect against substitutes.
Rivalry	Better able to compete on price.	Brand loyalty to keep customers from rivals.	Rivals cannot meet differentiation-focused customer needs.

Figure 4.3: Generic Strategies and Industry Forces

COMPETITIVE INTELLIGENCE

Competitive intelligence is the publicly available information on competitors, current and potential, that serves as an important input in formulating marketing strategy. No general would order an army to march without first fully knowing the enemy's position and intentions. Likewise, before deciding which competitive moves to make, a firm must be aware of the perspectives of its competitors. Competitive intelligence includes information beyond industry statistics and trade gossip. It involves close observation of competitors to learn what they do best and why and where they are weak. No self-respecting business admits to not doing an adequate job of scanning the competitive environment, but what sets the outstanding companies apart from the merely self-respecting ones is that watch their competition in such depth and with such dedication that, as a marketing executive once remarked to the author, "The information on competitive moves reaches them before even the management of the competition company learns about it."

Three types of competitive intelligence may be distinguished: defensive, passive, and offensive intelligence. **Defensive intelligence**, as the name suggests, is gathered to avoid being caught off-balance. A deliberate attempt is made to gather information on the competition in a structured fashion and to keep track of moves that are relevant to the firm's business. **Passive intelligence** is ad hoc information gathered for a specific decision. A company may, for example, seek information on a competitor's sales compensation plan when devising its own compensation plan. Finally, **offensive intelligence** is undertaken to identify new opportunities. From a strategic perspective, offensive intelligence is the most relevant.

Strategic Usefulness of Competitive Intelligence

Such information as how competitors make, test, distribute, price, and promote their products can go a long way in developing a viable marketing strategy. The Ford Motor Company, for example, has an ongoing program for tearing down competitors' products to learn about their cost structure. Exhibit 4.4 summarizes the process followed at Ford. This competitive knowledge has helped Ford in its strategic moves in Europe. For example, from regularly tearing down the Leyland Mini (a small truck), the company concluded that(a) Leyland was not making money on the Mini at its current price and (b) Ford should not enter the small truck market at current price levels. Based on these conclusions, Ford was able to arrive at a firm strategic decision not to assemble a "Mini".

The following example compares two companies that decided to enter the automatic dishwasher market at about the same time. One of the companies ignored the competition, floundered, and eventually abandoned the field; the other did a superior job of learning form the competition and came out on top. When the CEO of the first company, a British company, learned from his marketing department about the market growth potential for dishwashers and about current competitors' shares, he lost no time setting out to develop a suitable machine.

EXHIBIT 4.4 Ford Motor Company's Competitive Product Tear-Down Process

1. **Purchase the product:** The high cost of product teardown, particularly for a carmaker, gives some indication of the value successful competitors place on the knowledge they gain.
2. **Tear the product down - literally:** First, every removable component is unscrewed or unbolted; the rivets are undone; finally, individual spot welds are broken.
3. **Reverse-engineer the product:** While the competitor's car is being dismantled, detailed drawings of parts are made and parts lists are assembled, together with analyses of the production processes that were evidently involved.
4. **Build up costs:** Parts are costed out in terms of make-or-buy, the variety of parts used in a single product, and the extent of common assemblies across model ranges.

   Among the important facts to be established in a product teardown, obviously, are the number and variety of components and the number of assembly operations. The costs of the processes are then built up from both direct labor requirements and overheads (often vital to an understanding of competitor cost structures).
5. **Establish economies of scale:** Once individual cost elements are known, they can be put together with the volume of cars produced by the competitor and the total number of people employed to develop some fairly reliable guides to the competitor's economies of scale. Having done this, Ford can calculate model-run lengths and volumes needed to achieve, first, break even and then profit.

Source: Robin Leaf, "How to pick up Tips form your Competitors," Director (Feb-1978):60

Finding little useful information available on dishwasher design, the director of research and development decided to begin by investigating the basic mechanics of the dishwashing process. Accordingly, she set up a series of pilot projects to evaluate the cleaning performance of different jet configurations, the merits of alternative washing-arm designs, and the varying results obtained with different types and quantities of detergent on different washing loads. At the end of the year she had amassed a great deal of useful knowledge. She also had a pilot machine running that cleaned dishes well and a design concept for a production version. But considerable development work was still needed before the prototype could be declared a satisfactory basis for manufacture.

To complicate matters, management had neglected to establish effective linkages among the company's three main functions - marketing, technology, and production. So it was not until the technologies had produced the prototype and design concepts that marketing and production began asking for revisions and suggesting new ideas, further delaying the development of a marketable product. So much for the first company, with its fairly typical traditional response to market opportunities. The second company, which happened to be Japanese, started with the same marketing intelligence but responded in a very different fashion.

First, it bought three units of every available competitive dishwasher. Next, management formed four special teams: (a) a product test group of marketing and technical staff, (b) a design team of technologies and production people, (c) a distribution team of marketing and production staff and (d) a field team of production staff.

The conclusion of this story is what one might expect: the competitive Japanese manufacturer brought its new product to market two years ahead of the more of the traditionally minded British manufacturer and achieved its planned market share 10 weeks later. The traditional company steadily lost money and eventually dropped out of the market.

TURNAROUND STRATEGY

IBM Becomes "Internet Business Machines"

During the 1970s and 1980s, IBM dominated the computer industry worldwide. It was the market leader in both large mainframe and small personal computers. Along with Apple Computer, IBM set the standard for all personal computers. Even until recently when IBM no longer dominates the field-personal computers are still identified as being either Apple or IBM-style PCs.

IBM's problems came to a head in the early 1990s. The company's computer sales were falling. More companies were choosing to replace their large, expensive mainframe computers with personal computers, but they were not buying the PCs from IBM. An increasing number of firms like Hewlett-Packard, Dell, Gateway and Compaq had entered the industry. They offered IBM-style PC "clones" that were considerably cheaper and often more advanced than IBM's PCs. IBM's falling revenues meant corporate losses-$15 billion in cumulative losses from 1991 through 1993. Industry experts perceived the company as a bureaucratic dinosaur that could no longer adapt to changing conditions. Its stock price fell to $40 with no end in sight.

IBM's Board of Directors in 1993 hired a new CEO, Louis Gerstner, to lead a corporate turnaround strategy at "Big Blue" (the nickname IBM earned from its rigid dress code policies). To stop the flow of red ink, the company violated its long-held "no layoffs" policy by reducing its workforce 40%. Under Gerstner, IBM reorganized its sales force around specific industries such as retailing and banking. Decision making was made easier. Previously, according to Joseph Formichelli, a top executive with the PC division, he "had to go through seven layers to get things done." Firing incompetent employees could take a year, "so he pawned them off on another group." Strategy presentations were hashed over so many times "they got water down to nothing." Under Gerstner, formal presentations were no longer desired. The emphasis switched to quicker decision making and a stronger customer orientation.

At the same time that Gerstner was beginning his turnaround strategy in 1994, David Grossman, a recently hired IBM programmer, was arguing that the future of the computer lay in the developing Internet. According to Grossman, "I came from a progressive computing environment and was telling people at IBM that there was this thing called UNIX there was an Internet. No one knew what I was talking about." Teamed with John Patrick, a career person with IBM who also served on a strategy task force, and David Singer, a researcher who had written one of the first Gopher programs, Grossman began building a corporate internet and eventually created a formal Internet group with Patrick as Chief Technical Officer. Recalled Patrick, "A lot of people were saying, "How do you make money at this? I said, 'I have no idea. All I know is that this is the most powerful, important form of communication both inside and outside the company that has ever existed.' From the beginning our goal was to help IBM become the Internet Business Machines Company."

From 1994 to 2000, the company transformed itself from being a besieged computer marker to a dominant service provider. Its Global Services unit has grown from almost nothing to a $30 billion business with more than 135,000 employees. By the end of 1998, IBM had completed 18,000 e-business consulting engagements a third of which were Internet-related. In a 1999 report to financial analysts, CEO Gerstner stated." . IBM is already generating more (e-business) revenue and certainly more profits than all of the top Internet companies combined."

Sources: G, Hamel, "Walking UP IBM," Harvard Business Review (July-August 2000), pp. 137-146; I. Sager, "Inside IBM: Internet Business Machines," Business Week E. Biz (December 13, 1999), pp. EB20-EB40; B. Ziegler, "Gerstner's IBM Revival: Impressive, Incomplete," Wall Street Journal (March 25, 1997), pp. B1, B4.

Sell-Out/Divestment Strategy

If a corporation with a weak competitive position in its industry is unable either to pull itself up by its bootstraps or to find a customer to which it can become a captive company, it may have no choice but to **sell out**. The sell-out strategy makes sense if management can still obtain a good price for its shareholders and the employees can keep their jobs by selling the entire company to another firm. The hope is that another company will have the necessary resources and determination to return the company to profitability. The sale of Tata Oil Mills (Tomco) to Hindustan Lever (HLL) is a good example of a sell out.

If the corporation has multiple business lines and it chooses to sell off a division with low growth potential, this is called **divestment**. This was the strategy used by fast-moving consumer goods major Hindustan Lever Ltd (HLL) when it announced the divestment of its edible oil business to American company Bunge Co. According to the deal, the Dalda brand along with related brands, Masterline, Gold Seal, Silver Seal, Marvo, Biskin and Lily and HLL's edible oil manufacturing facilities in Trichy, Tamil Nadu, are to be sold to the U.S.-based farm-to-consumer major for Rs. 90 crore. Since Bunge Co does not have a presence in India, HLL will continue marketing the Dalda brand for a fee, which means that there will be no changes for the distributors and stockiest of the brand? While the divestment makes eminent business sense for HLL, which wants to exit out of the low margins commodities market and increase its presence in the highly profitable value-added foods business, the decision marks the exit of one of its oldest brands.

Bankruptcy/Liquidation Strategy

When a company finds itself in the worst possible situation with a poor competitive position in an industry with few prospects, management has only a few alternatives-all of them distasteful. Because no one is interested in buying a weak company in an unattractive industry, the firm must pursue a bankruptcy or liquidation strategy. **Bankruptcy** involves giving up management of the firm to the courts in return for some settlement of the corporation's obligations. Top management hopes that once the court decides the claims on the company, the company will be stronger and better able to compete in a more attractive industry. Established in 1993 and headquartered at Secunderabad, the Global Trust Bank (GTB) was promoted as a private sector bank by Ramesh Gelli, Jayanta Madhab and Sridhar Subasri against the backdrop of the government's policy of deregulation and liberalization. GTB has been running its operations successfully (Rs. 11.8 crore in net profits for the nine-month period ending December 31, 2003) and setting records until it collapsed under the pressure of bad loans. In 2004, it became bankrupt and merged with a Public Sector bank, Oriental Bank of Commerce.

In contrast to bankruptcy, which seeks to perpetuate the corporation, **liquidation** is the termination of the firm. Because the industry is unattractive and the company too weak to be sold as a going concern, management may choose to convert as many saleable assets as possible to cash, which is then distributed to the shareholders after all obligations are paid. The benefit of liquidation over bankruptcy is that the board of directors, as representatives of the shareholders, together with top management makes the decisions instead of turning them over to the court, which may choose to ignore shareholders completely. As an example, Precision Thermoforming & Packaging (PTP) was a successful company whose main business had been making, assembling and mailing computer disks to prospective customers of America Online (AOL). When AOL failed to pay $2.2 million for the 170 million disks it had ordered, PTP was unable to pay its debtors and went out of business. Although the company sued AOL for its money, management raised $3 million by auctioning off the firm's $6.2 million worth of equipment to partially pay the creditors. The PTP facility stood vacant while its owners awaited the result of the lawsuit.

At times, top management must be willing to select one of these less desirable retrenchment strategies. Unfortunately, many top managers are unwilling to admit that their company has serious weaknesses for fear that they may be personally blamed. Even worse, top management may not even perceive that crises are developing. When these top managers do eventually notice trouble, they are prone to attribute the problems to temporary environmental disturbances and tend to follow profit strategies. Even when things are going terribly wrong, top management is greatly tempted to avoid liquidation in the hope of a miracle. Thus, a corporation needs a strong board of directors who, to safeguard shareholders' interests, can tell top management when to quit.

TURNAROUND MANAGEMENT

Turnaround is of considerable importance to strategic management. However, the process of turnaround (how firms move away from deterioration in performance to enduring success) has not received sufficient attention in management literature. Not enough literature is available on turnarounds because of the wide gap between empirical findings (which may be based on large samples or case studies) and the work done towards uncovering the causal structure of events from the start of a firm's decline to its ultimate recovery or death. Here we will discuss the framework of the turnaround process developed by Shamsud Chowdhury and relate it to the turnaround process of three companies, Chrysler, IBM and Nissan. These three companies went through the same turnaround process.

The Turnaround Process

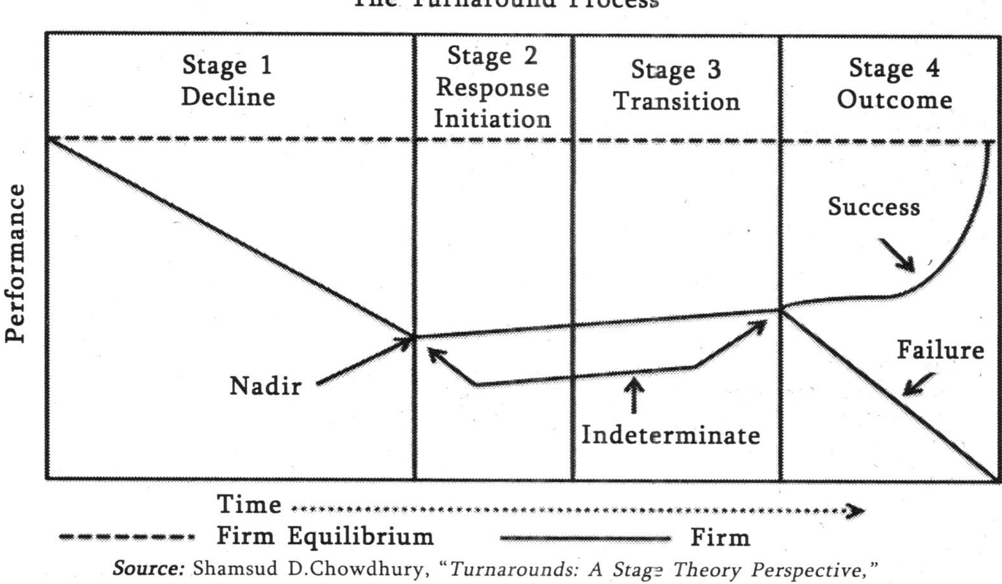

Source: Shamsud D.Chowdhury, "*Turnarounds: A Stage Theory Perspective,*" *Canadian Journal of Administrative Sciences, 19(a), 2002, @ ASAC.*

Figure 4.4 The Turnaround Process

A turnaround occurs when "a firm perseveres through an existence-threatening performance decline; ends the threat with a combination of strategies, systems, skills and capabilities; and achieves sustainable performance recovery. The obverse of performance recovery is failure and eventual death." This definition identifies four key attributes of a turnaround. First, declining performance is the trigger for turnaround. Second, turnaround involves a series of activities. Third, a turnaround is undertaken with a definite purpose. And fourth, turnaround activities continue for a number of years. Chowdhury suggested the use of a stage theory to study the turnaround process. He identified four stages of the turnaround process: decline, response initiation, transition and outcome. Figure 4.4 shows the four stages of the turnaround process. According to Chowdhury, though external forces such as competitive strategies of immediate competitors and pressure from shareholders influence the outcome of the turnaround, top management can still control the outcome to a great extent.

During the first stage, (decline stage), decline starts from firm equilibrium and reaches a nadir. As the firm's performance reaches its nadir, the management begins to take corrective actions - this is the second stage of the turnaround process. According to Chowdhury, the third stage of the turnaround process, the transition stage, is the most complex of all the stages. At this stage the firm experiments with different strategies, structures, cultures and technologies. During the fourth stage, the outcome stage, the outcome of the activities undertaken during the third stage is realized. The outcome could be either success or failure.

The various stages of the turnaround process are discussed in detail below.

Stage 1: Decline

There are two theoretical perspectives that provide reasons for the decline of firms: K-extinction and R-extinction. The K-extinction perspective suggests that macro or external factors are responsible for the decline. According to this perspective, as the concerned firm is part of an industry, any decline in the industry will result in the decline of the firm. According to the R-extinction perspective, the decline in the firm is due to a reduction in resources within the firm, independent of the external environment. However, both internal and external factors will contribute to deterioration in financial performance and reduction in resources within the firm. But the magnitude of decline will vary depending on whether this is externally or internally induced. It is necessary to identify the various factors that contribute to each type of decline and the way the decline type approaches its nadir. It is also necessary to identify the sources of intervention that trigger action. Usually more than one source of intervention or stimuli can be identified in a turnaround situation. Pressure from one or more triggers (banks, creditors, government, press, stockholders) can bring a change in management and even lead to the removal of the CEO of the firm.

Stage 2: Response Initiation

Turnaround responses can be categorized into strategic and operating responses. Strategic responses involve changing or adjusting the businesses the firm is currently involved in. Some of the changes include diversification, vertical integration and divestment. Operating responses focus on the way the firm conducts its businesses. These include short-run tactics aimed at cost cutting and revenue generation. This type of turnaround response used depends on the cause of a firm's decline. If the decline is due to structural shifts in the market, a strategic response should be used; if the decline is due to inefficiency an operating response should be initiated.

Stage 3: Transition

According to Chowdhury, "a substantial amount of time has to pass before the results of turnaround strategies show." For example, it took Ford four years to introduce its successful Taurus/Sable line in response to its declining market share. According to some other researches, on an average, performance improvement takes place after around 7 years.

Stage 4: Outcome

The fourth stage involves determining whether a turnaround has been accomplished. According to Chowdhury, a cut off point of performance measures can be used to determine this. The measures used to determine the outcome are the same as those that are used to identify the decline at the first stage of the turnaround (Refer Table 4.1 for key events and core concepts in turnaround).

Let us use the turnaround framework to understand the turnarounds of Chrysler, IBM and Nissan. Exhibits 4.5, 4.6 and 4.7 discuss the turnarounds of Chrysler, IBM and Nissan.

EXHIBIT 4.5 Turning Around Chrysler

Chrysler Corporation's decline started in the early 1970s. its market-share in the US car market went down from 16.1% in 1970 to 9.6% in 1979. In 1978, when GM and Ford sold 5.4 million and 2.6 million cars respectively, Chrysler sold less than 1.2 million cars. Chrysler recorded a loss of $1 billion in 1979, the largest in USO corporate history.

Chrysler's decline can be attributed to both internal and external factors. The internal or R-extinction factor that contributed to the decline was the inefficiency of the top management. The top management lacked an understanding of the strategic direction of the company and the dynamics of the industry in which the firm was operating. Some of the top management blunders that contributed to the erosion of competitiveness were poorly conceived overseas expansion and participation in the used cars business. Chrysler had 35 vice presidents, each with his own turf. According to Iacocca, the man behind Chrysler's turnaround, "There was no real committee set up, no cement in the organizational chart, no systems of meetings to get people talking to each other." The external or K-extinction factors which contributed to Chrysler's decline were excessive government regulation, the recession and the energy crisis.

In the response-initiation stage, Chrysler made changes at both strategic and operational levels. It divested its tank operation to raise cash; it closed down two of its plants in Michigan, it sold all the dealership real estate it owned, which included hundreds of strategic downtown locations; and it also divested some of its overseas operations in Argentina, Australia, Brazil and Venezuela. To reduce fixed costs, Chrysler also lowered the salary of its top executives and cut its employee stock option plans.

The key events in the transition stage as shown in Table 11.1 also occurred at Chrysler. Although Iacocca joined Chrysler in November 1978, it was only in July 1983 that Chrylser announced that it would repay the entire $1.5 billion government backed loan by the end of 1983. Thus there was a gap of about five years between the time Iacocca joined Chrysler and the official announcement of the repayment of the loan amount. Over a period of three years, Iacocca fired 33 of the 35 vice presidents of the company. There were massive layoffs at other levels also. In 1979-80, 15,500 workers were laid off, saving Chrysler $500 million in annual costs.

The transition stage was also marked by cooperation and communication among the employees. Employees had to be convinced of the rationale for drastic pay cuts and massive layoffs. Iacocca visited every single Chrysler plant, conducted sessions with plant supervisors and spoke directly with workers. By taking prompt and decisive steps, Chrysler gained new commitments from its key stakeholders such as suppliers, bankers, dealers and state and local governments.

The outcome of the transition stage was seen in many performance measures. By 1982, signs of a healthy Chrysler could be seen. At the end of 1982, Chrysler generated a modest profit and in 1983 made an operating profit of $925 million. By 1983, Chrysler offered 26 million shares and its stock price rose from $ 16 t $ 35 within weeks. Chrysler paid off its entire loan seven years before it was due. Chrysler's achievements showed that it had accomplished a turnaround.

(**Source:** ICFAI Centre for Management Research)

EXHIBIT 4.6 Turning Around IBM

IBM's decline started in the late 1980s. During the period 1986-1992, IBM's overall marketshare in the IT industry in the US fell by 37%, while its global market share fell by 30%. In 1993, it reported a record net loss of $8.1 billion.

IBM's decline can be attributed more to R-extinction than to K-extinction factors. The company had 24 product units functioning independently, even though they were a part of IBM. John Akers, who was the CEO before Louis Gerstner took over, had even announced a restructuring plan that aimed at splitting the company into independent units. To make matters worse, the mainframes and storage systems division, which contributed nearly half of IBM's revenues, was losing ground both in terms of revenues as well as market share. Moreover, the company's personal computers division was not generating any profits.

IBM response initiation stage was marked by changes at both strategic and operational levels. It strategically positioned its server family to suit the needs of the emerging Enterprise Resource Planning (ERP) and e-commerce applications. IBM also shifted from being product-centric to customer-centric in order to provide complete solutions to its clients. Gerstner, who turned the company around, brought about a radical change in the work culture of IBM. In July 1993, he reduced the workforce by 35,000 and undertook many other cost-cutting initiatives. These included the sale of the Federal Systems unit (a division which sold computers and electronic components to defence and public agencies of the US Government) for $12.575 billion, the sale of IBM's art collection (a collection of paintings which was started by IBM's founder, Thomas Watson Sr.) (valued at $25 million) and the sale of IBM property (valued at $248 million).

The transition stage was marked by the decision to reverse Aker's plans to split IBM into 11 entities. Gerstner felt that the different business units of IBM needed to be integrated in order to produce quality products within a specified time frame. He argued that customers wanted IBM to remain a single entity. During this stage, Gerstner summoned the top twelve managers of IBM and asked them to clearly define their respective businesses in terms of parameters such as nature of their business, its customers, competitors and markets. Gerstner also abandoned the lifetime employment policy followed by the company. Though this policy was aimed at increasing the loyalty of employees towards the organization, Gerstner felt that it was no longer relevant in the highly competitive business scenario. He tried to foster a performance driven culture at IBM and insisted on results.

In 1994, Gerstner made efforts to improve reporting procedures across different units of the firm. This helped him closely monitor production schedules, cost schedules and the sale of different products. He also started focusing on specific problems related to individual units. He realized that the personal computer division, which had good potential, was performing very poorly. The division was facing tough competition from companies such as Dell, HP and Compaq. With the objective of improving the situation, Gerstner appointed Richard Thomson, who was his colleague at American Express and RJR Nabisco, as the head of the unit.

The outcome of the steps taken at the transition stage was seen after eight years in 2001. In that year, the company reported a net income of $7.7 billion. During the period 1993-2001, the share price of IBM shot up by nearly 800%.

(**Source** :ICFAI Centre for Management Research)

EXHIBIT 4.7 Turning Around Nissan

Nissan's problems (decline) started in the early 1990s. its market-share in Japan decline from 34% in 1974 to 19% in 1999. Its global market-share went down from 6.6% in 1991 to 4.9% in 1999.

Nissan's decline, like that of Chrysler, was caused by both internal and external factors. In the early 1990s, the once young and dynamic management of Nissan became oblivious to market changes and customer needs. Its organizational structure was also responsible for its decline. The company's global divisions, such as Nissan North America and Nissan Europe, operated like separate entities when it came to finance, sales and marketing. The culture at Nissan was such that everyone was eager to blame someone else for poor performance. Sales blamed product planning and vice versa. Also, there was lack of communication between the different departments.

The external factor responsible for Nissan's decline was low growth in the Japanese economy in the 1990s. Post World War II, the Japanese economy grew rapidly and Nissan seized this opportunity and expanded not only within Japan but also overseas. This expansion was funded through debt. But once the economy slowed down, Nissan and other Japanese companies had to deal with excess capacity and low demand. This turn of events, seriously hurt the company. The decline in vehicle sales, loss of market share, huge debt and low stock price brought Nissan to near bankruptcy.

Carlos Ghosn, who became Chief Operating Officer (COO) of Nissan in 1999, turned the company around. The response initiation stage involved changes at both strategic and operational levels. One of the biggest challenges was gaining control of Nissan's communications, both internal and external. Nissan treated external communications as a reactionary tool by telling as little as possible to the general and investment public. This created an environment of distrust among the Japanese media. Nissan's internal communications was equally bad. Ghosn believed in transparency. He wasted no time in building a proactive approach with the media and employees. He used communications as a primary management tool and paid close attention to presentations and press releases.

When Ghosn realized that the regionalization of Nissan and its lack of a central strategy were impediments to the company's revival, he formed cross functional teams which were assigned specific focus areas, such as business development, purchasing, manufacturing and logistics, research and development, sales and marketing, general and administrative, finance and cost, phase out of products and parts complexity management and organization. The cross functional teams consisted of middle level managers from different disciplines and operational regions, who had previous specific line responsibilities. The managers were asked to identify problems and recommend solutions to Ghosn and the executive committee.

The Nissan Revival Plan marked the transition stage of the company's turnaround. This plan was made public in October 1999. The plan aimed at reducing operating costs by 1 trillion yen in three areas: global purchasing, manufacturing and general administrative costs. The plan also aimed at reducing net debt from 1.4 trillion yen to less than 700 bn yen by the year 2000; reducing the workforce by 21,000; reducing the number of vehicle assembly plants in Japan from seven to four; and reducing the number of manufacturing platforms in Japan from twenty-four to fifteen. As part of the plan, the company decided to launch 22 new models by 2002. The Nissan Revival Plan would start in fiscal 2000 and would continue till 2003.

To reduce global purchasing costs, Nissan centralized purchasing. It further reduced costs by centralizing global financial operations, reducing bureaucracy and selling off non-core assets such as land and securities. To bring about changes within Nissan, Ghosn introduced a new organizational structure. Seniority was eliminated and those who had few responsibilities were given new assignments. In addition, compensation packages were revamped to reflect performance.

The outcome of all these measures was that Nissan turned around faster than expected. In the fiscal year 2000, sales increased by 4%; 20 new models were launched: management was streamlined; purchasing costs were reduced by 11%, and the company earned 5.4% operating income on sales.

(**Source:** ICFAI Centre for Management Research)

Table 4.1: Key Events and Concepts in Turnaround

STAGES				
Incidents	Decline	Response Initiation	Transition	Outcome
Key Events	K extinction	Domain Definition	Elapsed Time	Success
	R extinction	Scope Overlap	Resource Commitment	Failure
	Stimulus	Strategic Contours	Policy/Programs	
			Structure	
			Rewards	
			People	

Source: Shamsud D. Chowdhury, "Turnarounds: A stage Theory Perspective," Canadian Journal of Administration Sciences, 19 (3), 2002.

SUMMARY & KEY TERMS

Competition is a strategic factor that affects marketing strategy formulation. In a generic mode the marketers have considered competition as one of the uncontrollable variable to be reckoned within developing the marketing mix. It is becoming more and more evident that a chosen marketing strategy should be based on competitive advantage to achieve sustained business success. There are two very different types of competition i.e., natural and strategic. Natural competition implies survival of the fittest in a given environment. In business terms, it means firms compete from very similar strategic positions relying on operating differences to separate the successful from the unsuccessful.

With strategic competition on the other hand underlying strategy differences vis-a-vis. market segments, product offerings, distribution channels and manufacturing processes become paramount considerations.

The major thrust of economic theories has centered on the model of perfect competition. Firms compete to satisfy customer needs, which may be classified as existing, latent or incipient .A firm may face competition from different sources which may be categorized as industry competition, product line competition or organizational competition.

The Porter's 5 Forces tool is a simple but powerful tool for understanding where power lies in a business situation. This is useful, because it helps to understand both the strength of the firm's current competitive position and the strength of a position the firm considering moving into. There are five important forces that determine competitive power in a business situation and they are Supplier Power, Buyer Power, Competitive Rivalry, Threat of Substitution and Threat of New Entry.

A competitive advantage is an advantage over competitors gained by offering consumers greater value, either by means of lower prices or by providing greater benefits and service that justifies higher prices, Michael Porter suggested three "generic" business strategies that could be adopted in order to gain competitive advantage. Michael Porter has argued that a firm's strengths ultimately fall into one of two headings: cost advantage and differentiation. By applying these strengths in either a broad or narrow scope, three generic strategies result: *cost leadership, differentiation and focus.* These strategies are applied at the business unit level.

A firm needs competitive intelligence to keep track of various facets of its rivals businesses. The system includes proper data gathering and analysis of each major competitor's current and future perspectives.

The turnaround process consists of four stages. During the first stage, (the decline stage), decline starts from firm equilibrium and reaches a nadir. As the firm's performance reaches its nadir, management begins to take corrective actions - this is the second stage of the turnaround process. The third stage of the turnaround process, the transition stage, is the most complex of all the stages. At this stage a firm experiments with different strategies, structures, cultures and technologies. During the fourth stage, the outcome stage, the outcome of the activities undertaken during the third stage is realized. The outcome could be either success or failure.

KEY TERMS

- Natural Competition
- Strategic Competition
- Existing demand
- Latent demand
- Incipient demand
- Porters five forces model
- Competitive advantage
- Monopoly
- Oligopoly
- Vertical Integration
- Competitive Intelligence
- Divestment
- Turnaround strategy
- Generic strategies

DISCUSSION QUESTIONS

1. Explain various theory of competition and also differentiate between natural and strategic competition with examples.
2. Identify with examples the different sources of competitions.
3. What do you mean by competitive advantage? Explain Porter's Generic Competitive Strategies in detail.
4. What is competitive analysis? Explain it using Porter's five forces model for competitive environment.
5. Write Short notes on:

a. Competitive Rivalry

b. Cost Leadership Strategy

c. Focus Strategy

d. Explain the generic strategies and industrial forces in the context of the Porter's five forces model.

e. Explain industrial organizational perspective of competition.

f. What are the factors contributing to competitive rivalry?

g. What is turnaround strategy? Explain the turnaround process in detail.

OPENING CASE: BASKIN-ROBBINS 31 FLAVORS: MANAGING "COOPERATIVE" ADVERTISING

Done Wilson, owner of two Baskin- Robbins franchises in a medium-sized Midwestern metropolitan area, was concerned about the results of the recent year's cooperative advertising program. The program had been greeted with great enthusiasm by most franchises at the previous year's national franchisee meeting and Don strongly supported the concept. He had been chosen "market captain" for his area and worked hard to develop a successful program. As he reflected over the past several months, however, he was disappointed with the results and wondered what changes might be necessary.

BACKGROUND

Don's two Baskin-Robbins ice cream stores were located about 8 miles apart, in a metropolitan area of about 250,000 people. It was a good, healthy market for franchised food operations. The local economy was diverse, including state government, automobile manufacturing, and a major state university. Don's first store was located across from a university campus, in a free-standing building. There was excellent access from a major highway and considerable walk by traffic from off-campus students. The closeness of a Burger King, Pizza Hut and local restaurants helped the in-store traffic for his store. As long as he had sufficient supply of chocolate flavors, Wilson's campus store was a big hit with the students.

Don acquired his second store a year after he bought the first; This store was located in a neighborhood strip centre. The neighborhood was largely residential and contained a good mix of government workers and employees of the nearby auto assembly plant. Family groups made up the principal customer base-birthday parties to be catered and walk-in traffic from the strip-center business.

While the first store had been profitable from the day it became a Baskin-Robbins franchise, the second store had a troubled past. Two prior owners in the past three years had given poor customer service, which led to bad reputation. Don bought the store at a good price-and had managed a turnaround to profitability in two years of consistent management. Don was considered to be an excellent franchisee: young and aggressive, with excellent store results.

BASKIN-ROBBINS' ADVERTISING PROGRAM

Each Baskin-Robbins store was responsible for all local-market-area advertising. The company provided advertising. The company provided advertising materials in the form of ad slicks, preprinted billboard posters, television spots on videotape, radio copy and other promotional items. Most of these materials were available free or at very low cost to the franchises. Media costs and placement were the responsibility of the individual franchisee, who designed promotional campaigns that seemed desirable for the local market.

The company also provided a national-spot television campaign each year. The campaign was paid for entirely by Baskin-Robbins and for over twenty-five years had been handled by a major advertising agency in Los Angeles, near the company's headquarters in Glendale. The television campaign focused on six major ice cream "holidays"-Valentine's Day, Easter, Mother's Day, Thanksgiving and Christmas. The advertisements promoted the extensive line of custom-made deserts-festive ice cream pies, cakes and novelty items-made by the franchises for customer to take home for special occasions. While franchises were informed of the items to be promoted on television, they had to input into the selection of the items not into any other aspect of the campaign decisions.

Baskin-Robbins has over 3000 franchised stores in the United States. Placement of the company-paid advertising was based on the number of stores in each television market area. Each market area received an allocation of gross rating points (GRPs) based on the number of stores in the market. Allocations were not based on dollars, with the idea being to maximize the impact of high-store-density markets through more GRPs. This decision had been made by the company and its advertising agency.

The national advertising program had always been administered by the company, with no formal input from the franchises. Many franchises were unhappy with previous campaigns and media placement so the company proposed to open up the process for franchises.

THE COOPERATIVE ADVERTISING PROGRAM

At the national franchisee convention, Jerry Salter's, regional vice president of operations for Baskin-Robbins, presented a new proposal for television advertising. Jerry opened the discussion by introducing Barbara Sutton from the Olander and Mays advertising agency located in Los Angeles. Mr. Sutton's presentation is summarized below.

As all of you know, we've always done national television advertising from Los Angeles. We have an exciting new campaign prepared for next year and I wanted to be here in person to tell you about it and answer your questions. The new campaign will effectively double our GRPs in each market and we are very pleased to involve you as franchises in our national television campaign for the first time. Before I get to the details, I want to share with you some of the creative executions already prepared for the Valentine's Day and Easter promotions and show you the proposed storyboards for the remaining four holiday pushes.

The agency had created a thirty-second and a fifteen-second advertisement for each of the holidays. A videotape showed each of the commercials three times. The ads had a unique style catchy theme and cute humorous touches:

Roses are red

Violets for lovers;

Baskin-Robbins has hearts

In 31 Flavors

When the tape ended, the franchises broke into applause. Obviously, there was support for these new spots. Barbara also narrated storyboards that were projected from sliders, and the additional advertising to be produced appeared that they would be a good follow-up to the early advertising in the campaign. Barbara explained the new advertising program.

We have worked hard to make your limited advertising budget pay off. We have always encouraged your company to spend more on television nationally. In the past years, the company has always given us slight increases in funds for media placement. But as media prices have risen, it has been difficult to maintain our share of media voice around the holidays. We considered moving our advertising to less competitive. Periods, but decided the we'd be shooting ourselves in the foot. If there's one thing the franchises seem to agree on is the importance of dessert advertising around the holidays.

Most franchises agreed. Store sales of desserts were very important in countering weather cycles in the northern climate of the Midwest. Four of the holidays occurred during slack walk-in periods, when the extra sales meant the difference between profit and loss for a month. Ice cream desserts also paid the highest profit margins of any product sold in a Basking-Robbins store.

"We've brainstormed on how to increase our GRPs without additional funds from the company. We've developed the first National cooperative campaign ever placed by your company. The company has committed itself to spending dramatically more than in past years on television advertising. The amount they actually spend will depend on you, the franchises. Beginning with the Valentine's Day campaign, the company will match dollar for dollar the advertising contributions of the franchises in each market area. This program is entirely voluntary for franchises. We are suggesting that each franchisee contribute 1 percent of each month's gross store sales to the national cooperative Advertising campaign. The company will match the money raised in each market area, effectively doubling what had been done before. The great thing about this plan is that there is no limit to the company's contribution. If you'd like to contribute 2 percent or 3 percent to the fund, the company will match you dollar for dollar.

Under the terms of the existing franchise agreements, the company cannot compel you to participate. If advertising is placed in a market area, all franchises in that area will benefit from it. We are counting on your cooperative spirit as fellow franchisees to make this cooperative campaign a success.

The program was to be administered by having the franchises from each market area elect a market captain to collect and disburse the advertising funds. The arrangements for collection were entirely up to the franchisees in the market area. Two months before the beginning for each campaign, the market captain would contact the agency and report how much money the market franchisees wished to spend on that holiday push. The agency arranged for matching funds from the company and for the media placement. Two weeks before the push was to begin, funds were due at the agency. When funds are received, the agency notified the television stations involved, and the campaign began.

The discussion at the meeting became quite lively, with numerous questions which Jerry and Barbara attempted to answer.

"What happens if we decide not to participate?

Jerry explained, "If one store declines, it becomes a free-rider. It will benefit from the contributions made by other area franchisees. Its absence will hurt the campaign because there will be less funding available locally and obviously less for matching from the company. If an entire market declines, the company will place no television advertising in that market area. You'd have to count on spillover effects through cable TV, but that would be sketchy at best".

"Is this program a foregone conclusion?"

Jerry answered, "Yes, the company believes this is the only fiscally sound approach it can take the short term. We've talked about rewriting franchise agreements to include a mandatory fee for national advertising, similar to that used by McDonald's and Burger King. But we don't want to renegotiate everyone's franchise agreement before its due date. We're confident that a cooperative spirit among franchisees will carry this program and that no mandatory advertising contribution clauses will have to be included in your franchise renewal when your five-year term rolls along."

"What kinds of input do we have into designing the advertising?"

Barbara answered "Some-quite a bit actually. The film you saw today is locked in but the storyboards are still subject to change. We appreciate your input and would consider any changes that make life easier for you and still keep us within the campaign objectives."

"What about placement? Last year in our market, we had Mother's Day ads placed on the David Letterman show. I don't like that show. I don't think any viewers would order a Mother's Day cake from my store."

Barbara continued, "Well, rather than talk about specific placements, let me just say that we examine each television program for the type of demographics it delivers. We attempt to match the delivered demographics with our targets for that holiday push, and place ads to generate maximum GRPs. For Mother's on her day. Without checking my records, I'd have to say the David Letterman Show have fit our program profile. But, if we argue over each placement, we'll have a very difficult time buying your advertising. At the agency, we have very expert people who select our advertising buys. I'm not an expert in this area and I trust our pros. I have you will trust them, too."

"What happens to me if I don't participate?"

"Well, nothing at first. But I certainly hope that peer pressure will help you see the light on this one. The company can't do anything to you directly. But we hope everyone will get into the spirit of this and pitch in their fair share."

PROGRAM IMPLEMENTATION

Don was chosen market captain for his area. There were three other owners in the market, each of whom he knew well. Each owned one Baskin-Robbins store. Two of Don's fellow franchises were within the same city; one was located in an adjacent urban area some 35 miles from Don's stores. This urban area was small and considered a part of Don's television market.

Adam Sleight owned the oldest store in the market. It was located in an older regional strip center that had been converted into a covered mall. While two major regional malls had been built in recent years, Adam's center retained a high traffic count due to its major anchor, sears. Adam's store was estimated to have over $250,000a year in gross sales.

Sal Bodoni owned the store that was out of town. Sal felt isolated from the other three owners, simply because he didn't meet for coffee as often as the others. Sal owned the only Baskin-Robbins store in his own, which was generally regarded as a well-run store. He'd been talking about selling his franchise because his wife Jean was in poor health and he wanted to retire.

Mara Orlowski a store on the west side of town. It was the newest Baskin-Robbins store in the market, having been open just a little over a year. Mara and her family were recent immigrants from Poland, who pooled family money to make a start in business. Mara and her husband Arkady had two daughters in high school and the family ran the store with no outside employees.

Don proposed that the store owners in his market go along with the 1 percent contribution rate. Mara and Sal agreed, but Adam wanted each store owner to contribute whatever they felt they could afford each month. After considerable discussion and other proposals, they finally settled on the 1 percent rate. Most other market areas agreed to similar proposals, although the contribution levels varied from .5 percent to 1.5 percent.

Over the course of the next several months, a number of problems arose in managing funds for the program. The following summaries of several phone calls between Don and the franchisees provide evidence of these problems.

Month One

"Adam, Don here. I didn't get your cheque for advertising yet. Oh, no, not postmarked by the tenth; in the bank by the tenth. Okay, what was your contribution?

Month Two

"Sal! Heard you put the store up for sale! Well, it's probably for the better. I didn't get your cheque this month, yet. Oh , well I understand you have to do remodeling before you sell, but remember we all agreed to participate. Okay. Next month, you'll make it up?"

Month Three

"Adam? Don. I got your cheque this month, but it's only for 50 dollars. Did you send me the wrong cheque? Hamm, well, no I didn't think they did a bad job of placing the last holiday push. Well, we can't penalize them by placing less advertising in our market. That's just hurting ourselves. If you don't like it. You should call Barbara. No it's not just me who can talk to her-call her yourself?"

Month Four

"Mara? Don. I didn't get your cheque yet this month. Well, yes, I realize it's getting into spring and we all need to build up our inventory levels. But advertising is what helps us to move that inventory. Please, send what you can this month and make it up next month."

"Sal? Don. About that back amount you owe to the advertising fund. Of course I understand it's voluntary, but it's also cooperative. No I'm not accusing you of being uncooperative. Hmm..... well, okay, I mean, if that's how you feel, contribute what you want.

Month Five

"Jerry? Don from store 181. This cooperative advertising fund is a pain in the rear! I'm the captain, and no one is 'cooperating!' Everyone has got an excuse each month. I feel like I'm carrying the ball here, and if I stopped hassling them, I'd be the only contributor. No it's more than Adam this time. Mara's short on cash this year and Sal's remodeling seems more important to him than promotion. I know there's nothing you can do to enforce it, but could you use some gentle persuasion?"

Month Six

"Hello? Adam How's it going? You're what? You can't pull out just because the Mother's Day ads didn't say 'order early!' you have to plan ahead for the demand. It was a good spot. I had enough stock on hand and you should have too! Won't you rethink this? I'll have to let Sal and Mara know about it if you pull out. What? You already talked with them?"

Month Seven

"Mara? Don. Will you contribute while it's busy this summer so we can have some TV in our market for Christmas? Anything would help. Thanks."

"Sal? Don. Mara says she'll kick in some advertising money during the busy months so we can buy some Christmas time on TV. Yeah, I know Adam's getting a free ride on this, but not contributing to the fund is like cutting off your nose to spite your face! C'mon, help us all out. Yes, I know you won't benefit if your store is sold by then, but think of the new owner."

Don felt he'd been a failure as a market captain. Other markets didn't seem to be having problems. Jerry and the company had not offered any help. Their hands were tied, it was a voluntary program. Don wondered how he could salvage the remainder of the television advertising campaign. He hoped the company would come up with something different for the next year.

❖ ❖ ❖

Chapter: 5

Distribution Strategies

Learning Objectives

In this chapter the main stress is given on :

- The evolution of distribution strategy.
- Understanding the Key Performance Indicators (KPIs) & Critical Success Factors (CSFs).
- An overview of distribution channel.
- Channel design model and its usage in distribution decisions..
- Understanding Exclusive, Intensive and Selective distribution.
- Managing channel conflict strategically.

EVOLUTION OF DISTRIBUTION STRATEGY

The company's marketing strategy is part of the overall business plan of the company and its corporate strategy. Distribution, being part of the marketing effort, forms a critical part of the changed as it requires building a network based on sound and long-term relationships. The overall strategy and direction for the company is spelt out in its corporate strategy. The marketing strategy outlines how this overall company strategy will be achieved using the company products and its distribution network. Organizing and managing the distribution function forms the part of the distribution strategy.

The distribution strategy could be looking at some of these factors:

- ***Defining customer service levels.*** This is the most critical factor in designing the channel strategy. The customer service level is what the customer is most interested in and hence requires extra care in defining.
- ***Defining the distribution objectives*** to achieve these service levels.
- ***Outlining the steps or activities*** required to achieve the distribution channel objectives.

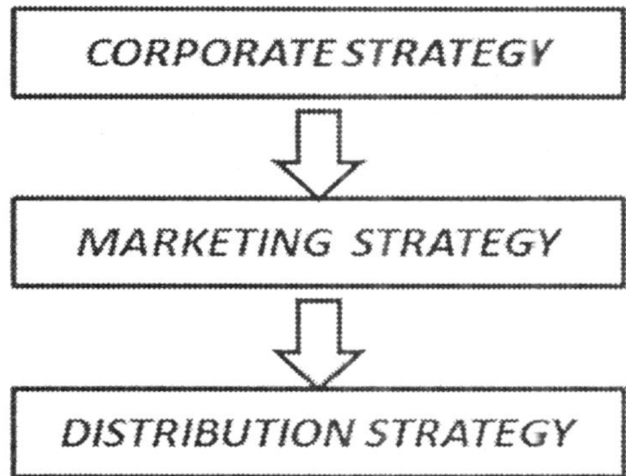

Figure 5.1 Evolution of a Distribution Strategy

- ***Deciding on the structure*** of the network to implement these activities to achieve the distribution objectives. These could be a combination of inside resources like the sales personnel and the outside resources like C&FAs, distribution and others.
- ***Clearly defined policy and procedure*** for the network to carry out its daily activities to achieve the objectives. Most companies cover this through and operations manual for the field operations so that there is no ambiguity or difference in interpretation.
- ***Starting the key performance indicators.*** This is only to check that the strategy is working well. This has to be worked out separately for each channel member.
- ***Understanding the critical success factors*** to make the distribution strategy effective.

We will discuss briefly each of the elements of the distribution strategy.

Customer service levels

The nature of the industry in which the company is operating, its products and services, its market share and the nature of competition help define the level of customer service the firm can promise its customers. Sometimes the affordability also dictates the service level. Companies could even think in terms of categorizing their customers into A, B and C (Pareto's Law) to decide different levels of service.

- Category A customers, who contribute the maximum to the company volumes and revenue, will obviously get special treatment. A customer product company could take extra care of its distributions. An automobile company takes extra care of the defense services who may contribute to maximum sales of its trucks.

- B category is the next set of customers who contribute who contribute regularly but in moderate levels to the business. They get second priority in service but are important as they have potential to become A category.
- C category customers are low contributors and may not even be regular. They can be handled as part of the routine marketing plans.

The extent of competition could also decide the level of service to be provided. The firm may increase the service levels in a prominent market where its share of the market is to be improved. Service levels could be in terms of number of distributors servicing the market, frequency of visits to the customers both by the channel partners and the company sales personnel, ready availability of stocks to service the market and so on. Once the service levels are decided, the distribution objectives can be set.

Setting distribution objectives

Apart from the firm's decision on the service levels to be provided, the customers also have certain expectations from the company and its channel partners. For example, retailers selling HLL products would want the company and its distribution to service them in such a way that they hold minimum stocks and at the same time never run out so stock. The distribution objectives to be worked out by HLL in this case would take care of this requirement of the customers also. The distribution objectives clearly spell out as to what is expected out of the network in ensuring the desired levels of customer service to meet the expectations of its customers. The expectations could only be in terms of the time, place and possession utilities as well as the period of credit which the company may be willing to offer its customers.

Set of activities

This part of the distribution strategy defines the manner in which the company and its channel partners go about actioning the customer the customer service objectives set earlier. This task is normally performed jointly by the company sales personnel along with the channel partners. Some of these steps could be:

- Periodic (normally monthly) sales forecasts by geography.
- Arranging for dispatch of the products from the plants or C&FAs to a point closest to the market-normally the distributor point based on some pre-agreed stock norms. The agreed levels of inventory at different points in the network are to be maintained.
- Developing beat plans for market coverage.
- Developing journey and beat plans for service engineers.
- Market visits to sell the products.

- Collection of sales proceeds.
- Carrying out promotional activities.
- Calling regularly on A category customers to build long term relationships.

It is necessary to clearly define these steps at this stage of the distribution strategy so that the company can also decide as to who has to perform each step defined here. Obviously some of the steps are to be taken by the company sales personnel and the others by the channel partners.

The distribution organization

Having established the service levels to be provided, the distribution objectives and the steps and activities to achieve the objectives, the firm has to now determine as to who will do what. This step will help define the organization structure to support the entire strategy. Decision points here could be:

- Extent of in-company support (own sales team) and outsourcing (use of channel partners). The planning of inventory, arranging for dispatches, credit management and collection of sales proceeds are activities normally done by the company personnel. This is accomplished by the sales people and the logistics function.
- Like it was mentioned earlier, this is also based on 'affordability'. Own sales team may mean higher fixed costs whereas a bigger outsourced network may mean higher variable costs if the volume goes up. Normally the channel partners are compensated based on percentage of sales value. Firms are now shifting to a method of mark-up rather than margins to avoid this problem. Either way, it indirectly affects the margins of the company.
- Selecting the channel partners including C&FAs and distributors, stockists or agents. This 'establishes' the channel that cannot be easily and frequently changed. The strategy also defines the guidance and rules for selection and appointment of partners.
- Setting clear objectives for each of the channel partners and systems to monitor the activities and measure the performance of the channel partners.
- Ensuring the correct and agreed level of financial investments by the channel partners in the company business. For example, leading companies specify the size of the warehouse which the distributor should have, the number of vans he should operate to cover the market, the number of sales and back office people he has to employ, his beat plans and the amount of credit he is expected to give in the market.

Policy and procedure

It is expected that the company sales personnel and its channel partners understand what is expected of them and discharge their roles and responsibilities faithfully. But as the salespeople may charge and the network is so vast with a large number of channel partners, not all of them may understand the policy and implementation guidelines in the same manner. Hence, companies clearly define policy and implementation guidelines. Normally this is in the form of operating manuals which are in the custody of the salespeople. The operations manual is capable of answering any query on procedure which the sales people or the channel partners may have on what action is to be taken in a given situation. The operation manual is an important tool to manage the distribution organization.

Apart from routine procedure, policy guidelines are also required on:

- System for redressal of complaints from the channel partners.
- System for setting disputes.
- Any additional payments to the channel members-for example in difficult territories or for covering rural markets, the firm may decide to subside the freight costs for carrying the goods to these markets for sometime till the volumes pick up.
- Coverage of institutional business and service levels to be extended.

Key Performance Indicators (KPIs)

The effectiveness of the strategy can only be judged if the company has agreed on certain measurement criteria with its channel partners. It is obvious that these KPIs all revolve around the promised service levels to the customers. If the service levels as perceived by the customer are being consistently achieved, the strategy and the implementation plans are working well. Some of the most popular KPIs are listed below:

- Consistent achievement of target by product groups, period and territories.
- Achievement of market shares.
- Achievement of profitability.
- Zero complaints from the customers.
- No stock returns.
- Ability to handle emergencies and sudden spurts in demand.
- Balanced sales achievements rather than period/month-end sales skews.
- Market coverage with ready stocks.
- Excellent management of accounts receivables.
- Minimize sales losses on account of stock-outs.
- Minimize damages to product.
- Critical Success Factors (CSFs)

Like any strategy, the distribution strategy also will be successful if it has the support and backing of the top management of the company. This can be achieved by involving them in the formulation of the strategy. Some of the other CSFs are outlined below:

- Clear, transparent and unambiguous policy and procedure.
- Serious commitment of the channel partners.
- Fair dealing of the company with all its partners. No undue favors to some of them at the cost of the others.
- Clearly defined customer service policy.
- High levels of integrity to be demonstrated by all the channel members.
- Equitable distribution in times of shortage of a product.
- Compensation to channel on special promotional activity should be prompt and not delayed.

An overview of Distribution Channels

A distribution channel is a group of people and firms involved in the transfer of title or ownership as the product moves the producer to the ultimate consumer.

The American marketing Association describes a distribution channel as: the structure of intra company organization units and extra company agents, dealers, wholesalers and retailers through which a commodity, product or service is marketed.

Distribution channels are nothing but intermediaries or middlemen between the producer and the customer. Further:

- They are there as the producers cannot reach all their consumers.
- They multiply reach and provide efficiency to the marketing process.
- They facilitate smooth flow and create time, place and possession utilities.
- They have the core competence and the reach which the company may not have and they can do this entire process more cost effectively.
- They also provide contact, experience, specialization and scales of operation. Distribution channels can broadly be classified as:
- Sales channel- which has the functions of motivating buyers, sharing information between the customer and the company, negotiating fair bargains for the consumer and financing the transactions.
    - A distribution for Nestle would perform all these functions for the company by dealing with the retailers and wholesalers who stock and sell the company products.
    - A franchisee for Pepsi would act in a similar manner.

- Delivery channel- which is only meant for physical transactions.
  - This is the primary job of a carrying & Forwarding Agent. A C& FA for Marico would ensure that the orders received from the company for the company for the company distributors would be physically delivered to them on time in full. The C& FA would also receive and stock the company products for distribution.
- Service channel- which performs after sales service like a Maruti service station.
  - A franchise for HP would help its customers either service or repair the PCs or other hardware bought by the customers from HP.

Distribution channels normally include the following:

- Company owned distribution centers (DCs) or carrying & forwarding Agents (C&FAs) or consignment selling Agents (CSAs)
- Distributors, stockists, value added resellers and agents-who could be exclusive or shared.
- Wholesalers who stock and sell a variety of products including that of competition.
- Retailers who are the ultimate and direct connect with the end user or consumer.
- For industrial products, the company's own sales force and marketing team could also serve as a part of the channel system.

Each channel member has unique characteristics and serves some objectives for the companies doing business in given market or geography. We will look at the brief profile of each of them here:

C&FAs, CSAs

This category is known as facilitators. Carrying and Forwarding agents are basically transporters who act as a mid way point between the company and its distributors. Their role is to collect the products from the company plant and store them in a central location for breaking bulk and dispatching to the distributors against indents from the company. C&FAs take physical possession of the goods but do not pay for it. The goods in the C&FA warehouse still belong to the company. In India, before the introduction of value Added Tax (VAT) the sales tax rules were so difficult that it was required that companies with a national distribution had to keep one distribution centre of their own or at least one C&FA in each state.

Consignment Selling Agents act as C&FAs or CSAs are on contract with the company.

Distributors, dealers, stockists, agents

This set of channel members are also known as stockists, agents and guarantors depending on the extent of re-distribution undertaken by them for the companies they represent. Agents do not invest in the company's products. All belong to the same category of company outsourcing to help distribute products to retailers. Some characteristics of distributors are:

- They are required to invest in the product by buying it from the company.
- They are on commission, margin or mark-ups.
- They may or may not get credit from the company. They, however, give credit to their customers who are wholesalers or retailers.
- Commission or margin is percentage of the price at which they buy the product from the company.
- Mark-up is still a percentage but based on the selling price to the customer/retailer.

Distributors work in the market and redistribute the stocks to the customers-wholesalers and retailers. Stockists may just invest in the products but expect the company to sell the products to the customers. Agents, dealers are only helping distribution with their contacts in the market place either with wholesalers/retailers or institutions, Distribution may be exclusive for the company or shared with others. Normally they sign some kind of an agreement or contract with the firm.

Wholesalers

They normally operate out of the main markets in a city. They deal with a large number of companies' products and packs. They have their own shops in busy trading areas. They depend on large volumes of business as their margins are quite low. In some cases it is know that wholesalers manage their margins on some products just by selling empty cases or cartons in which the products are received. Their features are:

- They choose and decide what products they will sell.
- They are not on contact with any company.
- Their customers are other wholesalers, retailers and institutions.
- They negotiate about 15 days credit from the distributors and special privileges on giving purchase requests more than once a week even though the beat plan of the distributors may give them one visit a week.
- They extend credit terms to their loyal customers.

With the increase in the number of supermarkets, the role of wholesalers is getting diluted.

Retailers

They are the shopkeepers who set up shops in the market place to cater to the needs of hundreds of consumers. If the retailer is located in a busy part of the market where the consumer traffic is large, he can command a lot of profitable terms from the distributors and companies- like credit, promotions, renting display space and so on. Anyway, the retailer makes the highest margins in the entire supply chain. Retailers extend credit to only about 25 per cent of their customers. They have also started home delivery to their regular customers close to their outlet.

Value added resellers purchase the incomplete product or kit and add value by assembling it and selling to the customer depending on his specifications. Example could be of personal computers or even bicycles.

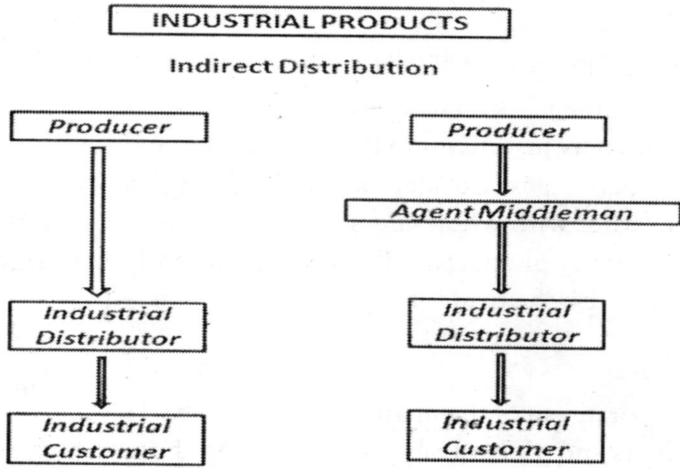

Figure 5.2(a) Distribution Channels for Industrial Products

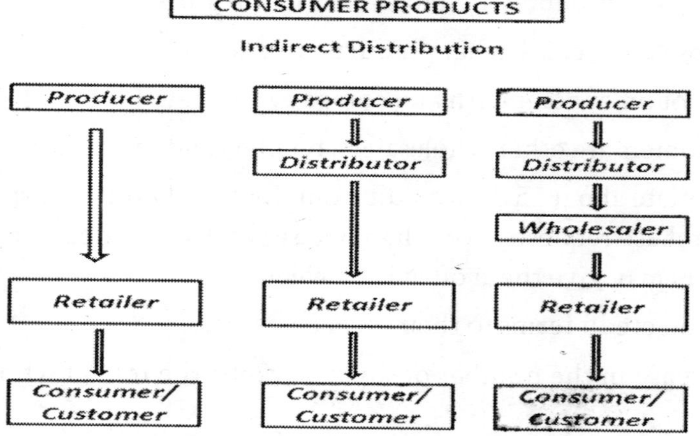

Figure 5.2(b) Distribution Channels for Consumer Products

CHANNEL- STRUCTURE STRATEGY

The channel-structure strategy refers to the number of intermediaries that may be employed in moving goods from manufacturers to customers. A company may undertake to distribute its goods to customers or retailers without involving any intermediary. This strategy constitutes the shortest channel and may be labeled a direct distribution strategy. Alternatively, goods may pass through one or more intermediaries, such as wholesalers or agents. This is an indirect distribution strategy. Figure 5.2(a) & 5.2(b) shows alternative channel structures for consumer and industrial products. Decisions about channel structure are based on a variety of factors. To a significant extent, channel structure is determined by where inventories should be maintained to offer adequate customer service, fulfill required sorting processes and still deliver a satisfactory return to channel members.

An underlying factor in determining channel-structure strategy is the use of intermediaries. The importance of using intermediaries is illustrated with reference to an example of a primitive economy used by Alderson. In a primitive economy, five producers produce one type of item each: hats, hoes, knives, baskets or pots, because each producer needs all the other producers' products, a total of 10 exchanges are required to accomplish trade. However, with a market (or middlemen), once the economy reaches equilibrium (i.e., each producer consumer has visited the market once), only five exchanges need to take place to meet everyone's needs. Let n denote the number of product-consumers. Then the total number of transactions (T) without a market is given by:

$$\text{Twithout} = \frac{n(n-1)}{2}$$

and the total number of transactions with a market is given by:

$$T_{\text{with}} = n$$

The efficiency created in distribution by using an intermediary may be viewed using this equation:

$$\text{Efficiency} = \frac{T_{\text{without}}}{T_{\text{with}}} = \frac{n(n-1)}{2} \times \frac{1}{n} = \frac{n-1}{2}$$

In the example of five producer-consumers, the efficiency of having a middle man is 2. The efficiency increases as n increases. Thus, in many cases, intermediaries may perform the task of distribution more efficiently than manufacturers alone.

Postponement-speculation Theory

Conceptually, the selection of channel structure may be explained with reference to Bucklin's postponement-speculation framework. The framework is based on risk, uncertainly and costs involved in facilitating exchanges. Postponement seeks to eliminate risk by matching production/distribution with actual customer demand. Presumably should produce efficiency in marketing channels. For example, the manufacturer may produce and ship goods only on confirmed orders. Speculation, on the other hand, requires undertaking risk through changes in form and movement of goods within channels. Speculation leads to economies of scale in manufacturing, reduces costs of frequent ordering and eliminates opportunity cost.

Exhibit 5.1 shows the behavior of variables involved in the postponement speculation framework. The vertical axis show the average cost of undertaking a function for one unit of any given commodity; the horizontal axis shows the time involved in delivering a confirmed order. Together, the average cost and the delivery time measure the cost of marketing tasks performed in a channel with reference to delivery time. The nature of the three curves depicted in Exhibit 5.1 should be understood: C represents costs to the buyer for holding an inventory; AD', costs involved in supplying goods directly from a manufacturer to a buyer; and DB, costs involved in shipping and maintaining speculative inventories (i.e., in anticipation of demand).

EXHIBIT 5.1 Using the Postponement-Speculation concept to determine channel structure

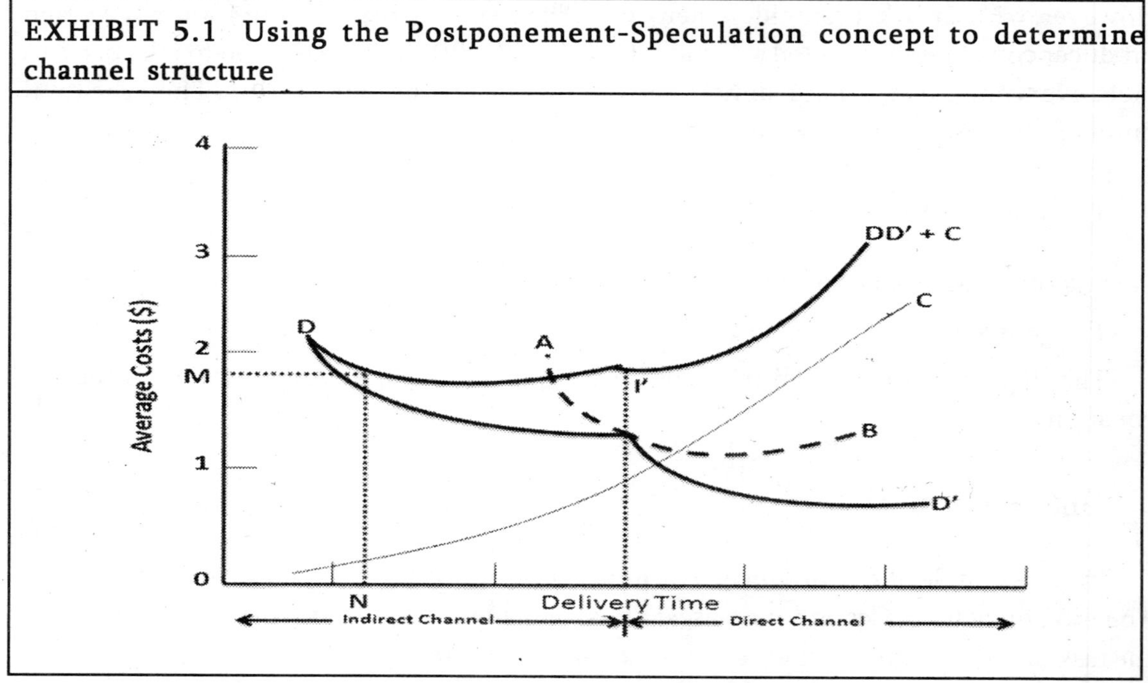

Source: Louis P Bucklin and Leslie Halpert, "Exploring Channels of Distribution for Cement with the Principle of postponement-speculation," in Marketing and economic development,ed.Peter D. Bennett(Chicago: American Marketing Association,1965):698

Following Bucklin's framework, one determines the channel structure by examining the behavior of the C,AD', and DB curves:

1. The minimal cost of supplying the buyer for every possible delivery time is derived from curves AD' and DB. As may be seen in Exhibit 5.1, especially fast delivery service can be provided only by the indirect channel (i.e., by using a stocking intermediary). However, at some delivery time, I' the cost of serving the consumer directly from the producer will intersect and fall below the cost of indirect shipment. The minimal costs derived from both curves are designated DD'. From the perspective of channel cost, it will be cheaper to service the buyer from a speculative inventory if delivery times shorter than I' are demanded. If the consumer is willing to accept delivery times longer than I', then direct shipment will be the least expensive.
2. The minimal total cost curve for the channel with respect to delivery time is derived by summing the cost of moving goods to the buyer, DD' and the buyer's costs of holding inventory, C. The curve is represented in Exhibit 5.1 by DD'+ C Total channel costs initially fall as delivery time lengthens because increased buyer expenses are more than made up for by saving in other parts of the channel. Gradually, however, the savings from these sources diminish and buyer costs begin to rise more rapidly. A minimal cost point is reached and expenses for the channel rise thereafter. Channel structure is controlled by the location of this minimum point. If, as in the present case, it falls to the left of I', then goods would be expected to flow through the speculative inventory (i.e., an intermediary). If on the other hand, the savings of the buyer from postponement had not been as great as those depicted, the minimum point would have fallen to the right of I' and shipments would have been made directly from the producer to the consumer.

Benetton, an Italian apparel maker, offers an excellent example of a distribution strategy that combines speculation with postponement in an effort to optimize both service and cost. Speculation involves commitment by retailers to specific inventory items months before the start of the selling season. It leads to such advantages for Benetton as low-cost production (via use of subcontractors) and good quality control (via centralized warehousing and assembly of orders). Postponement of orders requires last-minute dyeing of woolen items at an added cost. The advantages of speculation are flexibility in meeting market needs and reduced inventory levels.

Additional Consideration in Determining Channel Structure

The postponement-speculation theory provides an economic explanation of the way the channels are structured. Examined in this section are a variety of environmental influences on channel-structure strategy formulation. These influences may be technological, social and ethical, governmental, geographical or culture.

Many aspects of channel structure are affected by technological advances. For example, mass retailing in food has become of the development of automobiles, highways, refrigerated cars, cash registers, packing improvements and mass communications (television). In the coming years, television shopping with household computer terminals should have a far-reaching impact on distribution structures. Technological advances permitted Sony to become dominant in the U.S. market for low-priced CD players. Sony developed prepackaged players that could be sold through mass retailers so that even sales clerks without technical know-how could handle customers.

How technology may be used to revamp the operations of a wholesaler, marketing it worthwhile to adopt indirect channels, is illustrated by the case of Foremost-McKesson, the nation's largest wholesale distributor. A few years ago the company found itself in a precarious. Distribution, through one of the company's most pervasive business functions, did not pay. Foremost-McKesson merely took manufacturers' goods and resold them to small retailers through a routine process of warehousing, transportation and simple marketing that offered thin profits. As a matter of fact, at one time the company came close to selling off drug wholesaling, its biggest business. Instead, however, its new chief executive decided to add sophisticated technology to its operations in order to make the company so efficient at distribution that manufacturers could not possibly do as well on their own. It virtually redefined the function of the intermediary. Having used the computer to make its own operations efficient, it devised ways to make its data processing useful to suppliers and customers, in essence making foremost part of their marketing teams. Since the company computerized its operations, foremost has turned around dramatically.

Here are the highlights of foremost are steps in reshaping its role:

- Acting as middleman between drugstore and insurance offices by processing medical insurance claims.
- Creating a massive "rack jobbing" service by providing crews to set up racks of goods inside retail stores, offering what amounts to a temporary labor force that brings both marketing know-how and foremost merchandise along with it.
- Taking waste products as well as finished goods from chemical manufactures, and recycling the wastes through its own plants-its first entry into chemical waste management.
- Designing, as well as supplying, drugstores.
- Researching new uses for products it receives from manufacturers. Foremost found new customers, for example, for a Monsanto Co. food preservative from among its contacts in the cosmetics industry.

Another example of the use of technology to overhaul distribution is provided by Britain's supermarket chain Tesco. The firm's nine composite (variable temperature) distribution centers use a just-in-time system (known as pick-by-line or cross-docking). That means goods amounting to around 40% of total sales go straight out to the stores within hours of arrival.

Social taboos and ethical standards may also affect the channel-structure decision. For example, Mallen reports that Viva, a woman's magazine, had achieved a high circulation in supermarkets and drugstore in Canada. When Viva responded to readers' insistence and to competition from playgirl by introducing nude male photos, most supermarkets banned the magazine. Because supermarkets accounted for more than half of Viva's dropped the photos so that it could continue to be sold through this channel.

The channel-structure strategy can also be influenced by local, state and federal laws in a variety of ways. For example, door-to-door selling of certain goods may be prohibited by local laws. In many states (e.g., California and Ohio) wine can be sold through supermarkets, but other states (e.g., Connecticut) do not permit this.

Geographic size, population patterns and typology also influence the channel-structure strategy. In urban areas, direct distribution to large retailers may make sense. Rural areas, however, may be covered only by wholesalers.

With the inception of large grocery chains, it may often appear that independent grocery stores are dying. The truth is, however, that independent grocery stores as recently as 1992 accounted for 46 percent of all grocery sales in the country-over $175 billion. Thus, a manufacturer can ill afford not to deal with independents and to reach them it must go through wholesalers, Watteau, for example, is a grocery wholesale firm in Hazelwood, Missouri, which did over $6 billion worth of business serving almost 3,000 retail grocery stores. It does not do any business with chain stores. But because of Wetterau's determination to offer its customers relatively low prices, a wide selection of brands, service programs carefully designed to make brands more profitable and a personal interest in their sources, its customers are almost fanatically loyal. The company offers its customers-small independent retail stores-a variety of services, including lease arrangements, store design, financing packages, training and computerized inventory systems. These services tend to enhance customers competitiveness by reducing their operating costs and by simplifying their bookkeeping, which in turn helps Wetterau to earn profits. The Wetterau example shows that to reach smaller retailers, particularly in areas removed from large metropolises, the indirect distribution strategy is appropriate. The wholesaler provides service to small retailers that a large manufacturer can never match on its own.

Finally, cultural traits may require the adoption of a certain channel structure in a setting that otherwise might seem an odd place for it. For example, in many parts of Switzerland, fruits and vegetables are sold in central marketplace in the morning by small vendors, even though there are modern supermarkets all over. This practice continues because it gives customers a chance to socialize while shopping. Similarly, changing lifestyles among average American consumer and their desire to have more discretionary income for life-fulfillment activities appear to be making warehouse retailing (e.g., Sam's Club) more popular. This is so because prices at warehouse outlets-grocery warehouses, for example- are substantially lower than at traditional stores.

CHANNEL DESIGN MODEL.

Presented below is a channel design model that can be used to make the direct/indirect distribution decision. The model involves six basic steps.

1. List the factors that could potentially influence the direct/ indirect decision. Each factor must be evaluated carefully in terms of the firm's industry position and competitive strategy.
2. Pick out the factors that will have the most impact on the channel design decision. No factor with a dominant impact should be left out. For example, assume that the following four factors have been identified as having particular significance:
   (i) Market concentration,
   (ii) Customer service level,
   (iii) Asset specificity
   (iv) Availability of working capital.
3. Decide how each factor identified is related to the attractiveness of a direct or an indirect channel. For example, concentration reflects the size distribution of the firm's customers as well as their geographical dispersion. Therefore, the more concentrated the market, the more desirable the direct channel because of the lower costs of serving that market (high=direct; low = indirect). Customer service level is made up of at least three factors: delivery time, lost size, and product availability. The more customer service required by customers, the less desirable is the direct channel (high=indirect; low=direct). The direct channel is more desirable, at least under conditions of high uncertainly in the environment, with a high level of asset specificity (high=direct; low=indirect). Finally, the greater the availability of working

capital, the more likely it is that a manufacturer can afford and consider a direct channel (high=direct; low=indirect). Note that a high level on a factor does not always correspond to a direct channel.

4. Create a matrix based on the key factors to consider the interactions among key factors. If only two factors are being considered, a two-by-two matrix of four cells would result. For three, a three-by-three matrix of nine cells would result. For four factors, a four-by-four matrix of sixteen cells would result and so on. If more than five or six factors are involved, a series of smaller models could be constructed to make this fourth step more manageable. Exhibit 5.2 presents a four-by four matrix developed for this example.
5. Decide (for each cell in the matrix) whether a direct channel, an indirect channel or a combination of both a direct and an indirect channel is most appropriate, considering the factors involved. Combination channels are becoming more common in business practice, especially in industrial markets. For some cells in the matrix, deciding which channel design is best is rather easy to do. For example, Cell 1 in Exhibit 5.2 has all four factors in agreement that an indirect channel is best. This is also true for Cell 16: a direct channel is the obvious choice. For other Cells, choosing between a direct channel and an indirect channel is not as easy because factors conflict with each other to some extent. For example, in Cell 14, asset specificity is low, suggesting that an indirect channel is best. The other three factors suggest otherwise, however; the market is concentrated, customer service requirements are low and the availability of capital to the manufacturer is high. Taken together, the factors in Cell 14 reveal that a direct channel would be most attractive. In the cells that have factors that conflict with one another, the strategist must make trade-offs among them to decide whether a direct channel, indirect channel or combination of channels is best.
6. For each product or service in question, locate the corresponding cell in the box model. The prediction in this cell is the one that should be followed or at least the one that should be most seriously considered by the firm.

The accuracy of the model generated by this method depends totally on the expertise and skills of the person who builds and uses it. If a carefully constructed such a model can be invaluable in designing more efficient and effective channels of distribution.

EXHIBIT 5.2

			Asset Specificity: Low		Asset Specificity: High	
			Capital Availability		Capital Availability	
Market Concentration	Customer Service Level		Low	High	Low	High
Low		High	Cell 1 indirect	Cell 3 indirect	Cell 2 indirect	Cell 4 combination
Low		Low	Cell 5 indirect	Cell 7 combination	Cell 6 combination	Cell 8 direct
High		High	Cell 9 indirect	Cell 11 combination	Cell 10 direct	Cell 12 direct
High		Low	Cell 13 combination	Cell 15 combination	Cell 14 direct	Cell 16 direct

Designing a Distribution Channel Matrix

Source: Gary L. Frazier, "Designing Channels of Distribution," The Channel for communication(Seattle, Wash.: Centre for Retail Distribution Management, University of Washington, 1987):3:-7.

DISTRIBUTION-SCOPE STRATEGY

For an efficient channel network, the manufacturer should clearly define the target customers it intends to reach. Implicit in the definition of target customers is a decision about the scope of distribution the manufacturer wants to pursue. This determines the intensity of desired distribution after a firm has decided on the most appropriate channels of distribution. In a way, the intensity denotes the service level that the organization provides to customers. There are three types of strategic alternatives distribution intensity.

- Exclusive distribution
- Intensive distribution
- Selective distribution

A detail explanation of the three different patterns of distribution strategy is as follows:

Exclusive Distribution

Exclusive distribution means that one particular retailer serving a given area is granted sole rights to carry a product. For example, coach leather goods are distributed exclusively through select stores in an area. Several advantages may be gained by the use of exclusive distribution. It promotes tremendous dealer loyalty, greater sales support, a higher degree of control over the retail market, better forecasting and better inventory and merchandising control. The impact of dealer loyalty can be helpful when a manufacturer has seasonal or other kinds of fluctuating sales. An exclusive dealership is more willing to finance inventories and thus bear a higher degree of risk than a more extensive dealership. Having a smaller number of dealers gives a manufacturer or wholesaler greater opportunity to provide each dealer with promotional support. And with fewer outlets, it is easier to control such aspects as margin, price and inventory. Dealers are also more willing to provide data that may be used for marketing research and forecasts. Exclusive distribution is especially relevant for products that customers seek out. Examples of such products include Rolex watches, Gucci bags, Regal shoes, Celine neckties and Mark Cross wallets.

On the other hand, there are several obvious disadvantages to exclusive distribution. First, sales volume may be lost. Second, the manufacturer places all its fortunes in a geographic area in the hands of one dealer. Exclusive distribution brings with it the characteristics of high price, high margin and low volume. If the product is highly price elastic in nature, this combination of characteristics can mean significantly less than optimal performance. Relying on one retailer can mean that if sales are depressed for any reason, the retailer is then likely to be in a position to dictate terms to other channel members (i.e., the retailer becomes the channel captain).

This is more selective than the earlier example. Only one outlet in a market may keep the product. In addition, the outlets set up by companies for their own products could also be counted among these. Example is of Bata outlets or Titan showrooms. The producer is interested in keeping a close watch and controls on the distribution of his products. It requires a good relationship between the producer and the reseller. Examples include exclusive women's apparel and electronic appliances.

The last disadvantage of exclusive distribution is one that is easy to overlook. In certain circumstances, exclusive distribution has been found to be in violation of antitrust laws because of its restraint on trade. The legality of an exclusive contract varies from case to case. As long as an exclusive contract does not undermine competition and create a monopoly, it is acceptable. The courts appear to use the following criteria to determine if indeed an exclusive distribution lessens competition:

1. Whether the volume of the product in question is a substantial part of the total volume for that product type.
2. Whether the exclusive dealership excludes competitive products from a substantial share of the market.

Thus, a company considering an exclusive distribution strategy should review its decision in the light of these two ground rules.

Intensive Distribution

The inverse of exclusive distribution is intensive distribution. Intensive distribution makes product available at all possible retail outlets. This may mean that the product is carried at a wide variety of different and also competing retail institutions in a given area. The distribution of convenience goods is most consistent with this strategy. If the nature of a product is such that a consumer generally does not bother to seek out the product but will buy it on sight if available, then it is to the seller's advantage to have the product visible in as many places as possible. The Bic Pen Corporation is an example of a firm that uses this type of strategy. Bic makes its products available in a wide variety of retail establishments, ranging from drugstores, to "the corner grocery store", to large supermarkets. In all, Bic sells through 250,000 retail outlets, which represent competing as well as noncompeting stores. The advantages to be gained from this strategy are increased sales, wider customer recognition and impulse buying. All these qualities are desirable for convenience goods.

There are two main disadvantages associated with intensive distribution. First, intensively distributed goods are characteristically low-priced and low-margin products that require a fast turnover. Second, it is difficult to provide any degree of control over a large number of retailers. In the short run, uncontrolled distribution may not pose any problem if the intensive distribution leads to increased sales. In the long run, however, it may have a variety of devastating effects. For example, if durable products such as Sony television sets were to be intensively distributed (i.e., through drugstores, discount stores, variety stores, etc.,) Sony's sales would probably increase. But such intensive distribution could lead to the problems of price discounting, inadequate customer service and noncooperation among traditional channels (e.g., department stores). Not only might these problems affect sales revenues in the long run, but the manufacturer might also lose some of its established channels. For example, a department store might decide to drop the Sony line for another brand of television sets. In addition, Sony's distinctive brand image could suffer. In other words, the advantages furnished by intensive distribution should be related carefully to product type to decide if this form of distribution is suitable. It is because of the problems outlined above that one finds intensive distribution limited to such products as candy, newspapers, cigarettes, aspirin and soft drinks. For these types of products, turnover is usually high and channel control is usually not as strategic as it would be, for television sets.

This strategy is to make sure that the product is made available in as many outlets as possible so that anywhere the consumer goes, he or she should be able to get the product of his choice.

- If HUL is proud of the fact that its products are available in 3 million outlets, it can be the best example of intensive distribution.
- This system helps increase coverage and hence sales, and is most suitable for FMCG products.

- Automobile manufacturers would prefer this intensity of distribution for their spare parts.

Selective Distribution

Between exclusive and intensive distribution, there is selective distribution. Selective distribution is the strategy in which several but not all retail outlets in a given area distribute a product. ***Shopping goods***-goods that consumers seek on the basis of the most attractive price or quality characteristics-are frequently distributed through selective distribution. Because of this, competition among retailers is far greater for shopping goods than for convenience goods. Naturally, retailers wish to reduce competition as much as possible. This causes them to pressurise manufacturers to reduce the number of retail outlets in their area distributing a given product in order to reduce competition.

The number of retailers under as selective distribution strategy should be limited by criteria that allow the manufacturer to choose only those retailers who will make a contribution to the firm's overall distribution objectives. For example, some firms may choose retail outlets that can provide acceptable repair and maintenance service to consumers who purchase their products. In the automotive industry, selective criteria are used by manufacturers in granting dealerships. These criteria consists of such considerations as showroom space, service facilities and inventory levels.

It is obvious that in this case only a few select outlets will be permitted to keep the company products. The outlets are carefully selected by the company in line with the image it wants to project about itself and its exclusive products. This may be dictated by the value of the product. For example if one is shopping for Tanishq jewellery, it would be available in a few exclusive outlets only. Selective distribution gives the advantage of making the product available in outlets that matters the most and keeping distribution costs lower.

The point may be illustrated with reference to Pennsylvania House, a furniture company. The company used to have 800 retail accounts, but it cut this number to 500. This planned cut obviously limited the number of stores in which the company's product line was exposed. More limited distribution provided the company with much stronger support among surviving dealers. Among these 500 dealers there was a higher average amount of floor space devoted to Pennsylvania House merchandise, better customer service, better supplier relations and most important for the company, substantially increased sales per account.

Selective distribution is best applied circumstances in which high sales volume can be generated by a relatively small number of retailers or in other words, in which the manufacturer would not appreciably increase its coverage by adding additional dealers. Selective distribution can also be used effectively in situations in which a manufacturer requires a high- caliber firm to carry a full product line and provide necessary services. A dealer in this position is likely to require promotional and technical assistance. The technical assistance is needed not only in conjunction with the sale but also after the sale in the form of repair and maintenance service. Again, by limiting the number of retail outlets to a select few capable of covering the market, the manufacturer can avoid unnecessary costs associated with signing on additional dealers.

Obviously, the greatest danger associated with a strategy of selective distribution is the risk of not adequately the market. The consequences of the error are greater than the consequences of initially having one or two extra dealers. Therefore, when in doubt, it is better to have too much coverage that not enough.

In selective distribution, it is extremely important for a manufacturer to choose dealers (retailers) who most closely match the marketing goals and image intended for the product. There can be segments within retail markets; therefore, identifying the right retailers can be the key to penetrating a chosen market. Every department store cannot be considered the same. Among them there can be price, age and image segmentation. One does not need to be very accurate in distinguishing among stores of the same type in the case of products that have no special image (i.e., those that lend themselves to un-segmented market strategies and mass distribution). But for products with any degree of fashion or style content or with highly segmented customer groups, a selective distribution strategy requires a careful choice of outlets.

To appraise what type of product is suitable for what form of distribution, refer to Exhibit 5.3. This exhibit combines the traditional threefold classification of consumer goods (convenience, shopping and specialty goods) with a threefold classification of retail stores (convenience, shopping and specialty stores) to determine the appropriate form of distribution. This initial selection may then be examined in the light of other considerations to make a final decision on the scope of distribution.

EXHIBIT 5.3
Selection of Suitable Distribution Policies Based on the Relationship between Type of Product and Type of Store

Classification	Consumer Behavior	Most likely From of Distribution
Convenience store/ Convenience good	The consumer prefers to buy the most readily available brand of a product at the most accessible store	Intensive
Convenience store/shopping good	The consumer selects his or her purchase from among the assortment carried by the most accessible store.	Intensive
Convenience store/specialty good	The consumer purchases his or her favorite brand from the most accessible Store carrying the item in stock.	Selective/ exclusive
Shopping store/ convenience good	The consumer is indifferent to the brand of product he or she buys but shops different stores to secure better retail service and/or retail price.	Intensive
Shopping store/ shopping good	The consumer makes comparisons among both retail-controlled factors and factors associated with the product (brand).	Intensive
Shopping store/specialty good	The consumer has a strong preference as to product brand but shops a number of stores to secure the best retail service and/or price for this brand.	Selective/ exclusive
Specialty store/convenience good	The consumer prefers to trade at a specific store but is indifferent to the brand of product purchased.	Selective/ exclusive
Specialty/store/shopping good	The consumer prefers to trade at a certain store but is uncertain as to which product he or she wishes to buy and examines the store's assortment for the best purchase.	Selective/ exclusive
Specialty store/specialty good	The consumer has both a preference for a particular store and for a specific brand.	Selective/ Exclusive

Source: Louis P.Bucklin, " Retail Strategy and the Classification of Consumer Goods," Journal of Marketing (Jan 1963):50-55;published by American Marketing Association.

MULTIPLE-CHANNEL STRATEGY

The multiple-channel strategy refers to a situation in which two or more different channels are employed to distribute goods and services. The market must be segmented so that each segment gets the services it needs and pays only for them, not for services it does not need. This type of segmentation usually cannot be done effectively by direct selling alone or by exclusive reliance upon distributors. The Robinson-Patman Act makes the use of price for segmentation almost impossible when selling to the same kind of customer through the same distribution channel. Market segmentation, however, may be possible when selling directly to one class of customer and to another only through distributors, which usually requires different services, prices and support. Thus, a multiple-channel strategy permits optimal access to each individual segment.

Basically, there are two types of multiple channels of distribution, complementary and competitive.

Complementary channels

Complementary channels exist when each channel handles a different noncompeting product or noncompeting market segment. An important reason to promote complementary channels is to reach market segments that cannot otherwise be served. For example, Avon Products, which had sold directly to consumers for 100 years, broke the tradition in 1986 and began selling some perfumes (e.g., Deneuve fragrance, which sells for as much as $165 an ounce) through department stores. The rationale behind this move was to serve customer segments that the company could not reach through direct selling. Samsonite Corporation sells the same type of luggage to discount stores that it distributes through department stores, with some cosmetic changes in design. In this way the company is able to reach middle and low-income segments that may never shop for luggage in department stores. Similarly, magazines use newsstand distribution as a complementary channel to subscriptions. Catalogs serve as complementary channels for large retailers such as J.C. Penney.

The simplest way to create complementary channels is through private branding. This permits entry into markets that would otherwise be lost. The Coca-Cola Company sells its Minute Maid frozen orange juice to A&P to be sold under the A&P name. At the same time, the Minute Maid brand is available in A&P stores. Presumably, there are customers who perceive the private brand to be no different in quality from the manufacturers brand. Inasmuch as the private brand is always a little less expensive than a manufacturer's brand, such customers prefer the lower-price private brand. Thus, private branding helps broaden the market base.

There is another reason that may lead a manufacturer to choose this strategy. In instances where other firms in an industry have saturated traditional distribution channels for a product, a new entry may be distributed through a different channel. This new channel may then in turn be different from the traditional channel used for the rest of the manufacturer's product line. Hanes, for example, decided to develop a new channel for L'eggs (supermarkets and drugstores) because traditional channels were already crowded with competing brands. Likewise, R. Dakin developed nontraditional complementary channels to distribute its toys. Although most toy manufacturers sell their wares through toy shops and department stores,

Dakin distributes more than 60 percent of its products through a variety of previously ignored outlets such as airports, hospital gift shops, restaurants, amusement parks, stationery stores and drugstores. This strategy lets Dakin avoid direct competition. In recent years, many companies have developed new channels in the form of direct mail sales for such diverse products as men's suits, shoes, insurance, records, newly published books and jewelry.

Still yet to come is electronic commerce. The internet is going to change where and how consumers shop and retailers sell. It will become the location to buy almost anything a person wants-fast, easy and whenever he/she wants it. But that does not mean that traditional retail stores will become relics. For one thing, it is going to be a long time before the majority of consumers do most of their shopping on the Web. Further, the physical limits of buying on the Web mean that not every product is suited to online purchasing.

U.S. consumers spent $5 billion on purchases on the Web in 1997. The number was likely to be $11 billion in 1998 and would soar to $95 billion in 2002. As personal computers and online service penetrate more and more households, the number of cybershoppers will grow. By 2022, 22% of U.S. households will use internet services and 30% are expected to use the Internet to do a large part of their shopping.

A company may also develop complementary channels to broaden the market when its traditional channel happens to be a large account. For example, Easco Corporation, the nation's second-largest maker of hand tools, had for years tied itself to Sears, Roebuck and company, supplying wrenches, socket and other tools for the retailer's Craftsman line. Sears accounted for about 47 percent of Easco's sales and about 62 percent of its pretax earnings in the mid-1980s. But as Sear's growth showed, Easco had a critical strategic dilemma: what do you do when one dominant customer stops growing and starts to slip? The company decided to lessen its dependence on Sears by adding some 500 new hardware and home-center stores for its hand tools.

To broaden their markets in recent years, many clothing manufacturers, including Ralph Lauren, Liz Claiborne, Calvin Klein, Anne Klein and Adrienne Vittadini, have opened their own stores to sell a full array of their clothes and accessories Again to broaden the market, brand-name fast-food companies, Pizza Hut, Subway Sandwiches, Salad Kiosk and others, have started selling their products in public school cafeterias.

Complementary channels may also be necessitated by geography. Many industrial companies undertake direct distribution of their products in such large metropolitan areas as New York, Chicago, Detroit and Cleveland. Because the market is dense and because of the proximity of customers to each other, a sales person can make more than 10 calls a day. The same company that sells directly to its customers in urban environments, however, may use manufacturers' representatives or some other type of intermediary in the hinterlands because the market there is too thin to support full-time salespeople.

Another reason to promote complementary channels is to enhance the distribution of noncompeting items. For example, may food processors package fruits and vegetables for institutional customers in giant cans that have little market among household customers. These products, therefore, are distributed through different channels Procter & Gamble manufactures toiletries for hotels, motels, hospitals, airlines and so on, which are distributed through different channel arrangements. The volume of business may also require the use of different channels. Many appliance manufactures sell directly to builders but use distributors and dealers for selling to household consumers.

The basis for employing complementary channels is to enlist customers and segments that cannot be served when distribution is limited to a single channel. Thus, the addition of a complementary channel may be the result of simple cost benefit analysis. If by employing an additional the overall business can be increased without jeopardizing quality or service and without any negative impact on long-term profitability, it may be worthwhile to do so. However, care is needed to ensure the enhancement of the market through multiple channels does not lead the justice Department to change the company with monopolizing the market.

Competitive Channels

The second type of multiple-channel strategy is the competitive channel competitive channels exist when the same product is sold through two different and competing channels. This distribution posture may be illustrated with reference to a boat manufacturer, the Luhrs Company. Luhrs sells and ships boats directly to dealers, using one franchise to sell Ulrichsen wood boats and Alura fiberglass boats and another franchise to sell Luhrs wood and fiberglass/wood boats. The two franchises could be issued to the same dealer, but they are normally issued to separate dealers. Competition between dealers holding separate franchise is both possible and encouraged. The two dealers compete against each other to the extent that their products satisfy similar consumer needs in the same segment.

The reason for choosing this competitive strategy is the hope that it will increase sales. It is thought that if dealers must compete against themselves as well as against other manufacturers' dealers, the extra effort will benefit overall sales. The effectiveness of this strategy is debatable. It could be argued that a program using different incentives, such as special discounts for attaining certain levels of sales could be just as this type of competition. It could be even more effective because the company would eliminate costs associated with developing additional channels.

Sometimes a company may be forced into developing competing channels in response to changing environments. For example, nonprescription drugs were traditionally sold through drugstores. But as the merchandising perspectives of supermarkets underwent a change during the post-world War II period, grocery stores became a viable channel for such products because shoppers expected to find convenience drug products there. This made it necessary for drug companies to deal with grocery wholesalers and retail grocery stores along with drug wholesalers and drugstores. In the 1980s, Capital Holding Corp. (a life insurance company located in Louisville, Kentucky) adopted a variety of marketing innovations. For example, in 1985 it began selling life insurance in novel ways, notably through supermarkets. Impressed by Capital Holding's steady growth and strong financial performance, many other insurance companies were forced to develop new channels to sell their insurance products.

The argument behind the competitive channel strategy is that, although two brands of the same manufacturer may be essentially the same, they may appeal to different sets of customers. Thus, General Motors engages different dealers for its Buick, Cadillac, Chevrolet, Oldsmobile and Pontiac cars. These dealers vigorously compete with one another. A more interesting example of competing multiple channels adopted by automobile manufacturers is provided by their dealings with car rental companies. Carmakers sell cars directly to car rental agencies. Hertz, for example, buys from an assembly plant and regularly resells some of its slightly used cars in competition with new cars through its more than 100 offices across the United States. Many of these offices are located in close proximity to dealers of new cars. Despite such competition, a manufacturer undertakes distribution through multiple channels to come off, on the whole, with increased business.

In adopting multiple competing channels, a company needs to make sure that it does not overextend itself; otherwise it may spread itself too thin and face competition to such an extent that ultimate results are disastrous. Mccammon cites the case of wholesaler who adopted multiple channels and thus exposed itself to a grave situation:

Consider, for example the competitive milieu of Stratton & Terstegge, a large hard ware wholesaler in Louisville. At the present time, the company sells to independent retailers, sponsors a voluntary group program and operates its own stores. In these multiple capacities, it competes against conventional wholesalers (Belknap), cash and carry wholesales (Atlas), specialty wholesalers (Garcia), corporate chains (Wiches) voluntary groups (Western Auto), cooperative groups (Colter), free-form corporations (Interco) and others. Given the complexity of its competitive environment, it is not surprising to observe that Stratton & Terstegge generates a relatively modest rate of return on net worth.

One of the dangers involved in setting up multiple channels is dealer resentment. This is particularly true when competitive channels are established. When this happens, it obviously means that an otherwise exclusive retailer will now suffer a loss in sales. Such a policy can result in the retailer electing to carry a different manufacturer's product line, if a comparable product line is available. For example, if a major department store such as Lord & Taylor is upset with a manufacturer such as the Hathaway Shirt company for doing business with discounters (i.e., adopting competing channels), it can very easily give its business to another shirt manufacturer.

Consider the following examples. Hill's Science Diet pet food lost a great deal of support in pet shops and feed stores as a result of the company's experiments with a "store within a store" pet shop concept in the competing grocery channel. In the auto market, ATK, the dominant seller of replacement engines for Japanese cars, lost its virtual monopoly when it attempted to undercut distributors and sell direct to individual mechanics and installers.

Quaker Oats's recent $1.4 billion write-off from the divestiture of its Snapple business was caused in part by channel conflict. Quaker had planned to consolidate its highly efficient grocery channel deporting the Gatorade brand with Snapple's channels for reaching convenience stores. Snapple distributors were supposed to focus on delivering small quantities of both brands to convenience store accounts while Gatorade's warehouse delivery channel handled larger orders to grocery chains and major accounts, leveraging Quaker's established strength in this area.

However, the strategy backfired. As Quaker suggested moving larger Snapple accounts to Gatorade's delivery system, Snapple's distributors revolted. They saw the value of their Snapple business as an exclusive geographic franchise that the split channel strategy would undermine. Several Snapple distributors took legal action against Quaker. The company ultimately backed down, but the dispute had created a considerable distraction at a time when competition from Arizona and Nantucket Nectars was intensifying.

Multiple channels also create control problems. National Distillers and Chemical Corporation had a wholly owned New York distributor, Peel Richards that strictly enforced manufacturer-stipulated retail prices and refused to do business with price cutters. Since R.H. Macy discounted National Distiller's products, Peel Richards stopped selling to them. R.H. Macy retaliated by placing an order with an upstate. New York distributor of National Distillers. National Distillers had no legal recourse against either R.H. Macy or the upstate New York distributor, who was an independent businessperson.

These problems do not diminish the importance of multiple distribution: they only suggest the difficulties that may arise with multiple channels and the difficulties with which management must contend. A manufacturers. failure to use multiple channels gives competitors an opportunity to segment the market by concentrating on one or the other end of the market spectrum. This is particularly disastrous for leading manufacturer because it must automatically forgo access to a large portion of market potential for not being able to use the economies of multiple distributions. If a manufacturer determines that multiple channels could cause problems, solutions must be found to resolve those problems. Exhibit 5.4 outlines variety of ways to tackle multiple channel conflicts at different stages in its development. For example, if conflict has recently arisen between channels focused on the same segments, suppliers might respond by introducing separate products or brands tailored to each channel.

EXHIBIT 5.4 Ten Ways to Manage Channel Conflict

Ten ways to Manage Channel Conflict

Two or more channel target the same customer segment ➡	Channel economics deteriorate ➡	Threatened channel stops performing or retaliates against the supplier
1. Differentiate channel offer 2. Define exclusive territories 3. Enhance or change the channel's value proposition (e.g., by building skills in value chain)	4. Change the channel's economic formula: - Grant rebates if an intermediary fulfills certain program requirements - Adjust margins between products to support different channel economics - Treat channels fairly to create level playing field 5. Create segment-specific programs (e.g., certain services not available via direct channels) 6. Complement value proposition of the existing channel by introducing a new channel 7. Foster consolidations among intermediaries in a declining channel	8. Leverage power (e.g., a strong brand) against the channel to prevent retaliation 9. Migrate volume to winning channel (e.g., to warehouse clubs for packaged goods) 10. Back off

(**Source**: Christine B. Bucklin, Pamela A. Thomas-Graham and Elizabeth A. Webster, "Channel Conflict: When it is dangerous?" The McKinsey Quarterly, No.3, 1997, p.38)

CHANNEL-MODIFICATION STRATEGY

The channel modification strategy is the introduction of a change in existing distribution arrangements based on evaluation and critical review. Channels should be evaluated on an ongoing basis so that appropriate modification may be made as necessary. A shift in existing channels may become desirable for any of the following reasons:

1. Changes in consumer markets and buying habits.
2. Development of new needs in relation to service parts or technical help.
3. Changes in competitors' perspectives.
4. Changes in relative importance of outlet types.
5. Changes in a manufacturer's financial strength.

6. Changes in the volume level of existing products.
7. Changes in product (addition of new products) price (substantial reduction in price to gain dominant position) or promotion (greater emphasis on advertising) strategies.

To illustrate the importance of modifying channel arrangements to keep up with changing climate, consider GM's efforts to remake its distribution system. GM's objective is to catch up with population shifts by moving stores out of small towns and declining cities and into bustling retail zones along suburban highways. At the same time, it is pushing dealers to reconfigure their holdings to match the way GM has realigned its divisions and either to spiff up stores or build new ones. The company's ultimate goal: fewer but better dealers. Although the auto maker had made progress in revamping the distribution, the going has been tough as expected. GM launched a $1 billion project in 1990 to relocate some dealers, merge others and shrink its dealer count from 9,500 in 1990 to 7,000 by the end of 2000.

Channel Evaluation

Channels of distribution may be evaluated on such primary criteria as cost of distribution coverage of market (penetration), customer service, communication with the market and control of distribution networks. Occasionally, such secondary factors as support of channels in the successful introduction of a new product and cooperation with the company's promotional effort also become evaluative criteria. To arrive at a distribution channel that satisfies all these criteria requires simultaneous optimization of every facet of distribution, something that is usually not operationally possible. Consequently a piecemeal approach may be followed.

Cost of distribution: A detailed cost analysis of distribution is the first step in evaluating various channel alternatives on a sales-cost basis. This requires classification of total distribution costs under various heads and subheads. The question of evaluation comes up only when the company has been following a particular channel strategy for a number of years. Presumably, the company has pertinent information to undertake distribution cost analysis by customer segment and product line. This sort of data allows the analyzer to find out how cost under each head varies with sales volume; for example, how warehousing expenses vary with sales volume, how packaging and delivery expenses are related to sales and so on. In other words, the purpose here is to establish a relationship between annual sales and different types of cost. These relationships are useful in predicting the future cost behaviors for established dollar-sales objectives, assuming present channel arrangement are continued.

To find out the cost of distribution for alternative channels, estimates should be made of all relevant costs under various sales estimates. Cost information can be obtained from published sources and interviews with selected informants. For example, assume that a company has been selling through wholesalers for a number of years and is now considering distribution through its own branches. To follow the latter course, the company needs to rent a number of offices in important markets. Estimates of the cost of renting or purchasing an office can be furnished by real estate agents. Similarly, the cost of recruiting and hiring additional help to staff the offices should be available through the personnel office. With the relevant information gathered, simple break-even analysis can be used to compute the attractiveness of the alternative channel.

Assume that a company has 20,000 potential customers and on an average, that each of them must be contacted every two weeks. A salesperson who makes 10 calls a day and who works five days a week can contact 100 customers every two weeks. Thus, the company needs 20,000/100=200 salespeople. If each salesperson receives $30,000 in salary and $20,000 in expenses, the annual cost of its salespeople is $10,000,000. Further, assume that 10 sales managers are required for control and supervision and that each one is paid, say, $50,000 a year. The cost of supervision would then be $50,000. Let $9,500,000 be the cost of other overhead, such as office and warehouse expenses. The total cost of direct distribution will then be $10,000,000+$9,500,000, or $20 million. Assume that distribution through wholesalers (the arrangement currently being pursued) costs the company 25 percent of sales. Assuming sales to be $x, we can set up an equation, 0.25x+$20 million and solve for x (x+$80 million). If the company decides to go to direct distribution, it must generate a sales volume of $80 million before it can break even on costs. Thus, if sales potential is well above the $80 million mark, direct distribution is worth considering.

One problem with break-even analysis is that distribution alternatives that are considered equally effective may not always be so. It is a pervasive belief that the choice of a distribution channel affects total sales revenue just as the selection of an advertising strategy does. For example, a retailer may receive the same number of calls under either of two channel alternatives: from the company's salesperson or from a wholesaler's salesperson. The question, however, is whether the effect of these calls is the same. The best way to handle this problem is to calculate the changes that would be necessary in order to make channel alternatives equally effective. To an extent, this can be achieved either intuitively or by using one of the mathematical models reported in the marketing literature.

Coverage of the market: An important aspect of predicting future sales response is the penetration that will eventually be achieved in the market. For example, in the case of drug company, customers can be divided into three groups: (a) drugstores, (b) doctors and (c) hospitals.

One measure of the coverage of the market (or penetration of the market) is the number of customers in a group contacted or sold, divided by the total number of customers in that group. Another measure may be penetration in terms of geographical coverage of territory. But these measures are too general. Using just the ratio of customers contacted to the total number of customers does not give a proper indication of coverage because not all types of customers are equally important. Therefore, customers may be further classified, as shown in the accompanying display:

Customer Group	Classification	Basis of Classification
Drugstores	Large ,Medium, Small	Annual Turnover
Hospitals	Large ,Medium, Small	Number of Beds
Doctors	Large ,Medium, Small	Number of patients attended

Then the desired penetration for each subgroup should be specified (e.g., penetrate 90 percent of the large, 75 percent of the medium and 50 percent of the small drugstores). These percentages can be used for examining the effectiveness of an alternative channel.

An advanced analysis is possible, however, by building a penetration model. The basis of the model is that increments in penetration for equal periods are proportional to the remaining distance to the aimed penetration. The increments in penetration in a period t will be:=rp(1-r)t-1, where p = targeted or aimed penetration and r= penetration ratio. This ratio signifies how rapidly the cumulative penetration approaches aimed penetration. For example, if aimed penetration is 80 percent and if= 0.3, then first-year penetration is 80x0.3=24 percent. Next year the increment in penetration will be 80x0.3x0.7=16.8 percent. Hence, cumulative penetration at the end of the second year will be 24+16.8=40.8. The value of p for each subgroup is a matter of policy decision on the part of the company. The value of r depends on the period during which aimed penetration is to be achieved and on sales efforts in terms of the number of medical representatives/salespeople and their call pattern for each subgroup. For the existing channel (selling through the wholesalers), the value of r can be determined from past records. For the alternative channel (direct distribution), the approximate value of r can be computed in one of two ways:

1. Company executives should know how many salespeople would be kept on the rolls if the alternate channel were used. The executives can also estimate the average number of calls a day a salesperson can make and hence the average number of customers in a subgroup he or she can contact. With this information, the value of r can be determined as follows:

$$\frac{\text{No. of customers in a subgroup contacted under existing channel}}{\text{No. of customers in a subgroup that would be contacted in alternative channel}} = \frac{\text{Value of r for existing channel}}{\text{Value of r for alternate channel}}$$

2. A second approach may be to find out (or estimate) the penetration that would be possible after one year if the alternate channel is used, then to substitute this in the penetration equation to find r when p and t are known.

The penetration model makes it easier to predict the exact coverage in each subgroup of customers over a planning period (say, five years hence) The marketing strategist should determine the ultimate desired penetration p and the time period in which it is to be achieved. Then the model would be able to predict which channel would take the penetration closer to the objective.

Customer Service: The level of customer service differs from customer to customer for each business. Generally speaking, the sales department, with feedback from the field force, should be able to designate the various services that the company should offer to different consumer segments. If this is not feasible, a sample survey may be planned to find out which services customers expect and which services are currently being offered by competitors. This information can be used to develop a viable. Service package. Then the capability and willingness of each channel alternative to provide these services may be matched to single out the most desirable channel. This can be done intuitively. A more scientific approach would be to list and assign weights to each type of services, then rate different channels according to their ability to handle these services. Cumulative scores can be used for the service ranking of channel alternatives. Conjoint measurement can be used to determine which services are most important to a particular segment of customers.

Communication and control: Control may be defined as the processing steps to bring actual results and desired results closer together. Communication refers to the information flow between the company and its customers. To evaluate alternate channels on these two criteria, communication and control objectives should be defined. With reference to communication, for example, information may be desired on the activities of competitors, new products from competitors, the special promotional efforts of competitors, the attitudes of customers towards the company's and towards competitors' services, and the reasons for success of particular product line of the company. Each channel alternative may then be evaluated in terms of its willingness, capabilities and interest in providing the required information. In the case of wholesalers, the communication perspective may also depend on the terms of the contract. But the mere fact that they are legally bound by a contract may not motivate wholesalers to cooperate willingly. Finally, the information should be judged for accuracy, timeliness and relevance.

Channel Modification

Environmental shifts, internal or external, may require a company to modify existing channel arrangements. A shift in trade practice, for instance, may render distribution through a manufacturer's representative obsolete. Similarly, technological changes in product design may require frequent service calls on customers that wholesalers may not be able to make, thus leading the company to opt for direct distribution.

To illustrate the point, consider jewelry distribution. For centuries, jewelry was distributed through jewelry shops that relied on uniqueness, craftsmanship and mystique to reap fat margins on very small volumes. Traditionally, big retailers shunned jewelry as a highly specialized, show-moving business that tied up to much money in inventory. But this attitude has changed in the last few years. For example, between 1978 and 1982, jewelry stores' share of the jewelry market declined from 65 percent to less than 50 percent. On the other hand, relying on hefty advertising and deep discounting, mass merchandisers (e.g., J.C. Penney, Sears, Montgomery Ward, Target and others) have been making fast inroads into the jewelry business. For example, in 1983J.C. Penney became the fourth-largest retail jewelry merchant in the United States behind Zale, Gordon Jewelry and Best Products, the catalog showroom chain. Such a shift in trade practice requires that jewelry manufacturers modify their distribution arrangements.

Similarly, as computer makers try to reach ever-broadening audiences with lower-price machines, they need new distribution channels. Many of them, IBM and Apple, for example, have turned to retail stores. In the 1970s, people would have laughed at the idea of selling computers over the counter; how it is a preferred way of doing business. The tantalizing opportunity to sell computers to consumers has also given birth to specialty chains specializing in computer and related items.

Ben & Jerry's Homemade Inc. had to change their distribution arrangements for a different reason. Dreyer's Grand Ice Cream controlled 70 percent of its distribution, and the relationship was regarded as a cornerstone of Ben & Jerry's success. Then, Dreyer made an unwanted takeover offer which Ben & Jerry's resented. The company decided to end the relationship with Dreyer and forged a new alliance with Diage PLC's Haagen-Dazs, until now regarded as an arch competitor, to deliver its products.

Generally speaking, a new company in the market starts distribution through intermediaries. This is necessary because, during the initial period, technical and manufacturing problems are big enough to keep management busy. Besides, at this stage the company has neither the insight nor the capabilities needed to deal successfully with the vagaries of the market. Therefore, intermediaries are used. With their knowledge of the market, they play an important role in establishing a demand for a company's product. But once the company establishes a foothold in the market, it may discover that it does not have the control of distribution in needs to make further headway. At this time, channel modification becomes necessary.

Managerial astuteness requires that the company do a thorough study before deciding to change existing channel arrangements. Taking a few halfhearted measures could create insurmountable problems resulting in loose control and poor communication. Further, the intermediaries affected should be duly taken into confidence about a company's plans and compensated for any breach of terms. Any modification of channels should match the perspectives of the total marketing strategy. This means that the effect of a modified plan on other ingredients of the marketing mix (such as product, price and promotion) should be considered. The managers of different departments (as well as the customers) should be informed so that the change does not come as a surprise. In other words, care needs to be taken to ensure that a modification in channel arrangements does not cause any distortion in the overall distribution system.

The point may be illustrated with reference to caterpillar. A decade ago, many observers predicted Caterpillar's. Yet today the company's overall share of the world market for construction and mining equipment is the highest in its history. And the biggest reason for the turnaround has been the company's system of distribution and product support and the close customer relationships it fosters. The backbone of that system is Caterpillar's 186 independent dealers around the world. They have played a central role in helping the company build close relationships with customers and gain insights into how it can improve products and services. The company's success may be attributed to several factors. For one thing, the company stands by its dealers in goods times and in bad. In addition, it gives them extraordinary support, helps ensure that the dealership are well run and emphasizes full and honest two-way communication. Finally, it stresses the emotional ties that have developed between the company and its dealers over time.

CHANNEL-CONTROL STRATEGY

Channel arrangements traditionally consisted of loosely aligned manufacturers, wholesalers and retailers, all of whom were trying to serve own ends regardless of what went on elsewhere in the channel structure. In arrangements, channel control was generally missing. Each member of the channel negotiated aggressively with others and performed a conventionally defined of marketing functions.

Importance of Channel Control

For a variety of reasons, control is a necessary ingredient in running a successful system. Having control is likely to have a positive impact on profits because inefficiencies are caught and corrected in time. This is evidenced by the success of voluntary and cooperative chains, corporate chains, franchise alignments, manufacturers' dealer organizations and sales branches and offices. Control also helps to realize cost effectiveness vis-à-vis experience curves. For example, centralized organization of warehousing, data processing and other facilities provide scale efficiencies. Through a planned perspective of the total system, effort is directed to achieving common goals in an integrated fashion.

Channel Controller

The focus of channel control may be on any member of a channel system: the manufacturer, wholesaler or retailer. Unfortunately, there is no established theory to indicate whether any one of them makes a better channel controller than the others. For example, one appliance retailer in Philadelphia with a 10 percent market share, Silo Incorporated, served as the channel controller there. This firm had no special relationship with any manufacturer, but if a supplier's line did not do well, Silo immediately contacted the supplier to ask that something be done about it. Wal-Mart (in addition to K-Mart and Target) can be expected to be the channel controller for a variety of products. Among manufacturers, Kraft ought to be the channel controller for refrigerated goods in supermarkets. Likewise, Procter & Gamble is a channel controller for detergents and related items. Ethan Allen decided to control the distribution channels for its line of Early American furniture by establishing a network of 200 dealer outlets. Sherwin- Williams decided to take over channel control to guide its own destiny because traditional channels were not showing enough aggressiveness. The company established its own chain of 2,000 retail outlets.

These examples underscore the importance of someone taking over channel leadership in order to establish control. Conventionally, market leadership and the size of a firm determine its suitability for channel control. Strategically, a firm should attempt to control the channel for a product if it can make a commitment to fulfill its leadership obligations and if such a move is likely to be economically beneficial in the long run for the entire channel system. For example, the thought of winning a contract to supply a mass retailer may lead a company to modify existing channel arrangements. After all, Toys "R" Us accounted for a fifth of the U.S. toy market in 1996. The Home Depot sold more home improvement products than all hardware stores combined and the quarter of the underwear purchased by Americans came from Wal-Mart (an estimated 23 percent of the U.S. population shops in Wal-Mart on an average day). Landing an account with one of these mass retailers can double or even triple a supplier's annual sales. However, rapid revenue growth is not always accompanied by a surge in profits. The strain of coping with high volumes and the service needs of powerful customers can put tremendous pressure on suppliers' profit margins if they attempt to conduct business as usual. Some manufacturers that supply mass retailers even find that although their sales rise faster than those of other manufacturers, their earnings growth is slower.

Vertical Marketing Systems (VMS)

Vertical marketing systems may be defined as:

> Professionally managed and centrally programmed networks [that] are pre-engineered to achieve operating economies and maximum market impact. Stated alternatively, vertical marketing systems are rationalized and capital-intensive networks designed

to achieve technological, managerial and promotional economies through the integration coordination and synchronization of marketing flows from points of production to points of ultimate use.

The vertical marketing system is an emerging trend in the American economy. It seems to be replacing all conventional marketing channels as the mainstay of distribution. As a matter of fact, according to one estimate, vertical marketing system in the consumer-goods sector account for about 70 to 80 percent of the available market. In brief, vertical marketing systems (sometimes also referred to as centrally coordinated systems) have emerged as the dominant ingredient in the competitive process and thus play a strategic role in the formulation of distribution strategy.

Vertical marketing systems may be classified into three types: corporate, administrate red and contractual. Under the corporate vertical marketing system, successive stages of production and distribution are owned by a single entity. This is achieved through forward and backward integration. Sherwin-Williams own and operate its 2,000 retail outlets in a corporate vertical marketing system (a case of forward integration). Other examples of such systems are Hart, Schaffner and Marx (operating more than 275 stores), International Harvester, Goodyear and Sohio. Not only a manufacturer but also a corporate vertical system might be owned and operated by a retailer (a case of backward integration). Sears, like many other large retailers, has financial interests in many of its suppliers' business. For example, about one-third of Desoto (a furniture and home furnishings manufacturer) stock is owned by Sears. Finally, W.W. Grainger provides an example of a wholesaler-run vertical marketing system. This firm, an electrical distributor with 1998 sales of $900 million, has nine manufacturing facilities.

Another outstanding example of a vertical marketing system is provided by Gallo, the wine company.

The [Gallo] brothers own Fairbanks Trucking Company, one of the largest intrastate truckers in California. Its 200 semis and 500 trailers are constantly hauling wine out of Modesto and raw materials back in including lime from Gallo's quarry east of Sacramento. Alone among wine producers, Gallo makes bottles- who million a day- and its Midcal Aluminum Co. spews out screw tops as fast as the bottles are filled. Most of the country's 1,300 or so wineries concentrate on production to the neglect of marketing. Gallo, by contrast, participates in every aspect of selling short of whispering in the ear of each imbiber. The company owns its distributors in about a dozen market and probably would buy many. more if the laws in most states did not prohibited doing so.

In an **administered vertical marketing system**, a dominant firm within the channel system, such as the manufacturer, wholesaler or retailer, coordinates the flow of goods by virtue of its market power. For example, the firm may exert influence to achieve economies in transportation, order processing, warehousing, advertising or merchandising. As can be expected, it is large organizations like Wal-Mart, Safeway, J.C. Penney, General Motors, Kraft, GE, Procter & Gamble, Lever Brothers, Nabisco and General Foods that emerge as channel captains to guide their channel networks, while not actually owning them, to achieve economies and efficiencies.

In **a contractual vertical marketing system**, independent firms within the channel structure integrate their programs on a contractual basis to realize economies and market impact. Primary, there are three types of contractual vertical marketing systems: wholesaler-sponsored voluntary groups, retailer-sponsored cooperative groups and franchise systems. Independent Grocers Alliance (IGA) is an example of a wholesaler-sponsored voluntary group. At the initiative of the wholesaler, small grocery stores agree to form a chain to achieve economies with which to compete against corporate chains. The joining members agree to adhere to a variety of contractual terms, such as the use of common name, to help realize economies on large order. Except for these terms, each store continues to operate independently. A retailer-sponsored cooperative group is essentially the same. Retailers form their own association (cooperative) to compete against corporate chains by undertaking wholesaler functions (and possibly even a limited amount of production); that is, they operate their own wholesale companies to serve member retailers. This type of contractual vertical marketing system is operated primarily, though not exclusively, in the food line. Associated Grocers Co-op and Certified Grocers are example of retailer-sponsored food cooperative groups. Value-Rite, a group of 2,298 stores, is a drugstore cooperative.

A franchise system is an arrangement whereby a firm licenses others to market a product or service using its trade name in a defined geographic area under specified terms and conditions. In 1994, there were more than 2,800 franchisers in the United States, twice as many as in 1984. Practically any business that can be taught to someone is being franchised. In 1995, sales of goods and services by all franchising companies (manufacturing, wholesaling and retailing) exceeded $600 billion. Approximately one-third of all U.S. retail sales flow through franchise and company-owned units in franchise chains.

In addition to traditional franchising business (e.g., fast-food), banks are doing it, as are accountants, dating services, skin care centers, tub and title refinishers, tutors, funeral homes, bookkeepers, dentists, nurses, bird seed shops, gift wrappers, wedding consultants, cookie bakers, popcorn poppers, beauty shops, baby-sisters and suppliers of maid service, lawn care and solar greenhouses.

Four different types of franchise systems can be distinguished:

1. The manufacturer-retailer franchise is exemplified by franchised automobile dealers and franchised service stations.

2. The manufacturer wholesaler franchise is exemplified by Coca-Cola and Pepsi Co, who sell the soft drink syrups they manufactur to franchised wholesalers who, in turn, bottle and distribute soft drinks to retailers.
3. The wholesaler retailer franchise is exemplified by Rexall Drug stores, Sentry Drug Centers and Comp USA.
4. The service sponsor-retailer franchise is exemplified by Avis, Hertz and National in the car rental business; McDonald's, Chicken Delight, Kentucky Fried Chicken, and Taco Bell in the prepared foods industry; comfort Inn and Holiday Inn in the lodging and food industry; Midas and AAMCO in the auto repair business; and Kelly Girl and Manpower in the employment service business.

Vertical marketing systems help achieve economies that cannot be realized through the use of conventional marketing channels. In strategic terms, vertical marketing systems provide opportunities for building experience, thus allowing even small firms to derive the benefits of market power. If present trends are any indication, by the year 2000 vertical marketing systems should account for almost 90 percent of total retail sales. Considering their growing importance, conventional channels will need to adopt new distribution strategies to compete against vertical marketing systems. For example, they may

1. Develop programs to strengthen customers' competitive capabilities. This alternative involves manufacturers and wholesalers in such activities as sponsoring centralized accounting and management reporting services, formulating cooperative promotional programs and cosigning shopping center leases.
2. Enter new markets, for example, building supply distributors have initiated cash-and-carry outlets. Steel warehouses have added glass and plastic product lines to their traditional product lines. Industrial distributors have initiated stock less buying plans and blanket order contracts so that they may compete effectively for customers who buy on a direct basis.
3. Effect economies of operation by developing management information systems. For example, some middlemen in conventional channels have installed the IBM-IMPACT program to improve their control over inventory.
4. Determine through research the focus of power in the channel and urge the channel member designated to undertake a reorganization of marketing flows.

Despite the growing trend towards vertical integration, it would be naïve to consider it an unmixed blessing. Vertical integration has both pluses and minuses- more of the latter, according to one empirical study on the subject. For example, vertical integration requires a huge commitment of resources: in mid-1981, Du Pont acquired Conoco in a $7.3 billion transaction. The strategy may not be worthwhile unless the company gains needed insurance as well as cost savings. As a matter of fact, some observers have blamed the U.S. automobile industry's woes, in part, on excessive vertical integration: "In deciding to integrate backward because of apparent short-term rewards, managers often restrict their ability to strike out in innovative directions in the future.

STRATEGIC MANAGEMENT OF CONFLICT

It is quite conceivable that the independent firms that constitute a channel of distribution (i.e., manufacturer, wholesaler and retailer) may sometimes find themselves in conflict with each other. The underlying causes of conflict are the divergent goals that different firms may pursue. If the goals of one firm are being challenged because of the strategies followed by another channel member, conflict is the natural outcome. ***Thus, channel conflict may be defined as a situation in which one channel member perceives another channel member or member to be engaged in behavior that is preventing or impeding it from achieving its goals.***

Disagreement between channel members may arise from incompatible desires and needs. Wigand and Wasson give four examples of the kinds of conflict that may arise:

A manufacturer promises an exclusive territory to a retailer in return for the retailer's "majority effort" to generate business in the area. Sales increase nicely, but the manufacturer believes it is due more to population growth in the area than to the effort of the store owner, who is spending too much time on the golf course.

A fast-food franchiser promises "expert promotional assistance" to his retails as partial explanation for the franchise fee. One of the retailers believes that the help he is getting is anything but expert and that the benefits do not correspond with what he was promised.

Another franchiser agrees to furnish accounting services and financial analysis as a regular part of his service. The franchisee believes that the accountant is nothing more than a "glorified bookkeeper" and that the financial analysis consists of several pages of ratios that are incomprehensible.

A third franchiser insists that his franchisees should maintain a minimum stock of certain items that are regularly promoted throughout the area. Arguments arise as to whether the franchiser's recommendations constitute a threat, while the franchisee is particularly concerned about protecting his trade name.

Types of Conflict

Simply stated potential conflict occurs wherever channel members have distinctly different opinions or perceptions about distribution channel affairs. Conflict in distribution channels occurs in many different forms. In his pioneering work, Joseph C. Pala Mountain identified three types of distributive conflicts: **(1) horizontal, (2) intertype and (3)**

vertical. Before examining vertical conflict, which is of primary importance to channel management, an examination of the two other forms provides useful background.

Horizontal Conflict: Horizontal conflict is normally treated in microeconomics because it relates to competition. The term horizontal conflict is used because it occurs among firms at the same level in a distribution channel. Retailers such as two hardware stores in competition with each other for the consumer's dollar are involved in horizontal conflict. Similarly, a wholesaler competing against another wholesaler or a manufacturer is other examples of horizontal conflict.

Intertype Conflict: Intertype conflict refers to competition between different intermediaries at the same level in a channel. Intertype conflict differs from horizontal in that it occurs among dissimilar institutions competing for the same customer. The emergence of warehouse furniture outlets has spurred development of new distribution channels that compete with traditional forms of distribution. Intertype competition has significantly intensified since the advent of scrambled merchandising by retailers. Scrambled merchandising is the practice among retailers of offering consumers product lines unrelated to the retailers normal business. Some supermarkets, for example, have added house wares, clothing and other nonfood items to their merchandising profile in an effort to achieve higher margins. In doing so, they compete with the traditional channels for those products.

Manufacturer may also create intertype competition when they attempt to develop new channels of distribution. An excellent example is the Hanes Hosiery Company and its development of L'eggs pantyhose. Until Hanes introduced L'eggs most hosiery was sold in department and specialty stores. Hanes pioneered new product packaging and unique supermarket distribution to cultivate retail exposure. Today, about 50 percent of all hosiery sales take place in grocery store and drugstore outlets.

Intertype competition is a significant form of conflict because it stimulates firms to remain efficient and respond to changing market conditions. It is also significant for the ramifications it has on a firm's existing channel relationships and its potential for breeding vertical conflict.

Vertical Conflict: Vertical Conflict refers to competition between different levels within a given channel of distribution. When Hanes decided new retail outlets for hosiery, management expected and received considerable negative reaction from department and specialty store buyers who had traditionally handled their products. Such problems among channel members are potentially devastating to the cooperative relationships existing within a channel because of the disruptive nature of detailed investigation of the vertical conflict process.

Causes of Conflict

A basic of conflict theory is that if no interdependence exists will be no basis for conflict. Thus, mutual dependence creates the basis for conflict. Given the fact that the most common types of VMS behavior are cooperative, it follows that there must be some reason or combination of reasons for the development of disagreement.

Social scientists have carefully studied the basic causes of conflict. From the view point of distribution channels, conflict typically results from: ***(1) goal incompatibility, (2) position-role-domain in congruency, (3) communication breakdown, (4) differing perceptions of reality and (5) ideological differences.***

Goal Incompatibility All members of a VMS presumably share the common goal of maximizing their joint effectiveness. It may be assumed that each firm's man agreement anticipates that VMS involvement will facilitate attainment of individual organization goals. However, each firm remains a separate legal entity. Each has its own employees, stockholders or owners and interest groups who help shape goals and strategies. Thus, each firm has goals, some of which overlap and may not be totally compatible with those of other channel members. This incompatibility may be the underlying cause of stress, which will ultimately create conflict.

A typical example of goal incompatibility leading to conflict often occurs in disagreements over the appropriate share of channel profits. Naturally, each institution desires the highest possible profit for the channel as a whole. Each individual firm also desires the largest obtainable share of total channel profits. A predictable result is conflict over the allocation process. Disagreement over trading margins represents one such form of conflict. Another form of conflict may result from the financial aid granted for performance of cooperative marketing functions. Some retailers feel that traditional cooperative advertising agreements providing 50 percent support from manufacturers are inadequate due to the high cost of color newspaper advertisements.

Even when goals of firms in a VMS are compatible, disagreement may develop as to methods. All channel members may agree that volume increases are desirable, but they may be in disagreement about how to accomplish them. Manufacturers might desire more shelf space or better positioning of their products. Retailers might feel that more advertising by the manufacturer would better accomplish the objective. Disagreement over which a tactic to use in an effort to increase sales could lead to conflict and unexpected actions. For instance, if better shelf position is assigned, the retailer may raise prices to compensate for the improved space and precipitate conflict concerning the objectives of the two firms.

Position Role and Domain In-congruency The concepts of position role and domain must be recognized and agreed to by channel members. Changes in specification of position or poorly defined roles may precipitate conflict among channel members. A firm can perform or fill a position only if all other channel members agree. Thus incompatibility can develop channel arrangements as roles and methods of operation change.

In some situations, a position may be clearly specified but the expected behavior of a channel member may not be. There may be considerable ambiguity among channel members concerning the appropriate behavior of each member. Rarely are the roles of channel members static. They can be expected to vary over time and under different circumstances. In cases in which roles change, VMS participants must agree upon the acceptable behavior of involved firms. When consensus is not reached, conflict is likely to result.

Because role definition represents a code of conduct defining a channel member's expected contribution, adequate performance is critical to maintaining harmony. The roles specified for a given channel position permit other members to predict behavior and measure contribution. A wholesaler, for example, expects certain types of behavior and levels of performance from its suppliers. Manufactures might be expected to ship orders within forty-eight hours after receipt. A well run wholesaler will plan inventory replenishment base on such performance expectations. If the manufacturer consistently fails to perform as expected or as promised, the wholesaler is most likely will consider an alternative supply. At the very least, conflict will exist between the two channel members. Inadequate role performance or failure to behave in the prescribed manner frustrates attempts by one firm to predict what the other will do. This frustration is as major cause of channel conflict. Of course, actual behavior will deviate from the expected since a firm's ability to maintain control results from many situational factors.

Conflict may also arise in distribution channel in which there is a lack of agreement concerning appropriate domain. Domain dissension is a likely precipitator of hostility in at least two situations: (1) when channel members do not know or do not agree on the appropriate operational scope of other firms in the VMS and (2) when domains overlap and two or more firms lay claim to the same functions, products or customers. Both of these result in frustration, stress or tension.

An excellent example of role and domain dissension is the conflict that arose between Quaker State Oil and a group of its distributions and jobbers. Quaker State adopted a policy discouraging its distributors from selling oil to discount stores. This policy was aggressively supported by retail service-station operators who felt that they were losing market share to the discount outlets. Some distributors continued to sell to discounters in violation of the policy. Apparently, these distributions believed that a manufacturer (Quaker State) had no right to limit the customers they service in their geographic area. The distributors that did not confirm to policy concerning their roles behaved in a manner that caused dissension with Quaker State. In order to determine which distributors were violating the prescribed behavior, Quaker coded its packages with ink visible only under special lighting. Once the violators were traced, Quaker responded with threats to reduce or terminate deliveries. While there are legal implications to this conflict episode, it should be noted that the basic cause of hostility was dissension concerning organizational domains and role performance.

Communication Breakdown As highlighted earlier, the importance of communication to smooth functioning of a channel system cannot be overemphasized. Communication breakdown that results in conflict can occur in at least two ways. The first way communication can break down is by a firm failing to exchange vital information with other channel members. A manufacturer wishing to maintain competitive advantage may decide not to announce a new product until a national distribution program is developed. Retailers, on the other hand, want information about new products as soon as possible to prepare their own strategies for the introductory period. Another example is a manufacturer failing to pass along vital information when products are recalled. Such recall notices, which often appear in newspapers, instruct consumers to return the product to retailers for a refund for replacement. A retailer's first awareness of a recall may be when consumers enter the store demanding compliance with the manufacturers instructions. In such a situation, the retailer can be expected to resent and complain about the manufacturer's failure to communicate. The second way that communication breakdown can occur is through nice and distortion. In a distribution channel, communication noise can arise from incomplete messages or language connotations. When various members of a distribution channel attach different meanings to specific terminology, the potential for stress increases. Such terminology distortion is illustrated by Warren Witteich's classical example of brewery executives trying to communicate with tavern owners:

> *To him (the tavern owner) "profit's a highfalutin' word used by wise guys who think they are better than he is "Being in business to "make money" he is more likely to respond to arguments or appeals which are supposed to lead to "better profits" By the same token, talk about "merchandising" or "promotion" is likely to sail over his head. In order to get him to act you have to speak to him in terms which are familiar and meaningful to him and which promise concrete rewards that he can grasp and understand.*

Such communications breakdowns are common in business. Often noise arises because a functional specialist develops terminology that may mean little to anyone except another specialist. Confused meanings that occur when a specialist communicates with a non-specialist may play a major part in the development of conflict. Recently a major advertising agency realized that many non-advertising executives did not understand such terms as "weighted target audience" and "pulsing" Consequently, the agency published a twelve-page brochure that defined key advertising terminology and explained methods of computing such measures as "readers per copy". In this manner the agency avoided potential conflict from misunderstood communication with its clients.

Differing Perceptions of Reality Conflict may occur when VMS members differ in methods of achieving mutual goals or have different solutions to a mutual problem. Even when channel members have a strong desire to cooperate, conflict can result from perceptions of what the real facts are. The problem of varied perceptions occurs because all channel members have different backgrounds, prejudices and positions in the channel. In any given situation, facts are likely to be interpreted in light of prior experience and access to available information. All members may agree that the channel is not functioning as effectively as desired. However, each member may perceive a different reason for the lack of effectiveness. The manufacturer may feel that the retailer's stock-outs are caused by a failure to maintain adequate safety stock levels. The retailer may feel that inventory polices are realistic and that the problem is caused by the manufacturer's inability to provide reliable inventory replenishment. Each party is interpreting the situation based on past experience and prejudices associated with its VMS position and role.

An interesting example of conflict resulting from different perceptions of channel members occurred when Cotton Incorporated, the marketing arm of the cotton industry, became angry with one of the primary users of cotton. Levi Strauss & Company. When Levi began making and promoting a line of denim jeans that contained 35 percent polyester, Cotton Incorporated began an advertising campaign using network television, trade journals and consumer magazines such as sports illustrated and play boy. Although Levi was not specifically named in the advertisements, the basic theme was that unless denim jeans are 100 percent cotton, they are not in fact denim jeans. Believing that the cotton-polyester blend is easier to care for than pure cotton, Levi countered with: "It's the performance of the fabric and the weave that makes it denim. "Thus, conflict was spurred by a very basic difference in perception as to which characteristics constitute denim fabric. The cotton industry felt that denim has to be pure. Levi viewed performance and weave as prime determinants of denim fabric.

Ideological Differences Ideological or value conflicts are similar to those resulting from differences in perceived roles and expected behaviors. Fundamental ideological conflict can result from big-business and small-business perceptions of the appropriate role of management. A large manufacturer may be so satisfied with the performance of a wholesale distributor that pressure is exerted to expand the business, hire new employees and move into new territories. The wholesaler, a small individual proprietorship, may be satisfied with the existing business. Expansion may mean loss of personal control because of a need to hire additional managers. Or the expansion may require longer working hours and cause more personal frustration. The small business owner may indeed value leisure time and fewer headaches and thus may resist expansion pressures. In such a situation, management of the larger organization may fail to understand the value system of the small business. Conflict can be expected.

In summary, conflict has many origins. Although actual events that precipitate conflict among channel members are limitless, mutual dependence in the channel system carries with it the potential for stress and conflict concerning incompatible goals, position-role domain incongruence, communications breakdown, differing perceptions of reality and different ideological values of the involved institutions.

Results of Conflict

Conflict in which channel members exhibit overt hostile behavior needs to be resolved in some way. A number of methods for conflict resolution are available. However, most of the means by which conflict is resolved in a channel rely to a greater or lesser extent upon some form of power or leadership.

Regardless of the method used for conflict resolution, the resulting behavior adjustment made by channel members will depend upon whether the conflict was functional or dysfunctional. Early literature viewed all over conflict as dysfunctional or disruptive because if forced channel members away from their cooperative relationship. More recently, however, conflict has been considered to have certain beneficial qualities that can enhance the solidarity of a channel. There is no doubt, however, that in some situations dysfunctional conflict may be so pronounced that an effective channel cannot be said to exist. The results of functional and dysfunctional conflicts are discussed below.

Functional System Results The consequences of functional channel conflict can be observed in two distinct situations. The first situation involves unification of the channel system. Channel members may eventually conclude that no alternative relationship exists that could satisfy goals as adequately as the current alignment. A retailer may determine that although the supplier delivers a high percentage of damaged or defective merchandise, no other manufacture exists that does better. In such a situation, the basic problem still exists but stress is reduced. Cooperation may be fostered in such a situation if the retailer's satisfaction with the manufacturer is increased as a result of the search for alternative supply sources. Increased cooperation may produce more unified efforts to solve other problems in the channel system. In a VMS two involved firms can work together to improve their joint situation.

The second situation in which channel conflict produces functional consequences is when a change in the system results. If the conflict episode precipitates changes in the system and this improves performance, then the conflict can be judged to be functional. For example, a conflict episode may lead a retailer to integrate operations and reduce dependence on suppliers. If the integrated retailer is able to operate more efficiently, the outcome of the conflict is positive. In essence, contrary to popular belief, *conflict that results in the disintegration of old alliances and relationship is not necessarily dysfunctional.*

Rather, such consequences may be positive if the new alliances enable channel members to be serviced better, which results in an improvement in the meeting of customer's needs.

Dysfunctional System Results Under what circumstances, then, might channel conflict be considered to be dysfunctional or harmful?. To answer this question, it is necessary to take perspective similar to that used in judging functional conflict. Two situations represent dysfunctional conflict: (1) when duplication of effort results and (2) when channel members dissipate their resources in prolonging heightening of conflict rather than seeking constructer solutions.

The duplication of effort that results from channel conflict is illustrated in the following series of relationships:

1. The higher the level of perceived vertical conflict among channel members within any given channel system, the lower the probability of functional cooperation among members.
2. The lower the probability of functional cooperation, the greater the duplication of effort among channel members.
3. The greater the duplication of effort, the lower the performance of the channel system.

If, for example the conflicting channel members remain in a VMS relationship but choose not to cooperate in performing marketing functions, it is quite likely that duplication of effort will result. The reduction in efficiency would be dysfunctional. In addition, the increased cost that would result from duplication would probably impair the system's ability to compete effectively.

Conflict that wastes the resources of all channel members and fails to result in formation of a more effective distribution system is dysfunctional. Kenneth Boulding once termed such conflict "pathological" because, in attempting to injure or restrict, a firm's resources are expended and self-desired goals are thwarted. In such situations, the conflicting parties lose sight of the original issues and allow. Such emotions as revenge, distrust or insecurity to proliferate and escalate the conflict.

The aim of the marketing manager involved with channel strategy is not necessarily to avoid all conflict; rather, it is to avoid conflict that will have dysfunctional consequences. A level of tension that drives members to seek better solutions to common problems may not only lead to more satisfactory attainment of individual organizational goals but also will improve the competitive posture of the overall VMS. Thus, the major interest of the channel strategist is conflict management rather than conflict avoidance.

Conflict Resolution

. It is obvious that power and conflict have close ties. Both result from mutual dependence.

It is apparent that a principal factor differentiating vertical conflict from horizontal and intertype competition is that it is so directly a power conflict. Power relationships among horizontal competitors occasionally are significant but this power usually is narrowly limited. This later type of competition (intertype) is almost devoid of power relationships. In the plane of vertical conflict; however, power relationships are direct, obvious and important to the extent that the market is imperfect.

Attempts to utilize power may actually precipitate conflict episodes. If a channel member has a low level of tolerance for control and another system member attempts to exercise leadership, a situation of stress and conflict will develop. It is important to note that the conflict will surface over the issue of attempted leadership, but the underlying cause of conflict may be more difficult to identify. It could stem from such basic causes as goal incompatibility or dissatisfaction over distribution of rewards. But it is important to understand that when an attempt is made to control a channel member's decisions or behavior and when the level of influence exerted exceeds that firm's tolerance, conflict will result.

Conflict may also develop from a firm's attempt to gain more power. What is not clear is whether the attempt is to gain power or to satisfy the firm's goals. A retailer that undertakes a market study to gain information may simply desire better knowledge so that internal decisions can be made more effectively. However, the information will most likely also serve to increase the retailer's expert power.

The balance of power in itself may create conflict. A relationship in which one party maintains a relative advantage may be considered unstable because it encourages the use of power. The implication is that the more powerful channel member over time will become insensitive to the tolerance level of VMS members.

Although power can precipitate conflict, it is also the means by which conflict or hostility is resolved. Each method of resolution involves, to a greater or lesser extent, a power relationship among conflicting channel members. A marketing manager must be sensitive to the ways in which power is directly or indirectly related to attempts among channel members to maintain cooperative relationships. Once an established channel experiences conflict, a natural tendency exists to seek a satisfactory solution. Four basic processes by which conflict may be resolved have been identified in the field of organizational behavior. **These four methods are:**

1. *Problem solving* It is assumed in problem solving that conflicting parties share mutual objectives and that the solution is to find a way to satisfy shared goals.

2. *Persuasion.* In persuasion, it is assumed that the goals of the conflicting parties differ, but that they are subject to modifications if basic agreement exists regarding objectives.
3. *Negotiation.* In negotiation, disagreement over goals is assumed to be fixed. An end of conflict is sought by the development of new agreements with no attempt to refer to common objectives.
4. *Politics.* Politics is similar to bargaining, except participants attempt to increase the number of parties involved in the resolution process.

These four processes for conflict resolution and the ways in which they relate to channel management are explained in greater detail.

Problem Solving A number of problem-solving techniques exist within distribution channels. The two most important are the development and emphasis of super ordinate goals and improvement of the communications process among channel members.

Super-ordinate Goals Since each VMS member has joined to achieve goals that could not be obtained otherwise, a basis for problem solving exists. Essentially, a super-ordinate goal is one that all channel member's desire but that cannot be achieved by any one firm acting alone. All channel members have a stake in the operating efficiency of the channel system and most likely have as an overriding goal a desire to increase total performance. By increasing total output, all firms may be better off than if they allowed conflict to limit or restrict the system's ability to produce. In such instances, appeals to the super-ordinate goal may aid in ending a conflict episode.

The establishment of super-ordinate goals becomes most likely when a channel confronts an external threat. Only a few years ago conflict between gasoline service station operators and oil refineries was common. In recent years, however, this conflict has been reduced as the overall petroleum distribution system has been confronted with numerous threats such as supply shortages and potential congressional actions. Similarly, conflict among members of a channel seems to dissipate when an alternative distribution system arises. The development of super-ordinate goals and reduction of conflict may be temporary. When the outside threat is removed, internal stress and conflict is likely to occur again.

Communication Processes A number of methods exist to alleviate communication noise in distribution channels. More efficient flow of information and/or communications in the channel will permit channel members to find solutions to their conflict bases on common objective

Many industries have established trade organizations that include as members firms from all levels of the distribution channel. The International Foodservice Manufacturers Association (IFMA) is a trade group that deals in distribution of food to the away from home market. The membership of the IFMA includes not only food processors, but also equipment manufacturers. Through meetings and trade publications, channel members are able to share information and improve communications. In addition, meetings permit member firms to develop solutions to common problems; thus, they reinforce channel relationships.

To some extent, all channel communications are efforts to decrease or avoid conflict. The use of sales representatives by a manufacturer to convey information to and from wholesalers and/or retailers implies that the manufacturer is attempting to encourage attainment of its individual goals as well as common goals. The function of a sales representative for a manufacturer has often been described as that of a problem solver.

Persuasion Persuasion as a means of resolving conflict implies that the involved institutions draw upon leadership. By its very nature, persuasion involves communication between conflicting parties. The emphasis is upon influencing behavior through persuasion rather than only by the sharing of information. Specifically, the purpose of persuasion in the resolution of conflicts is primarily to avoid or reduce conflict about domain.

Disagreement about or overlap in domains is a primary cause of channel conflict. Since channel members may agree upon super ordinate goals, persuasion may be employed to help members resolve differences concerning territories, functions or customers. The important point is that the persuading member should appeal to the conflicting channel members and remind them of their commitment to superordinate goals of the channel. Agreement that is reached through the process of persuasion alleviates or reduces stress. It also usually results in redefinition among channel members of their domain

Negotiation In negotiation no attempt is made to fully satisfy a channel member. Instead, the objective of negotiation is to halt a conflict. Such compromise may resolve the episode but not necessarily the fundamental stress over which the conflict erupted. If stress continues, it likely that some issue or another will cause future conflict.

Compromise is one means by which bargains can be reached among channel members. In compromise situations, each party gives up something it desires in order to prevent or to end conflict. Often, compromise is necessary so that consensus about domain can be reached in situation in which persuasion is ineffective.

Both persuasion and negotiation draw upon abilities of the involved parties to communicate. In fact, the resolution of conflicts by the utilization of either of these processes requires that each party develop a strategy to ensure a favorable resolution. Both parties must reach a satisfactory agreement that does not increase hostility. It is extremely important for the marketing manager to understand how effective negotiation strategies are developed.

Politics Politics refers to the resolution of conflict by the involvement of new organizations or parties in the process of reaching an agreement. Examples of such solutions are ***coalition formation, arbitration or mediation and lobbying or judicial appeal.***

Coalitions The formation of coalitions among channel members is, in effect, an attempt to alter the channel power structure. The National Automobile Dealer's Association offers dealers the capability to deal effectively with manufacturers. Voluntary and cooperative retail chains allow smaller retailers to negotiate with food processors on an equal basis with large supermarket chains. The formation of such coalitions represents a political move by channel members. Once a coalition is formed, however, the conflict resolution process may be achieved through problem solving, persuasion or negotiation. In addition, coalitions may become involved in additional forms of political activity that are discussed below.

Mediation and Arbitration Both mediation and arbitration involve a third party in the conflict resolution process. In mediation, the third party may suggest a solution to the conflict but channel members are not required to accept that solution. In arbitration, the solution suggested by the intermediary is binding upon the conflicting parties. Although there are many reasons to submit to mediation or arbitration for the resolution of distribution conflicts actual example of the use of these mechanisms are rare. Perhaps the major reason for this is that it is difficult to find a neutral third party whose decision would be acceptable to the conflicting channel members.

It is often suggested that trade associations undertake the mediator or arbitrator function. At least two factors usually preclude involvement by trade association. The first is the fact that trade associations normally have predominant membership from one channel level; thus, members views will most likely be biased and unacceptable to one or more of the conflicting parties. The second factor concerns the nature of the arbitration or mediation process, which may require the proprietary information be revealed. Neither channel member is likely to want to share this information with other trade members.

Lobbying and Judicial Appeal Channel members may resort to the governmental process in order to resolve conflicts. Attempts to influence the legislative process through lobbying activities are frequent. Court litigation is also a popular means for the resolution of conflict by the drawing of outside parties into the relationship.

Withdrawal An additional method for the termination of conflict is the withdrawal of one firm from the relationship so that the hostile behavior existing in the channel can be avoided. Withdrawal is a relatively common method of conflict resolution. A firm that decides to terminate its existing channel relationship should have an alternative available or must be willing to change the nature of its business and goals if such alternatives are not available.

If a firm decides to continue in the same business, channel alternatives must exist; either the cost of the alternative should be no greater than the cost of the existing system or the firm should be willing to incur higher costs to avoid the hostility inherent in the existing channel. A retailer may choose to end a relationship with a current supplier because of a specific activity on the part of the supplier. The retailer can easily do so as long as alternative sources of supply exist and can provide essentially the same mix of product and services as the current supplier.

A firm may choose to withdraw from a channel if it decides to alter its mission. In this case, benefits obtained from the existing channel are reduced in important or at least the goals of the firm have changed so that they are less important. A manufacturer, for example, may terminate relationships with an entire retail chain or group because the profits obtained from a specific line of private-label merchandise are not sufficient to compensate for the effort involved in conflict resolution.

In addition to the above mentioned conflict resolution methods, there are five additional strategic alternatives available for resolving conflicts between channel members and these are ***bargaining, boundary, interpenetration, superorgnizational strategies and arbitration.. Under the bargaining strategy***, one member of the channel takes the lead in activating the bargaining process by being willing to concede something, with the expectation that the other party will reciprocate. For example, a manufacturer may agree to provide interest-free loans for up to 90 days to a distributor if the distributor will carry twice the level of inventory that it previously did and will finish warehousing for the purpose. Or a retailer may propose to continue to carry the television line of a manufacturer will supply television sets under the retailer's own name (i.e., the retailer's private brand). The bargaining strategy works out only if both parties are willing to adopt the attitude of give-and take and if bottom-line results for both are favorable enough to induce them to accept the terms of the bargain.

The boundary strategy handles the conflict through diplomacy; that is by nominating the employee most familiar with the perspectives of the other party to take up the matter with his or her counterpart. For example, a manufacturer may nominate a veteran salesperson to communicate with the purchasing agent of the customer to see if some basis can be established to resolve the conflict. For example, North Face, the manufacturer of high-performance outdoor clothes is expanding beyond the $5 billion specialty outdoor market to the broader $30 billion casual sportswear market. To implement the strategy, it plans to increase the number of stores selling North Face after 2001, from 1,500 specialty stores up to 4,000 retailers.

This is upset the specialty stores since they fear that the expansion will undercut the brand, putting pressure on their margins. To resolve the conflict the North Face salesperson may meet the specialty store buyers to talk over business in general. In between the talks, he or she may indicate in a subtle way that the company's decision to broaden the distribution would be mutually beneficial. In the end, the specialty stores will reap the benefits of the brand name popularity triggered by the mass distribution. Besides, the salesperson may be authorized to propose that his or her company will agree not to sell the top of the line to new retailers, "thus ensuring that it will continue to be available only through the specialty stores. In order for this strategy to succeed, it is necessary that the diplomat (the salesperson in the example) be fully briefed on the situation and provided leverage with which to negotiate.

The **interpenetration strategy** is directed towards resolving conflict through frequent informal interactions with the other party to gain a proper appreciation of each other's perspectives. One of the easiest ways to develop interaction is for one party to invite the other to join its trade association. For example, several years ago television dealers were concerned because they felt that the manufacturer of television sets did not understand their problems. To help correct the situation, the dealers invited the manufacturers to become members of the National Appliance and Radio-TV Dealers Association (NARDA). Currently, manufacturers take an active interest in NARDA conventions and seminars.

Finally, the focus of **super organizational strategy** is to employ conciliation, mediation and arbitration to resolve conflict. Essentially, a natural third party is brought into the conflict to resolve the matter. Conciliation is an informal attempt by a third party to bring two conflicting organizations together and make them come to an agreement amicably. For example, an independent wholesaler may serve as a conciliator between a manufacturer and its customers. Under mediation, the third party plays a more active role. If the parties in conflict fail to come to an agreement, they may be willing to consider the procedural or substantive recommendations of the mediator.

Arbitration may also be applied to resolve channel conflict. Arbitration may be compulsory or voluntary. Under compulsory arbitration, the dispute must by law be submitted to a third party, the decision being final and binding on both conflicting parties. For example, the courts may arbitrate between two parties in dispute. Years ago, when automobile manufacturers and their dealers had problems relative to distribution policies, the court arbitrated. Voluntary arbitration process whereby the parties in conflict submit their disputes for resolution to a third party on their own. For example, in 1955 the Federal Trade Commission arbitrated between television set manufacturers, distributors and dealers by setting up 32 industry rules to protect the consumer and to reduce conflicts over distribution. The conflict areas involved were tie-I sales; price fixing; mass shipments used to clog outlets and foreclose competitors; discriminatory billing; and special rebates, bribes, refunds and discounts.

Of all the methods of resolving conflict, arbitration is the fastest. In addition, under arbitration, secrecy is preserved and less expense is incurred. Inasmuch as industry experts serve as arbitrators, one can expect a fairer decision. Thus, as a matter of strategy, arbitration may be more desirable than other methods for managing conflict. Exhibit 5.5 (*Ten ways to manage Channel Conflict*) lists different ways of managing channel conflict.

CLOSING CASE: OAKVILLE MALL

In the fall of 1998, Ms. Roberta Brent, president of E.L. Lint Company, a department store firm with branches in three mid-Michigan cities, was concerned about reports that another major department store chain, well-known in several states, was considering opening branch stores in Lint's market areas. In December, Ms Brent's fears were confirmed when it was announced that the firm, Deming Stores, planned to open two branches in Lint's major market. One of the branches was to be located in a new mall to be developed and built by Deming's Properties. Brent realized that this new mall would present substantial competition for all area retailers, but there was little that could be done to prevent entry by this source of competition. She was extremely concerned, however, about the announcement that Deming also planned to open a store in Oakville Mall, an existing shopping center in which Lint's maintained a large branch store.

OAKVILLE MALL

Oakville Mall opened in 1974. The developer of this shopping center project was Cal Martin properties; Inc. Oakville was the first enclosed regional shopping center in its market, a standard metropolitan statistical area (SMSA) with a population of over 250,000. The original development contained a gross leasable area of 300,000 square feet. Besides the Lint's store, which was the largest in the shopping center, there were two other large general-merchandise stores in the mall as well as a number of smaller specialty stores. In the original development, however, Cal Martin had considered Lint the primary traffic generator for the project. Lint was in the centre of the mall; the other two major tenants were at opposite ends.

As in most shopping centers, lease arrangements between Cal Martin and the tenants of Oakville Mall varied. Lint's contract the most favorable rental rates for any tenant, with the store paying a guaranteed minimum rent of $1.25 per square foot of area occupied. Thus, Lint's minimum rent during a year was $112,500. The contract also called for Lint to pay 3 percent of its sales revenue as rent, if that figure exceeded the $112,500 minimum.

The highest rental paid by any of the tenants in Oakville Mall called for a $12 per square foot minimum or 16 percent of net sales. The candy shop that signed this lease had a prime location in the centre of the main aisle.

After a poor first-year start, Oakville Mall became quite profitable for Cal Martin properties. Sales volume for most tenants grew steadily and very few tenants went out of business because of poor performance in the shopping center. However, one of the large general-merchandise stores closed in early 1988. Although this store was paying rent above its minimum, indicating a satisfactory sales volume, the national chain of which it was only one unit filed for bankruptcy in 1988 and closed all its stores in the United States. The closing of this branch, therefore, was not due to any specific problems with the Oakville Mall unit.

Roberta Brent was particularly pleased with the performance of the Lint store in Oakville Mall. Although sales volume in early years had not been great enough to require that the percentage rental clause be in effect, Lint paid a total of $158,600 in rent to Cal Martin in 1986. Ms. Brent considered the Oakville Mall branch of Lint's one of the most successful units operated by the firm.

PROPOSED EXPANSION OF OAKVILLE MALL

The proposal expand Oakville Mall with the addition of Deming's would also add many new specialty stores. As a result, the total size of Oakville Mall would be increased to 578,000 square feet, with Deming occupying 103,000 square feet. The expansion was to be constructed on vacant land on the westernmost portion of the Oakville Mall site, the only vacant land available. Exhibit 5.5 contains a site plan of the 1988 Oakville Mall as well as the proposed addition. Brent commented that she was not pleased that Deming's had decided to enter the market. She knew that the competition would be very strong. Deming's was well known as a retailer of fashion oriented, quality merchandise. With Deming's having tremendous resources at the disposal of the regional firm, Lint would probably have a difficult time maintaining its dominant position in the local market. Brent did say, however that the competition could force Lint's management out of its complacency and into a new era of aggressiveness. The firm had never been challenged in its dominant position.

EXHIBIT 5.5 Oakville Mall site plan, including proposed additions

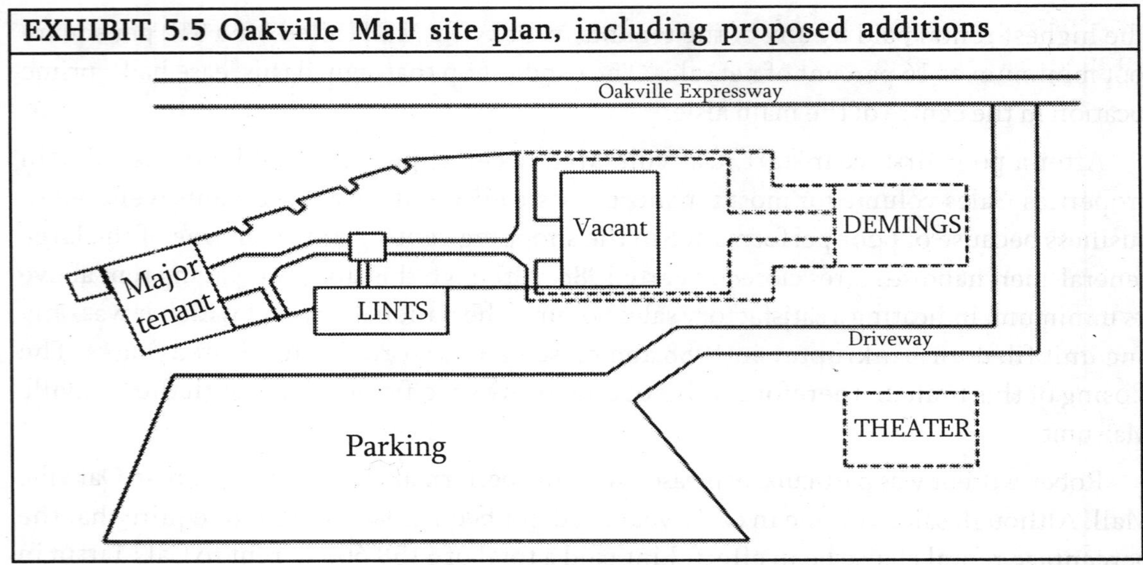

Although concerned about the new competition, she was also very angry about the proposed changes at Oakville Mall. "I want to make it very clear to everyone that we think competition will be beneficial to areas consumers and we therefore welcome Deming's to the market," Ms. Brent said in a newspaper interview. "We even think that their coming to Oakville Mall will be good for all parties concerned. As long as they are going to locate in this area we would rather see them in Oakville than any other shopping center. However, we do not think that there is any need to destroy the present configuration of the mall just to get them into the location. They could move into the recently vacated store which contains 50,000 square feet and begin operations immediately. This would be good for all parties concerned. Cal Martin would have its vacant store leased Deming's could open its doors sooner and the present mall configuration would be preserved.

"The major problem with the proposed expansion is that it totally changes the site plan. Whereas our Lint store is presently in the centre of the mall, after the expansion we will be at the east end. We contend that this change would greatly inconvenience our customers and would ultimately result in a decline in our sales. Therefore, we must be opposed to this proposal.

In a later conversation, Ms. Bent continued her thoughts: "you know, it is interesting how conditions change. In 1973, when Cal Martin approached us about Oakville Mall, he needed us very badly. Without Lint as a tenant in his project, he could not get mortgage financing to build the mall. Since we were the major retailer in the market, no financial institution would agree to a mortgage unless we were included. We saw it as a worthwhile project, however and agreed to lease space once the mall was underway. With our promise, he was able to obtain financing, find other tenants and build Oakville. Now that the mall is a tremendous success, he wants to expand. We are in favor of expansion, but it will put us in an inferior position."

CAL MARTIN'S POSITION

Cal Martin said that he really didn't understand Lint's objections to the mall expansion. He felt that since Deming's entry to the area was inevitable, his efforts to have them locate in Oakville Mall were good not only for him but also for all the Oakville tenants: "After all, with Deming's located in our mall and the tremendous increase in the number of other stores, we should draw many more customers than ever before. Why, instead of a decline in sales, I expect to see everyone's sales climb after the expansion is completed."

Martin agreed with Brent's contention that Oakville Mall would not have become a reality in the 1970s without Lint's agreement to locate in the shopping center. He went on to say, however, that the original development had always been considered only the first phase of a major commercial development that was planned ultimately to include office and residential areas as well as the shopping center itself. He said the final project would include 2 million square feet of leased space. Martin claimed that the development was always envisioned as including the area of the proposed expansion and that it should have been obvious to anyone that the acreage west of the mall was intended to be part of the mall someday. "Why else", he asked, "Would I have built the driveway where it is and located the movie theater so far from the mall itself? It was general knowledge that I planned to expand the mall as soon as I became financially able to do so."

To summarize position, Martin said: "I don't know what all the fuss is about. Everyone is going to be better off when I finish this project."

DEMING'S POSITION

A representative of Deming's commented that Deming's entry to this new market represented the first time the firm had planned to open two stores at one time in a new area. It was felt that such an opening thrust would allow the firm to penetrate the market rapidly. The representative also commented that the firm definitely intended to develop its own mall on the opposite side of town from Oakville Mall, approximately twenty minutes driving time away.

SUMMARY & KEY TERMS

Distribution strategies are concerned with the flow of goods and services from manufacturer to customers. Businesses differ in their abilities and desire to perform overall marketing functions. Therefore, through the process of specialization, they often align themselves with other firms into organized marketing channels. As a result of this combination, each firm becomes dependent upon others in the channel system for the accomplishment of its objectives. This mutual dependence lays the foundation for three types of behavior that are critical to channel management: cooperation, power and conflict.

A key to channel management is leadership. Most leadership in marketing results from power. In all situations, potential channel members have limited tolerance for following others. The leadership process in a channel can become complex. In advanced situations, what can result is what amounts to an extended enterprise that links a firm with its customers, service suppliers and materials vendors.

The discussion in this chapter was conducted from the manufacturer's viewpoint. Six major distribution strategies were distinguished: channel-structure strategy, distribution-scope strategy, multiple-channel strategy, channel-modification strategy, channel-control strategy and conflict-management strategy. Channel-structure strategy determines whether the goods should be distributed directly from manufacturer to customer or indirectly through one or more intermediaries. Formulation of this strategy was discussed with reference to Bucklin's postponement-speculation theory. Distribution-scope strategy specifies whether exclusive, selective or intensive distribution should be pursued. The question of simultaneously employing more than one channel was discussed under multiple-channel strategy. Channel strategy. Channel-modification strategy involves evaluating current channels and making necessary changes in distribution perspectives to accommodate environmental shifts. Channel-control strategy focuses on vertical marketing systems to institute control. Vertical marketing systems (VMSs) represent channel structures that build upon cooperative behavior. VMS arrangements are characterized by repeat business situations. All VMS arrangements are based upon acknowledged dependence among participants. The chapter looked at basic principles that guide formation of VMS agreements and the attributes of a successful arrangement. Examples of guidelines to build successful alliances were illustrated from the perspective of manufacturer and a service specialist. Some clear reasons why VMS arrangements fail were also reviewed

Channel conflict occurs in three forms. The first is horizontal conflict or competition, which takes place among firms at the same level of distribution. The second is intertype, which takes place between two competing or alternative channel systems of particular interest to channel management is the third form of hostility, vertical conflict, which occurs among different levels of a marketing channel.

Finally, resolution of conflict among channel members was examined under conflict-management strategy

KEY TERMS

- Assortment
- Carrying & Forwarding Agents(C&FAs)
- Customer Service
- Distribution Channel
- Distribution Management
- Horizontal Conflict
- Key Performance Indicators(KPIs)
- Vertical Conflict
- Intertype Conflict
- Vertical Marketing System(VMS)
- Exclusive Distribution
- Intensive Distribution
- Selective Distribution
- Critical Success Factors(CSFs)
- Consignment Selling Agents(CSAs)

DISCUSSION QUESTIONS

1. What factors may a manufacturer consider to determine whether to distribute products directly to customers? Can Air Conditioners be distributed directly to customers?
2. What is the most appropriate strategy for resolving channel conflict?
3. Explain the three alternatives of distribution scope strategy with example.
4. What is VMS? Explain it with an example.
5. Explain the ten ways to manage Channel Conflict.

Finally, resolution of conflict among channel members was explored under conflict management strategy.

KEY TERMS

- Assortment
- Carrying & Forwarding Agents (C&F)
- Customer Service
- Distribution Channel
- Distribution Management
- Horizontal Conflict
- Key Performance Indicators (KPI)
- Vertical Conflict
- Intertype Conflict
- Vertical Marketing System (VMS)
- Exclusive Distribution
- Intensive Distribution
- Selective Distribution
- Critical Success Factors (CSF)
- Consignment Selling Agent (CSA)

DISCUSSION QUESTIONS

1. What factors may a manufacturer consider to determine whether to distribute products directly to customers? Can Air-conditioners be distributed directly to consumers?
2. What is the most appropriate strategy for resolving channel conflict?
3. Explain the three alternatives of distribution coverage strategy with example.
4. What is VMS? Explain it with an example.
5. Explain the ten ways to manage Channel Conflict.

OPENING CASE: EASTWOOD CORPORATION

INTRODUCTION

The GM of Eastwood knew that he had just been given the most difficult challenge of his career. Only hours earlier, he had met with the executive committee of Eastwood's parent, Pelican Corporation. He had been warned prior to his arrival that the corporation's expectations for its 10 operating divisions had been changed. He discovered that the original business plan for his division (see Exhibit 6.1), submitted a month earlier in August 2001, would need to be revised to account for the corporate change in goals. Despite his requests for more reasonable expectations and more time, he had to accept what he considered to be very difficult improvement goals for his division. He now had two weeks to submit a revised business plan outlining a formal strategy for achieving or exceeding the new objectives.

EXHIBIT 6.1 2002 Projection-business plan for Eastwood Corporation, submitted in August 2001 ($ in millions)

Income Statement	*2001*	*% of Sales*	*2002*	*% of Sales*
Sales	$30.7		$28.9	
Sales Growth		N/A		(7.1)
COGS	30.9	100.7	25.0	37.7
Gross Margin	(0.2)	(0.7)	3.5	12.3
SG&A	4.9	16.0	3.0	10.5
Misc. Expenses & Income	1.8	5.9	1.9	6.6
Profit Before Tax	(3.3)	(10.7)	2.4	8.4
Taxes (35%)	(1.2)		0.8	
Net Income	($2.1		$1.6	
Cash Flow				% of FA
Net income			$1.6	
Depreciation			0.6	5.3
Change in working capital			1.7	
Change in Fixed & Other Assets			1.6	
Cash Flow			$5.5	
Assets	*2001*	*% of Sales*	*2002*	*% of Sales*
Current Assets	$14.9	48.5	$13.7	48.0
Current Liabilities	4.3	14.0	4.8	16.8
Fixed and Other Assets	10.7	34.9	8.5	29.8
Net Assets	$21.3		$17.4	
Return on Net Assets	(104%)		9.1%	

EASTWOOD CORPORATION'S PRODUCTS, MARKETS, AND PERFORMANCE

Eastwood was a manufacturer of high quality electrical switching components for aerospace, defense, telecommunications, and industrial applications. From the division's founding, Eastwood was one of only a few suppliers to these niche markets. The lack of competition during those years had allowed Eastwood to enjoy high margins and a captive customer base. Unfortunately, Eastwood was unable to protect the niche markets that it had created and dominated.

Partly because of the success of Pelican and partly because of its own failures, Eastwood allowed inefficiencies to develop in its operations. To maintain the margins that the company had enjoyed for many years, Eastwood raised its prices rather than address the underlying cost drivers of its products. As prices climbed and quality deteriorated, competitors began entering the market. By 1994, Eastwood had lost most of its share of the telecommunications and aerospace markets as a result of high prices, late deliveries, and an indifference to customer needs and requests. Similarly, by the mid-1990s, Eastwood had witnessed the erosion of its market share in the defense and industrial applications markets.

In 2000, a new GM was appointed to lead Pelican's floundering Eastwood division. By that time, the division was plagued by high prices, declining profit margins, long-term contracts that obligated Eastwood to sell its products at a loss, large inventories, high fixed costs, late deliveries, and an indifference to its customers. The GM's first action was to implement several quality assurance programs designed to improve customer service, lower costs, and improve productivity.

A study of Eastwood's performance during the most recent five-year period compared key operating results to those of a representative set of comparable companies in the same SIC code. The calculation of relative economies of scale revealed just how inefficient the division was in comparison with its industry competitors. At its current sales volume, the company was only half an efficient as the industry average, requiring approximately 16 employees per $1 million in sales. The company, however, was improving. Eastwood had recently achieved annual productivity growth rates of 6 per year, which were higher than the industry average productivity growth rate.

Improvement efforts had been interrupted unexpectedly in 1998, when the corporation decided to relocate the division's operations from Texas to North Carolina. Despite this setback, the GM still believed that the company could return to its status as a market leader within the next five years. Unfortunately, Pelican had given him no more than one year to turn things around.

PELICAN'S EXPECTATIONS FOR EASTWOOD

The GM was moderately surprised by the new division goals, because he believed that the division's original plan was aggressive and contained realistic performance targets. In 2001, Eastwood's cost of goods sold was expected to be 101 percent of revenues, and SG$A 16 percent of revenues. As a result, Eastwood would suffer a loss of $2.2 million during the year. Under Eastwood's original plan for 2002, cost of goods sold were expected to be 88 percent of sales and SG&A would be 10 percent of sales, which was expected to result in a profit of $1.6 million.

The parent company, however, believed that Eastwood was capable of even better results. Pelican's new expectations called for at least 1 percent (of sales) improvement in sales growth, gross margin and SG&A expense, above the company's original business plan. To assess the impact that such improvements would have on the division's cash flow and net income, the GM asked his finance manager to perform a sensitivity analysis on these variables. The analysis showed that attainment of these new goals would increase the division's net income by about $390,000 and its cash flow by about $200,000.

The GM knew that corporate management was conducting a review of the viability and attractiveness of each of the 10 operating units. Although he was not sure which methods of analysis were being used by the corporation to assess the business strengths and industry attractiveness of each operating unit, he was aware of the existence of a corporate strategic analysis matrix that considered several factors in performing such an assessment. He thought it would be prudent to consider how Eastwood would be characterized using such a tool.

The result of Pelican's strategic analysis of the division likely would determine Eastwood's fate within the corporation. To estimate the current value of his division, the GM collected data on Eastwood's recent financial performance as well as information on completed financial transactions involving comparable companies. His analysis yielded an estimated valuation for the company of nearly $31 million.

CHALLENGES FACING EASTWOOD

Any realistic strategic plan that the GM and his team developed had to account for the many problems that plagued the division as it approached 2002. In preparing Eastwood's original business plan several months earlier, the GM had asked his management team to list the critical problems confronting the division in the coming year. His staff identified key problem areas that Eastwood would have to address in 2002.

First, the prices of Eastwood's products were higher than those of competitor's products. Unlike earlier years when Eastwood was the sole producer in its markets, the current markets were saturated and no one company could dictate the selling price of the products. Despite this competitive environment, however, Eastwood had continued to raise prices over the last few years to reflect higher overhead costs. The price increases were not accepted by the market and Eastwood's customers began finding alternative sources to replace Eastwood's products.

Second, Eastwood had a reputation of being unable to meet delivery deadlines. A typical comment voiced by customers was, "Eastwood has a good product, if you can get it." Late deliveries, in conjunction with higher prices, led customers to second-source of drop Eastwood's products altogether.

Third, Pelican's financial difficulties had made many of Eastwood's suppliers and customers uneasy. Many existing customers had expressed their concerns about Pelican's financial stability and in turn, the ability of Eastwood to satisfy its obligations to both customers and suppliers.

Fourth, the decision to move Eastwood's operations from Texas to North Carolina caused several important customers to find alternative suppliers. These customers were geographically closer to Texas and believed that the increased distance would lead to even higher prices and further delays in delivery. Eastwood lost key personnel as a result of the decision to move operations to North Carolina. When the decision to move Eastwood was announced, many of the division's seasoned engineers and other key personnel chose to remain in Texas. Several of these former employees either joined competitors or started their own companies to compete directly with Eastwood.

Last, the division no longer had original equipment manufacturer (OEM), aftermarket (replacement parts) or international representation. Until recently, Eastwood had relied on a very effective representative in these markets. The representative had unexpectedly announced three months previously that it would no longer represent third parties. Unfortunately, the division was a party to several long-term contracts that required Eastwood to deliver custom-made systems to major customers in the aerospace industry at a substantial loss. These contracts had been executed prior to the GM's arrival at Eastwood and he was uncertain how difficult it would be to renegotiate them.

OPPORTUNITIES

In spite of the difficulties noted above, the GM felt that the division had weathered the storm. Eastwood was expected to produce a positive cash flow with minimum capital requirements for the foreseeable future. The Eastwood brand, while experiencing some erosion, maintained excellent name and recognition in the niche markets in which it is operated. Additionally, over the last year, the division had greatly improved delivery performance, the quality of its products and the attentiveness of its personnel to customer needs and complaints. It was believed that additional opportunities for improvement existed in each of Eastwood's functional departments, described below.

Sales and Marketing

The loss of the distributor was believed to be more of a benefit to Eastwood than a setback. The use of a third-party distributor had contributed to the decline in division responsiveness to customer needs and problems. With significant growth potential in the national and international OEM markets, the GM believed that direct marketing and sales efforts would reestablish Eastwood as the OEM market leader for switching systems.

Manufacturing

The sales and marketing efforts were dependent upon continued improvement by manufacturing. If production costs could be reduced further, sales and marketing could reduce prices and make their products more competitive. The following manufacturing objectives were thought to be achievable:-

1. **A reduction in rework in the fabrication area.** In 2001, the fabrication area had reduced rework from 16 percent to 4 percent. It was believed that another 2 percent decrease was possible in 2002.
2. **A reduction in scrap.** In 2001, manufacturing had reduced scrap from 10 percent to less than 2 percent. In 2002, it was felt that a further reduction in scrap to 0.5 percent was attainable.
3. **Productivity increases in fabrication and assembly.** For 2002, it was projected that productivity could be increased by 7 percent in fabrication and 5 percent in assembly.
4. **Additional improvements in the Quality Improvement Department.** Improvements should result from the quality assurance programs implemented by the division several years earlier. The quality assurance programs would be upgraded by the addition of experienced personnel, implementation of statistical process control (SPC) and other statistical control programs. The adoption of a vendor qualification program, the development of an internal audit department and the formation of a continuous training program would also improve quality.

Engineering

Because of the relocation from Texas to North Carolina, Eastwood lost many of its talented engineers to competitors. A successful turnaround would depend heavily on the division's ability to attract and retain qualified personnel. The re-staffing efforts to date had been extremely successful. In addition to the personnel issue, several initiatives had been undertaken by the engineering department and were expected to be completed in 2002. These include the following:

a. **The redesign of the switching systems currently marketed and sold to the aerospace industry.** Currently, the weight and size of the systems exceeded customer specifications and were higher than those offered by competitors. The new systems would be superior in quality to those of competitors.

b. **A formalized program designed to increase coordination between the marketing and engineering departments, including increased visits to customers.** This initiative was aimed at decreasing total production costs and improving customer service.

c. **A reduction in product lines within certain product families.** Fewer product offerings would decrease setup times and increase the capacity of each of the machines. The net result would be greater operational efficiencies and lower total costs.

STRATEGIES ANALYSIS: STRENGTHS AND WEAKNESSES

The GM understood the magnitude of the challenges facing his division. As he reviewed the problems and opportunities confronting him, he wondered what actions should be taken and what priorities should be assigned.

Strengths

- Strong brand equity despite recent slippage.
- Productivity improvements two times the predicted level of 2.8 percent for Eastwood's growth rate
  - 2001: 6.2 percent, projected 2002: 5 to 7 percent
- Improved product quality
- Previously implemented quality assurance programs taking effect
- Rework in fabrication reduced from 16 percent in 2000 to 4 percent in 2001
- Scrap reduced from 10 percent in 2000 to 2 percent in 2001
- Improved delivery performance
- Increased customer focus
- Loss of distributor, beneficial in this respect
- Success in replacing personnel lost in move
- SG&A expense ratio below industry average of 24.8 percent
  - 2001: 16.0 percent, projected 2002: 10.5 percent

Weaknesses

- Small size - a disadvantage in an industry with significant economies of scale
- Poor productivity
  - 16 employees per $1 million sales - well above expected level of 11 employees
  - The most efficient firms employed 8 employees per $1 million of revenues and had revenues of approximately $200 million
- Critical engineering personnel lost in move to North Carolina
- Market share declines resulting from customer defections driven by the following eight factors, below
  - High prices
  - Poor delivery
  - Move from Dallas to North Carolina is inconvenient to some customer, suppliers and employees
  - Customers have concerns about Pelican
  - Majority of market share lost in all segments
  - Locked into long-term loss-generating contracts in aerospace
  - Lacking distribution in OEM, aftermarket and international markets
  - Loss of distributor
- Must develop marketing and sales for segments previously serviced by distributor
- Growth projection well below industry five-year average of 10.9 percent
  - 2001: 11.8 percent, projected 2002: -7.1 percent
- Gross margins well below industry five-year average of 35.7 percent
  - 2001:-0.7 percent, projected 2002: 12.3 percent
- ROS well below industry five-year average of 6.2 percent
  - 2002: 6.8 percent, projected 2002: 5.5 percent
- RONA well below industry five-year average of 12.4 percent
  - 2001:-10.4 percent, projected 2002: 9.1 percent

Industry Characteristics

- Strong industry growth, five-year average of 10.9 percent
- Potential growth in OEM markets, both internationally and domestically
- Crowded industry with high level of competitive intensity

- Many large competitors
- Competition on the basis of price
- Pricing power controlled by buyers
- Economies of scale up approximately $200 million, slight diseconomies about that
- Very large growth economies
- Attractive industry returns
- Industry RONA: Five-year average 12.4 percent, high 15.7 percent in 1999; low 6.3 percent in 1997

STRATEGIC SUMMARY

Business Strengths

Eastwood Products retained the strong brand recognition that it had always had, but little else. In 2000 it lost over $9 million on revenue of $27 million. Its losses narrowed considerably in 2001, when it generated revenue of $30.7 million and produced a loss of $3.3 million (pre-tax). In 2002, Eastwood was forecast to earn $2.4 million on revenue of $28.5 million. Based on these somewhat optimistic assumptions, the company would still trail the industry in gross margin, revenue per employee, return on sales and return on net assets.

Recent efforts to improve the performance of the division had resulted in significant progress. Rework and scrap rates had fallen dramatically. Delivery performance had improved and replacement efforts for personnel lost due to move to North Carolina had gotten off tc a good start. Additionally, plans to build a marketing and sales force portended improved customer service.

Despite these efforts to improve, Eastwood remained a small and inefficient firm in an industry dominated by larger and more efficient firms. In the industry, smaller firms had consistently lost money. Its size was an inherent disadvantage, which was compounded by its inefficiency. The negative growth forecast for 2002 did not appear to offer any hope of rectifying the situation.

Overall business strength: Low.

Industry Attractiveness

The switching systems industry was a crowded one, which was dominated by large firms. It had exhibited strong growth over the past five years, averaging almost 11 percent. Returns on investment during this period had averaged over 12 percent and had never been negative. Opportunities in the OEM market would provide continued room for growth.

An increasing trend towards price competition had the potential to depress returns. The larger firms controlled pricing in the crowded industry. As a result of significant economies of scale, firms of approximately $200 million were the best positioned for efficient manufacturing. Smaller firms had traditionally seen lower returns in this industry than their larger competitors. In addition, economic cycles tended to exaggerate the swings in performance of smaller competitors in the switching systems industry.

Overall industry attractiveness: Medium.

RECOMMENDATIONS

Pelican Corporation should divest Eastwood. Although the switching systems industry was reasonably attractive, Eastwood was not well positioned to regain a leadership position. Improvements in performance such that the division could return to a stable and profitable position in the industry were unlikely. Even if such improvements were likely, they would lead to little more than marginal improvements, because the division's small size severely limited its potential in this scale-driven industry. Additionally, the modest size of the potential returns indicated that Pelican's attention and resources would be better spent on more competitive businesses.

If Retained, What Should Eastwood Do?

- Continue emphasis on improved operational efficiency
- Go for productivity improvement of 7 percent in fabrication and 5 percent in assembly, achievable in 2002
- Renegotiate money-losing long-term contracts in the aerospace market
- Continue emphasis on improved quality
- Scrap reduction from 2 percent to 0.5 percent, possible in 2002
- Rework reduction from 4 percent to 2 percent, possible in 2002
- Implement SPC, vendor qualification, internal auditing, continuous training and improved scheduling and ordering system
- Begin product redesign program
- Redesign products for cost reduction and performance improvement
- Improve coordination between engineering and marketing by more frequent customer contact
- Prune product lines
- Free up capacity on constrained production lines
- Eliminate marginally profitable products

If Divested, What Price Could Be Expected?

The data on nine completed transactions involving the sale of comparable companies provided multiples for revenue, total assets, net assets and EBIT. These multiples provided a wide range of estimates for the market value of Eastwood. Asset multiples provided high-end values of approximately $30 to $34 million but did not reflect the questionable value of the continued operations of the firm. An EBIT multiple supported these estimates and assumed future performance consistent with historical levels. A revenue multiple provided a low-end value of approximately $28.5 million. A grand average of all of these values provided an estimate of the market value of Eastwood of approximately $31 million.

Chapter: 6

Corporate Strategies

Learning Objectives

In this chapter the main stress is given on :

- Understanding the nature, scope and concerns of corporate strategies and its significance to the firm and its main constituents.
- To understand the linkage between corporate objectives and corporate strategies.
- An overview of Innovative strategies.

INTRODUCTION TO CORPORATE STRATEGY

Capitalism, Diversification and Corporate Goals

A major strength of the U.S. free-enterprise system is the capability of major corporations to amass large sums of required investment capital. These funds come from both institutional and individual investors who purchase debt and equity instruments based on their assessments of the company's future prospects. The costs of these funds to a firm are largely dependent upon the past financial performance of the firm and the investors' and lenders' expectations of the risks inherent in projected future performance. This contingency leads to a practice in which the chief executive officers (CEOs) of corporations interested in influencing investors make public projections of their corporate goals and their strategies for achieving those goals. These projections, along with the company's past success at achieving its stated goals, allow the investment community to rationally choose preferred investments.

The most important measures of corporate performance assessment are the interrelated goals of return on investment (ROI); growth in revenues, earnings or market share; and the adequacy of cash flow to fund the growth. The efficacy of corporate goals and performance are measured by comparisons with companies in the same industry and, ultimately, with the wider array of investment opportunities across the spectrum of all industries.

The natural development of most corporations during the last 30 years has resulted in some degree of diversified, decentralized operations. The tendency to lower investment risk by diversifying a company's businesses and product lines has made it difficult for corporate executives to manage the myriad of operational details in a wide range of businesses. The investment community in recent years has pressurised companies to become less diversified by rewarding focused companies with significantly higher multiples of stock price to earnings. In spite of this pressure, the diversified, decentralized form of corporate organization is still the dominant mode of operation of most large, public U.S. companies.

Diversification, despite all its advantages in avoiding risk, has one major disadvantage: the difficulty of achieving reasonably stable corporate results. Each industry has its inherent pattern of investment intensity, gross profit margins, degree of labor intensity, rate of new product development and introduction, prevailing rate of research and development expenses and degree of market elasticity. Each operating unit (a division or subsidiary company) of a diversified company has a characteristic set of feasible financial results based on the industry competitive structure it faces. The performance of the divisions on the variables listed above leads to a set of boundaries that define reasonable corporate expectations with regard to return on investment, growth and cash flow.

Achieving high returns on investment in industries that are highly investment-intensive is difficult. So is growing significantly faster than the industry's market growth rate. Finally, growing significantly faster than the market if the product or service is a commodity is almost impossible. Typically, any attempt to capture market share by reducing prices in this situation will lower the prices and margins of all of the competitors, because competitors will meet the lower prices to protect their market shares. It is also axiomatic that fast-growing businesses require injections of cash to grow capacity and to provide the necessary working capital to fund their growth.

Many focused businesses seem to have difficulties achieving high returns on investment, high relative growth rates and self-sustaining cash flow simultaneously. If the business were to grow rapidly over a long time, it would need continuous injections of cash. If it were required to maintain some level of debt to total capital, it would invariably and continually reach points in time at which its debt would encounter limits imposed by lenders and it would have to issue additional equity in order to continue to grow. This process would relentlessly dilute the ownership of the company and would be counterproductive from an investor standpoint.

Some businesses with market leadership through new product innovation or through patents are able to earn sufficient profit margins and the resultant cash flow, to support almost any market growth rate. But such situations are very rare and they are most often found in so-called high-technology, research-oriented businesses. Finally, investment-intensive businesses producing commodity products or any business facing price pressures from strong foreign competition will find it difficult to earn an attractive ROI.

These challenges, however, are offset in each situation by concomitant advantages to a company with a portfolio of businesses. In spite of their needs for cash, fast-growing businesses provide their corporate parent with the growth for which financial analysts long. Businesses with market leadership provide their parent company with high profit margins. And investment-intensive businesses, in spite of thin margins and low returns on investment, often provide steady, high levels of cash flow, resulting largely from high levels of depreciation. As a result, many companies resist pressures from the financial analysts for more focus and prefer to operate through a portfolio of business units, which brings the mix of desirable results to the corporate totals.

This advantageous combination of performance measures does not necessarily represent synergy among the businesses of the portfolio. Many companies seek synergies among operating divisions, such as supposed advantageous supplier/customer relationships created through vertical integration. The advantages would seem to be the capturing of the supplier margins, which would tend to increase the company's profits. In reality, the disadvantages inherent in attempting to achieve synergy often greatly outweigh the advantages, because of the internal squabbles that naturally arise over fair transfer prices, reasonable inventory levels and delivery dates.

Many well-run companies have come to realize the power of the free enterprise system in resolving these situations. The divisions are left to do business with one another at their discretion, based on arm's-length relationships, without corporate edicts in regard to transfer prices or schedule dates. Division managements are left to fill their procurement needs on the open market, with a caveat that they should "buy internal," all other things being equal. Supplier division must compete by meeting market standards for prices and delivery. One very successful company went so far as to institute a policy that if a division did not sell more than 50 percent of its output on the open market, then another division in the same company purchasing more than 50 percent of its output would subsume it. The general notion throughout this book is that synergies are advantageous, when the free enterprise system is left to work, and the only effective rules are those provided by competition.

The concept of corporate strategy is viewed from the dual perspectives of both the parent company and the operating divisions of a diversified, decentralized corporation. The corporate challenge is to provide an effective set of consistent results over the long term from a given mix of businesses, each of which has some inherent pattern of achievable results. The divisions are charged with producing outstanding results compared to similar companies, their own past performances and that of other well-run companies. In such a corporation, the results of the total enterprise are very much the sum of the results of the operating units.

Evidently, the only way the corporate office can make significant changes in the important performance measures of return on investment, growth and cash flow is to make changes in the portfolio of businesses. That is, it can choose to acquire new, more desirable businesses and/or it can choose to divest less-attractive businesses. In the end, its long-term results will be determined by the mix of businesses and their potential for contributing to the crucial performance measures. Corporations that perform superbly will find ready access to equity markets, will enjoy lower interest rates than competitors and will be able to use strong stock prices to acquire additional businesses. The overriding objective of contemporary corporate management is to enhance shareholder value.

CORPORATE-LEVEL STRATEGY

In a diversified, decentralized corporate setting, strategy at the corporate level may be narrowed to a choice or set of choices, which are not mutually exclusive. First among these, a corporation may choose to continue operations as an ongoing enterprise with the business units currently in its portfolio. This strategy more or less commits the corporation to the pattern of results reasonably available from the current business units. If the business units compete in attractive industries and are well managed, this strategy may be viable and desirable. The growth of the company is this committed to the limits imposed by the natural growth rates available to the several business units.

A corporation may instead opt to sell one or more of its current business units. This choice could result from a perception that these units lack long-term prospects consistent with the company's objectives. The decision could follow from environmental or other regulatory requirements that call for extensive capital investments for continued operations in one or more business units. The company may not have the cash for such investments or may not wish to commit the investment at the time. The company may not have the time or resources to focus on a particular division. Either way, selling the unit would bring in cash that could be used in what would be considered more advantageous ways. It may also improve performance relative to the company's specific goals.

A corporation may also choose to spin off one or more of its current business units. Spin-offs offer certain advantages to a company and to its shareholders, as compared to the sales of operating divisions, especially related to taxes. Spin-offs occur when management feels that greater shareholder value can be achieved by separating operations. In such a case, the shares in the newly separated business are distributed pro rata to the holders of the parent company's shares. Because this transaction is considered a substitution of one item of a stipulated value for another item of similar value, it is deemed to create no gain for either party and is, thus, a tax-free exchange. Understandably, spin-offs are becoming increasingly popular because of this advantage. This process allows the individual shareholder to decide whether to sell or hold the new stock thus controlling the occurrence of a taxable event. Alternatively, a parent company may choose to sell one or more of its businesses, either by negotiating or by auction to the highest bidder. Naturally, a selling price in excess of the book value of the business would create a taxable event. Whether the mechanism is a sale or a spin-off, the result is the same - a leaner, more focused corporation.

Occasionally, a company may find itself in a strategic and/or operational situation from which it cannot readily extricate itself. A competitive advantage formerly enjoyed might have been neutralized by an aggressive competitor. The firm may face prohibitive labor or material costs that are uncontrollable. It may find itself "in play" as a result of an unsolicited offer for its shares. The company may find that its focused market segment is vanishing as a result of shifting consumer trends or substitute products. For these and other reasons, the corporation may conclude that shareholder interests are best served by "going out of business." The company would thus sell out to another company and its shareholders would receive cash or stock in the acquiring company in return for their shares.

Alternatively, a company may choose to invest cash accumulations into strategic acquisitions. The management may feel that the company should proceed in a different direction and that certain focused acquisitions may enhance the competitive position of one or more of the corporation's business units. This choice precludes simply reinvesting all available cash into existing operations. These acquisitions, if carefully thought out, can improve the company's performance in regard to return on investment, growth and/or cash flow.

Finally, a company may choose to use its cash accumulations to buy back its own shares. This option has become increasingly popular in recent years as many companies, faced with holding levels of cash beyond their reasonable operating needs and believing their stock to be underpriced, reason that buying their own shares constitutes the best use of these funds from the shareholder's point of view. The cash accumulates as a result of an imbalance among the company's growth rate, its needs for cash and its ability to generate cash. After debt is paid down to optimal levels, the cash in excess of internal needs normally earns less than the prevailing ROI from operations. Thus it lowers the overall average ROI for the corporation. It does so because public companies normally invest excess cash only in risk-free government bonds; the management is not expert at investments and companies are not normally formed for the purpose of investing in other companies. We note that the repurchase of shares is effectively a tax-free dividend, increasing the shareholders' investment with no tax penalty.

Many variations or combinations of these corporate-level strategies exist. All essentially constitute the types of actions feasible for the corporate management to undertake to improve performance, as measured by the increase in shareholder value. Most extended efforts to pressure business-unit managers to improve performance are fruitless. Corporate management must establish limits for business units to conform to corporate goals and forgo the common "hockey-stick" effect of promised future improvements. If a business is well-positioned in an attractive industry and if it is well-managed, then the corporate management must accept the results. If many believe that the unit could be managed better, then a management change is in order. In the final analysis, the corporate performance is largely determined by the performance potential of the several business units.

This determination is, of course, predicated on the premise that corporate overhead is in line with that of other well-run companies. No amount of divisional excellence can overcome the negative effects of a bloated, out-of-control level of corporate overhead expenses and punitive interest charges brought on by excessive levels of corporate debt.

STRATEGIES FOR DIVISIONS AND FOCUSED COMPANIES

The term division stand for such business designations as "subsidiaries," "business units," or stand-alone "focused companies" that may be part of a corporate portfolio. In fact, from corporation to corporation, these terms are used interchangeably. The strategic challenge in a division is quite different from that of its diversified, decentralized parent. The first major distinction between division and parent is that a division must normally obtain any needed cash from its parent company rather than the capital markets. It must prepare detailed plans for its future operations, carefully spelling out its needs for capital expenses and for working capital. It must also determine its product, marketing and pricing strategies in a way that is consonant with overall corporate goals and objectives.

The details follow from a systematic answering of a series of strategic questions. Does the division intend to grow rapidly or slowly? Is this projected growth rate slower than the market growth rate, at the market growth rate or faster than the market growth rate? Will the division need to have excess (for now) capacity in place to accommodate the growth? Is the division the cost leader (the low-cost producer) in its industry? Are there structural or other restrictions, if any, labor related, supplier related or management related? Are the restrictions, if any, labor related, supplier related or management related? Is the division a leader or a follower in the market-place? Does the division command a premium price for its product or, does the market dictate the prices? Is the product line a "full" line or a "narrow" line? Through which channels are the products marketed?

Does the quality level of the products meet industry standards or are the products quality leaders? The answers to these and other strategic questions help define the basic strategies of divisions. Michael Porter defined three basic, generic strategies available to any business that produces goods and services and faces a complex marketplace. These generic strategies are:

- Market a differentiated product
- Focus on or dominate, a market niche
- Be the low-cost producer

A firm may choose to differentiate its products as sufficiency high in quality to command a premium price. Products can also be differentiated by the diversity of the product line, by the offering of features not matched by competitors or by their reliability.

A firm may choose to compete in a narrow market niche, such as the standard line of bearings or the specially line of bearings. It may choose the lowest-cost market segment or the small (in units), highest-priced segment. It may choose to market a limited line of children's clothes, as contrasted with a full line of clothing for all segments of the population. In addition, the firm may choose a geographic niche, limiting its distribution to a well-defined region, typically prescribed by transportation economies.

A firm also may strive to be the lowest-cost producer of its products. This means that no competitor can produce and deliver an equivalent product a lower price. To be in this situation provides a firm with many strategic advantages, including the ability to punish competitors by lowering prices, which competitors would have trouble meeting.

Finally, these alternatives strategies are not mutually exclusive. Pursuing one generic strategy does not preclude a firm simultaneously striving to implement the others, although Porter argued that most firms found the successful implementation of a single strategy a daunting task. On the other hand, some companies can set all three strategies in place and execute them effectively and simultaneously, which enables them to become the dominant firms in their industries. Some competitors, however, cannot survive the product, marketing and pricing advantages that accrue to firms that successfully pursue the three generic strategies simultaneously.

NATURE, SCOPE AND CONCERNS OF CORPORATE STRATEGY

The strength of the entire process of strategic planning is tested by the efficacy of the strategy finally forged by the firm. The ultimate question is whether the strategy ironed out is the appropriate one - whether it would take the firm to its objectives. Corporate strategy is the game plan that actually steers the firm towards success. The degree of aptness of this game plan decides the extent of the firm's success. That is precisely why formulation of corporate strategy forms the crux of the strategic planning process. The ramification of this vital task forms the theme of the series of chapters commencing with the present one.

Corporate strategy is basically the growth design of the firm; its spells out the growth objective of the firm the direction, extent, pace and timing of the firm's growth. It also spells out the strategy for achieving the growth. Thus, we can also describe corporate strategy as the objective-strategy design of the firm. And, to arrive at such an objective-strategy design is the basic burden of corporate strategy formulation.

Corporate strategy is basically concerned with the choice of businesses, products and markets. To be more specific, it is concerned with what Ansoff refers to as changes/addition/deletions to the firm's Business-Product-Market posture. Exhibit 6.2 describes in a nutshell the nature, scope and concerns of corporate strategy.

EXHIBIT 6.2 NATURE, SCOPE AND CONCERNS OF CORPORATE STRATEGY
• Corporate strategy is the growth design of the firm; it spells out the growth objective of the firm - the direction, extent, pace and timing of the firm's growth; it also spells out the strategy for achieving the growth. • It can also be viewed as the objective-strategy design of the firm. • It is the design for filling the firm's strategic planning gap. • It is concerned with the choice of the firm's products and markets; it actually denotes the changes/additions/deletions in the firm's existing product-market postures. It spells out the businesses in which the firms will play the markets in which it will operate and the customer needs it will serve. • It ensures that the right fit is achieved between the firm and its environment. • It helps build the relevant competitive advantage for the firm. • Corporate objectives and corporate strategy together describe the firm's concept of business

WHAT DOES CORPORATE STRATEGY ENSURE FOR THE FIRM?

What does corporate strategy ensure? Corporate strategy in the first place ensures the growth of the firm and ensures the correct alignment of the firm with its environment. It serves as the design for filling the strategic planning gap. It also helps build the relevant competitive advantages as:

Ensures right environmental fit: Masterminding and working out the right fit between the firm and its external environment is the primary contribution of corporate strategy. We have seen that basically the purpose of corporate strategy is to harness the opportunities available in the environment, countering the threats embedded therein. How does corporate strategy actually accomplish this task? It is by matching the unique capabilities of the firm with the promises and threats of the environment that it achieves this task.

It is obvious that responding to environment is part and parcel of a firm's existence. The question is how good or how methodical is the response. This is where strategy steps in. Strategy is the opposite of adhoc responses to the changes in the environment - in competition, consumer tastes, technology and other variables. It amounts to long-term, well thought-out and prepared responses to the various forces in the business environment. When the responses are right it implies that the right fit has been created between the firm and its environment.

Right now many Indian firms are busy seeking the right alignment with environment .In the Indian context, the current times provide an apt setting for highlighting the powerful role of corporate strategy in ensuring the right fit between the firm and its environment. The business environment of India is now replete with changes. The suddenness and the vastness of these changes proved a real test for the firms, of their competence at forging the right fit between the firm and the environment.

Helps fill the firm's strategic planning gap, selecting the appropriate strategy route

The difference between the firm's desired performance and its achievable performance is its strategic planning gap. The firm seeks to fill this gap through the strategy exercise. In fact, strategy is nothing other than the plan for bridging the strategic planning gap. In its search for filling this gap the firm considers different strategy routes and arrives at an appropriate strategy choice.

Helps build competitive advantages

Creating sustainable competitive advantage is a major concern of corporate strategy. As we know that for a strategy to work, it must be backed by relevant competitive advantage. Quite often, companies fail not because their strategy is inherently hopeless but because they had not taken care to endow themselves with the relevant competitive advantages. Whatever the strategy route chosen by a firm, it should ensure that the competitive advantages essential for the pursuit of the chosen strategy are present. Since building such competitive advantages is a long-term process, and a corporate level concern, automatically it becomes a responsibility of corporate strategy. The interesting point is that while competitive advantage is a constituent of corporate strategy, competitive advantage is also built through corporate strategy. Corporate strategy uses competitive advantage; it also builds competitive advantage. As successful firms ensure that their corporate strategy includes conscious moves for building competitive advantages, so that they will serve as the backup for their strategies.

THE LINKAGE BETWEEN CORPORATE OBJECTIVE AND CORPORATE STRATEGY

While objectives indicate where the firm wants to reach, strategy provides the design for getting there. While the objective specifies the results the firm seeks in a given timeframe, the strategy spells out the program of action for achieving the results. In finally deciding the business-product-market choices for the firm, corporate strategy fills in those areas left blank in the objective formulation stage.

Objectives and strategy together describe the firm's concept of strategy

The firm raises many questions before finally clinching its growth objective. For instance, it agitates questions such as: What part of its overall growth ambition it should target for realization during the present planning period? To what extent can its existing businesses contribute to this target? To what extent they can grow and to what extent can new markets be found for these businesses? From where else can the desired growth come? To what extent do the firm's capabilities match the desired growth? The firm clinches its growth objective after agitating all such questions in detail. Even after clinching the growth objective in this way, the firm is not totally clear about the specific routes through which the growth gap is going to be filled.

Subsequently, in the strategy formulation stage, these explorations continue; and it is at this stage that it is finally clinched as to how and through which businesses/products/markets the intended quantum of growth will be actually achieved. In other words, the scope of the existing businesses, the choice of additional businesses and deletions from the existing basket are all concluded at this stage. The contributions of existing businesses, their expansions and that of new businesses to the total growth are ascertained. In other words, even the objective becomes complete only when the strategy component, i.e., the business choices, is finalized. And, objective and strategy together fully clarify the future plan.

Reliance Industries
For instance, when Reliance Industries fixes Rs. 20,000 crore annual turnover and 20 percent, RONW by 2002 and 20 percent CAGR in EPS over the five-year period as its objective, the future plan of the company is still not clear in full measure. For example, it is not clear as to how and wherefrom the additional growth of Rs. 11,000 crore over and above the present level of Rs. 9,000 crore would materialize, or more precisely, how the strategic planning gap of Rs 11,000 crore would be filled, ensuring simultaneously other parameters such as profitability. The picture becomes clear only when the strategic choice is made and decisions are taken on the businesses the company will pursue. When it is finally fixed that approximately 30 percent of the gap will be filled through expansions in existing businesses, viz., textiles, fibers and petrochemicals and 45 per cent through

power and 25 percent through telecom, the future programme of the company becomes fully clear. In other words, while objective fixes the planning gap, strategy decides how and through what businesses the firm will fill the gap. Objectives and strategy take together fully clarify the firm's future plan.

THE CONSTITUENTS OF CORPORATE STRATEGY

We have seen that objectives, product-market scope, growth vector, competitive advantage and synergy are the constituents of corporate strategy. Let us elaborate here these constituents of corporate strategy. Objectives have been handled already in detail in the preceding chapter. We shall elaborate the others here.

Product-market posture

The corporate strategy is largely concerned with the choice of the firm's product market postures or more precisely, changes/additions/deletions to the firm's business-product-market postures. That product-market posture is the crux of strategy would be evident, since any shift in strategy, in effect, results in a realignment of the firm's product-market posture.

Corporate strategy ensures that the product-market choices are made wisely, providing for the best utilization of the firm's resources among the various product-market opportunities. Quite naturally, while formulating corporate strategy, the firm raises several questions relating to its product-market posture. For example, the firm raises and answers questions such as:

What businesses/product-markets should it stay with?

Which ones should it intensify?

Which ones it should quit?

What new businesses it should pursue?

What should be the relative priorities of these businesses?

What level of resource/support should be given to each of these businesses?

Through what strategy routes will it gain entry into new businesses or expansions?

What competitive advantages, core competencies and synergies are available/required for pursuing these businesses?

What are the conditions that govern success in these businesses? To what extent does the firm possess them?

There will be several alternative product-market choices before the firm, all generated by the strategic planning process. When a firm is choosing its strategy from a basket of strategy options, in a base sense, it is assessing the effect of the alternatives in terms of changes/additions/deletions to the firm's existing product-market posture. Wrong product-market choices can be catastrophic. And here lies the main risk as well as responsibility of corporate strategy formulation. How to arrive at correct business/product/market choices is the real question.

Growth vector

Growth vector indicates the direction or path in which the firm is moving and the pace at which it is moving with respect to its product-market posture - whether the firm opts for intensification, integration or diversification. Growth vector basically means the path of growth adopted by the firm.

Competitive advantage and synergy

Strategy will identify the competitive advantage that will back up the chosen. Here, we are concerned specifically with the fact that competitive advantage forms one essential constituent of corporate strategy. Corporate strategy will identify the competitive advantages available with the firm which will form the support for the chosen strategy. Likewise, it will also identify the competitive advantages additionally required for working the strategy, which are not presently available with the firm. Corporate strategy will also help build the latter category of competitive advantages so that the strategy would have the required back-up.

Corporate strategy will also indicate the extent and nature of synergy available to the firm, which can be of support to the chosen strategy. Synergy is the benefit emanating from linkages and joint effects between the existing transactions of the firm and its chosen strategy. It can show up as operational synergy or management synergy. Corporate strategy clarifies this aspect.

Corporate strategy of a firm can be stated in concrete and precise terms. Corporate strategy of a firm is not a vague idea; it can be described in concrete terms, without any ambiguity. It has specific constituents and when there is clarity about these constituents, the firm's corporate strategy can be expressed through a precise and easily understandable statement. Once the five constituents of corporate strategy explained in the foregoing paragraphs are stated clearly, we get the full shape of the firm's corporate strategy. Using this framework illustration of a corporate strategy of a firm is done in Exhibit 6.3.

EXHIBIT 6.3

An example of how corporate strategy can be stated in concrete and precise terms

Corporate strategy statement

Firm	ITC
Planning Period	1998-2003
Corporate objectives	Income to reach Rs 10,000 crore by 2003 from the present level of Rs. 6,000 crore per annum; RONW should reach 22% Foreign exchange earnings in the coming five years should be Double that of preceding five years of US$ 1100 million
Product-market posture	Tobacco & cigarettes Hotels and tourism Packaging & printing and Paper and paperboards Will be the main businesses
Growth vector	Expansion in the above businesses through intensification and integration Divestment of troubled businesses like agri-business, financial Business and global trading if repositioning and JVs do not work out
Competitive advantage & synergy	In cigarettes: Strength in tobacco farming, Strength in cigarette brands, BAT connection and the permission to use BAT international Brands in India In hotel and tourism: Sheraton connection This will be used better to strengthen the Welcomgroup Chain; already more than 60% of Welcomgroup turnover is in Forex thanks mainly to Sheraton connection In packaging:

The "leading supplier status" to cigarettes and liquor Industries

In paperboards:

Bhadrachalam's international quality plus its cost advantage with the recent modernization, the new captive power facility; captive farms with heavy expansion in social forestry to provide the raw material at lower cost

An international alliance will also be sought to strengthen Bhadrachalam brand.'

The actual task of formulating the strategy

The firm looks at the opportunity-threat profile derived from the survey of the environment and its own strength and weaknesses, competitive advantages and resource position derived from the internal appraisal. It then weighs the pros and cons of the various strategy options and makes the final choice of strategy.

PRODUCTIVITY AND COMPETITIVE ANALYSIS

Competitive analysis is critical for managers formulating corporate and divisional strategies. Executives and planners must be aware of the levels of and trends in performance of their competitors to determine the best directions for their divisions and parent corporations. They also must be capable of critically assessing their own organization's performance, over time, relative to its competitive peers.

Competitive analysis are typically based on historical data, which allows managers to review how their firm has compared to competitors in the past. Current data are more difficult to come by and future performance must be estimated. Managers and planners use the information gathered in the process of competitive analysis to develop strategic plans and to set realistic goals and objectives. The analysis should focus on those performance measures that are central to gaining competitive advantage in the business's marketplace. We will concentrate here on measures that are significant in most competitive settings.

We begin here with recognition of the value of a simple rank ordering of comparable firms on various measures of interest and discuss at length two-way performance mapping, which we illustrate with two performance measures, introduced in the economies-of-growth analysis: a firm's corporate growth rate and its labor-productivity growth rate.

A Generic First Step

A straightforward first step in competitive analysis is to develop ordinal rankings of a group of comparable firms for each element in a set of given performance measures. For example, with an identified performance measure, such as revenues, the firms being compared are listed in rank order, from the largest to the smallest. Listing the comparable firms in rank order on such variables as return on sales, gross margin percentage and asset turnover provides valuable comparisons. The development of such lists requires that a group of comparable firms must be identified. Such a group might consist of firms in the same industry or firms from different industries facing similar competitive environments. At least some of the firms examined should make up a competitive circle - businesses competing for orders in the same or overlapping markets. For the identified firms, performance measures vital to competitiveness should be tracked on a regular basis.

These aid managers in understanding how their firms compare to the competition, assist them in recognizing their organizations' strengths and weaknesses and provide guidance in the goal-setting process. Some managers have demeaned this process and discounted its results for failing to provide a rich review of the actual circumstances of the competitive environment. No doubt, every figure has a story behind it and qualitative details or perceptions might enrich our understanding of a given competitive situation. More often than not, however, those who are most critical of the comparison process represent organizations ranking at or near the bottom of their peer groups. Strong organizations want to "keep score" and never lost sight of the necessity for continuous improvement, and an organization can't measure its improvement if it does not know its relative effectiveness.

The rank orderings of firms on a number of attributes may be refined slightly to aid in the goal-setting process. We recommend dividing the list of ranked firms into four equal groups of firms, with each of the separating values called a quartile. From the divided list, managers may readily determine the quarter within which their firms are positioned, as well as which competitors are in similar situations to their own. A powerful motivator to which all members of the organization can relate is to have the goal of performing above the top quartile or in the top quarter, for each of the key performance indicators of the firm and its industry. In the spirit of continuous improvement, after a level of performance in the top quarter is reached on any measure, the goal should be redefined to be reaching number one or number two among the comparable companies.

Economies of Scale in Labor

The productivity of a firm's work force is a decisive contributor to competitiveness in most situations. We can use an analysis of economies of scale in labor to determine both the levels of productivity among a set of comparable firms and whether or not the sizes of the firms significantly influence the productivity levels. We can then determine the level of productivity a firm "should" be achieving to meet the industry average, taking into account the size of the firm. This measure then should be compared to the actual productivity level of the firm to determine whether the firm's performance meets, exceeds or falls short of its expected level.

To determine whether or not economies of scale in labor are present, a regression analysis can be performed using data from a set of comparable firms. For each year of analysis, two elements of data for each of the firms in the sample are needed: scale (size) and labor productivity, measured as input per unit of output. Revenue dollars are used as a measure of scale and employees per million dollars revenue as the labor-productivity measure. In banking institutions total assets are substituted for revenues because total assets normally are used to measure the size and growth of banks.

An example of economies of scale is shown in Exhibit 6.4. The illustration is based on actual data from a mature, old-economy U.S. industry, where all of the 18 competitors were constituents of the Fortune 500. Five years of data were gathered and plotted for each of the firms and the regression model was found to be highly significant. We are interested in the performance of Firm R, the smallest of the 18 comparable firms. We would expect that the smallest firm would have lower-than-average productivity as a result of the presence of economies of scale. But what level of productivity would be reasonable to expect for Firm R, given the economies of scale? The fitted regression line answers this question for us.

EXHIBIT 6.4 Economies of Scale

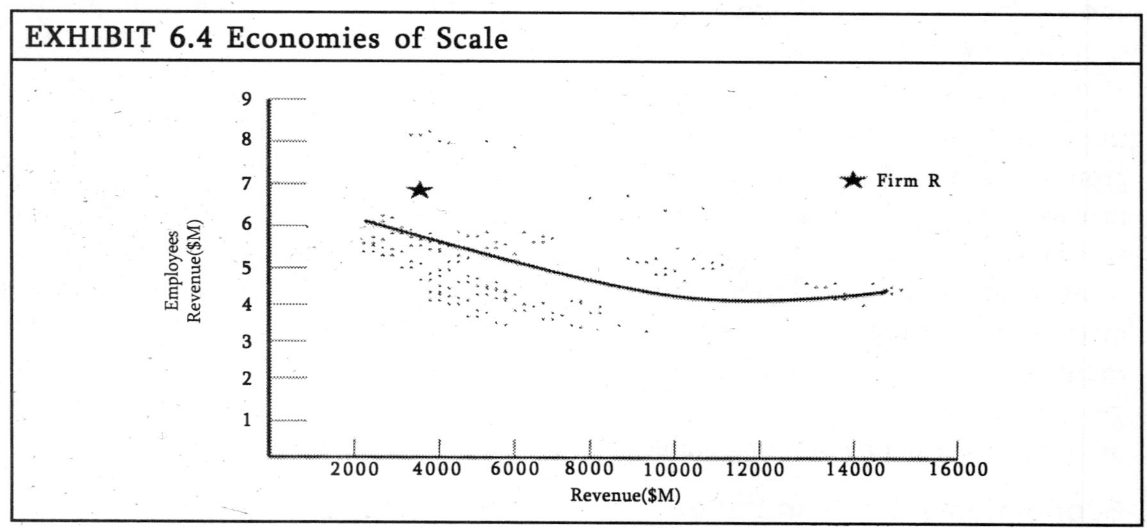

The line represents the productivity values that are expected for the range of firm sizes, based on the sample of firms used in the analysis. Accordingly, we use the equation for the line to determine the expected productivity value for a given size firm. As shown in the Exhibit 6.4, Firm R reported revenues of approximately \$2.7 billion and labor productivity of 7.0 employees per million dollars of revenue. If we drop down vertically to the line from the point representing Firm R, we will find the productivity level expected for a firm with \$2.7 billion in sales to be approximately 5.5 employees per million dollars of revenue. As an alternative to estimating the number of employees per million dollars of revenues from the plotted graph, the expected number could be calculated from the fitted equation. In either case, Firm R's productivity level is above (or worse than) this expected value.

It is important to recognize that all of the firms in the competitive circle must compete with one another regardless of their sizes. Scale economies may explain a smaller firm's lower productivity level, but they do not influence the fact that the larger, more-efficient firms, which have found ways to gain an advantage from their size, remain the smaller firm's competition. Firm R must compete with the firms demonstrating productivity in the range of 3.0 employees per million dollars revenue, productivity that is over twice as effective as its own.

Economies of Growth

The economies-of-growth analysis allows us to examine the rate at which the productivity levels of these firms have been changing over time - to review trends in improvement deterioration. The economies-of-growth analysis also reveals whether a firm's corporate growth rate influence the rate at which labor productivity changes. Similar to our analysis of economies of scale, the analysis of economies of growth allows us to determine the rate at which the productivity of a given firm "should" be improving to meet the industry average, taking into account the growth rate of the firm. We then may compare that level to the actual performance of the firm.

We can determine whether or not economies of growth are present by performing a regression analysis on data from a set of comparable firms. For the period of the analysis, we need two elements of data for each of the firms in the sample: the corporate growth rate and the labor productivity growth rate. The corporate growth rate is to be the compound annual growth rate (CAGR) in revenues and the labor-productivity growth rate to be the compound annual growth rate of revenues per employee. Note that our measure of productivity for economies of growth is the inverse of the measure used for the economies-of-scale analysis.

Exhibit 6.5 provides a graphical illustration of economies of growth. In this industry, the competitors produce precision-measuring instruments. Five years of data were gathered, the growth rates were calculated and plotted for each of the firms and the model was found to be highly significant. We are interested in the performance of Riviera Corporation, which is one of the slower-growing firms in the group of comparables. We would expect that a slower-growing firm would have a lower-than-average productivity growth rate because of the presence of economies of growth, but we do not yet know what level of productivity growth should reasonably be expected of Riviera given the industry trend. As we saw with the economies-of-scale discussion previously, the fitted regression line will provide the answer.

The line represents the productivity growth rate values that are expected for the range of corporate growth rates shown, based on the sample of firms used in the analysis. As a result, we use the equation for the line to determine the productivity growth rate value expected for a given growth rate of sales. We can see from the figure that Riviera has a very small growth rate of sales during the five years analyzed. In fact, Riviera's compound annual growth rate of revenues rounds to zero, while its compound annual growth rate of labor productivity was 9 percent. If we drop down vertically to the line from the point representing Riviera, we will find the productivity growth rate expected for a firm with no average growth in sales to be about 5 percent. Riviera's actual productivity growth rate is substantially better than this expected value. Thus, Riviera is improving its labor productivity faster than the industry trend would predict for a firm with effectively no growth in sales over five years. Its productivity growth rate, however, is slightly below the industry average of 9.2 percent.

EXHIBIT 6.5 Economies of Growth

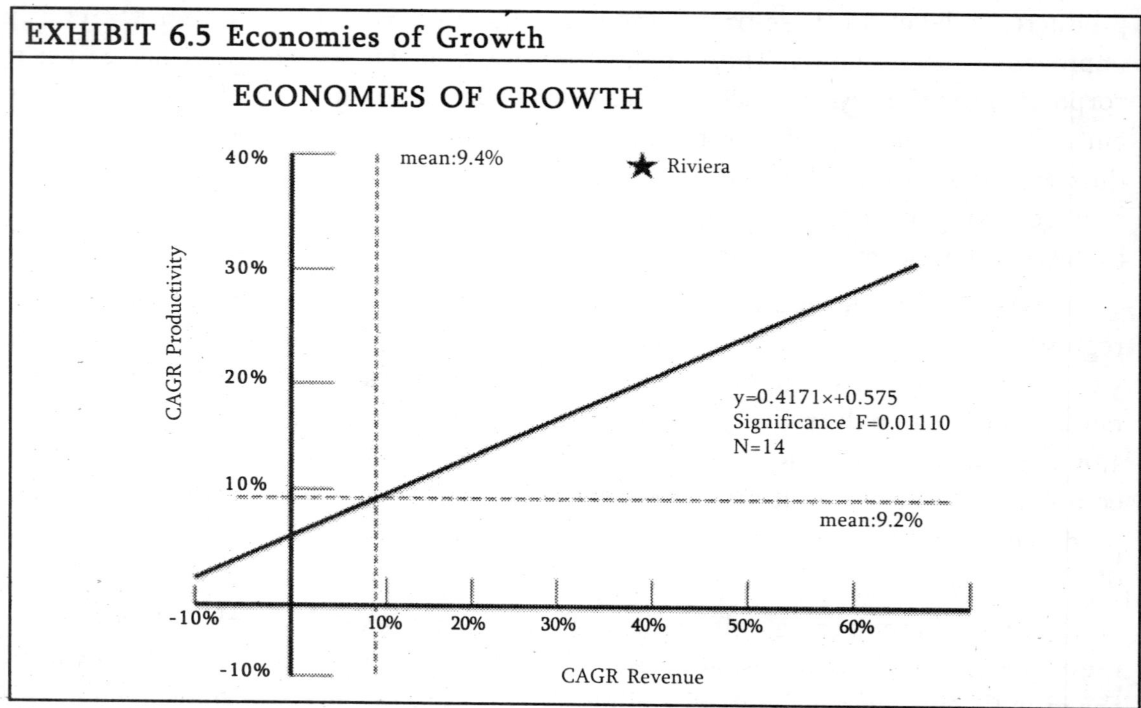

Once again, it is valuable to recognize that all of the firms in the identified circle remain competitors regardless of their growth rates. Economies of growth may explain why a slower-growing firm would demonstrate a slower rate of productivity growth than the faster-growing one, but they do not change the competitive reality than the slower-growing firms must contend with the faster-growing firms in the marketplace. Even for those firms such as Riviera, with a productivity growth rate that exceeds expectations, managers must be cognizant of their actual productivity growth rate and how it compares with the same measure for the firm's competitors.

Economies of scale and economies of growth are separate phenomena related to productivity. Economies of scale provide a static picture of how firms in the industry have been performing. In the context previously highlighted, economies of scale provide a view of the competitive landscape based on labor productivity. Economies of growth, on the other hand, provide a glimpse of the dynamics of the direction in which firms are headed, based on their past records of improvement (or decline). Some industries demonstrate significant economies of scale and virtually nonexistent economies of growth, and other industries have the converse being true. When both effects are present, we find a confluence of events that managers should recognize. In such a situation, growth leads to economies of scale and improved productivity levels (when firms have not passed the size at which diseconomies arise). Faster growth produces economies of growth and faster improvement in productivity. The two are a powerful, mutually reinforcing combination. In industries in which both are at work, growing firms will have the advantage in productivity improvement and slow-growing or stagnant firms should beware.

TWO-WAY PERFORMANCE MAPPING

Two-way performance mapping is another general method of competitive analysis that may be used with any two performance measures. It allows managers to review their organizations' histories relative to their peers' on the chosen two measures simultaneously. Mapping the two measures in a graphic format creates four quadrants into which the firms can be divided. We will demonstrate this technique using the measures employed in the economies-of-growth analysis - corporate growth and growth rate of labor productivity.

Particularly when economies of growth are not present in an industry, we recommend the use of the two-way performance mapping as a means of comparing firms' rates of productivity improvement. With this method, the average of a group of competitors is used as a straightforward and convenient dividing point. It is always useful to determine how many and which competitors are above (or below) average, as well as their relative rankings on a given measure.

As shown in Exhibit 6.6 the axes of the graph should be drawn in the same orientation that they were for the economies-of-growth analysis, with corporate growth rate serving as the horizontal axis and labor productivity growth rate as the vertical axis. The axes also should be drawn at the industry-average values. Thus, the horizontal axis, representing corporate growth rate, will cross the vertical axis at the industry average value of labor productivity growth, dividing the firms with above-average productivity growth (above the horizontal axis) from those with slower-than-average productivity growth (below the horizontal axis). Similarly, the vertical axis, labor productivity growth, will cross the horizontal axis at the average value of corporate growth rate, separating firms with above-average growth rates (to the right) from those with below-average growth rates (to the left). This creates a convenient system of four quadrants.

Meticulous Example

An example of this type of two-way performance mapping is shown in Exhibit 6.6. The illustration is based on actual data from the same entrenched, industrial U.S. industry for which we saw economies of scale in labor earlier in the chapter. The identification of the firms is based on size (revenue dollars), with Firm A being the largest and Firm R the smallest. We can see from the figure that the industry-average corporate growth rate is 10 percent, and the industry-average productivity growth rate is 10.85 percent, as shown in the top half of Exhibit 6.6. The growth rates were calculated over a five-year period. The bottom half of Exhibit 6.6 provides data on the CAGR of revenues and the CAGR of productivity for each company.

As we saw earlier, economies of scale in labor were found to be present in this industry, with diseconomies setting in for the largest of the firms. Economies of growth were not statistically significant, however, which makes performance mapping particularly effective for this industry. An examination of the quadrants in Exhibit 6.6 provides some insight into why the economies of growth were not present.

Firms in Quadrant I, which showed above-average corporate growth rates and above-average productivity growth rates, had been successful in growing both of these measures. Of the four companies in this quadrant, only one had eliminated jobs over the five years examined; the other three had created jobs. As a general rule, jobs have been eliminated when created when the CAGR of productivity exceeds the CAGR of revenues. Jobs have been created when revenues have grown faster than productivity. Firms in Quadrant II had rapidly-growing revenues, but they had not taken advantage of the opportunity for growth in productivity. All three of the firms in this quadrant had expanded their employment rolls over the five-year period. Companies in Quadrant III had not demonstrated substantial growth for either of the two measures. Four of six firms here had eliminated jobs during the five years. Finally, the firms in Quadrant IV had grown more slowly than average but had achieved above-average productivity gains through restricting and downsizing. All of the firms in this quadrant had eliminated jobs over the five-year period.

Managers may find this approach revealing for their own industries. They would naturally want to position their firms in Quadrant I. Executives whose firms are not in this attractive position, however, might use the information on the graph in their goal-setting processes to attempt to move their organizations towards more-promising competitive positions on these measures, with the ultimate aim of creating value for their shareholders.

We will focus on one of the firms in the industry, Firm R, to illustrate the importance of productivity improvement to a firm's financial health and its potential to create value for the shareholders. We know that Firm R was the smallest firm in the industry based on revenues, ranked fifth in corporate growth rate and ranked seventeenth of eighteen in productivity growth rate. Firm R is in Quadrant II on the two-way performance map, with above-average revenue growth and below-average productivity growth.

The table in Exhibit 6.7 shows actual performance data for Firm R over the five-year period examined. We see that Firm R's revenues grew from $1.7 billion in year 1 to $2.7 billion in year 5 and its employees grew from approximately 14,500 to 19,000 during the same period. We know from the performance map that Firm R's productivity growth rate was less than half the industry-average value. We would like to examine the effect this lower-than-average rate had no Firm R's earnings, as well as the potential effect it might have had on Firm R's stock price.

To begin with, we will examine how Firm R's employment levels would have looked had the organization improved its labor productivity at the industry-average rate. We assume that revenues followed their actual pattern of growth. Exhibit 6.8 reveals the results. Notice that the revenues used in the projection are the actual revenues shown earlier in Exhibit 6.7. The actual number of employees are shown for comparison purposes. In year 1, the actual labor productivity figure of revenues per employee of $117,119 is shown. This value, then, is grown

EXHIBIT 6.6 Two way performance map for an entrenched manufacturing industry

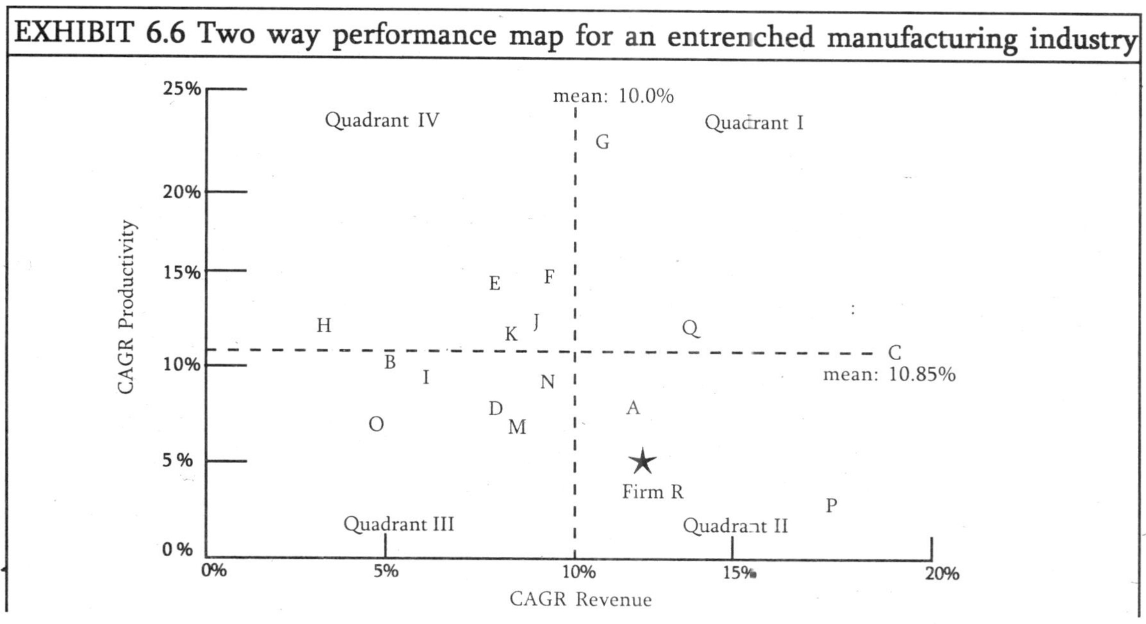

Quadrant IV			CAGR Revenue mean: 10.85%	Quadrant I	
	CAGR Revenue	*CAGR Productivity*		*CAGR Revenue*	*CAGR Productivity*
Firm E	8.1%	13.8%	Firm C	19.4%	11.0%
Firm F	9.9%	13.5%	Firm G	10.5%	21.1%
Firm H	3.1%	12.6%	Firm L	17.9%	13.6%
Firm J	9.2%	11.8%	Firm Q	13.7%	12.6%
Firm K	8.6%	11.7%			
Firm B	5.5%	10.5%			CAGR Productivity mean: 10.85%
Firm D	7.9%	7.3%			
Firm I	6.5%	9.1%			
Firm M	9.4%	6.8%	Firm A	11.7%	7.8%
Firm N	9.2%	9.5%	Firm F	15.3%	4.2%
Firm O	5.2%	7.8%	Firm R	12.4%	5.0%
Quadrant III				Quadrant II	

at a rate of 10.85 percent per year, the industry average, to arrive at productivity figures for each of the remaining four years. Using these projected productivity figures and the actual revenues, we have calculated the expected number of employees Firm R would have had if it had grown its productivity at the industry average rate of 10.85 percent per year. Projected employees equal revenues divided by the projected productivity level. The cumulative effect is rather startling, with the difference in employment accounting for nearly one-fifth of the firm's employment by year 5.

An identical analysis was performed to determine how Firm R's employment levels would have looked had the company improved its labor productivity at a rate equal to the average rate of the firms in Quadrant I of our two-way performance map. Exhibit 6.9 reveals these results. As one would expect, the results would be even more dramatic. Had Firm R grown its productivity at 14.57 percent per year, it would have had nearly 30 percent fewer employees by year 5.

EXHIBIT 6.7 Firm R Actual Performance History

Performance Measure	*Year 1*	*Year 2*	*Year 3*	*Year 4*	*Year 5*	*5-Year CAGR*
Revenue ($M)	1697	1838	1947	2300	2706	–
Annual Revenue Growth	–	8.3%	5.9%	18.1%	17.7%	12.4%
Employees		14490	14780	16472	17200	19000–
Revenue per Employee	$117,119	124,359	118,728	133,728	142,430	–
Annual Productivity Growth	–	6.2%	-4.9%	13.1%	6.5%	5%

EXHIBIT 6.8

Projected productivity and employment levels based on competitor analysis (b)

Scenario 1: Industry comparison starting in Year 1 and forecasting forward

Grow productivity at industry-average growth rate

	Year 1	*Year 2*	*Year 3*	*Year 4*	*Year 5*
Firm R's Revenue ($M)	1697	1838	1947	2300	2706
Firm R's Actual Employees	14,490	14,780	16,472	17,200	19,000
Revenue per Employee Growth by 10.85%	$117,119*	129,827	143,913	159,523	176,836
Projected Employees	14,490*	14,168	13,531	14,418	15,303
Differences in Employees		622	2941	2782	3697
Differences as % Actual		4.2%	17.9%	16.2%	19.5%

*Actual

EXHIBIT 6.9

Projected productivity and employment levels based on competitor analysis.

Scenario 2:

Industry comparison starting in Year 1 and forecasting forward

Grow productivity at industry-average growth rate of Quadrant firms

	Year 1	Year 2	Year 3	Year 4	Year 5
Firm R's Revenue ($M)	1697	1838	1947	2300	2706
Firm R's Actual Employees	14,490	14,780	16,472	17,200	19,000
Revenue per Employee Growth by 14.57%	$117,119*	134,184	153,734	176,133	201,796
Projected Employees	14,490*	13,698	12,666	13,059	13,410
Differences in Employees		1082	3806	4141	5590
Differences as % Actual		7.3%	23.1%	24.1%	29.4%

*Actual

Continuing on, we examine the potential effects these different productivity growth rates would have had on Firm R's earnings. Exhibit 6.10 provides the details of one analysis of this question. A number of relevant pieces of information and assumptions are shown at the top of the figure. A conservative estimate of $40,000 pre-tax expense per employee was employed in the analysis; this value should include all direct employment expenses. For both of the scenarios examined, the financial effects are shown for year 5 only, when the employment differences are the greatest. Scenario 1 reveals the potential differences that might have the industry-average rate. Scenario 2 presents the same information for improvement at the average rate of the firms in Quadrant I.

Exhibit 6.10 begins the analysis by reporting the number of employees that Firm R would not have had on its employment rolls in year 5 had it improved its productivity at the two identified rates. These values - 3,697 and 5,590 - were previously calculated in Exhibits 6.8 and 6.9, respectively. These differences in employment were then multiplied by the assumed expense of $40,000 per employee to arrive at the total pre-tax savings that would have resulted from the reduced number of employees. The pre-tax savings were then converted to after-tax values using the assumed tax rate of 39 percent. We can see that these potential after-tax savings would have been quite substantial: $90 million for Scenario 1 and $136 million for Scenario 2.

It is interesting to examine the potential effects of these earnings differentials on the firm's stock price. The after-tax savings must first be converted to per-share values by dividing by the number of shares outstanding.

EXHIBIT 6.10		
Potential impact of productivity growth rate on net income and stock price		
Assumptions		
Estimated expense per employee	$40,000	
Assumed tax rate	39%	
Firm R's shares outstanding (current)	90,021,489	
Firm R's share price (current)	$24.43	
Firm R's P/E multiple (current)	15	
Industry average P/E multiple (current)	23	
	Scenario 1	Scenario 2
Year 5 difference in employees	3697	5590
Pre-tax payroll savings	$147,880,000	$223,600,000
After-tax savings	$90,206,800	$136,396,000
Savings/incremental earnings per share	$1,00	$1.52
Potential stock price increase = P/E multiple x incremental earnings per share		

Potential stock price increase At Firm R's P/E multiple	$15.03	$22.73
Potential stock price increase At industry average P/E multiple	$23.05	$34.85

*Actual

In doing this, we find that $1 per share in after-tax earnings could have been generated or saved in year 5 under Scenario 1 and $1.52 per share under Scenario 2. We are able to translate these incremental earnings per share into potential or hypothetical stock price increases by multiplying them by Firm R's price-earnings multiple. Using the P/E multiple of 15 noted in the assumptions, we find that Firm R's stock price might have increased by as much as $15 under Scenario 1 and nearly $23 under Scenario 2. Because Firm R traded at a below- average multiple, the effects of the incremental earnings were less than they might have been for a firm trading at the industry average. To demonstrate the average effect such incremental earnings might have had on a firm's stock price, we multiplied the earnings by the industry-average P/E multiple of 23 (which is over 50 percent higher than Firm R's multiple). This resulted in values of $23.05 increase per share for Scenario 1 and $34.85 per share for Scenario 2.

The potential impact of the incremental earnings on Firm R's stock price is extraordinary, based on the analysis of Exhibit 6.10. Following the steps of the analysis, which we recognize as hypothetical and assume changes only in the earnings, we see that Firm R's stock price might have doubled from what it actually was in year 5 had the organization maintained a rate of productivity growth equal to the industry average. The increase might have been 150 percent with a productivity growth rate equal to the average of the firms in Quadrant I of the two-way performance map.

Such dramatic results do not arise from a one-time slowdown in productivity improvement. They are the result of an ongoing pattern of performance that creates a widening gap between a below-average firm and the top performers over time. In the case of Firm R, we saw that a substantial gap was created between the firm and even the average performer. We saw in Exhibit 6.7 that firm R's productivity improved at an above-average rate (over 10.85 percent) only once in the five years examined. Furthermore, from year 2 to year 3, Firm R's productivity actually declined 4.9 percent, putting the firm at a significant disadvantage when compared to the average 10.85 percent improvement. An average cost per employee of $40,000 multiples rapidly into considerable foregone earnings when a firm does not keep a tight rein on its headcount. Moreover, this figure is conservative for many organizations, making it all the more imperative for managers to manage their organizations' productivity closely.

We should recognize that Firm R would not have had to cut employment over the five years to have achieved the industry-average productivity growth rate of 10.85 percent. Rather, the firm could have added jobs, but obviously it should have added considerably fewer than it actually did. On the other hand, Firm R would have had to eliminate jobs to achieve the average productivity growth of the Quadrant I firms. Growth creates an environment in which organizations are able to increase employment while simultaneously improving productivity. Without growth, productivity improvements come only through job elimination. As a general rule, a firm's productivity growth equals its revenue growth when employment remains constant.

INNOVATIVE STRATEGIES

History shows that the companies that continue to invest in their innovative capabilities during tough economic times are those that fare best when growth returns. In a challenging business climate, focus is crucial. Open innovation can play an important part in the solution by breaking down the traditional corporate boundaries, open innovation allows intellectual property, ideas, and people to flow freely both in and out of an organization.

"I'll be happy to give you innovative thinking. What are the guidelines?"

FIVE OPEN-INNOVATION MOVES

1. **Become a customer or supplier of your formal internal projects:** If your business is pursuing an important capability that it can neither afford to develop itself nor acquire on the open market and others in or beyond your industry. Then join with those others to fund, develop and launch it as an independent business and become its first customer

2. **Let others develop your non-strategic initiatives:** If your business is reinforcing on its core activities and you have identified adjacent complimentary initiatives that drain too much attention, time and capital but that might attract outside interest and investment. Then spin them out to investors who can take over the development burden. Others will fund the progress and you can keep some equity in case they make it big.

3. **Make your intellectual property work harder for you and others:** If a lot of your company's intellectual property sits on a shelf and generates no direct financial benefit & you understand that its value, to you and to others then let outside partners benefit from what you've created, continue its development and pay you licensing fees. Many businesses recover their R&D expenses spending in this way
4. **Grow your ecosystem, even when you are not growing:** If your company is an active innovator, continually engaging with its customers, collaborators, industry expert's trade associations and others to identify future opportunities, then build on your ecosystem of potential innovation partners. Be like a Major League baseball general managers, who always know which team will be interested in which player at what price
5. **Create open domains to reduce costs and expand participation:** If your internal ideas are likely to attract interest from valuable outside communities, potentially creating breakthrough advances or even changing the game within our industry, then consider establishing open domains that either exchange information and ideas or provide shared facilities and services.

Taken together these are complicated activities that should be approached holistically, under the leadership of senior executives in strategic roles. Darwin taught us that it's neither the strongest nor the most intelligent species survive; it's those that adapt best to changes in the environment.

SUMMARY & KEY TERMS

For operating divisions of diversified, decentralized companies, the strategic questions (problems or opportunities) relate to their interfaces with their competitive market-places. They must determine which of the three generic strategies they will follow. Will they seek to differentiate their products, attempt to compete in a particular niche and/or strive to be or to become the low-cost producer?

The bottom line is that the parent corporation and its divisions have very different strategic issues. The corporate office operators in one orbit, facing its set of unique problems and opportunities. The more diversified the corporation, the more difficult it is for corporate executives to understand the detailed problems and opportunities faced by its operating divisions. Division executives, on the other hand, operate in a financial structure created and managed by the corporate office. This setup allows them to create effective divisional marketing and operational strategies that will be of maximum utility in creating value for the shareholders of the parent company.

The corporate strategy is largely concerned with the choice of the firm's product market postures or more precisely changes/addition/deletions to the firm's business product market postures. The growth vector indicates the direction or path in which the firm is moving and the pace at which it is moving with respect to the product market postures. Strategy will identify the competitive advantage .Corporate strategy will identify the competitive advantages available with the firm which will form the support for the chosen strategy.

Open innovation can play an important part in the solution where the problem is to have best returns even in the tough economic times.

KEY TERMS

- CAGR-Compound Annual Growth Rate
- ROI-Return on Investment
- Competitive Advantage
- Growth Vector
- Competitive analysis
- EOS-Economies of Scale
- EOG-Economies of Growth
- Performance Mapping
- Innovative Strategies

DISCUSSION QUESTIONS

1. What s the practical importance of competitive analysis?
2. What do you mean by Innovative Strategies? Explain the open innovation moves with examples.
3. How can two-way performance mapping assist a manager in understanding the competitive structure of his or her industry?
4. What does corporate strategy ensure for the firm?
5. Explain the linkage between corporate objective and corporate strategy.

❖ ❖ ❖

OPENING CASE: STARBUCKS COFFEE "ENSURING CUSTOMER VALUE AND SATISFACTION"

In 1971, three lovers named Gerald Baldwin, Gordon Bowker and Zev Siegl decided to set up Starbucks for selling whole coffee beans. During the initial year, they sold other items as well like bulk tea, spices, etc., the coffee beans were sold to various local restaurants and by 1982, it had set up give retail stores that also offered freshly roasted coffee beans. Afterwards, Starbucks introduced whole bean coffees, espresso beverages along with bakery products. By the mid 90s, it had also introduced ice creams and tea though most of the earnings still came from the coffee bars where people could order pastries and coffee while taking home coffee beans for brewing at home.

Starbucks had always charged a premium price for its offerings and compared to the local cafe's it cost several times more. When the typical café charged 50 cents, Starbucks charged $1.75 for a cup of basic coffee while the special concoctions cost anywhere between $3.50 and $4.50. The reason why customers patronized Starbucks was because of the baristas who were willing to accommodate the special requests, customers made for preparing the brew. So, personalization helped in creating the desired customer value and justified the premium price. Though the cafe's were initially frequented by the young, trendy, up-market customers, very soon older customers and those belong to even minority ethnic communities started thronging the cafe's. The acceptance of the value could be conjectured from the motley customer base that Starbucks had begun to attract.

The customer value was created not just through the quality of the coffee that was served but also through the ambience and the experience offered to the customer at the café. Howard Schultz, the chairman of Starbucks had commented: "We are not in the coffee business, serving people. We are in the people business, serving coffee." Schultz wanted customers to get the right kind of experience and invested in comfortable, velvety chairs, appropriately chosen ambient music and the aroma that should advertise the quality of the coffee that was served. To ensure that the aroma of fresh brewed espresso reached customers, smoking was banned in the cafe's. Essentially, Starbucks aimed at becoming a place for customers where they could be their own selves and do their own things. This meant that customers would just come to the café and read their favorite books seated on plush couches or plug in their laptops to reach their favorite websites and shop on online portals or conduct net meetings. Market research had shown that more than 10% of customers visited Starbucks twice a day. Howard Schultz commented that Starbucks had become the 'third place' for customers (the first being the home and the second the place of work).

A very noteworthy aspect of Starbucks that ensures that it offers desirable customer value even in countries like China, Japan, France, Greece or Kuwait is of serving food with a local flavor (maintaining the flavor of the espresso coffee to ensure a consistent brand experience). To ensure that the cafe's were offering the desired level of customer value and satisfaction, Starbucks has avoided taking the franchising route. Since Starbucks did not invest in mass media advertising, it paid great attention to customer satisfaction to ensure high word of mouth publicity and customer loyalty.

To ensure that customers were offered the right experience, Starbucks made sure that the employees were imparted adequate knowledge about the products and paid enough attention in detail to ensure that nothing was left to chance. The employees were chosen taking into account their personality and the ability to communicate the company's passion for coffee to customers properly. It was important to deliver a pleasing experience to customers every time they came to Starbucks and this required tremendous commitment on the part of the employees. Some of the employees at Starbucks were college students who worked part time but had mastered the art of being a barista. The challenge for Starbucks was to attract the right set of employees and to reward and motivate them properly. In the words of Howard Schultz: "The relationships that we have with our people are the driving force of innovation at Starbucks."

To enhance the value it was offering to the young customers, Starbucks extended its brand to music in 1999. Media bars were created to sell the CDs and also enabled customers to legally download music and burn them on CDs after paying a fee. The charges for this service were fixed at $9 for 7 songs. Though this was more than what customers would have had to bear by using their home PCs, the service was still found attractive by customers.

In an effort to ensure a consistent experience for customers across stores and also pass on the benefits of reduced costs, Starbucks undertook certain measures. The average store opening costs in 1995 was $350,000 which was a concern for Starbucks. It began consolidating the orders across the stores and going in for bulk purchases to get the price advantage. The high volumes enabled the company to get 20-30% discounts from the chosen vendors and also ensured that the stocks were delivered in just-in-time basis to the stores. To facilitate the unified approach, some standardization was also necessary. Modular designs were created for the display cases in the stores and the store layouts were designed using a computer, enabling the calculation of costs while the design evolved on screen. These initiatives enabled reduced costs for opening new stores and also helped in getting the time taken for developing a new store from 24 weeks down to 18 weeks. Despite being customer focused and desirous of offering customer value, Starbucks also ensured it was business savvy. It had developed 20,000 permutations of various drink combinations and took care to take off the slow moving low margin products from the menu. By May 2004, the plain espresso coffee was not available on the menu but if a customer specially asked for it, Starbucks made it especially for that customer.

The speed of service was enhanced with the installation of automated espresso machines at 800 locations. Since customers ended up being hassled over paying through cash after finishing the meal, Starbucks offered prepaid Starbucks Cards starting from as low as $5 and going up to $500. These could be used for quick payments through swiping of the cards and the transaction time was reduced considerably. Starbucks even got into a strategic alliance with Bank One to offer the Starbucks Card Duetto Visa which possessed the dual benefits of being a stored value card as well as a credit and became an instant success.

In 2005, Starbucks had created a customer base of 33 million customers on an annual basis. The heartening factor was getting the typical customer to visit 18 times a month - which was the highest among any retailer in the US. The typical Starbucks store conducted 636 daily transactions and the average value of each was $4.05 essentially comprising of coffee and food.

Chapter: 7

The Strategies in Action

Learning Objectives

In this chapter the main stress is given on :

- Understanding CRM and its strategic perspectives.
- The criticality of customers relationships
- The Strategic orientation of CRM
- How to extend the concept of CRM to create more value through loyal customers.
- The changing role of the relationship manager.
- Understanding Communication Strategy
- The Pricing strategies
- Advertising and sales promotion strategies.
- Brand building strategies.

INTRODUCTION

Customer Relationship Management (CRM) has emerged as a popular buzzword in the business press as well as academic publications. In this chapter, we start by listing some indicators of the popularity of CRM in marketing as well as in Information Technology (IT). Academic conferences, journal articles and special issues of academic publications and academic centers at leading universities are a few measures of the increased attention to CRM among academicians. On the practice side, the increasing number of CRM product vendors, entry of leading software players. CRM implementations and investments by business are cited as indicators of CRM's growing appeal among corporate executives. In the second section, we examine the key macro-environmental factors responsible for the explosion of interest and investment in CRM around the world. The emergence of service as well as market economy, global orientation of businesses and ageing population of the economically developed economies have been identified as the growth drivers for CRM.

In the third section, we focus on challenges faced by businesses in the twenty-first century. These challenges, arising from non -traditional competition, market maturity and misalignment between revenue and profits, will increase the importance of customer relationships for businesses to survive and also thrive. In the fourth section, we discuss the demand and supply factors, which are likely to motivate more businesses to adopt CRM in the future. We have identified increasing customer expectations and affordable technology advances, as primary drivers of CRM adoption. In the fifth section, we present our perspective on CRM implementation experiences. Finally, in the sixth section, we conclude with a summary of the discussions.

Explosion of CRM both in Marketing and IT

In the 1990s, CRM started attracting attention of academicians as well as practitioners from marketing and IT. A series of research conferences on various aspects of buyer-seller relationships were organized by the Center for Relationship Marketing at the Emory University (1994-2000), the Scandinavian academics at the Swedish School of Economics and Business Administration in Finland and Stockholm University in Sweden, the Industrial Marketing and Purchasing Group (IMP) and the annual International Colloquium in Relationship Marketing (from 1993 onwards). Leading academic journals including the Journal of the Academy of Marketing Science (Fall 1995), the Asia-Australia Marketing Journal (issue 1, 1994) and (issue 1, 1997), Industrial Marketing Management (issue 2, 1997) and the European Journal of Marketing (issue 2, 1997) published special issues on relationship marketing (Payne, 2000). The Journal of Marketing is publishing a special section on CRM in its October 2005 issue. Journals focusing on CRM like the Journal of Relationship Marketing (Haworth Press), forums and associations like the CRM Community (http://www.crmcommunity.com) and the Association for the Advancement of Relationship Marketing as well as the American Marketing Association's (AMA) academic Special Interest Group (SIG) on Relationship Marketing have played a significant role in advancing the understanding and practice of relationship marketing. The academic interest in CRM has been sustained by research centers established at business schools, many of them with corporate support, e.g., the Teradata Centre for CRM at Duke University's Fuqua School of Business.

The academic interest in CRM paralleled the explosive growth and adoption of relationship orientation and implementation of CRM solutions across different businesses. The early adopters of CRM in the business to consumer markets were financial services, retailing, telecommunication, travel and hospitality, utilities and automotive (Herschel, and Maoz, 2003). Developments in information and communication technology, especially in the 1990s, have helped these large businesses recreate the personal relationships once enjoyed by the small businesses (Peppers and Rogers 1999); Zineldin 2000). The IT solutions for automating the sales process initiated the trend, which expanded to include automation of services and marketing as part of comprehensive CRM solutions. Leading CRM vendors included Siebel Systems, SAP, Oracle, PeopleSoft, Interact Commerce and Epiphany. Enterprise Resource Planning (ERP) majors like SAP, Oracle and PeopleSoft have entered the CRM market in recent years to tap the emerging opportunities.

Siebel Systems Inc., the worldwide leader in the CRM market, has implemented its products at 3,500 customer organizations around the world for over 2 million users (Siebel Systems, Financial Results for the Quarter ended December 31, 2003). SAP has deployed its mySAP CRM at more than 2,300 businesses around the world. The startling success of the CRM solutions is evident. In less than decade, the global market for CRM products and services has grown to about US$ 42.8 billion (Forrester Research estimates, July 2002). There was no surprise when Microsoft, the world's largest software company, entered this market. Microsoft launched its CRM product in early 2003 after acquiring two specialized CRM firms, Great Plains and Navision.

The last decade witnessed an explosion of CRM in marketing and IT. In the next section, we will explore the reasons for the growth of this phenomenon, which many have termed as a 'new-old concept' (Berry, 1995; Gronroos, 1994; Sheth and Parvatiyar, 1995).

Enablers for the growth of CRM

The tremendous growth of interest and investments in CRM across the globe can be attributed to the following macro-environmental factors:

(a) Emergence of service economy,

(b) Emergence of market economy,

(c) Global orientation of business and

(d) Ageing population of the economically advanced economies.

Emergence of service economy

The emergence of service economy is a global phenomenon. In the US, the service sector accounts for over 75 per cent of GNP and employs 80 per cent of the workforce (Czinkota and Ronkainen, 2002). The service sector contributes to 60-70 per cent of the GDP of economically advanced nations of Western Europe, Canada and Japan. The increasing contribution of the service sector is not limited to developed countries. Developing economies like China, Indonesia and Thailand employ about 40 per cent of the workforce in the service sector (Wirtz, 2000). In the year 2001, the service sector contributed to 48 per cent of the GDP in India, 54 per cent in Philippines and 33 per cent in China. The average annual growth rate of the services during the decade of 1990s was 8 per cent in India, 9 per cent in China and 4.1 per cent in the Philippines (Statistical Outline of India, 2002-2003).

Advanced countries progressed from agricultural to industrial and then to post-industrial economies. The shift from manufacturing to services was spread over a few decades of the last century. However, in developing countries, the growth is led by all three sectors of the economy in varying proportions.

The growing importance of services resulted in greater customer orientation as services are characterized by simultaneity/inseparability (Berry and Parasuraman, 1991). It implies that the production and consumption of services are inseparable. In services, one needs to be close to customers to deliver the service offering. The factory is where the customer is and service is offered in real time. The customer perceives the production process as part of the service consumption, not just the outcome of a production process as in traditional marketing of physical goods (Gronroos, 1998). Therefore, it is not surprising that service business like hotels, airlines, banking, financial services, telecom and retailing were the early adopters of CRM.

Emergence of market economy

In addition to the shift towards service, there is a global emergence of the market economy. The power is more to the market as compared to the controlled economy. Market regulation was in place all over the world including the US, Europe, USSR, China and India. The 1990s witnessed acceleration in the deregulation of many large industries including banking, telecommunications, broadcasting and airlines across the world. As a result, market-oriented firms operating in intensely competitive markets now take a decision that was once controlled by the government (Vietor, 1994). The focus has shifted from capacity creation under control to the markets. Market-oriented economy necessitated a customer focus and boosted the importance of CRM.

Global orientation of businesses

National boundaries are giving way to either a borderless world or at least a regional world resulting in the emergence of trading blocks like North American Free Trade Agreement (NAFTA), European Union and the Association of South-East Asian Nations (ASEAN). The abolishment of the General Agreement on Tariffs and Trade (GATT) and the emergence of World Trade Organization (WTO) helped create a global orientation for business establishments. Increasing international trade became the growth engine for the global economy. Liberalization of markets and trade proved to be a far stronger growth engine. It has eased the entry into foreign markets. Firms need stronger customer-orientation to be able to tap opportunities in new markets while defending themselves in their home markets.

Aging population in Economically Developed Countries (EDC)

The economically advanced nations are witnessing an aging of their population. In 2000, 12.6 per cent of the US population was 65 years of age or older. The comparative figures for Sweden and Japan were 17.2 per cent and 17 per cent of their respective population (Sheth and Mittal 2004). This trend is visible in most parts of Europe, except in Ireland (Leefland and Raij 1995). Aging of population has been attributed to the combined effects of a slowdown in birthrate and an increase in life expectancy. While an ageing population creates new opportunities for wellness, financial well being, safety and security and recreation (Sheth and Mittal 2004), it has also slowed the markets for traditional goods and services designed for a younger population. Therefore, in these markets, growth is being achieved by increasing the 'share of wallet' and not through 'growth of markets' driven by a growing population. Marketers are now forced to develop a deep understanding of their existing customers and meet their ever changing needs through suitable products and services. Indeed, most large companies, especially the services sector, wants to become One-Stop-Shop for the customers.

After identifying and discussing the factors responsible for the growth of CRM across the globe, we now evaluate the reasons as to why managing customer relationship has become critical for businesses.

THE CRITICALITY OF CUSTOMER RELATIONSHIPS

In recent years, businesses are facing new challenges. These challenges have increased the critically of customer relationships. The three key challenges include:

(a) Non-traditional competition,

(b) Market maturity and

(c) Misalignment between revenue and profits

In the following paragraphs, we shall discuss these challenges.

Non-traditional Competition

Porter (1985) identified five forces that determine the intrinsic long-run attractiveness of a market. These forces include industry competitors, potential new entrants, substitutes, buyers and suppliers. Many markets have experienced upheavals in recent times due to the entry of non-traditional competitors. Traditionally, the competition was limited to rivalry among existing players. Non-traditional competitors include:

(i) New entrants from outside the industry like Reliance Industries in the telecom sector in India. Reliance transformed the telecom market in India through an aggressive entry backed with a huge capital investment of approximately US$ 4 billion. It adopted a rapid market penetration entry strategy with low prices supported with heavy promotional spending. These strategies helped Reliance attract over 9 million subscribers to emerge as the second largest player in the Indian telecom industry. In the domestic airlines industry in India, Jet Airways has emerged as the largest player in less than a decade by targeting the business travelers through better service on the profitable domestic trunk routes. Similarly, Virgin Air and Ryan Air have turned the European airlines market upside down by following unconventional strategies.

(ii) Substitute technology - Traditional leaders like Kodak and Fuji in the cameras and photography market lost out to Sony due to substitution of chemical by digital technology. Mobile handset makers like Samsung have emerged as large players in this market with their phone cameras. At the industry level, wireless as well as Voice over IP (VOIP) is replacing the traditional telecom providers for local and long distance communication.

(iii) Supplier as a competitor - The supplier becomes a competitor when the buying industry has a high margin and the supplier has low margin. It motivates the suppliers to do forward integration (move downstream). Examples include, raw material companies moving into component manufacture and product companies entering into retailing.

(iv) Customer becomes a competitor - This has coincided with the emergence and consolidation of organized retailing. Retail giants like Wal-Mart and Carrefour compete with the national brands through their own private labels. Also, many enterprises after many years of outsourcing are now in-sourcing many corporate support services such as legal, human resources, finance and information services.

Non-traditional competitors often enter the markets with a lower cost structure and offerings targeting the most profitable customers of the incumbents. It is forcing companies to become relationship oriented to retain their customers and protect themselves from the threat of these non-traditional competitors.

Market Maturity

After World War II, most countries focused on building capacities to fulfill the pent up demand. Now there is excess capacity in industries, especially those located in the developed economies. Therefore, the focus is no longer on capacity creation but on capacity utilization. Globally, excess capacity exists in industries like agriculture, commodity materials, aircrafts, automobiles, appliances and even telecom bandwidth.

Therefore, capacity is now searching for market. More companies from the developed countries, facing slow or zero growth markets, now rely on repeat customers in their domestic markets. Businesses were used to rapid or stable rates for most of the last five decades in developed countries. But now the growth has shifted to emerging markets in developing countries like India and China. Understanding customers is critical to succeed in these markets due to the inherent differences in the customer needs, cultural, social, economic and also regulatory environments. So, market maturity is forcing companies to be more customer-oriented to retain their customers in their home markets and also to attract customers in emerging markets.

Misalignment between Revenue and Profit

In the 1990s companies realized that in their efforts to acquire customers and market share, they had also built inefficiencies through customer subsidization. While managers knew subsidization across product and markets, they had never looked at subsidization by customers. Companies adopted Activity Based Costing (ABC) for analyzing the cost of business with customers and comparing it to the revenue generated by them (Shapiro et al. 1987 and Foster et al. 1996). If we plot the revenue and profits by customers, the misalignment between revenue and profits will be clearly visible. Typically, the distribution of revenues is exponential, while costs are distributed in a more linear relationship with customer size. Thus, while the revenue curve slopes down exponentially, the cost curve slopes down gradually (Sheth and Sisodia 1999).These profitable customers are very attractive targets for many of the non-traditional competitors who can exploit this distribution of revenues and costs to their advantage. In recently deregulated industries such as banking, airlines, telecommunications and electric utilities, for example, new entrants target the most profitable large customers and heavy users, leaving the incumbent with unprofitable customers.

In many instances, data often shows that the biggest and the smallest customers are the least profitable. For example, in the business markets, companies do not get high margins in large accounts as large buyers negotiate a lower price. But in consumer markets, profit margins are higher in large accounts and heavy users. For example, AT&T in August 1998 announced that it was losing money on approximately 25 million of its 70 million residential customers (Sheth and Sisodia, 1999). These 25 million customers never made a long distance call or used any of their value-added services. On an average AT&T was spending US$ 6 per month on its customers for support and care. So each of these customers made AT&T loss US$ 72 a year.

Customer subsidization is a problem created primarily by the traditional accounting systems. Traditional accounting was usually organized around products and sometimes around markets. When companies began to disaggregate revenues and costs at the customer or account level due to improved information and accounting systems, they discovered previously hidden subsidies by customers. It also resulted in companies paying attention to their most profitable customers by adopting a relationship orientation.

Thus we have seen that in the last decade or so, the criticality of customer's relationship increased due to non-traditional competition, maturing of traditional markets and the misalignment of revenue and profits. These challenges were faced by businesses across industries and stronger customer relationships helped mitigate the impact of these challenges. We foresee these challenges to intensify in the coming years. However, more and more businesses will adopt CRM practices. Rising customer expectations and affordable technology advances will drive these adoptions.

WHY BUSINESSES SHOULD ADOPT CRM?

We believe that a combination of demand and supply led factors will accelerate the adoption of CRM in the coming years. On the demand side, rising customer expectations will force businesses to adopt CRM. And on the supply side, technological advances and the declining costs of information and communication technology will reduce the barriers to adoption of technology led CRM initiatives.

Rising Customer Expectations

Customer expectations are rising due to increasing affluence in the emerging economies, greater awareness due to media explosion and increasing customer diversity.

(a) Increasing affluence in the emerging economies: The economic growth in the emerging has created a large middle class, estimated at 250 and 300 million people conscious. The transition of these markets from sellers to a buyers market and the buying power of the middle class make them attractive to all businesses. Taken together, nine developing nations - China, India, Brazil, Mexico, Russia, Indonesia, Turkey, South Africa and Thailand - have a combined GDP that is larger, in purchasing power parity, than the combined GDPs of Japan, Germany, France, UK and Italy.

The middle class has a large proportion of professional class with greater global awareness and influence. For example, in India every year over 3,00,000 engineers and about 1,00,000 MBAs join the workforce. They can afford and are willing to pay for better and customized products and services. Many of them are nuclear families and have double income with the spouses employed. This has resulted in a lot of the traditional homemaking activities like cooking, cleaning and childcare being outsourced to service providers. All these will drive the service economy. In services, the customers are a collaborative partner and a co-producer who routinely offers direct input into the making of the offering.

(b) Greater awareness due to explosive media growth: Customers in the emerging markets have greater access to marketplace information about products, services and lifestyles through the explosion in the traditional media like the newspaper and television as well new media like cable television and the internet. The total number of TV homes has remained stable at about 100 million in the US in the last decade while it has exploded in the developing countries. China (341 million), India (80 million) and Brazil (44 million) have witnessed some of the fastest penetration growth of TV in homes in the last decade. The information explosion has played a significant role in raising customer aspirations as well as expectations.

(c) Customer diversity: Increasingly customer prefers choices, tailored to their needs and is personalized in nature. Many of the mass marketing practices fail with customers who are diverse in their lifestyles, age, income and ethnicity. In the last decade, more people have migrated to obtain better living standards after the economic integration of Europe. In the US, ethnic pluralism is increasing as some minority groups like the Hispanic, Afro-American and the Asian are growing rapidly (Cory 1995). About 29 per cent of the workforce in the US is minorities. One-third of all children in the US in 1995 were Asian, African American or Hispanic (Francese 1995).This increase in diversity will greatly increase the diversity in demand and expectations. Rising customer expectations will make CRM a necessity for businesses to be able to customize all elements of marketing mix to satisfy these customers. Fortunately for businesses, advances in affordable technology will help them meet these divergent needs from demanding customers.

Affordable Technological Advances

Advances in technology have made an impact on all stages from production to final consumption. They are allowing marketers to offer unique solutions to individual customers.. We describe some of the key technology advances in production, distribution, facilitation and consumption and their impact on marketing practices.

(a) Production: Breakthroughs, including computer-aided design and computer-aided manufacturing (CAD-CAM) and processes like flexible manufacturing systems (FMS) and just-in-time operations (JIT), have helped improve the quality while reducing the costs across the supply chain. Production technology leaders like Toyota and Dell Computers have gained significant competitive advantage in their respective markets by being early adopters of these technologies. Consumers will benefit as they are offered products and services tailored to their specific requirements through mass-customization at prices comparable to mass-marketed products.

(b) Distribution: Distribution capabilities of firms have been enhanced due to computer-aided logistics (CALS) and scanner technology which allows faster response for replenishment with fewer stock-outs. Improvements in forecasting and database technologies allow fine tuned targeted approaches to marketing and close to real-time fulfillment in many cases, especially information intensive services. Distribution intermediaries and third party logistics providers leverage technology to rapidly deliver products at affordable prices and increase market coverage.

(c) Facilitation: The use of internet to connect enterprise within and outside with suppliers as well as customers through e-commerce technologies has resulted in major improvements in facilitating commercial as well informational exchanges. Dramatic reductions in transaction costs have allowed even small businesses to aspire for a global reach. Large businesses in the airlines, banking and financial services have leveraged the power of the internet to offer services directly to their customers at a lower cost to them as well as to customers. In many industries the sellers as well as the buyers have benefited by this process of disintermediation, i.e., cutting down layers of intermediaries. While the inefficiencies of the traditional intermediation process were reduced through disintermediation, a new class of intermediaries, e.g., Priceline.com and Freemarkets.com have emerged to facilitate transactions between sellers and buyers. Customer shopping habits are changing with the convenience of information availability, evaluation and purchase through the click of a mouse.

(d) Consumption: Breakthroughs in consumption occurred due to the development of affordable personal IDs, e.g., individual login which helped customize the consumption experience. It allows the seller to determine the transaction, purchase and usage history at the level of an individual to personalize the offerings. For the consumer, it has given the power to be a co-producer by intervening and providing direct inputs into the making of the product. Dell.com allows buyers to configure the computer of their choice by co-opting them as co-producers during the design stage. In addition to the personalized consumption, these technologies have allowed customers as well as marketers to overcome the limitations imposed by time and place. Customer's desire for instant gratification will drive businesses to provide access to their products anytime and anywhere. Banks have discovered that as customers shift from a time and place restricted channel like the branch to electronic channels like ATMs, call centers and internet, they save on costs and are able to provide improved services.

These technological developments are proving to be a win-win for companies as well as customers. Therefore it is not surprising that shopping on the internet is growing rapidly. According to an eSpending report by Goldman Sachs & Co., Harris Interactive Inc., and Nielsen/NetRatings Online holiday shoppers spent US$ 18.5 billion during the year end 2003 holiday season, excluding travel, an increase of 35 per cent from the US$ 13.7 billion spent during the 2002 holiday season, (Linda Rosencrance, Computerworld, January 6, 2004). Retailers have reworked their supply chain so that orders could be placed even two days before Christmas. Earlier this took two weeks. Shipping is free. Thus, the Internet has made e-commerce easy for customers as well as companies.

Even in emerging countries like India, customers have started shifting to electronic channels. ICICI Bank, the second largest bank in India, has reported that 70 per cent of its transactions are conducted through electronic channels (February 26, 2004, Economic Times). Its 1,800 ATMs account for 48 per cent of the transactions while the remaining 22 per cent is divided equally between call centre and internet banking.

We will witness greater adoption of these technologies as customers demand for hassle free product information, delivery, consumption and even disposal from businesses. Lowering costs of both information as well as communication technologies will attract firms to invest in these technologies.

IMPLEMENTING CRM

Developments in information technology, data warehousing and data mining have now made it possible for firms to maintain one-to-one relationships with their key customers. Many organizations initiated CRM project as they foresaw tremendous potential for benefits. The benefits come from lower costs of customer retention and increased profits due to lower defection rates (Reichheld and Sasser, 1990). But CRM may appear to be an expensive option to firms which have been practicing mass-marketing due to the relatively high initial investments in sophisticated IT systems required to acquire knowledge about individual customers (Davids 1999; Gupta, 2000). However, as discussed above, the improving performance and declining costs of technology is making it attractive, from a cost-benefit perspective, for them to adopt CRM.

In spite of the availability of multiple technological options, organizations face numerous challenges while selecting and implementing technology intensive CRM solutions. These include issues of top management commitment, change management, developing customer centric processes, integration with legacy systems, identifying and establishing performance metrices and evaluation of return on investments (Adolf et al., 1997; Goff et al., 1998; Ernst and Young, 1999; Sisodia and Wolfe, 2000).

Firms are investing expansively on CRM, focusing specially on the technology. Yet there has been considerable amount of frustration and disappointment with early efforts to apply technology to various aspects of the customer relationship. Many companies are sponsoring a number of CRM initiatives - often with little coordination or clarity of purpose. For instance, an astonishing 63 per cent did not know much their CRM efforts increased or decreased their profitability.

Poor technology choices and ill-conceived implementation plans have derailed many customer relationship projects. The failure rate for CRM projects has been estimated to be high (Davids, 1999; Ernst and Young, 1999, p. 74). The lure of early-mover advantages make many firms invest heavily in technology, statistical tools, databases and restricting which increases risk of these firms biting off more than they can chew (Adolf et al., 1997). Unfortunately, many of these challenges are still faced by managers, in spite of so many implementation experiences.

One major reason as to why CRM is such a challenge to implement is that customer relationship management attempts to tie together many people, processes and technologies within a firm that have, until now, been separate (Ernst and Young, 1999). In the context of banking, Adolf et al. (1997) had argued.

Day (2000) had identified their elements of market-related capability that a firm has to master in order to keep and maintain relationships with its most valuable customers on a durable basis for competitive advantage:

First, a relationship orientation must pervade the mindset, values, norms of the organization. Second, the firm must keep deepening its knowledge of these customers and putting it to work throughout the organization. Third, the key must be internally integrated and externally aligned with the corresponding of the firm's customers.

We believe that a process oriented strategic approach drive by the top management to link the operational, informational and the organizational components of CRM will be crucial for the success of CRM initiatives (Parvatiyar and Sheth, 2000; Pisharodi, Angur and Shainesh, 2003). The process approach helps better delineate the challenges of customer relationship formation, its governance, its performance evaluation and its evolution. Similarly the division of relationship strategy into its operational, informational and organizational components helps managers to understand, identify, measure and manage the impact of these individual components on overall relationship effectiveness.

In a similar vein, Goff et al. (1998) reported, Companies that have taken a comprehensive view are enjoying improved results; those that have not are struggling with technology for technology's sake. CRM is a fundamental requirement for the success of any enterprise and it requires a holistic strategy and process to make it successful.

STRATEGIC ORIENTATION FOR CRM

To enable effective CRM, a suitable strategy needs to be developed and implemented. This calls for a suitable 'strategic orientation' on the part of the organization to enable the CRM initiative. The key drivers of CRM need to be taken into account to ensure the right orientation. According to Arnett and Badrinarayan (2005), these include:

Trust: According to Morgan and Hunt (1994), one party should have confidence in the other party's reliability and integrity in situations of exchange.

Relationship commitment: According to Moorman et al. (1992), it is an enduring desire to maintain a valued relationship.

Communication: According to Anderson and Narus (1990), communication has been described as formal as well as informal sharing of meaningful and timely information between firms.

Therefore, the company should develop an orientation that would enable it to enjoy the trust of the customer, ensure commitment to the relationships and also undertake proper communication. According to Mack et al. (2005), it also involves a proper integration of the CRM strategy, technology, processes and the employees to ensure that the right orientation is achieved. Therefore, a different mindset and attitude is necessary for the company. Firstly, it involves slotting of customers into various segments based on the profitability, needs, purchase behavior, etc. Employing the resources of the company in an equitable manner on all customers is detrimental to the CRM initiative. Once the key customers have been identified, the attitude towards them needs to be perfected. This involves thinking of the key customer as a long-term 'friend' and the company as an 'ally' or a 'partner'.

The customer transactions in a non-CRM orientation are more sales oriented and therefore commercial in nature. The CRM orientation should involve taking active interest in the customer's spoken (and unspoken) needs and ensuring that the commitment is exhibited in the transactions. This, in no way, means that the customer should be pampered and showered with gifts and goodies. However, some necessary amenities should be made available for key customers. For example, ICICI Bank offers Private Banking for key customers (whom they call High Net worth Individuals or HNIs) - they are offered a well appointed private lounge facility with basic hospitability, a designated relationship manager available on call, etc. Likewise, Master Card offers exclusive benefits like access to a special lounge at airports for key customers (those who have opted for membership of a premier card).

The aspect of trust is often exhibited through subtle gestures. These could include:

- A key customer with regular payment record is not harassed for a delayed payment
- When new offers are sent to key customers, they are given time to respond instead of persistent calls being made by sales representatives to get a response
- In case there is a dispute that arises between the company and a key customer regarding some issue wherein the customer has a different standpoint, the company could give the benefit of doubt to the customer if it does not cause a significant financial loss or a tarnishing of the company's image.

Reinhartz et al. (2004) point out that certain factors should be taken into account while formulating the CRM strategy. These include:

- The relationships with customers evolve through distinct phases (Dwyer et al. 1987)
- The firm interacts with customers and has to manage the relationships as it passes through each phase (Srivastava et al. 1998)

The cause behind the above mentioned considerations are obvious. Customers with whom the company begins a relationship would go through various stages owing to their changing income, family lives, business requirements, etc. The company needs to recognize the stage of a relationship with a customer while practicing CRM.

The aspects that should be taken into account with respect to the phase of the relationship with a customer include:

1. Current trust level of the customer - is the customer a suspect, a prospect or a loyal customer?
2. Length of the relationship - how old is the relationship? Were there any break-offs when the customer began patronizing a competitor?
3. Cumulative value of transactions till date - total revenues received? What is the average billing done by the customer?
4. Profitability of the customer - based on the products purchased by the customer? On an average, what margin does the company get from the customer's purchase?
5. Cost to the company to render service - how much does it cost the company to maintain the customer's loyalty? What is the cost of the spare parts that have been offered as replacement (if any)?
6. Stage of customer in the lifecycle - for individuals and firms. Firms - how old is the firm? At what stage of their evolution is the firm currently in? For individuals - age, marital status, income, education, assets, psychographic profile, etc.
7. Relationship of customer with sales and other employees - is it formal or cordial or informal? Do the employees enjoy a good rapport with the customer and vice versa?

The other aspect that should be given due attention apart from customer orientation is of protecting the interests of the company with respect to CRM. Narver and Slater (1990) mention that looking after the customer's best interests may not result in company's profitability. In this context, Dwyer et al. (1987) mention that some customers may be unprofitable and may require being treated differently or even dropped altogether.

Extending the concept of relationships

Companies developing the CRM strategy should also plan how the relationship can be extended to create more value through the loyal customers. In this way, apart from leveraging the lifetime values of the customers, the companies can even extend the value that had been initially ascribed to the customer and create higher customer equity. The aspects that can help in this regard include:

Building a Community

The customers belonging to a particular segment can be grouped together to create a community. This would inculcate a sense of greater belonging among the customers and enable them to identify better with the company. For example, Indian Express newspapers has created the Express Youth Club which has become a community for readers belonging to the youth segment and enables them to participate in various contests and other functions that add value to their personality and gives them desirable exposure. The internet can also be used to build a community. The Sunsilk gang of girls website is a very good example which has enabled a large number of customers to connect with each other in a fruitful manner.

Extended Family

The company can become an extension of the family for the customer. In olden days, families considered various service providers like jewelers, doctors, etc., a part of the extended family and could not even dream of patronizing a competitor. In today's world, through social gatherings with customers, this feeling of extended family can be included which will help to extend the concept of the relationship.

Loyal Advocates

Once a customer has exhibited loyalty, the company can take the opportunity of making the customer an advocate. This should also benefit the customer financially or in some other fashion. For example, customers of Amazon.com can also sign up for the 'affiliate marketing program' which enables them earn referral fees.

The technological orientation

According to Anton and Petouhoff (2002), CRM technologies are best viewed as enables of the people and processes needed to effectively and efficiently manage customers. Campbell (2003) has given stress that the mere implementation of technologies would not result in sales effectiveness. In this context, Landry et al. (2005) mention that CRM can be conceptualized as an organizational mandate to direct structures within the organization in ways that optimize customer relationships in which technology plays an important part.

Therefore, the CRM strategy should also include a proper orientation to accept and make proper use of the technology that would help to facilitate the CRM initiatives.

Explaining the Role of Technology in CRM

Most employees tend to view technology as an enemy rather than a friend. The reason behind this mindset could perhaps be attributed to factors like losing control over one's data, being dependent on technology is an enabler and not a 'master' that will dictate terms to them. Secondly, technology will enable them to perform their tasks faster and in a more effective manner. Thirdly, technology will enable employees to stop performing repetitive tasks that can be better done using technology enabled tools.

Managing the Shift to New Technologies

The fear of the unknown is all-pervading. Anything that is new evokes a sense of fear, mistrust, anxiety and even helplessness. More so if it is a 'new technology' that is going to transform the employees' everyday work life. To allay fears and arrest the spread of unfounded rumors, adequate orientation to the 'new technology' should be done well in advance. Familiarity with the 'new technology' will surely result in employees becoming amenable to it. Also, intensive training (conducted in an informal manner) will serve the purpose well.

Up-gradation of Legacy Systems

Every company that embraces CRM and a new technology for its facilitation would have to take into account the legacy system that has been in use since some time. Employees may have become somewhat accustomed to it and have even grown 'fond' of it (owing to familiarity). The new technology should be able to ensure up gradation of the legacy systems and assure worried employees that they would still enjoy access to their old data.

The tasks to be performed using technology need to be decided while formulating the CRM strategy. Unless a judicious decision is taken with regard to the tasks to be performed, it could result in improper choices and waste of resources. The fate of the CRM initiative could be adversely affected as a result of the faulty choices made. Widmier et al. (2002) mention the various automations possible using technology:

- Organization - scheduling, forecasting, sales route planning software;
- Presenting - multimedia;
- Reporting (to management) - automated reporting;
- Informing (collecting information for sales use) - e-catalogs, internet;
- Supporting and processing transactions - information databases;
- Communicating - cell phones, e-mail and so on.

STRATEGIC FRAMEWORK FOR CRM

The CRM strategy should be encapsulated into a strategic framework which will serve as a guiding tool to be followed for the CRM initiative. Payne and Frow (2005) conducted research to develop a strategic framework for CRM. According to them, the key generic CRM processes can be summed up in five points viz.,

1. The Strategy Development Process

This can begin with a review of the company's vision as well as that of the industry and the competitors. Recent methods may be employed for conducting the analysis such as the impact of disruptive technologies by Christensen and Overdorf (2000).

2. The Value Creation Process

The company should judge the value that is being offered to the customer which can include aspects like co-creation of value with the help of the customer as well. Also, the company should judge the value being received from the customer - this can be done by taking into account the lifetime value of the customer, the profitability offered by the customer, etc.

3. The Multi-channel Integration Process

In this process, the channels are viewed from the customer's standpoint and taking into account the fact that hybrid channels have emerged as a means to customer access, the channel most suited for a customer should be offered to a customer or the customer could be migrated to that channel. The challenges lie in integrating the various channels that operates with different dynamics to ensure that the customer experience is standardized across channels. However, it should be noted that to offering a 'fantastic customer experience' should also be affordable for the company.

4. The Information Management Process

A critical role in the CRM process is played by the information management process. The parts that make up the information management system include - the data repository to receive all the data that is collected; the IT systems that includes the hardware, the software and the middleware; tools for analysis; and the front and back office applications that support the activities that are performed.

5. The Performance Assessment Process

The performance assessment should include the two components - shareholder results (what value is it creating for shareholders) and performance monitoring (enhancement of customer retention, satisfaction levels, etc.,) Cross-functional indicators such as the use of balanced scorecard, etc., could be beneficial for performance measurement.

PLANNING FOR SUCCESS

Beth (2003) mentions the following issues concerning metrics used for CRM:

1. According to Kellen (2002), the use of internal and external metrics should be made. External information with regard to customer perception and behavior should be gathered and help in creating customer insight in the value creation process. These would serve for internal metrics that would be focused on value production and value delivery.
2. On the other hand, Johnson and Gustafsson (2000) have attempted to link internal quality and external quality perception. According to them, this is linked with customer satisfaction, loyalty, retention and leads to cost savings and revenue growth.
3. Shaw (1998) takes into account not just the two easily measurable inputs (costs) and outputs (sales/profits) but two interim steps: customer motivation and customer behavior. The changes in motivation can be tracked through the changes in customer behavior and a model may be created for the same.

The findings of a global survey of over 370 companies across industries conducted by IBM Business Consulting Services suggests: "CRM is done right less than 15 per cent of the time across the globe. In America, Europe and Asia, 85 percent of companies, large and small, are not feeling fully successful with CRM." The highlight of this survey suggests that the success rate can be enhanced from less that 15% to over 70% by "focusing and prioritizing the key CRM approach steps". Surprisingly, the research highlights that the problems are not with 'technology implementation' or 'customer data integration' but with issues like 'change management' and 'process change.' Table 7.1 presents the noteworthy aspects with regard to CRM success from the study conducted by IBM.

Table 7.1 Global Drivers of CRM Success

Aspect	Major contributory factors
Differentiating steps	* CRM strategy and value proposition development
	** Budget process management
	** Change management
Contributing steps	* Customer data integration and data ownership
	** Senior executive and opinion leader buy-in
	** Prioritization of company initiatives
Foundation building steps	* Customer needs analysis
	** Organizational alignment
	** Metric development

CHANGE MANAGEMENT

In the CRM context, change management has been described by Hiatt (2004) as the convergence of two predominant fields - an engineer's approach to improving business performance and a psychologist's approach to handling the human side of change. In this context, Conner (2001) has opined: "When CRM is introduced in a work environment, it causes shock waves of disruption to emanate from the initial points of impact. These points of impact are the physical and political locations where the system is actually introduced and has its effects on the people it touches." In this regard, Hiatt and Creasay (2004) have defined change management in the following manner: "the process, tools and techniques to manage the people-side of business change to achieve the required business outcome and to realize that business change effectively within the social infrastructure of the workplace."

What is noteworthy is that all these researchers have stressed on the 'human aspect' when it comes to change management. In other words, it requires managing the people and their attitudes, mindset, motives and behavior in the right manner for effective change management. The shift to a CRM orientation calls for a radical change in the attitude of not just the sales and marketing people but also the people performing other functions. Even the Relationship Manager also needs to effect a change in the approach to fulfill the objectives of the CRM initiatives. The manner in which this change should be effected has been presented in Table 7.2.

Table 7.2 Changing Role of the Relationship Manager

Traditional role	Change role
Polite behavior with customers	Gaining insights into customer's needs
Selling the product	Offering the complete solution
Representing the sales department	Representing the entire company
Focus on the immediate transaction	Focus on the customer's lifetime value

Kale (2005) suggests the following methods to deal with change management to ensure that the CRM:

Selling Change

The role that needs to be played by the senior management in the change management process is significant and can make the desired impact. The cause of change management should be sold by the top management in no uncertain terms. Efforts should be made to ensure a buy-in by the internal customers and generate the right degree of loyalty, commitment and enthusiasm. It is necessary to mention the benefits to all layers of the organization and make the employees aware of how they can contribute to the betterment of the organization through the CRM initiative.

Change Infrastructure

The people behind the change management process needs to be identified and be empowered through adequate infrastructure. According to Smith and Mourier (1999), the roles could be played by these people would include: change agents, team leaders, content experts, steering teams and project managers.

Training

Training should be imparted in proper measure to ensure that the employees are prepared for the change. The training should not just cover the technical aspects (such as the new business processes) but also the behavioral and attitudinal aspects that would impact the success of the CRM initiative.

COMMUNICATIONS STRATEGY - MANAGING COMMUNICATIONS MIX FOR PRODUCTS, BRANDS

Modern marketing calls for more than just developing a good product, pricing it attractively and making it available to target customers. Companies must also communicate with current and prospective customers, and what they communicate should not be left to chance. For most companies, the question is not whether to communicate, but how much to spend and in what ways. All of their communications efforts must be blended into a consistent and coordinated communications program. As shown in the fig 7.1, completion of marketing process requires something of value with both producer and customer that should be communicated with each other for performing the exchange process

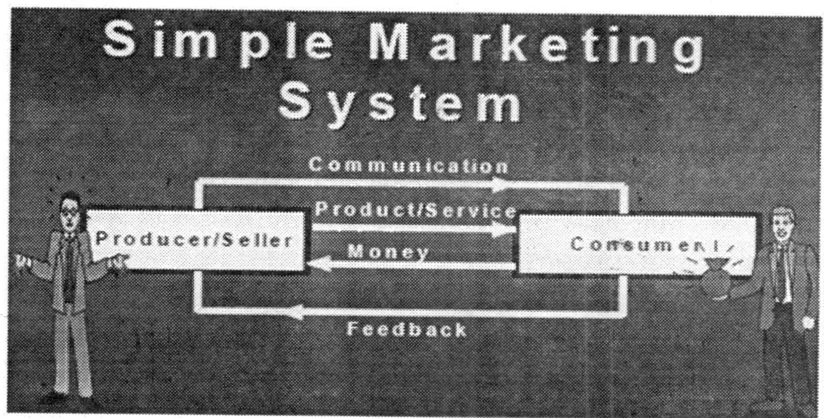

Figure 7.1 Simple Marketing System.

The Marketing Communication Mix for Products and Brands:

A company's total marketing communications mix-also called its promotion mix consists of the specific blend of advertising, personal selling, sales promotion, public relations and direct marketing tools that the company uses to pursue its advertising and marketing objectives.

Definitions of the five major promotion tools follow:

1. **Advertising:** Any paid form of non personal presentation and promotion of ideas, goods or services by an identified sponsor.
2. **Personal selling:** Personal presentation by the firm's sales force for the purpose of making sales and building customer relationships.
3. **Sales promotion:** Short-term incentives to encourage the purchase or sale of a product or service.
4. **Public relations:** Building good relations with the company's various publics by obtaining favorable publicity, building up a good corporate image and handling or heading off unfavorable rumors, stories and events.
5. **Direct marketing:** Direct connections with carefully targeted individual consumers to both obtain an immediate response and cultivate lasting customer relationships-the use of telephone, mail, fax, e-mail, the Internet and other tools to communicate directly with specific consumers.

Each category involves specific tools. For example, advertising includes print, broadcast, outdoor and other forms. Personal selling includes sales presentations, trade shows and incentive programs. Sales promotion includes point-of-purchase displays, premiums, discounts, coupons, specialty advertising and demonstrations. Direct marketing includes catalogs, telemarketing, fax, kiosks, the Internet and more. Put together, these promotional activities make up the promotional or communications mix with varying emphasis on each element according to the type of product or service, characteristics of consumers and company resources. Company size, competitive strengths and weaknesses and style of management all influence the promotional mix. Thanks to technological breakthroughs, people can now communicate through traditional media (newspapers, radio, telephone, television), as well as through newer media forms (fax machines, cellular phones, pagers and computers). The new technologies have encouraged more companies to move from mass communication to more targeted communication and one-to-one dialogue.

Other communications elements with which promotion must be coordinated are the product itself, price and distribution channels used. Product communication, including brand name, design of packaging and trade-marks are all product cues which convey a message about the total product offering. Price can communicate different things under varying circumstances, for instance conveying 'prestige appeal' for those buyers who perceive that a high price is equal to quality and prestige. The place in which the products are to be found also has notable communications value. Retail stores have 'personalities' that consumers associate with the products they sell. Products receive a 'halo effect' from the outlets in which they can be found and two stores selling similar products can project entirely different product images. For example, a perfume sold through an up market store will have a much higher quality image than one sold through supermarkets.

The Marketing Communications Process

Effective communication means effective marketing. Buyers' perceptions of market offerings are influenced by the amount and type of information they receive as well as their reaction to that information. There must be a good flow of information between seller and buyer to assist decision-making that precedes a purchase. An effective marketing communications system also allows feedback from the consumer to the seller.

Some people have a psychological predisposition to buy products and services that are 'new' to the market. This predisposition can be modeled with the use of a normal distribution. Certain people derive a great deal of pleasure from acquiring new products and being first in the market. Such people have a low level of perceived risk and in fact they positively like the risk and excitement associated with the purchase of new, innovative products. These people are referred to as 'innovators' and according to Everett Rogers account for about 2.5 % of the population. The next group of people displaying a tendency to buy new products are known as 'early adopters' and account for approximately 13.5 % of the market. These are still highly adventurous purchasers and the possession of innovative new products gives them a high present value. They still have a low level of perceived risk but are slightly more risk adverse than the 'innovator' category. The next two groups, 'Early Majority' and 'Late Majority' account for the bulk of the potential market, 64% in all. Most people fall into one of these categories. Finally the 'Laggards' are people who are not really infested in new product development and tend to purchase products only when their old product is worn out and stops working. This theme is returned to later under product issues.

A key question for the marketing communicator is: Are the innovators and early adopters also opinion leaders? The majority of potential customers are too risk adverse or too disinterested to be 'first in the market' for an innovation. They are largely unaffected by the media communication about the innovation. Instead, they are influenced by people that they know who they regard as opinion leaders. Although some individuals may be innovators for many products and services, it is more likely that they will be classified as such for a limited range of products. For example a computer enthusiast may be regarded as an 'innovator' for new computer products'. Similarly, someone who is interested in photography may be regarded as opinion leaders in relation to this product but not others.

A new brand of toothpaste containing baking soda is not really that new to people; after all, it is still just toothpaste. A vacuum cleaner for your garden is on the other hand quite a radical innovation. These products have recently come on to the market although most people, even keen gardeners seem a little unsure as to whether they should buy one or not. If these products are good, then the message will soon circulate by word of mouth and soon most households will own one, just as most own a lawn mower or a lawn edger and indeed these latter products were considered to be a radical innovation only a few years ago.

PRICING STRATEGY-VALUE PRICING, OPTIMIZATION OF PRICING

One of the four major elements of the marketing mix is price. Pricing is an important strategic issue because it is related to product positioning. Furthermore, pricing affects other marketing mix elements such as product features, channel decisions and promotion. Price is the amount of money charged for product and service of the sum of the values that customer exchange for the benefit of having or using the product or service. Price goes by many names such as rent, tuition fees, fare, rate, interest, toll, premium etc. Price is the only element in the marking mix that produces revenue, all other element represents costs. Price is also one of the most flexible elements in marketing mix.

While there is no single recipe to determine pricing, the following is a general sequence of steps that might be followed for developing the pricing of a new product:

1. Develop marketing strategy - perform marketing analysis, segmentation, targeting and positioning.
2. Make marketing mix decisions - define the product, distribution and promotional tactics.
3. Estimate the demand curve - understand how quantity demanded varies with price.
4. Calculate cost - include fixed and variable costs associated with the product.
5. Understand environmental factors - evaluate likely competitor actions, understand legal constraints, etc.
6. Set pricing objectives - for example, profit maximization, revenue maximization or price stabilization (status quo).
7. Determine pricing - using information collected in the above steps, select a pricing method, develop the pricing structure and define discounts.

These steps are interrelated and are not necessarily performed in the above order. Nonetheless, the above list serves to present a starting framework

Pricing Objectives

The firm's pricing objectives must be identified in order to determine the optimal pricing. Common objectives include the following:

i. **Current profit maximization** - seeks to maximize current profit, taking into account revenue and costs. Current profit maximization may not be the best objective if it results in lower long-term profits.

ii. **Current revenue maximization** - seeks to maximize current revenue with no regard to profit margins. The underlying objective often is to maximize long-term profits by increasing market share and lowering costs.

iii. **Maximize quantity** - seeks to maximize the number of units sold or the number of customers served in order to decrease long-term costs as predicted by the experience curve.

iv. **Maximize profit margin** - attempts to maximize the unit profit margin, recognizing that quantities will be low.

v. **Quality leadership** - use price to signal high quality in an attempt to position the product as the quality leader.

vi. **Partial cost recovery** - an organization that has other revenue sources may seek only partial cost recovery.

vii. **Survival** - in situations such as market decline and overcapacity, the goal may be to select a price that will cover costs and permit the firm to remain in the market. In this case, survival may take a priority over profits, so this objective is considered temporary.

viii. **Status quo** - the firm may seek price stabilization in order to avoid price wars and maintain a moderate but stable level of profit.

For new products, the pricing objective often is either to maximize profit margin or to maximize quantity (market share). To meet these objectives, skim pricing and penetration pricing strategies often are employed.

Skim pricing attempts to "skim the cream" of the top of the market by setting a high price and selling to those customers who are less price sensitive. Skimming is a strategy used to pursue the objective of profit margin maximization.

Skimming is most appropriate when:

i. Demand is expected to be relatively inelastic; that is, the customers are not highly price sensitive.

ii. Large cost savings are not expected at high volumes, or it is difficult to predict the cost savings that would be achieved at high volume.

iii. The company does not have the resources to finance the large capital expenditures necessary for high volume production with initially low profit margins.

Penetration pricing pursues the objective of quantity maximization by means of a low price. It is most appropriate when:

i. Demand is expected to be highly elastic; that is, customers are price sensitive and the quantity demanded will increase significantly as price declines.

ii. Large decreases in cost are expected as cumulative volume increases.

iii. The product is of the nature of something that can gain mass appeal fairly quickly.

iv. There is a threat of impending competition.

As the product lifecycle progresses, there likely will be changes in the demand curve and costs. As such, the pricing policy should be reevaluated over time.

The pricing objective depends on many factors including production cost, existence of economies of scale, barriers to entry, product differentiation, rate of product diffusion, the firm's resources and the product's anticipated price elasticity of demand.

Pricing Methods

To set the specific price level that achieves their pricing objectives, managers may make use of several pricing methods. These methods include:

i. **Cost-plus pricing** - set the price at the production cost plus a certain profit margin.

ii. **Target return pricing** - set the price to achieve a target return on investment.

iii. **Value-based pricing** - base the price on the effective value to the customer relative to alternative products. Its price the product based on the value it creates for the customer. This is usually the most profitable form of pricing, if you can achieve it. The most extreme variation on this is "pay for performance" pricing for services, in which you charge on a variable scale according to the results you achieve

iv. **Psychological pricing** - base the price on factors such as signals of product quality, popular price points and what the consumer perceives to be fair.

In addition to setting the price level, managers have the opportunity to design innovative pricing models that better meet the needs of both the firm and its customers. For example, software traditionally was purchased as a product in which customers made a one-time payment and then owned a perpetual license to the software. Many software suppliers have changed their pricing to a subscription model in which the customer subscribes for a set period of time, such as one year. Afterwards, the subscription must be renewed or the software no longer will function. This model offers stability to both the supplier and the customer since it reduces the large swings in software investment cycles.

Cost-based versus value-based pricing

Value-based pricing reverses this process. The company sets its target price based on customer perceptions of the product value. The targeted value and price then drive decisions about product design and what costs can be incurred. As a result, pricing begins with analyzing consumer needs and value perceptions and price is set to match consumers' perceived value (Fig 7.2.).

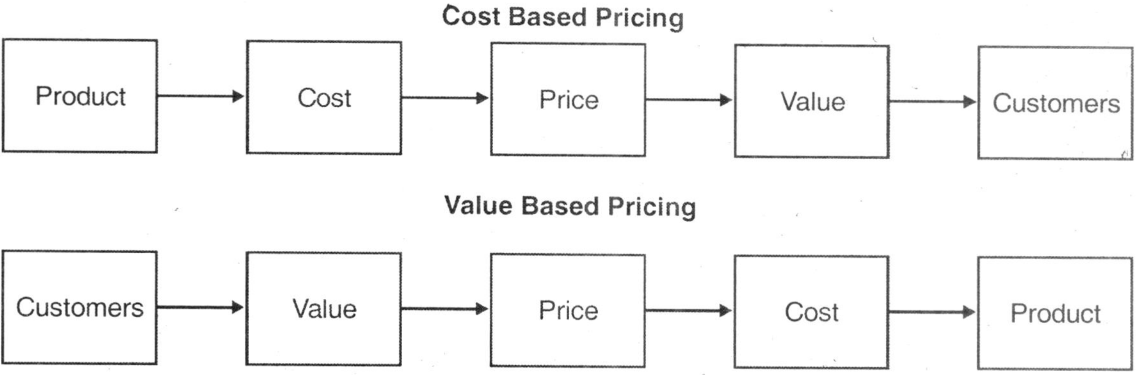

Figure 7.2 Cost-based versus value-based pricing

A company using value-based pricing must find out what value buyers assign to different competitive offers. However, measuring perceived value could be difficult. Sometimes, consumers are asked how much they would pay for a basic product and for each benefit added to the offer or a company might conduct experiments to test the perceived value of different product offers.

If the seller charges more than the buyers' perceived value, the company's sales will suffer. Many companies overprice their products and their products sell poorly. Other companies do under pricing. Under priced products sell very well, but they produce less revenue than they would have if price were raised to the perceived-value level.

During the past decade, marketers have noted a fundamental shift in consumer attitudes towards price and quality. Many companies have changed their pricing approaches to bring them into line with changing economic conditions and consumer price perceptions. The best way to hold your customers is to constantly figure out how to give them more for less."

Thus, more and more, marketers have adopted value pricing strategies-offering just the right combination of quality and good service at a fair price. In many cases, this has involved the introduction of less expensive versions of established, brand-name products. In many business to business marketing situations, the pricing challenge is to find ways to maintain the company's pricing power-its power to maintain or even raise prices without losing market share. To retain pricing power-to escape price competition and to justify higher prices and margins-a firm must retain or build the value of its marketing offer. This is especially true for suppliers of commodity products, which are characterized by little differentiation and intense price competition. In such cases, many companies adopt value-added strategies. Rather than cutting prices to match competitors, they attach value-added services to differentiate their offers and thus support higher margins.

OPTIMIZATION OF PRICING

In economies, Profit Maximization is the process by which a firm determines the price and output level that returns the greatest profit. There are several approaches to this problem. The Total Revenue -- total cost method relies on the fact that profit equals revenue minus cost and the Marginal Revenue -- marginal cost method is based on the fact that total profit in a perfectly competitive market reaches its maximum point where marginal revenue equals marginal cost.

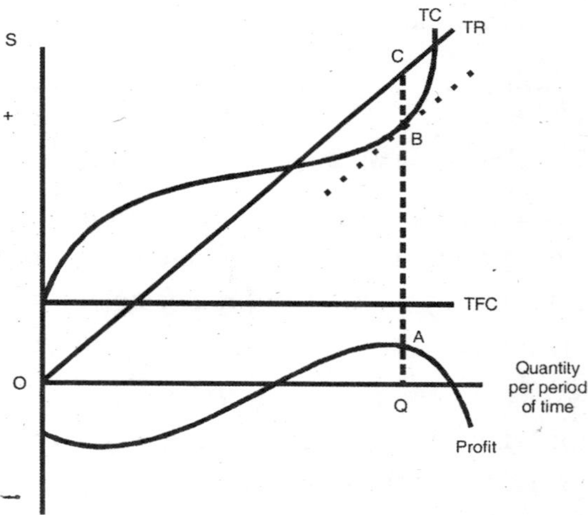

Figure 7.3 Profit Maximization - The Totals Approach

To obtain the profit maximizing output quantity, we start by recognizing that profit is equal to total revenue minus total cost. Given a table of costs and revenues at each quantity, we can either compute equations or plot the data directly on a graph. Finding the profit-maximizing output is as simple as finding the output at which profit reaches its maximum. That is represented by output Q in the diagram.

Profit Maximization - The Totals Approach (Fig 7.3)

There are two graphical ways of determining that Q is optimal. Firstly, we see that the profit curve is at its maximum at this point (A). Secondly, we see that at the point (B) that the tangent on the total cost curve (TC) is parallel to the total revenue curve (TR), the surplus of revenue net of costs (B, C) is the greatest. Because total revenue minus total costs is equal to profit, the line segment C,B is equal in length to the line segment A,Q. Computing the price at which to sell the product requires knowledge of the firm's demand curve. The price at which quantity demanded equals profit-maximizing output is the optimum price to sell the product.

Marginal Cost-Marginal Revenue Method(fig 7.4)

If total revenue and total cost figures are difficult to procure, this method may also be used. For each unit sold, marginal profit equals marginal revenue minus marginal cost. Then, if marginal revenue is greater than marginal cost, marginal profit is positive, and if marginal revenue is less than marginal cost, marginal profit is negative When marginal revenue equals marginal cost, marginal profit is zero. Since total profit increases when marginal profit is positive and total profit decreases when marginal profit is negative, it must reach a maximum where marginal profit is zero - or where marginal cost equals marginal revenue. This intersection of marginal revenue (MR) with marginal costs (MC) is shown in the next diagram as point A. If the industry is competitive (as is assumed in the fig 7.4), the firm faces a demand curve (D) that is identical to its Marginal revenue curve (MR), and this is a horizontal line at a price determined by industry supply and demand. Average total costs are represented by curve ATC. Total economic profits are represented by area P,A,B,C. The optimum quantity (Q) is the same as the optimum quantity (Q) in the fig 7.3

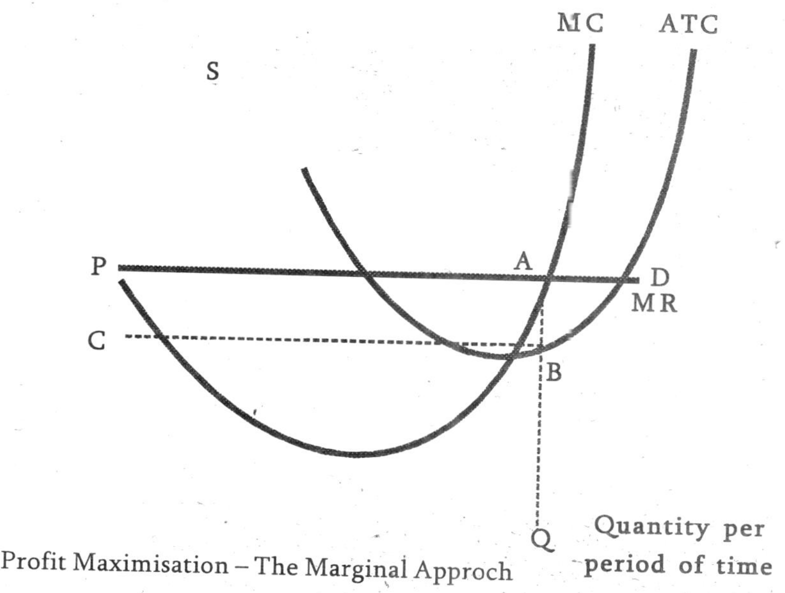

Profit Maximisation – The Marginal Approch

Figure 7.4 The Marginal Approach

Modes of Operation

It is assumed that all firms are following rational decision-making and will produce at the profit-maximizing output. Given this assumption, there are four categories in which a firm's profit may be considered. A firm is said to be making an **economic profit** when its average total cost is less than the price of the product at the **profit-maximizing** output. The economic profit is equal to the quantity output multiplied by the difference between the average total cost and the price. A firm is said to be making a normal profit when its economic profit equals zero. This occurs where average total cost equals price at the profit-maximizing output. If the price is between average total cost and average variable cost at the profit-maximizing output, then the firm is said to be in a **loss-minimizing** condition. The firm should still continue to produce, however, since its loss would be larger if it was to stop producing. By continuing production, the firm can offset its variable cost and at least part of its fixed cost, but by stopping completely it would lose equivalent of its entire fixed cost. If the price is below average variable cost at the profit-maximizing output, the firm is said to be in **shutdown**. Losses are minimized by not producing at all, since any production would not generate returns significant enough to offset any fixed cost and part of the variable cost. By not producing, the firm loses only its fixed cost.

ADVERTISING AND SALES PROMOTION STRATEGY

Advertising

Media advertising communicates information to a large number of recipients, paid for by a sponsor. It has three main aims:

1. To impart information
2. To develop attitudes
3. To induce action beneficial to the advertiser (generally the purchase of a product or service).

An advertisement for washing powder is paid for by the manufacturer to achieve greater sales; a party political broadcast aims to increase votes. It must be remembered that advertising is only one element of the communications mix, but it does perform certain parts of the communicating task faster and with greater economy and volume than other means.How large a part advertising plays depends on the nature of the product and its frequency of purchase. It contributes the greatest part when:

1. Buyer awareness of the product is low
2. Industry sales are rising rather than remaining stable or declining
3. The product has features which are not obvious to the buyer

4. The opportunities for product differentiation are strong
5. Discretionary incomes are high
6. A new product or new service idea is being introduced.

Advertising models

These have been drawn from several sources, particularly psychology and from advertising practitioners in order to explain how advertising works.

1. The stimulus/response formula

This was used at first, later models taking into consideration the environment in which the decision to buy is made. Daniel Starch said in 1925 'for an advertisement to be successful it must be seen, must be read, must be believed, must be remembered and must be acted upon'. This model assumed that the advertisement is the main influence on the state of mind of the consumer in respect of the product and makes no allowance for combined or multiple effects of advertisements.

2. The DAGMAR philosophy

Colley's DAGMAR model in 1961 (Defining Advertising Goals for Measured Advertising Results) allows for the cumulative impact of advertisements and also maps out the states of mind consumers pass through:

1. From unawareness to awareness;
2. To comprehension;
3. To conviction;
4. To action.

This is described as the marketing communications spectrum. Advertising, along with promotion, personal selling, publicity, price, packaging and distribution, move the consumer through the various levels of the spectrum as follows:

Unawareness/awareness The advertisement tries to make potential customers aware of the product's existence.

Comprehension The customer recognizes the brand name and trademark and also knows what the product is and what it does; knowledge gained from the advertisement or from an information search prompted by it.

Conviction The customer has a firm attitude, preferring a particular brand over all others. Preferences may have an emotional rather than rational basis.

Action Some move is made towards purchase, thus the advertisement has been acted upon.

This illustrates the concept that the purpose of advertising is to cause a change of mind leading towards purchase, but it is rare for a single advertisement to have the power to move a prospect from complete unawareness to action. Effectiveness is judged by how far an advertisement moves people along the spectrum.

3. The Lavidge and Steiner model

This consists of a hierarchical sequence of events on six levels:

1. Awareness
2. Knowledge
3. Liking
4. Preference
5. Conviction
6. Purchase

These steps divide behavior into three dimensions: cognitive (the first two), affective (the second two) and motivational (the third two). Although this differs from the 'DAGMAR' model in the number and nature of stages, there is agreement that purchase is the result of the persuasion elements, making the assumption between changes in knowledge and attitude towards a product and changes in buying behaviour there is a predictable outcome.

Dissonance theory, however, illustrates a two-way relationship, with behaviour influencing attitudes as well as attitudes influencing behaviour. After making a decision to purchase, the prospect will be involved in cognitive dissonance and will actively seek information to reinforce the decision, focusing on attractive features and 'filtering out' unfavorable data. The major implication of this is that advertising for existing brands in the repeat purchase market should be aimed at existing users to reassure them in the continuation of the buying habit at the expense of the competition.

4. The Unique Selling Proposition

This was developed by Rosser Reeves (1961) who reported the principles his agency had adopted for 30 years. This states that the consumer remembers one key element of an advertisement - a strong claim or concept. This proposition must be one that the competition does not offer, which will be recalled by the consumer and will result in purchase at the appropriate time.

5. The 'brand-image' school

This was led by advertising practitioner David Ogilvy who focused on non-verbal methods of communication to invest a brand with agreeable connotations aside from its actual properties in use, such as prestige and quality.

It must be remembered that an advertisement is the channel through which the sponsor communicates their message. The encoded message reaches recipients, through advertising or salespeople, who then decode and absorb it either fully or partly. The quality of the transmission can be distorted by 'noise' occurring because the receiver does not interpret the message in the way the source intended (due perhaps to differences in cultural backgrounds of the two parties). It may however be because of cognitive dissonance which occurs when peoples' receipt of the message does not agree with what they previously believed.

Dissonance may cause a number of different reactions by the receiver:

1. Rejecting the message
2. Ignoring the message
3. Altering the previous opinion
4. Searching for justifications

The first two reactions are of course negative and from this feedback the source may change the message or stop communicating altogether with a particular receiver who is not receptive to the source's ideas. It can, therefore, be seen that advertising does not always convert people into users of a particular product. It can, however, have a positive effect in preventing loss of users and increasing their loyalty.

6. Advertising by objectives

Advertising situations are so varied and unique that it is not possible to generalize about how advertising works. Any potential advertiser should therefore adopt an advertising-by-objectives approach that will make clear what they are trying to achieve, how they will achieve it and how they are going to measure its effects.

Few companies give any detailed scientific thought to exactly what they are trying to achieve through advertising. Clear objectives are needed to aid operational decisions, which include:

- The amount to be spent on a particular campaign
- The content and presentation of the advertisement
- The most appropriate media
- The frequency of display of advertisements or campaigns
- Any special geographical weighting of effort
- The best methods of evaluating the effects of the advertising.

Corkindale and Kennedy (1976) found that systematically setting and evaluating objectives provided the following benefits.

1. Marketing management has to consider and define in advance what each element in the programme is expected to accomplish.
2. An information system can be set up to monitor ongoing performance, with the nature of information required clearly defined.
3. Marketing management will learn about the system it is operating from accumulated experience of success (and failure) and can use this knowledge to improve future performance.

Majaro's (1970) major study on objective setting revealed that most managers saw increasing sales or market share as their main advertising objective. In fact, this is a total marketing objective and it is unreasonable to expect to achieve this objective through advertising alone (unless it was the only element of the marketing mix used, as in direct mail and mail order businesses). Majaro's study also revealed that methods of evaluation used by most companies were not relevant, and that clear, precise advertising objectives, known to all involved, would rectify this situation. The following advantages of the advertising-by-objectives approach became clear.

1. It helps to integrate the advertising effort with other ingredients of the marketing mix, thus setting a consistent and logical marketing plan.
2. It facilitates the task of the advertising agency in preparing and evaluating creative work and recommending the most suitable media.
3. It assists in determining advertising budgets.
4. It enables marketing executives and top management to appraise the advertising plan realistically.
5. It permits meaningful measurement of advertising results.

When setting objectives, all personnel in a company who have an interest in and influence on, advertising decisions have different ideas of the purpose of advertising. The Chairman may be concerned with corporate image, whilst the Advertising Manager may see it as an investment direct towards building a brand image and increasing market share. Marketing objectives have to be separated from advertising objectives. Overall marketing objectives should be defined and the next step is to determine the contribution that advertising can efficiently make to each of these. An advertising objective is one that advertising alone is expected to achieve.

Advertising objectives should be set with the following points in mind.

1. They should fit in with broader corporate objectives.
2. They should be realistic, taking into account internal resources and external opportunities, threats and constraints.

3. They should be universally known within the company, so that everyone can relate them to his or her own work and to the broader corporate objectives.
4. They need to be flexible, since all business decisions have to be made in conditions of partial ignorance.
5. They should be reviewed and adapted from time to time to take account of changing conditions.

Setting advertising objectives should not be undertaken until all relevant information on the product, the market and the consumer is available. Consumer behaviour and motivation must be thoroughly assessed, particularly that of the company's target group of customers. The statement of an advertising objective should then make clear what basic message is intended to be delivered, to what audience, with what intended effects and the specific criteria to be used to measure success.

Corkindale and Kennedy used five key words to summarize the elements of setting advertising objectives:

1. **WHAT** What role is advertising expected to fulfill in the total marketing effort?
2. **WHY** Why is it believed that advertising can achieve this role? (What evidence is there and what assumptions are necessary?)
3. **WHO** Who should be involved in setting objectives; who should be responsible for agreeing the objectives, coordinating their implementation and subsequent evaluation? Who is the intended audience?
4. **HOW** How are the advertising objectives to be put into practice?
5. **WHEN** When are various parts of the programme to be implemented? When can response be expected to each stage of the programme?

'Below-the-line' promotion:

The terms 'below-the-line' promotion or communications refers to forms of non-media communication, even non-media advertising. Examples of non-media 'promotions' are exhibitions, sponsorship activities, public relations and sales promotions such as competitions, banded packs and price promotions. Below-the-line promotions are becoming increasingly important within the communications mix of many companies, not only those involved in FMCG products, but also for industrial goods. For example dealer incentives, exhibitions and sponsorship activities are all growing in popularity. All forms of non-media communications are a form of 'promotion' if we use the word in the broadest sense. Specific forms of 'below-the-line sales promotion' are discussed below.

1. Below the line sales promotion

Below the line sales promotions are short term incentives, largely aimed at consumers, but also aimed at the 'trade' e.g., wholesalers, retailers, distributors, etc., along with company employees, usually the sales force. Over the past 20 years or so there has been greater pressure on marketing budgets and a greater demand on marketing management to achieve marketing communications objectives more efficiently. Hence marketers have been searching for a more cost-effective way to communicate with their target markets than conventional media advertising. A move to below the line promotion is one result of this. A definition of below-the-line sales promotion is given by Hugh Davidson:

'An immediate or delayed incentive to purchase, expressed in cash or in kind and having only a short term or temporary duration'.

This definition highlights one important characteristic of below-the-line sales promotion that is its short term nature. Most conventional above the line advertising campaigns are medium to long term in nature. Below the line sales promotions tend to be short term in nature. Rarely does a sales promotion last for more than six months and the majority last for much shorter periods.

All promotions are variations of one basic type or another, but since the sales promotion is dynamic by nature new types will be developed in the future. The sphere of sales promotions generally includes the following:

- Display materials (stands, header boards, shelf strips, 'wobblers')
- Packaging (coupons, premium offers, pack flashes)
- Merchandising (demonstrations, auxiliary sales forces, display arrangements)
- Direct mail (coupons, competitions, premiums)
- Exhibitions

Industrial promotions also include the above elements, but with modifications to make them closer in type to those used by manufacturers of consumer goods for their retailers; designed to gain orders over long periods.

2. Sales promotion planning

A full plan is needed to ensure that each stage of a promotion is reached:

1. Analyze the problem task
2. Define objectives
3. Consider and/or set the budget
4. Examine the types of promotion likely to be of use
5. Define the support activities (e.g., advertising, incentives, auxiliaries)

6. Testing (e.g., a limited store or panel test)
7. Decide measurements required
8. Plan timetable
9. Present details to sales force, retailers, etc.
10. Implement the promotion
11. Evaluate the result

3. Advantages and disadvantages of sales promotions

Advantages

- Easily measured response
- Quick achievement of objectives
- Flexible application
- Can be extremely cheap
- Direct support of sales force

Disadvantages

- Price-discounting can cheapen brand image
- Short-term advantages only
- Can cause stress with retailers
- Difficulty in communicating brand message

4. The importance of sales promotion

It is often difficult to know which 'marketing' expenditures can be attributed to sales promotion. For example price reduction can cause confusion - 10% off a packet of biscuits is a sales promotion, but what about price discounting by manufacturers?

Telephone marketing:

Telemarketing can be defined as 'any measurable activity that creates and exploits a direct relationship between supplier and customer by the interactive use of the telephone'. The American Telephone and Telegraph Company define it as 'the marketing of telecommunications technology and direct marketing techniques'.

Telephone marketing can take the forms of 'in-coming call' and 'out-going call'. In-coming call telephone marketing usually makes use of special numbers, which enables the caller to call 'free-phone' or at local call rates. Such campaigns are usually used in conjunction with other marketing communications 'tools'.

Direct mail and direct marketing:

Direct mailing is the use of the postal service to distribute promotional material directly to a particular person, household or firm. It is often confused with the following related activities, which all fall under the general heading of 'direct marketing'.

1. **Direct advertising** One of the oldest methods of reaching the consumer, with printed matter being sent directly to the prospect by the advertiser, often by mail, but sometimes through the letter box personal delivery, handing out to passers-by or left under the screen wiper of a car.
2. **Mail order** advertising aims to persuade recipients to purchase a product or service by post, with deliveries being made through the mail or other carrier or through a local agent. Thus it is a special form of direct mail, seeking to complete the sale entirely by mail and being a complete plan in itself. Mail order is a type of direct mail, but not all direct mail is mail order.
3. **Direct response advertising** This is a strategy of using specially designed advertisements, usually in magazines or newspapers, to invoke a direct response, such as the coupon-response press ad, which the reader uses to order the advertised product or request further information. Other variants offer money-off coupons and incentives to visit the retail outlet.

The usage and acceptance of direct mail is increasing rapidly and one reason for this is that the media has become increasingly fragmented, with many commercial TV channels and the rapid growth of 'free-sheets' and special interest magazines. This means that advertisers have to either spend more money to reach their audience or spread the same amount over a wider range of media. Improvements in the quality of large mail shots have attracted an increasing number of large advertisers. Direct mail, with increasing sophistication of computerization, now enables advertisers to segment and target their markets with greater flexibility, selectivity and personal contact.

Direct mail can be used to sell a wide range of products or services and its uses are also varied. To help define direct mail more fully, it is appropriate to deal with direct mail to consumers and businesses separately.

1. Consumer direct mail

Some of the most common uses of consumer-targeted direct mail are:

1. **Selling direct:** Direct mail is a good medium for selling a product directly to the customer by a company that has a convincing sales message. It provides a facility for describing the product or service fully and for an order to be sent straight back, cutting out the 'middlemen'.

2. **Sales lead generation** Some products/services require a meeting between the customer and a specialized salesperson and direct mail can be used to acquire 'qualified' leads. A mail-shot that has been well thought through can reveal the best prospects and rank other leads in terms of 'potential', enabling some responses to be followed up by a salesperson. An invitation can be made for the customer to view the product in a retail outlet, showroom or exhibition. Such 'cordial-contact' mailings can create a receptive atmosphere for salespeople by building on the reputation of the company and creating a good impression, which can be converted into buying action later.
3. **Sales promotion** Promotional messages such as special offers will reach specific targets through direct mail and in the same way prospects can be encouraged to visit showrooms or exhibitions.
4. **Clubs** The most popular users of direct mail here are book clubs and companies marketing 'collectibles'.
5. **Mail order** Direct selling and recruitment of new customers and agents are possible through direct mail.
6. **Fundraising** It is easy through direct mail to communicate personally with an individual and therefore it is an excellent method of raising money for charitable organizations. Large amounts of information can be included to induce the recipient to make a donation.
7. **Dealer mailings** Dealers or agents can use direct mail to reach the prospects in their own area.
8. **Follow-up mailings** These help to keep the company's name before the customer following a sale, for example checking that the customer is satisfied with a purchase. New developments, products and services can also be communicated or invitations issued, thus maintaining contact and increasing repeat sales.

2. Business direct mail

For business, this is more effective than mass advertising for identifying different market sectors and communicating to each an appropriate message. Some of the more common uses are:

1. **Product launch:** Direct mail is able to target the small but significant number of people who influence buying decisions.
2. **Sales lead generation:** Direct mail provides qualified sales leads, as well as doing some initial selling.
3. **Dealer support:** Dealers, retail outlets, franchise holders etc., can be kept fully informed of marketing promotions and plans.

4. **Conferences :** Potential delegates in specific business sections can be issued with invitations through direct mail.
5. **Follow-up mailing using customer base:** Mailing existing customers regularly encourages repeat sales.
6. **Market research/product testing:** Market research (especially amongst existing customers) can be very effective where it is possible to do this through direct mail, using questionnaires as part of a regular communication programme. Small-scale test mailings can give an accurate picture of market reaction, with low risk and a successful product can later be mailed to the full list.

3. Direct mail as part of the promotional mix

When direct mail is added to, say, a television or press campaign, the effectiveness of the overall campaign can be significantly raised. The media reaches a broad audience and can raise general awareness of the company and its products, while the direct mail campaign is targeted specifically at the groups of people or companies most likely to buy. Mailing lists of respondents to couponed press advertisements or television or radio commercials with a 'phone-in' number can be used for direct mail approaches.

Exhibitions

Exhibitions are another form of below the line promotional activity. As with many other below-the-line methods they are growing in use and popularity. They come in three basic forms.

1. those aimed at the consumer,
2. those aimed solely at the trade,
3. those aimed at and open to both.

The third category has become the most common. Most exhibitions start off as trade exhibitions and then after the first week or so when all of the 'trade' business has been conducted they are usually opened to the public. The public usually pays an entry fee that brings in revenue for the exhibition organizer and helps to pay for the costs of actually staging the exhibition. The general public may have an actual interest in the products and services being exhibited for example Clothes Shows, Motor Shows and Home Exhibitions. Sometimes the products and services are of little direct interest to the general public. That is, they are highly unlikely to buy any of the products on show, but nevertheless attendance at the exhibition can be a 'good day out' (e.g., an agricultural show or an air show) and the public is prepared to pay for this privilege.

Exhibitions tend to attract a high quality audience and company directors will often attend an important trade exhibition. Such trade exhibitions offer the marketing firm the opportunity to come in personal contact with high status decision making unit (DMU) members.

Sponsorship

Like most below the line activity, this is growing in popularity. In some ways sponsorship achieves many of the functions of exhibitions especially in terms of audience quality. We have already established that in business to business marketing environments, high status decision making unit members are notoriously difficult to contact on a personal basis. The firm sponsoring an event can invite important members of a prospective customer company's DMU to the event thereby enabling personal contact to be made in a social setting.

BRAND BUILDING STRATEGIES

Building a powerful brand by using a consistent marketing strategy is absolutely essential to having a successful and profitable small business. A powerful brand identity can influence the customers to buy the product or service over the competitors, even if they have to pay more for it! A powerful brand can influence the customers to think that no one else, but you or your company, can deliver the quality or the benefits that they want. By building a unique brand identity, a company can have the most powerful business edge that the competitors can NEVER take away from them!

What is a Brand?

A brand can be a name, a phrase, an image, a symbol or a combination of things that tend to identify the products or services of one company as unique or different from its competitors. A brand can represent something intangible about your company, your product or service. It can be a combination of feelings and perceptions about your name, image, quality, reputation and personality.

In other words "A Brand is a name, sign, symbol or design or a combination of these that identifies the marketer or seller of a product or service."

A Brand equity is the value of a brand, based on the extent to which it has high brand loyalty, name awareness, perceived quality, strong brand associations and other assets such as patents, trademarks and channel relationships.

A brand can convey various levels of meaning:-

1. **Attributes:** A brand brings to mind certain attributes. Like- Mercedes suggests expensive , durable, high prestige automobiles.
2. **Values:** The brand says something about the producer's values. Like- Mercedes stand for high performance, safety and prestige.

3. **Benefits:** Attributes must be translated into functional and emotional benefits.
4. **User:** The brand suggests the kind of consumer who buys or uses the products.

Branding decision:

The first decision is whether the company should develop a brand name for its product. The various branding decisions can be explained with the help of following Figure 7.5: Branding, Brand Sponsor, Brand Name, Brand Strategy, Brand Decision and Repositioning Decision.

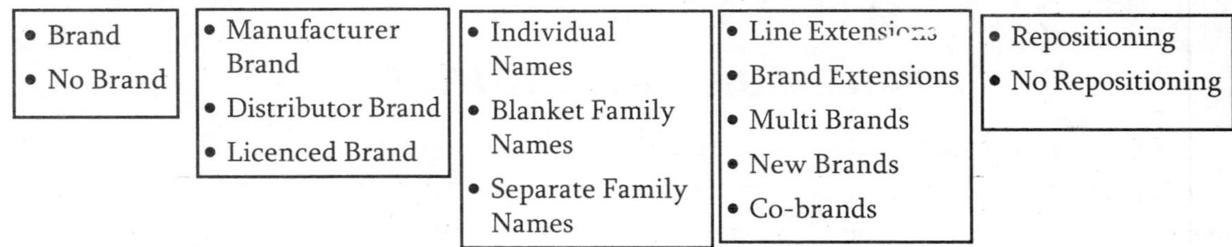

Figure 7.5 Branding Decisions

As pre-packed products, especially in FMCG (Fast Moving Consumer Goods) sector, come into common use and are accepted in different societies, manufacturers are presented with an opportunity to exercise some control over the way their products are accepted by a rapidly growing, dispersed mass market. As markets become impersonal, with increasing physical and time distance between the manufacturer or producer and the customer, some way has to be found to maintain the association of a name and a product with its producer. In these circumstances the evolution of brands affords customers the opportunity of forming product perceptions in terms of packaging and design, product quality and performance, value and image.

The branding of products basically serve three purposes :

1. To conform to the legal patent protection the inventor may have.
2. To guarantee quality and homogeneity in markets where buyers and producers cannot meet face to face.
3. To differentiate products in a competitive environment

How to build a brand?

Brand building is continuous process. It includes every implementation of the brand once it has defined. It is not focusing on the brand image but knowing the role of brand in driving choice. It is not just about advertising, but consistently managing the brand at all intersections with the customer. Brand building involves various inputs, outcomes and assessment. The model may be used to illustrate the salient steps of various inputs, outcomes and assessment Figure 7.6.

INPUTS:

- Identification of key customer groups or segments.
- Understanding customer expectations, needs and aspirations.
- Assessing competitive offering including substitutes.
- Building customer confidence by
  - customizing the product,
  - establishing the key image of the brand,
  - dealer support- easy availability and push,
  - innovative communication and promotion schemes, and
  - elegant packaging.
- Total brand management- both hardware and software aspects

OUTCOME:

1. Market share
2. New customers attracted
3. Customer loyalty index
4. Increased profitability
5. Brand knowledge

ASSESSMENT:

1. Continues feedback from customers as well as trade channels.
2. Scientific inquiry into customer satisfaction determining:
   i. Who is the customer and profile of the target segment?
   ii. What constitutes customer satisfaction?
   iii. Designing the scale to measure customer satisfaction.
   iv. Measuring current levels of customer satisfaction.
3. Brand strength scores - The overall brand strength score is a composite of different weighted factors, each of which can be measured on a suitable scale. The key questions of measurement are as follows:

- Leadership - Does the brand lead the market?
- Stability - Is there any established status of the brand?
- Market position - What are the prospects for the said brand in the current market?

4. Trend - Will the brand remain contemporary and relevant to target consumers in the long run? Ascertain the nature of market segment whether the said brand has still found its relevance.

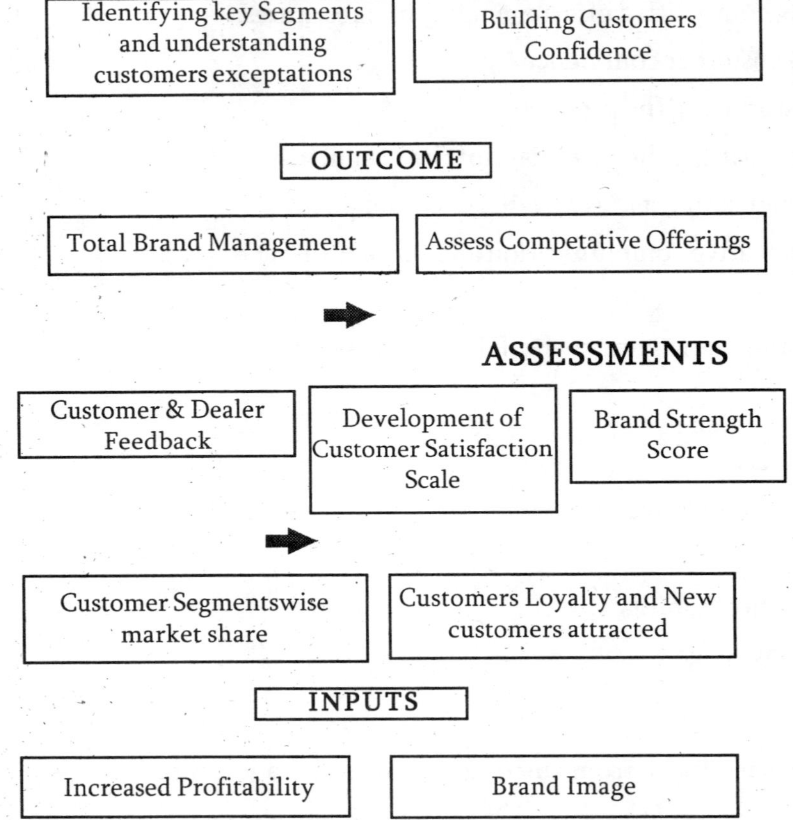

Figure 7.6 Brand Building: A Conceptual Framework

CHECKLIST FOR BUILDING A BRAND:-

1. What is your brands vision?
2. What values does your company subscribe to?
3. What are the good and bad features/attributes of your brand (company, product, service)?
4. What are the bad aspects of your brand and how can you dispose of them?

5. What are the practical benefits associated with each of the good features/ attributes?
6. Can you extend those features and benefits to form emotional characteristics for the consumer?
7. What are the emotional reasons why customers might buy your products/services?
8. What are the rational and emotional personality characteristics of your brand?
9. What can you do to bring these personality characteristics to life?
10. How can you use the brand personality to attract and retain more customers?
11. How are you going to generate more trust in your brand-customer relationship?

THE BRANDING CYCLE:-

Brand building, as the responsibility of brand management, is a continuous cycle of research, planning, implementation and control. Creating a new brand begins with research and its first cycle with the consumer. Thereafter, the cycle begins again, this time focusing on monitoring research, as part of the control process to ensure that the brand continues to meet consumer's needs.

PRINCIPLES OF BRAND BUILDING:-

It is the brand which speaks of the product. The various principles of building a brand are:-

1. Choosing products with a meaning:-

The more ambitious the brand and its system of values, the greater the degree of care required in choosing the product or service to launch the brand campaign. This should centre on the product which best represents the brands intention - the one which best supports brand potential to bring about change.

2. Brand language and Role of Communication:-

Brand language allows the brand to hold forth more freely. All communication must express the products specific attributes - personality, culture and value and allow the brand to be presented in an appealing way. The brand language should be in a unified format in which to express themselves, different subsidiaries worldwide can adapt the theme of their message to the local market.

BRANDING STRATEGY:

A company has four choices when it comes to **brand strategy**. It can:

1) **Introduce line extensions:** Existing brand names are extended to new forms, sizes and flavors of an existing product category. A company might introduce line extensions as a low-cost, low-risk way of introducing new products in order to:
   a) Meet consumer desires for variety.
   b) Meet excess manufacturing capacity.
   c) Simply command more shelf space.

Risks include:

a) An overextended brand might lose its specific meaning.
b) Can cause consumer frustration or confusion.

2) **Introduce brand extensions:** Existing brand names are extended to new or modified product categories. Advantages include:
   a) Helps a company enter new product categories more easily.
   b) Aids in new product recognition.
   c) Saves on high advertising cost.

3) **Introduce multi-brands:** New brand names are introduced in the same product category.

Advantages include:

a) They gain more shelf space.
b) Offering several brands to capture "brand switchers." The company can establish flanker or fighter brands to protect its major brand.
c) It helps to develop healthy competition within the organization.

Drawbacks include:

a) Each brand may only obtain a small market share and be unprofitable.

4) Introduce new brands: New brand names in new categories are introduced.

Advantages include:

a) Helps move away from a brand that is failing.
b) Can get new brands in new categories by corporate acquisitions. Some companies are now pursuing mega brand strategies.

Drawbacks can include:

a) Spreading resources too thin.

Seven main factors in building successful brands (Figure 7.7)

1. Quality:

Quality is a vital ingredient of a good brand. Remember the "core benefits" the things consumers expect. These must be delivered well, consistently. The branded washing machine that leaks, or the training shoe that often falls apart when wet will never develop brand equity. Research confirms that, statistically, higher quality brands achieve a higher market share and higher profitability that their inferior competitors.

2. Positioning:

Positioning is about the position a brand occupies in a market in the minds of consumers. Strong brands have a clear, often unique position in the target market. Positioning can be achieved through several means, including brand name, image, service standards, product guarantees, packaging and the way in which it is delivered. In fact, successful positioning usually requires a combination of these things.

Figure 7.7 Seven main factors in building successful brands

3. Repositioning:

Repositioning occurs when a brand tries to change its market position to reflect a change in consumer's tastes. This is often required when a brand has become tired, perhaps because its original market has matured or has gone into decline.

4. Communications:

Communications also play a key role in building a successful brand. It suggested that brand positioning is essentially about customer perceptions with the objective to build a clearly defined position in the minds of the target audience. All elements of the promotional mix need to be used to develop and sustain customer perceptions. Initially, the challenge is to build awareness, then to develop the brand personality and reinforce the perception.

5. First-mover advantage:

Business strategists often talk about first-mover advantage. In terms of brand development, by "first-mover" they mean that it is possible for the first successful brand in a market to create a clear positioning in the minds of target customers before the competition enters the market. There is plenty of evidence to support this. Think of some leading consumer product brands like Gillette, Coca Cola and cello tape that, in many ways, defined the markets they operate in and continue to lead. However, being first into a market does not necessarily guarantee long-term success. Competitors drawn to the high growth and profit potential demonstrated by the "market-mover" will enter the market and copy the best elements of the leader's brand. A good example is the way that Body Shop developed the "ethical" personal care market but were soon facing stiff competition from the major high street cosmetics retailers.

6. Long Term Perspective:

This leads onto another important factor in brand-building: the need to invest in the brand over the long-term. Building customer awareness, communicating the brand's message and creating customer loyalty takes time. This means that management must "invest" in a brand, perhaps at the expense of short-term profitability.

7. Internal Marketing:

Finally, management should ensure that the brand is marketed "internally" as well as externally. By this we mean that the whole business should understand the brand values and positioning. This is particularly important in service businesses where a critical part of the brand value is the type and quality of service that a customer receives. Think of the brands that you value in the restaurant, hotel and retail sectors. It is likely that your favorite brands invest heavily in staff training so that the face-to-face contact that you have with the brand helps secure your loyalty.

CLOSING CASE

ICICI BANK -ITS CRM STRATEGIES

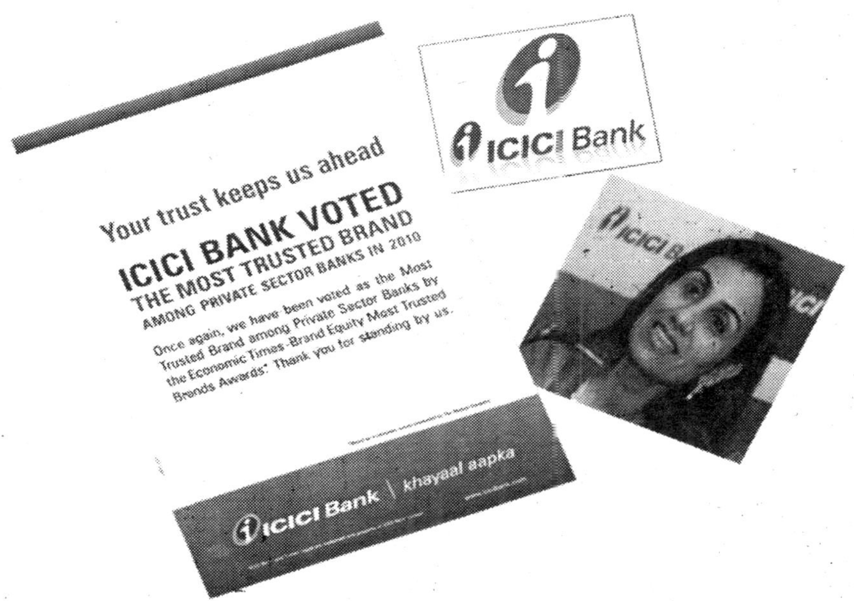

ICICI Bank began its retail operations in the mid nineties and as on March 31, 2007, had a total asset of about Rs. 3,446.58 billion (US$ 79 billion) as on March 31, 2007 and profit after tax of Rs. 25.40 x 109 (US$ 569 mn). It had built up a network of 614 branches (including extension counters) and over 2,200 ATMs. The services offered by the bank and its affiliates include financial services to corporate and retail customers in the areas of investment banking, life and non-life insurance, venture capital and asset management services. In terms of market capitalization, ICICI Bank is India's most valuable bank.

ICICI Bank has embarked on CRM with a cohesive and well-planned strategy. The noteworthy aspects of the CRM initiative include the following:

Multi-Channels

ICICI Bank has made concerted efforts at creating a number of channels to enable easy access for customers. Even at the pre-purchase stage, these channels can be used for getting information regarding the various products and services offered by the bank. The retail branches are open from 8 AM - 8 PM thereby enabling customers to visit the bank at their convenience (i.e., before or after office hours). Also, prospective customers can go to the nearest ATM and use the Hotline to speak to a representative of the bank. The customers can log onto the internet website www.icicibank.com which is fully functional and can be used for undertaking transactions. Apart from these, customers can use the

ATMs for transactions. The bank also offers phone banking and mobile banking. The phone banking facility can be used by customers to remain at home or office and undertake the transactions by having a representative of the bank come and visit them. Using the mobile phone, customers can find out critical about their account - such as being informed the moment a cheque gets cashed. ICICI Bank also enables customers to get in touch through email or through the 24 hour phone banking. By offering these multichannel, ICICI Bank ensures that customers can choose the most suitable and convenient way to reach the bank.

Cross-selling and Up-selling

ICICI Bank undertook data warehouse installation that focused on building a single customer view in the first phase. In the second phase, the objective was to use the information in understanding the customer using suitable tools. The system helped the bank to generate over 242,975 leads resulting in cross-selling leads as well. These leads have resulted in 24/5 of the bank's recent sales. Using the data warehouse, 300 marketing campaigns could be undertaken within one year. Personalization initiatives have been possible by scoring the transactions and extending overdraft limits on current accounts of good customers.

Business analytics have also been of use to banks in managing their credit card customers. Prior to using analytics, ICICI Bank offered all customers the same credit limit. Using analytics, the bank differentiated between customers and based on the low and medium risk profile of customers, the credit limits were suitably increased resulting in better matching of market averages.

Arresting Customer Churn

At ICICI Bank, the analytics involved reporting and analytical tools that offered standard and interactive reports, drill-down capabilities, cross-sell opportunities, channel usage by segment, etc. During the first year that the analytics were used, ICICI Bank has run over 40 cross-sell, up-sell and retention campaigns. The cross-selling campaigns enabled generating about 18-20% of the business from credit cards using analytics. This also helped in reducing customer acquisition costs despite the increasing competition.

Business analytics has also enabled banks to be alerted sufficiently in advance of customers who are at risk of cancelling their credit cards. The managers concerned can then prepare a strategy in retaining those customers that they deem worth keeping and reducing the probability of losing customers. ICICI Bank used past customer data to prepare a predictive model and assigning a score to each customer. The model made use of demographic and behavioral information. The outputs indicated the likelihood of a customer leaving in a certain time (for example 30, 60 or 90 days). The managers could then assign the required resources to ensure retention of the valuable customers. The scoring of customers was done on their likelihood of attrition. These scores were combined with the expected lifetime value of the customers and could be referred by the managers as a trade-off framework to help in negotiations with customers with regard to retention. The resources would be increased for customers who had maximum potential for profitability and were most likely to cancel the card.

Questions

1. Explain Cross-selling and Up-selling with reference to the above case.
2. "ICICI Bank has embarked on CRM with a cohesive and well-planned strategy" elucidate.
3. Read the case carefully and discuss about ICICI bank CRM strategies that made the most trusted bank among private sector banks in year 2010.

SUMMARY & KEY TERMS

Today's situation is where competitors use predatory pricing and heavy promotion to eliminate or undermine their rivals and this is nothing but the cutthroat competition. In this competitive environment the organizations are bound to adopt the strategic mode to be a leader in their segment. The concept of CRM i.e., Customer Relationship Management can be used as a result oriented tool to counter the pace of competition by the competitors. The process of personalization, individualization, anticipation and even prediction of the successful outcome of the customer's interactions with the business require companies to have as much up-to-date information as possible. In a challenging business climate and by the introduction of technological advancements the pressures of competitive and dynamic markets have contributed to the growth of CRM in almost all the sectors in general and major impact to banking, automobile hospitality sectors in particular.

Customer Relationship Management is the establishment, development, maintenance and optimization of long-term mutually valuable relationships between consumers and the organizations. Successful customer relationship management focuses on understanding the needs and desires of the customers and is achieved by placing these needs at the heart of the business by integrating them with the organization's strategy, people, technology and business processes. At the heart of a perfect CRM strategy is the creation of mutual value for all the parties involved in the business process. It is about creating a sustainable competitive advantage by being the best at understanding, communicating and delivering and developing existing customer relationships in addition to creating and keeping new customers. The growing pace of technology and that too the use of internet has revolutionized the business scenario. In a fraction of seconds heavy transactions crossing all the boundaries are taking place in this internet platform.

The companies developing the CRM strategies should also plan how the relationship can be extended to create more value through the loyal customers. Once a customer has exhibited loyalty the company can take this opportunity of making the customer an advocate. This should also benefit the customer financially or some other fashion.

A company's total marketing communications mix-also called its promotion mix consists of the specific blend of advertising, personal selling, sales promotion, public relations and direct marketing tools that the company uses to pursue its advertising and marketing objectives. The new technologies have encouraged more companies to move from mass communication to more targeted communication and one-to-one dialogue.

Effective communication means effective marketing. Buyers' perceptions of market offerings are influenced by the amount and type of information they receive as well as their reaction to that information.

One of the four major elements of the marketing mix is price. Pricing is an important strategic issue because it is related to product positioning. Furthermore, pricing affects other marketing mix elements such as product features, channel decisions and promotion. Price is the amount of money charged for product and service of the sum of the values that customer exchanges for the benefit of having or using the product or service. Price goes by many names such as rent, tuition fees, fare, rate, interest, toll, premium etc. Price is the only element in the marking mix that produces revenue, all other element represents costs. Price is also one of the most flexible elements in marketing mix.

Media advertising communicates information to a large number of recipients, paid for by a sponsor. It has three main aims:

1. To impart information
2. To develop attitudes
3. To induce action beneficial to the advertiser (generally the purchase of a product or service).

Advertising models have been drawn from several sources, particularly psychology, and from advertising practitioners in order to explain how advertising works. Colley's DAGMAR model in 1961 (Defining Advertising Goals for Measured Advertising Results) allows for the cumulative impact of advertisements and also maps out the states of mind consumers pass through: From unawareness to awareness; to comprehension; to conviction; to action.

A brand can be a name, a phrase, an image, a symbol or a combination of things that tend to identify the products or services of one company as unique or different from its competitors. A brand can represent something intangible about your company, your product or service. It can be a combination of feelings and perceptions about your name, image, quality, reputation and personality.

Building a powerful brand by using a consistent marketing strategy is absolutely essential to having a successful and profitable small business. A powerful brand identity can influence the customers to buy the product or service over the competitors, even if they have to pay more for it! A powerful brand can influence the customers to think that no one else, but you or your company, can deliver the quality or the benefits that they want.

KEY TERMS

- CRM- Customer Relationship Management.
- IMP-Industrial Marketing and Purchasing Group.
- VOIP-Voice over Internet Protocol.
- ABC-Activity Based Costing
- Personal selling
- Public relations
- Direct marketing
- Cost Based Pricing
- Skim pricing
- CALS- Computer Aided Logistics
- Loyal Advocates
- JIT-Just In Time
- ERP-Enterprise Resource Planning
- FMS- Flexible Manufacturing Systems
- HNIs-High Net Worth Individuals
- Advertising
- Sales promotion
- Marketing Communications
- Value based Pricing
- Sales promotion strategy

DISCUSSION QUESTIONS

1. Explain the Strategic orientation for CRM in view of extending the concept of relationship with the customers to create more values, also describe the strategic framework of CRM in detail.
2. Explain in detail the key generic CRM process

3. How the key customers are identified in CRM?
4. Explain the strategic framework for CRM.
5. Differentiate between traditional role and change role of the relationship manager.
6. What do you mean by pricing objectives? How status quo plays a vital role in pricing strategy?
7. Differentiate between skim pricing and penetration pricing.
8. Explain optimization of pricing in detail.
9. What are seven main factors in building successful brands?
10. Write short notes on:
    a. Fighter brands
    b. The Branding Cycle
    c. Branding decisions
    d. Telephone marketing
    e. Direct mail and direct marketing
11. Explain marketing communication mix for products and brands in detail.

Case Studies

Learning Objectives

This Chapter is focused on the following objectives:

Case Study- 1: eBay: "The world's largest online marketplace"

Case Study- 2: Competitive Strategies of a Market Leader- State Bank of India (SBI)

Case Study- 3: The Times of India vs Hindustan Times.

Case Study- 4: The Strategic Success story of Nirma

Case Study- 5: Bajaj Auto Limited - a strategic move.

Case Study- 6: The Health Drink War.

Case Study- 7: Kinetic Honda: The Breakup

CASE STUDY-01: EBAY: "THE WORLD'S LARGEST ONLINE MARKETPLACE"

eBay establishes itself as the "The world's Online Marketplace" .Coincidently, it is also the positioning statement of eBay, which itself means many things about the company's identity, it enables trade on local, national and international basis, with a diverse and passionate community of individuals and small businesses, eBay offers an online platform where millions of items are traded each day. According to company tradition, the idea for eBay came from founder Pierre Omidyar's wife, who wanted to trade Pez dispensers with other collectors over the Internet. In truth Omidyar had been pondering an Internet auction venture before he was ever aware of Pez mania. He says that he had been thinking about how to create an efficient marketplace-a level playing field, where everyone had access to the same information and could compete on the same terms as anyone else." After writing the code for the site, Omidyar launched eBay from his home in mid-1995.the concept of an Internet marketplace caught on so quickly that by the end of the year, eBay was getting a few thousand hits daily. Even more impressive the website was profitable from its inception. The objective at ebay was to develop the work ethics and culture of eBay as a fun, open and trusting environment and to keep the organization focused on the big picture objectives and key priorities. ebay went public in September 1998 at $18 a share. By early march 1999, the stock was trading approximately b$282 per share. The company market capitalization had surpassed that of even Amazon.com, making it the world's most valuable Internet retailer.

eBay's strategy

eBay community values are incredibly amazing since it focuses on trading millions of dollars on mere faith and trust among the community members. Its values can be sited as below,

"We believe people are basically good

We believe everyone has something to contribute

We believe that an honest, open environment can bring out the best in people.

We recognize and respect everyone as an individual.

We encourage you to treat others the way you want to be treated".

These community values mean that the entire strategy lies in "trust" to build e-loyalty, for long- term profitable relationships, these set of core values encourages open and honest communication between its members.

Corporate strategy

The whole foundation of eBay, lies on the idea that practically anything that can be bought and sold can be facilitated through this Internet retailer, and this auction platform provider was implementing the concept of e-commerce even more forcefully. "We help people trade practically anything on earth and conduct commerce through the Internet on a global basis" is certainly eBay's business model .This model was so effective and efficient in conducting transactions that more and more people preferred to trade online, so that they can enjoy the comfort at home or work-places and still buy things online just by the click of the mouse.

Today eBay users can bid anything from office equipments to real estate to cars. It is surprisingly true but perplexing that "Why has eBay prevailed, but others have failed?" Though many of its successes resulted from its adaptive approach, eBay's accomplishments can also be explained by the company's consistent focus on two long-term goals that is "becoming the world's largest consumer to consumer online auction house and building out each of the five core strategies". An analysis into these strategies reveal that eBay has applied sound strategic management as adopted from Porter and other Management experts. Its whole business revolves around creating an environment where everyone can come and transact without any second thought of being cheated or misguided in any form.

The first strategy is creating an insurmountable customer base, that is

(1) Establishing a larger user base : To attract new users, eBay established relationships with more than 60 websites, including America online which gave eBay the largest access to the largest user base on the internet and prevented AOL from entering the auction arena, bay also added dealer to person trading and addresses the fast growing and fragmented small business market by creating a feature called business exchange, where businesses could buy or sell new, used or refurbished business merchandise and professional tools in their local market.

The second strategy is:

(2) eBay concentrated on local and international trading: EBay has local sites in 53 U.S markets they deliver distinct regional flavors and give users the convenience of shopping locally for difficult -to ship items such as automobiles or antique furniture. The company also built a truly global presence with users in more than 150 nations.

The third strategy is:

(3) Creating a strong brand

For eBay's first few years it did not spend a single penny on marketing, relying instead on viral marketing and its ability to piggyback on competitors ceaseless (and expensive) efforts to retain market recognition. The company's brand building shifted though with the arrival of new top professionals.

The fourth strategy is:

(4) Broadening the trading platform

By 1999, eBay's fourth year, a host of competitors had entered the online auction market, while eBay had the first entry advantage, not all of its competitors were small start ups, some including yahoo and Amazon were internet significant players with extensive, established user bases. eBay's response was to extend its core business into other attractive niches, the company introduced higher priced product categories, a move that would increase its profit margin dramatically while requiring minimal infrastructure and operating expenditures. The only caveat was that the company needed to develop a new skill set-to overcome this obstacle. eBay made several acquisitions, starting with auction house Butterfield and Butterfield, the marriage of offline and online auction houses revolutionized the way that fine antiques and collectibles were bought and sold, allowing users to place real-time bids for items on offline auction house floors.

The fifth strategy is:

(5) Maintaining a strong community affinity

The company believes that fostering direct interaction between buyers and sellers with similar interest had enabled it to create loyal, active community of users, As noted earlier this emphasis on community building has been present since eBay's founding.

Applying the five external market tests

eBay can be understood to a common man who is not aware of online retailing and sites which provide such facilitaies, which could be some of the market test like Inimitability: is the resource hard to copy eBay's resource could easily be copied

Durability: how quickly does the resource depreciate? eBay is immersed in a very dynamic environment, thus the evolution and up gradation of its resources are crucial.

Appropriateness: who captures the value that the resource creates eBay certainly holds the most valuable resource for auction-like sites: critical mass, the company extracts profits from its community, making it one of a handful of profitable Internet companies.

Substitutability: can a unique resource be trumped by a different resource? A different format of seller/buyer transaction could undermine eBay's successful model-if eBay is not able to adapt quickly to the changing environment, which is unlikely. Auction aggregators also pose a significant threat.

Competitive superiority: whose resource is really better. eBay has improved substantially in terms of committing internal resources to improving customer experience. Other sites such as yahoo or Amazon, might still have better services, but eBay has the first mover advantage, and it has one resource in particular that cannot be replaced: a large and loyal community. SWOT Analysis of eBay is carried out to get onto the finer and intricate details that eBay has adopted in such a shorter span of time to achieve profits in millions and is able to maintain a customer base that is again unbelievable.

The strengths of eBay could be identified like:

eBay is the leading global brand for online auctions. The company is a giant marketplace used by more than 100 million people to buy and sell all manner of things to each other. Pierre Omidyar, a French entrepreneur, was just 28 when he sat down over a long holiday weekend to write the original computer code for what eventually became an Internet megabrand. The brand has grown tremendously over the decade or so since its inception.

The company exploits the benefits of Customer Relationship Management (CRM). Buyers and sellers register with the company and data is collected by eBay on individuals. This is the Business-to- Consumer (B2C) side of their business. However the strong customer relationships are founded on a Consumer-to-Consumer (C2C) business model, where strong interrelationships occur, for example where buyers and sellers leave feedback for each other and whereby awards are given to the most genuine of eBayers.

The term 'eBay' has become a generic term for online auctions. Other companies with such a strong position include Hoover for vacuum cleaners and Google for search engines. Today it is common to hear that someone is 'ebaying' or is an 'eBayer,' or that someone is going 'to eBay.'

Weaknesses of eBay were as below:

The organizations work tremendously hard to overcome fraud. However, the eBay model does leave itself open to a number of fraudulent activities. Often the company deals with such activities very quickly. Fraud includes counterfeit goods being marketed to unsuspecting (and suspecting!) eBayers. Other forms of theft could include the redistribution of stolen goods. It should be pointed out that fraud and theft are problems with individuals, not eBay. The weakness is that unscrupulous individuals can exploit the C2C business model. As with many technology companies, systems breakdowns could disturb the trading activities of eBay. In the past both eBay and its payment brand Pay pal have encountered shutdowns and outages. As technology improves such a weakness is less and less of an issue. Opportunities that eBay had were tremendous and invincible. They are: Acquisitions provide new business strategy opportunities. eBay's latest venture is it has agreed to buy online telephone company Skype Technologies in a deal reported to be worth $2.6 billion. Skype's software lets PC users talk to each other for free and make cut-price calls to mobiles and landlines. eBay has been buying up firms - including payment system PayPal - in an effort to increase the number of services it offers to consumers and keep its profits growing. New and emerging markets provide opportunities (Market Development).

Countries include China and India. There, consumers are becoming richer and have more leisure time than previous generations. Aspirating consumers are growing segments in many developing nations. There are also still opportunities in current markets (Market Penetration). Western Europe and the USA still have many potential consumers that have yet to discover the benefits of online auctions. Remember products have life cycles that eventually come to an end, and such products are ideal for selling and buying on eBay. Even a mammoth organization like eBay faces threats, which can be like as below: As with many of the global Internet brands, success attracts competition. International competitors competing in their domestic markets may have the cultural experience that could give them a competitive advantage over eBay. In fact eBay has found that it has met with other USA- based Internet companies when trading overseas. For example, Yahoo! Dominates the Japanese market.

Attack by illegal practices is a threat. As with weaknesses above, the brand is attacked by unscrupulous individuals. For example e-mails are sent to unsuspecting eBayers pretending to come from eBay. Logos and the design of the pages look authentic. However they are designed so that you input private information that the thieves can use to take passwords and identifications. -

So beware!

Some costs cannot be controlled by eBay. For example delivery charges and credit card charges. If fuel prices were to rise, the cost is passed on to the consumer in terms of delivery and postal fees. This could make the overall cost of an auctioned item too expensive. Similarly, if a credit card company such as Visa or Mastercard imposed a charge for online transaction, the total cost of the same items would increase with similar consequences.

Today, the eBay community includes more than a hundred million registered members from around the world. People spend more time on eBay than any other online site, making it the most popular shopping destination on the Internet.

Questions:

1. Evaluate the above case from strategic viewpoint.
2. Identify the SWOT factors mentioned in the above case and frame it in your own thought.
3. Conduct the value chain analysis to examine the development of competitive advantage for the above case.
4. Based on the five external market tests address the criticisms about these tests.
5. Analyze the five strategies given in the above case that has given a competitive advantage over other online marketing sites.

❖ ❖ ❖

CASE STUDY- 02: COMPETITIVE STRATEGIES OF A MARKET LEADER- STATE BANK OF INDIA (SBI)

State Bank of India (SBI) is the largest nationalized commercial bank in India in terms of assets, number of branches, deposits, profits and workforce. With the liberalization of the Indian banking industry in the mid-1990s, SBI faced stiff competition from the private sector and foreign banks which resulted in significant loss of its market share.

In March 2003, State Bank of India (SBI) and its associate banks had 13,579 branches, one of the largest branch networks for any bank in the world. It played a key role in providing working capital finance and term loans to Indian industry. In 2003, SBI had eight business units - corporate banking, international banking and domestic banking for concentrating on core business areas; associate banks unit for looking after these banks, credit division unit to monitor overall credit and three other business units including finance, corporate development and inspection for in-house work.

SBI was the largest commercial bank in India in terms of revenues, assets, deposits, branches and workforce. Since the late 1990s, SBI had been losing market share in the Indian banking industry due to the tough competition from private sector banks. By adopting modern technology and offering superior customer service, the private sector banks gained a significant share in urban banking. Expressing concern over this trend, in an interview to the Asian Banking Journal, AK Purwar, SBI's Chairman and Managing Director since November 2002, said, "The top most priority for the bank has been retention of market share. As a PSU bank, SBI was losing its market share. Although it was at a very slow pace, it was definitely losing its market share."To regain lost ground, SBI initiated a major internal restructuring exercise. The bank responded to competition by taking several measures including offering an array of new products and services, forging alliances with other business entities, entering new areas of business and adopting novel ways of reaching out to customers and providing them value-added services.

The origin of SBI dates back to the early 19th century, when the Bank of Calcutta was established in Calcutta (present day Kolkata in the state of West Bengal) in June 1806 under the aegis of the Government of Bengal. Three years after its inception, the bank was renamed Bank of Bengal on receiving its charter. It was a unique banking institution as it was the first joint-stock bank in British India. Next came, the Bank of Bombay in April 1840 followed by the Bank of Madras on July 1843. By 1876, the three presidency banks, together with their branches, agencies and sub-agencies, covered major inland trade centers in India. Bank of Bengal had 18 branches while the other two had 15 branches each. Initially, the business of these banks was restricted to discounting bills of exchange or other negotiable private securities, keeping cash accounts and receiving deposits and issuing and circulating cash notes. The last quarter of the 19th century witnessed rapid commercialization in India owing to the expansion of the railway network, to cover all major geographic regions of the country.

The three presidency banks were both beneficiaries and promoters of this commercialization process as they became involved in the financing of practically every trading, manufacturing and mining activity in the Indian sub-continent.The three presidency banks were amalgamated in January 1921 to form the Imperial Bank of India. The new bank performed the triple role of a commercial bank, a banker's bank and a banker to the government.

However, the quasi-central bank role performed by the Imperial Bank ended with the formation of the Reserve Bank of India (RBI) as the central bank of India in 1935. RBI's establishment was a catalyst in the conversion of the Imperial Bank into a purely commercial bank. At the time of Independence in 1947, the Imperial Bank had acquired a paramount position in the country's banking industry. It had a capital base of Rs.118.5 mn, deposits of Rs. 2.7514 bn and advances of Rs. 729.4 million. It had a network of 172 branches and over 200 sub-offices spread all over India. When the first Five Year Plan was launched in 1951, the rural sector was given top priority.

The Imperial Bank and other commercial banks too operated mainly in urban areas and had not yet penetrated the rural sector. To overcome this lacuna, it was recommended that a state-partnered and state-sponsored bank be created to take over the Imperial Bank and integrate the former state-owned or state-associated banks with it.Private sector banks made their first appearance in January 1993. During that period, PSBs accounted for over three-fourths of total banking industry assets. They were weighed down with huge NPAs(Non-Performing Assets), falling revenues, lack of modern technology and a massive and highly unionized workforce. New entrants began to erode the market share of the nationalized banks, especially in metro cities and urban areas. The PSBs found it increasingly difficult to compete with the new private sector banks and the foreign banks. These banks also employed state-of-the-art technology, which helped them to save on manpower costs and concentrate on providing better service.

To overcome the intense competition from private and foreign banks, SBI planned a major organizational restructuring exercise. The key aspects involved redesigning of branches, providing alternate channels; focus on a lean structure and technological up-gradation. A business process reengineering (BPR) team was constituted in June 2003 with McKinsey & Company as consultants. The BPR's basic goal was to create an operating architecture that would facilitate service delivery of international standards. The project objectives were defined as "increasing customer satisfaction and convenience, freeing up time for branch manager and branch staff to focus on sales and marketing, simplifying process for employees, enhancing SBI's competitiveness in the market, increasing the profitability through higher market share and improved process efficiency

Apart from restructuring, SBI launched several innovative, value-added products and services to project a customer friendly image. It launched a special service for corporate customers called 'tele-banking and remote login' to support transactional requests.

This facility would be available at 593 branches, and remote login at 269 branches. The bank's trade finance solution, called EXIMBILLS, was intended to handle trade finance transactions efficiently and enhance the range of services provided to corporates and network branches. In March 2004, SBI announced that it would introduce 'anywhere banking' facility for its customers from over 9000 branches across India in the next two years. All branches in Mumbai would provide this facility by December 2004. SBI also launched different customized loan programs to cater to various sections of society depending on income levels and repayment capabilities. Interest rates and repayment periods were tailor-made to suit the customer groups. To boost its business, SBI entered into several alliances and tie-ups with automobile, insurance, mutual fund, project finance and medical equipment companies.

Unlike other competitors that relied on reduced interest rates to get business, SBI extended the tenure of car loans from five to seven years, thereby lowering the monthly debt repayment burden of the loan seeker. SBI entered into a tie-up with Maruti, the largest automobile manufacturer in India, to provide loans for purchase of Maruti cars at the rate of 10.05 per cent and 11.25 per cent for three years and above three years respectively. After the scheme was introduced, SBI emerged as the largest financier for Maruti cars in India and the number of Maruti vehicles financed grew by 17 per cent in the fiscal 2003-04 over fiscal 2002-03

SBI carried out various marketing initiatives to enhance its reach. They included segregating and targeting existing high value customers, cross sales of other products, setting up call centers and outbound sales force to secure new customers. Plans were also made to utilize database marketing to pursue large and medium sized corporates, government and trade finance customers. Database marketing was expected to draw increased revenue from cross selling, lower costs and increased customer loyalty. SBI also introduced various other ways of reaching out to customers like extension of hours of work and aggressive marketing through print and television media. SBI increased daily working hours by two hours and Sunday banking was introduced.SBI's restructuring exercise and growth strategies resulted in an increase in profit.

Questions:

1. What are the strategies adopted by a market leader in the banking industry to retain its market share.
2. Explore the reasons how a market leader can lose its market share significantly.

3. Examine and analyze the key elements of the restructuring exercise undertaken by SBI.
4. Study the marketing initiatives adopted by SBI to reposition itself as a customer-oriented bank.
5. Examine the challenges that can be faced by a market leader due to the changes in the industry structure.
6. Study and analyze the structure of the Indian banking industry.

CASE STUDY- 03: THE TIMES OF INDIA VS HINDUSTAN TIMES

The fierce competition in Delhi and northern India between two major publishing houses - Hindustan Times and Times of India on the aggressive pricing strategies adopted by the companies to counter each other. However, to gain a bigger share, Hindustan Times' vice chairperson Shobhana Bhartia chalked out a restructuring plan with an investment of Rs.4 billion.

Newspaper companies in India came to be projected as public service institutions after independence. However, in the late 1980s, they became just another fast moving consumer commodity. The companies started aggressive marketing and promotional strategies to increase circulation and readership. The industry witnessed tough competition both regionally and nationally. In 1999, the top 10 newspapers accounted for about 90% of the readership and the top two made 90% of the profits. There was fierce competition for the advertising rupees By late 1990s, electronic media like television had made a dent into the print media revenues. Print media was facing a squeeze due to the increasing popularity of television-initially color television and then satellite television. The ad market worth about Rs.90 billion slowed down and newspapers saw a steady decline in advertising share - from about 75% in 1995 to almost 50% in 2000. Newsprint costs too spiraled. The companies survived by increasing the ad rates every year. However, analysts felt that newspapers could not survive for long by increasing advertising rates. In 2001, the print industry was expected to see a negative growth in revenues for the first time. The early 1990s saw HT and ToI engaged in a bitter battle for supremacy in Delhi, which is perceived to be the most important market in India. In 1991, ToI had a circulation of around 70,000 in Delhi as against 0.35 million for HT. In 1994, ToI slashed its price from Rs.2.30 to Rs.1.50. By 1998, the difference in circulation figures narrowed down to a few thousand copies. Since 1991, ToI's circulation has increased in percentage terms more than HT. Analysts felt that ToI increased its share largely by breaking into HT's readership. A fresh round of price-cuts began in 1999. On March 19, 1999, HT cut its price from Rs.1.50 to an all-time low of Re. 1 on all days except Sundays.

From a strong one-city brand in the early 1990s, ToI emerged as the only national newspaper with a circulation of 1.7 million all over the country by 2000. HT with a circulation of about 0.9 million in Delhi was still restricted to Northern India. With revenues of Rs.4.05 billion during 2000-01,HT's share was roughly a third of ToI in revenue. (Refer Exhibit I) To strengthen its presence in Delhi as well as to expand nationally, Shobhana Bhartia initiated a major restructuring plan in 2000-01. (Refer Exhibit II) As a first step towards realization of the plan, in September 2000, Vir Sanghvi was appointed editor of HT. Rajan Kohli, of Fujitsu-ICIM was brought in as the executive president to head a new team of 20, which redesigned the paper and made it more youthful. Five new supplements were introduced, and new editions were launched in nine cities in India. HT followed the ToI style of marketing blitzkrieg: events, promotions and ad campaigns.

Questions:

1. Analyze the Competition between Hindustan Times and Times of India
2. Evaluate the Pricing strategies of the two companies.
3. Evaluate the Restructuring plan for Hindustan Times
4. Understand and analyze the strategies of the two newspaper companies.
5. Analyze whether Hindustan Times should counter Times of India in Mumbai, Chennai and other cities or stick to northern India

CASE STUDY- 04: THE STRATEGIC SUCCESS STORY OF NIRMA

In 1969, Karsanbhai Patel (Patel), a chemist at the Gujarat Government's Department of Mining and Geology manufactured phosphate free Synthetic Detergent Powder and started selling it locally. The new yellow powder was priced at Rs. 3.50 per kg, at a time when HLL's Surf was priced at Rs 15. Soon, there was a huge demand for Nirma in Kishnapur (Gujarat), Patel's hometown. The use of detergent powder was pioneered in India by HLL's Surf in 1959. But by the 1970s, Nirma dominated the detergent powder market, simply by making the product available at an affordable price. Nirma carved a niche for itself in the highly competitive detergents and toilet soaps market in India.

Within a short span, Nirma had completely rewritten the rules of the game, by offering good quality products at an unbeatably low price. Nirma's success was attributed to its focus on cost effectiveness. Nirma also had innovative marketing strategies. In the mid-nineties, Nirma successfully extended its brand to other product categories like premium detergents (Nirma Super Washing Powder and Detergent Cake), premium toilet soaps (Nirma Premium, Nima Sandal, Nirma Lime Fresh).

Though Nirma was better known as a producer of low-cost economy range of products, it was successful in the middle- and up-market segments. But at the same time, competition was also increasing. While HLL continued to be a major competition, P&G and Henkel SPIC also adopted aggressive measures. Players from unorganized sector were also adding to the competition in the detergents and washing powder industry.

Question:

Understand and analyze the various factors that attributed to the success of Nirma.

CASE STUDY- 05: BAJAJ AUTO LIMITED - A STRATEGIC MOVE.

On July 18, 2009, India-based Bajaj Auto Limited (Bajaj Auto), a leading manufacturer of two wheelers and three wheelers, launched the 100 cc Discover DTS-Si motorcycle. The new product had several unique features such as a Digital Twin Spark-Swirl Induction (DTS-Si) engine, nitrox suspension, the longest wheelbase in the 100 cc segment, a 5 speed gear - the first in the 100 cc segment and a maintenance free battery. Commenting on the new product, Rajiv Bajaj (Rajiv), Managing Director, Bajaj Auto, said, "We are launching a bike which is not seen as a 100 cc bike and we wish to offer it to people who typically buy 100cc motorcycles but would like to upgrade.

For Bajaj Auto, the launch of the 100 cc Discover DTS-Si motorcycle served as a point of re-entry into the entry segment3 of the motorcycle market. The company had reduced its focus on the entry segment motorcycles three years earlier, citing low operating margins, even though the entry segment motorcycles accounted for about 50 percent of the company's total sales volumes in 2006. Commenting on the launch of the new product and the renewed focus on the 100 cc motorcycle segment, Rajiv said, "We are not changing our strategy. The 100 cc market has got numbers. All we wanted to do was give the commuter a choice, more value for money. We have no choice but to have substantial share here.

Bajaj Auto, which had been selling two wheelers in India since 1945, was the market leader in the Indian two wheeler industry till the 1990s, riding on the success of its popular scooter models. The history of the Indian two wheeler industry can be traced back to the mid-1900s. In 1952, Enfield India Limited (Enfield) started manufacturing motorcycles. In 1955, Automotive Products of India (API) began manufacturing scooters in the country. In the 1950s, two other companies, Ideal Jawa (India) Limited (Ideal Jawa) and Escorts India Limited (Escorts) also entered the motorcycle segment. Enfield, which initially imported the Bullet, a 350 cc motorcycle from the United Kingdom (UK), started producing it in India in 1956. Ideal Jawa and Escorts sold motorcycles under the brand names, Yezdi and Rajdoot. In 1971-72, the motorcycle segment held a 36 percent share of the total two wheeler sales

The company faced hardly any significant competition during that time, but this worked against the company. It grew complacent, with the result that it failed to realize the structural shift in demand towards motorcycles among Indian consumers.The history of Bajaj Auto dates back to the early 1900s. In 1930, the Bajaj Group was formed by Jamnalal Bajaj (Jamnalal). In 1945, Kamalnayan Bajaj, Jamnalal's elder son, established Bachraj Trading Corporation Limited (BTCL) to import and sell two and three wheelers in India. Till 1959, BTCL was importing two and three wheelers from Italy and selling them in India. In 1959, the company got a licence to manufacture scooters in India

In late 2001, Bajaj Auto started a new advertising campaign to change its image of being only a scooter manufacturer. In the advertisements, Bajaj Auto showed motorcycles instead of scooters as part of a conscious effort to change the company's image. The advertisements showed 'slice of life' situations of 'new age India'

According to industry experts, Bajaj Auto, in spite of being the oldest manufacturer of two wheelers in India, was not proactive enough to visualize the structural demographic changes happening in India. Till the late 1990s, it was the market leader in the two wheeler industry. However, it did not upgrade its scooter models, nor did it introduce new motorcycle models. Despite the opening up of the Indian economy and foreign players coming in with their innovative technology, it continued to rely on its old scooter models. However, with the competition growing, it was forced to focus on the motorcycle segment.

In the first quarter of the financial year 2009-10, the motorcycle unit sales of Bajaj Auto declined by 14 percent compared to the corresponding quarter of the previous year. However, the revenue sales figure grew by 29 percent compared to the fourth quarter of 2008-09. The company attributed this success to the launch of the XCD 135 DTS-Si, the new Pulsar 150 DTS-Si and the Pulsar 180 DTS-Si since February 2009.

Questions:

1. Analyze the structural changes happening in the Indian two wheeler industry in the 1990s and early 2000s and its implications.
2. Examine the growth strategy of Bajaj Auto over the decades.
3. Study the transformation process initiated by Bajaj Auto and its impact.
4. Analyze the shortcomings in the business strategy of Bajaj Auto.

CASE STUDY- 06: THE HEALTH DRINK WAR.

In late 2008, a legal battle broke out between GlaxoSmithKline Consumer Healthcare (GSK) and Heinz India (Heinz) over the advertisements of their respective health drinks Horlicks and Complan. The advertisements talked about how their respective brand was better than the other and showed the competitor's product in bad light when compared to the company's products. In September 2008, Heinz moved the Bombay High Court , objecting to advertisements of Horlicks which highlighted the nutritional content and price gap between the two brands and showed Horlicks as a better and more inexpensive health drink than Complan. The advertisement showed the competitor brand clearly while making the comparison. Heinz later followed up with its own ad comparing Horlicks unfavorably with Complan. This prompted GSK to file a case in the Delhi High Court. In December 2008 claiming that the ad released by Heinz disparaged its brand by calling it low priced and thereby damaging its reputation. Horlicks and Complan were popular health drinks in Indian households. The estimated Rs.18 billion health drinks market in India was growing at an annual rate of 20% as per AC Nielsen data. As of 2008, GSK was the market leader in the health drink category in India with a share of 55%, while Complan's market share was about 14%. The ongoing war for supremacy between these two brands in the Indian health drink market started as early as in the 1960s. According to analysts, the latest round in the health drink war was initiated by the makers of Horlicks; the makers of Complan retaliated.

About Horlicks

Horlicks was invented by William Horlick (William) and his brother James Horlick (James) (1844-1921) in 1873. The brothers belonged to Gloucestershire, England. James was a chemist and worked for a company which made dried baby food.

About Complan

Complan, owned by the Heinz Company, was one of the most popular health drinks in India. The name Complan was coined from the words "COMplete" and "PLANned". Complan was introduced by Glaxo Laboratories (Glaxo) in the UK during World War II (1939-1945), as an essential nutritional supplement for soldiers at the frontlines.

According to analysts, until the 1990s, Horlicks was the more aggressive player in the health drink market compared to Complan. While Horlicks introduced a series of variants aimed at the family segment and promoted its products well, Complan lay low on the promotional front, with its ads just focusing on the "extra growth" attribute.

Experts felt that in their quest to outdo their rivals, advertisers resort to comparative advertising and at times ends up denigrating the competitor brand. Some analysts felt that companies resorted to comparative advertising to gain publicity and to increase sales. Though both the companies backed their claims with scientific research data, they were still locked in a legal battle. Issues of disparaging ads by rival companies were often resolved by the ASCI. But with constant mudslinging at each other, the two companies decided to battle it out in the courts instead.

Questions:

1. Analyze the advertising strategies adopted by Complan and Horlicks over the years.
2. Analyze the issues and challenges faced by companies while using comparative advertising.
3. Examine the efficacy of comparative advertising in enhancing brand image and sales.
4. Study the implications of the advertising war between Complan and Horlicks.
5. Discuss and debate the legal/ethical issues involved in the case.

CASE STUDY- 7: KINETIC HONDA: THE BREAKUP.

It was in August 1998 that the first chinks in the Kinetic Honda Motors Ltd. (Kinetic Honda) armor were reported by Business India. Both Honda and the Firodias of Kinetic were quick to deny rumors of a split, though reports of the Firodias quietly raising resources to buy out Honda's stake kept surfacing. The Firodias were even reported to have securitized the assets of their two-wheeler finance company - 20th Century Kinetic Finance (TCKF) - to raise this money. Trouble had been brewing since the company recorded a loss of Rs. 6 crore in the first quarter of 1998. Eventually Honda decided to put the matter to rest and called Arun Firodia (Firodia) to Japan in December 1998.

Honda made Firodia an offer - either he buy their 51% stake or Honda would buy out his 19% stake. Analysts remarked that it was difficult for Firodia to let go of the company that he had nurtured for the best part of his life. Eventually, Firodia negotiated a deal with Honda, to acquire its stake at Rs 45 per share, (when the market price was almost double), at a total cost of Rs 35 crore. He also signed an agreement with them for continuing to manufacture and sell the existing Kinetic Honda models. Honda also agreed to continue providing technical know-how support in return for royalty and technical fees from Kinetic.

Considering the fact that Honda was the world's biggest and most successful scooter manufacturer, the pullout came as a surprise to industry observers, as it was quite uncharacteristic of Honda Motor to give up a segment. More so, as just a couple of months earlier, Honda had been reported to be planning to make further investments in Kinetic Honda. This was seen as a major setback for the company. It was also perhaps the only instance of a Honda failure anywhere in the world.

In 2001, the Kinetic Group had two automobile companies - Kinetic Engineering Ltd and Kinetic Motor Company Ltd. After the December 1998 deal, Kinetic Honda Motor Ltd was renamed Kinetic Motor Company Ltd. Kinetic's story began in 1972 with the founder H.K.Firodia buying the 'Luna' moped's design from a foreign company. The moped, which aimed at capturing the bicycle market, went on to become such a huge success, that Luna became a generic name for mopeds.

In 1985, under Arun Firodia's (H.K.Firodia's son) leadership, Kinetic tied up with Japanese auto major Honda Motor to form Kinetic Honda Motors Ltd. (KHML) with both the partners holding an equal stake of 28.56%. The company's primary business was manufacturing scooters. Sales of spare parts formed a minor part of the turnover. The 'KH-100,' the first ungeared scooter in India, proved to be a huge success in the initial stages.

Throughout the 1980s, Kinetic remained India's largest moped manufacturer with a 44% market share and a 15% share of the overall two-wheeler market. A decade later, the company's moped market share halved to 22% and the overall market share figure reached an abysmal 5%. Also, in 1991, Kinetic, with a turnover of Rs 121 crore, was competing on an equal turf with the Rs 140 crore TVS Suzuki and the Rs 150 crore Hero Honda. But by 1999, while TVS and Hero Honda grew seven times over to Rs 1,018 crore and Rs 1,146 crore respectively, Kinetic just managed to double its turnover.

A major reason for this was the fact that Kinetic seemed to have missed the pulse of the market, which was fast moving towards motorcycles. Kinetic had no motorcycles to offer - mainly due to the Honda joint venture stipulations. (Kinetic could not make motorcycles because that meant competing with Hero Honda.) Kinetic's financial position also took a beating in the late 1990s. While sales grew slowly, compared to its competitors, its operating margin was the lowest in the industry because of the high import content of raw materials. Kinetic also had to shelve its plans to launch a small, 500cc, 2-cylinder car after a substantial sum was spent on the project.

With Kinetic Honda's fortunes declining, Firodia agreed to let Honda increase its stake to 51% in 1993, perhaps hoping that if Honda were in control, it would bring in new products more quickly and thereby improve the company's prospects. But Firodia soon realized that this was not to be. At a time when its competitors were spending 1-1.5% of the turnover on R&D, Kinetic Honda did not move beyond 0.31%. On advertising, Honda spent just Rs 20 crore during 1993-98. As a result, Kinetic Honda's market share declined steadily during 1996-98.

In 1997-98, Kinetic Honda's sales grew marginally to Rs 353 crore over the previous year, but profit after tax dipped to Rs 2.16 crore from Rs 2.30 crore. This, coupled with the Rs 6 crore loss for the first quarter of 1998 made the Firodias give serious thought to parting ways with Honda. Firodia said, "There was no growth, so we decided to review the contract." The new agreement involving the Honda stake sell-off and the technical collaboration arrangement was signed after this. Commenting on this, Firodia claimed, "It's a win-win scheme for everybody."

Though Firodia claimed that Honda's equity sale decision was taken jointly by both partners, media reports had a different story to tell.Reports claimed that right from the beginning there had been differences between Honda and the Firodias over the issue of management of Kinetic Honda. Firodia admitted that there were serious differences over issues like introduction of new models, advertising expenditure, marketing strategies, etc., As a result, the company suffered in terms of growth and profitability.

Under the joint venture agreement, Kinetic Honda manufactured scooters and Kinetic Engineering made mopeds. Both of them could not manufacture each other's products or motorcycles. Because Honda was present in the motorcycle segment with Hero Honda, the Kinetic group remained in mopeds and scooters. This was not in favor of Kinetic because the moped market had declined considerably during the 1990s. Kinetic had ambitions of becoming a full range two-wheeler company as it was strong in operations and also had a large distribution network.

When Kinetic developed indigenous technology for its four-stroke step-through vehicle K400, a competitor to Hero Honda's Street model, Honda saw it as an unfriendly move.

The Firodias were unhappy about the fact that 'Kinetic,' as an umbrella brand was not being promoted. Consumers associated the name Kinetic with scooters and 'Luna' with mopeds, but did not see them as belonging to the same business house. To support the Kinetic brand as an umbrella brand with a number of products under it, the Firodias wanted to advertise heavily and bring out new products. According to Sulajja , "The tie-up with Honda was limiting our competitive capabilities."

Kinetic Honda insiders claimed that Honda had always taken a 'half-hearted approach' towards managing the company. They also said that Honda was too preoccupied with other markets such as Indonesia and Thailand which were growing much faster and where, unlike in India, Honda was doing well. Also, Honda's margins were much higher in these markets - even a 50cc Honda scooter cost more in other parts of the world than the lead model being sold in India. Yet, Honda scooters were considered expensive in India. Industry watchers pointed out that Honda, with all its resources, could have easily engineered a product for the Indian roads, but was simply not interested.

Honda claimed that it had decided to position itself as a niche player at the upper end of the segment and that segment did not grow as much as the company had anticipated. Company sources said, "We miscalculated the purchasing power of the Indian middle class. We thought it would go up, but it didn't. Instead, the economy went into a tailspin and we couldn't grow." However, Honda admitted that having just a single model for several years had worked to the company's disadvantage. But the investment required to develop and introduce new models was very high, rendering the end product uncompetitive and hence an unattractive proposition. Honda claimed that the Firodias did not have the marketing acumen of the Munjals of Hero Honda. Disagreements over advertising expenditure and the interference of the Firodias in the appointment of dealers widened the rift between the partners.

Kinetic wanted Honda to increase the advertising expenditure, but Honda did not agree. Being a large organization with various decision-making layers, Honda wasn't quick enough to react to the demands of the marketplace. The joint managing director, a Honda nominee, was changed every three years. Thus, by the time he understood the demands of the marketplace, it was time for him to be replaced.

Unlike the Hero Honda venture, where the Munjals and Honda showed complete faith in each other and worked together as a team right from the beginning, the Firodias and Honda reportedly never shared a good rapport. In Hero Honda, the partners had equal stakes and this made decision-making easier. Moreover, because of lack of competition for a long time, things were easier for Hero Honda. But Kinetic Honda had to compete with a giant like Bajaj. Also, while the cost of making the Kinetic scooter was higher than the cost of manufacturing a motorcycle, the selling price of the latter was Rs 10,000 more. The profitability of Hero Honda, therefore, was much more and they could afford to spend more on advertising. Also, the Munjals could take their own decisions regarding adspend. Firodia said, "If we could have done the same, it would definitely have increased Kinetic's visibility and volumes would have grown faster." Honda's exit raised questions about Kinetic's survival. It was thought that the Rs 35 crore the Firodias paid for acquiring the entire stake would put a great strain on their finances and weaken the company. Analysts were quick to comment that Kinetic would have problems regarding the development and induction of new products. Honda's technical support limited to the existing range of products. And as the existing products - Kinetic Honda and Marvel - were not doing very well at that time, the withdrawal was seen as an unwelcome development.

Firodia denied that the dropping of the Honda tag from its scooters would affect the sales. The company introduced tough measures to facilitate improvements on various fronts including input costs, asset management and inventory management. Kinetic realized that gaining customer and dealer confidence would be a key task if it wanted to survive without Honda. Kinetic told its dealers about its product plans for 1999-2001 and tried to convey to them that now on they would be selling not just Kinetic Honda scooters, but promoting the umbrella 'Kinetic' brand. This meant that they would also be selling mopeds and motorcycles. This in turn, meant higher volumes and, thus, higher profits in the coming years. Kinetic conducted training programs for its dealers to help them deal with customers in a better manner. On the distribution front, Kinetic gave its dealers full range or 'pavilion' dealership. A new Kinetic logo was adopted to give the company a new corporate identity.

However, after the breakup, Firodia's immediate strategy was to push up sales by getting the group's auto-finance companies - Kinetic Leasing & Finance Ltd. (KLFL), Kinetic Fincap and Kinetic Capital Finance (later merged with Kinetic Fincap) - to offer attractive finance schemes. Those finance companies were strategically located to service the three biggest markets for two-wheelers in India - north, west and south. They offered a wide range of finance schemes (termed as Wonder Loans) to suit various customer needs. The move paid rich dividends as sales picked up considerably. Kinetic Fincap and Kinetic Leasing & Fincap contributed 20% of Kinetic Honda's sales in 1999. Kinetic called dealer meetings in all regions of the country to assure them of the company's strong prospects even after Honda's departure, which had a very positive feedback. Kinetic also stepped up promotion of the Kinetic brand, using both television and newspaper ad campaigns. A considerable amount was spent on an image-building campaign for the group. Adspend was increased from Rs.12 crore in 1997-98 to Rs.20 crore in 1998-99. A new public awareness campaign on road safety was launched. The company set up a direct sales division as well, which had 50 teams of people going from shop to shop and door to door, informing people about the company's products and the finance schemes offered. The response was overwhelming and around 12% of the sales came from this division in 1999. A survey conducted across nine cities showed that Kinetic had maintained its hold, despite Honda's exit.

On the customer front, Kinetic launched a new, aggressive and consumer-focused marketing strategy, with the new motto 'Closer to You.' The group launched 'Kinetic Care,' a package of post-sale and post-warranty benefits for the consumers. Several 'Kinetic Mileage Advantage' service camps were held across the country where more than 25,000 scooters were tuned for optimal mileage free of cost. Scooter service campaigns were organized, where spares and lubricants were offered at a discount and labor charges for replacing these spares were waived. For popularizing the K4-100, 'Customer Satisfaction' camps were organized across the country. These were attended by over 18,000 customers, who got free spare parts even though the warranty period had lapsed.

Kinetic's moves on the operations front, included opening of more depots around the country and a change in the credit policy. The Honda stake came with Rs.400-500 million as outstanding with dealers. Once these were recovered, interest costs came down considerably. Kinetic decentralized the distribution network and thus reduced inventory costs. Kinetic Engineering already had 20 C&F agents across the country. Kinetic used these agents to extend its reach to semi-urban and rural areas. For example, Kinetic was able to reach places like Anand and Gandhinagar from a depot in Ahmedabad within 24 hours. From its Pitampur plant, this would have taken almost three days. Kinetic also approached banks and negotiated deals to reduce its cost of borrowings. Material costs were reduced by reducing unnecessary imports. To improve the mileage of its scooters, Kinetic consulted experts from around the world and introduced a new technology in its new series of scooters, raising the mileage from 30kmpl to 50kmpl.

All these efforts soon translated into improved performance, proving the company's detractors wrong. Kinetic posted good results for both KEL (sales rose by 20%) and KMCL (sales rose by 23%) for the first half of 1999. KMCL also wiped off the previous year's loss of Rs 6 crore and posted profits of Rs 3.69 crore for the same period. In fiscal 2000, sales increased by around 25%.

In August 1999, Honda announced that it was setting up a wholly-owned subsidiary to manufacture scooters in India with an initial capacity of one lakh units per year. The company set up an independent distribution network for the new venture. Through this $ 43 million subsidiary, Honda planned to focus on scooters for a period of five years. Later, Hero Honda and the Honda subsidiary were to be free to expand the range to include all two/three wheelers. Honda's first scooter model was launched in mid-2001. Around one-third of the total proposed outlay of Rs 150 crore had already been invested by that time. Though the contract with the Firodias prevented Honda from manufacturing the same scooter through a subsidiary or a joint venture, Honda got around the clause by introducing scooters in a different range. A Honda official said, "This is an extremely important market for us and there is no question of giving up the scooter business - we never give up."

Honda's decision sparked off debates in industry circles over guidelines regarding foreign companies being allowed to set up wholly owned subsidiaries in India, when they already had joint ventures here. The Confederation of Indian Industry (CII) expressed fears that this could develop into a trend that would adversely affect the local partners in these joint ventures.

Kinetic claimed they were not perturbed by Honda's announcement, as the group believed they were the de-facto leaders in ungeared scooters. Also, they had the exclusive rights to manufacture the 100cc and 110cc, Marvel, DX and ZX scooters. The Firodias were not really surprised by Honda's announcement, because at the time Honda was negotiating with them for the Kinetic Honda stake, such a possibility had been discussed. However, many felt that Honda could eventually enter the motorcycle segment as well - something which seemed strategically wrong given the success of the Hero Honda venture. Sulajja said, "If Honda was serious about its scooter business in India and wanted to grow in the market by introducing new models, then why did they not do so during the 12 years that it was present in India, through its JV with us? After all, it had a majority stake and full management control. Yes, it's true that Honda has said that it will start by manufacturing a 4-stroke scooter first through the new company. But what one fails to understand is why Honda should reenter a business by setting up a green-field project at a whopping investment of over Rs.200 crores, when it has barely 10 months ago exited that market, unless it has a larger game plan of manufacturing motorcycles too."

Question:

Understand and analyze the various factors strategically that attributed to the breakup of Kinetic Honda.